Ferrets FOR DUMMIES® 2ND EDITION

by Kim Schilling

Foreword by Susan Brown, DVM

1807 WILEY 2007

Wiley Publishing, Inc.

Ferrets For Dummies®, 2nd Edition

Published by
Wiley Publishing, Inc.
111 River St.
Hoboken, NJ 07030-5774
www.wiley.com

WILEY

About the Author

A Chicago native for all but two years of her life, **Kim Schilling** resides in a south suburb of Chicago with her husband, David, and son, Samuel. Kim published the first Edition of *Ferrets For Dummies* in 2000 after three grueling years of title changes, rewrites, and personnel turnovers. Today, her book is the bestselling ferret book on the market. Although writing is a passion of hers, and she vows to keep doing it, her true calling is her son, Sam. Her life changed forever in 2001 when she broke her back and pelvis — the result of a horseback-riding accident on Mother's Day. The traumatic injuries were the bad news; the good news was that she found out the baby she was told she'd never have was three weeks in the making. Born in 2002, this little miracle changed her life. At one time, Kim thought she knew what was important. Today, she knows without a doubt what's important. Sam, this wonderful, lit boy, has completed her life.

When Kim isn't working full time or being Mom, she's running Animals for Awareness, a USDA-licensed and -inspected facility. Created in the early 1990s — incorporated in 1997, with nonprofit status attained in 1999 — Animals for Awareness is dedicated to meeting the needs of wild and exotic animals. Its mission: *Protection Through Education.* Although Animals for Awareness doesn't adopt out exotic animals to the general public, it does find permanent USDA facilities for the bigger exotic animals and almost always has domestic critters such as ferrets up for adoption. Kim and many of her exotic critters frequently hit the road to educate as many people as possible. Her main goal is to promote responsible pet ownership and discourage the keeping of exotic, dangerous, or wild animals. Among the 50 species of animals she cares for, Kim dotes on her six ferrets — Squee, Gir, Gaz, Casanova, Dusk, and Macey — who reside peacefully with three happy little fennec foxes. You can learn more about Animals for Awareness at www.animals forawareness.org.

Dedication

For my beautiful son, Sam, for he is the brightest blessing in my life. For David, my husband, who stands by my side. For my dearest friend Dr. Mike Miller, whose untimely passing will always leave a gaping hole in my heart and whose wisdom filled my life with priceless knowledge. For my invaluable, precious friend Bob Church, whose immeasurable love and understanding of ferrets has so inspired and taught me.

Author's Acknowledgments

I have to start off by extending a big thank you to Dr. Susan Brown, my technical and medical editor, who went way above and beyond the call of duty by spending countless hours helping me research and answer my many questions. Susan was both my coach and my cheerleader. She is truly priceless and inspiring, and I value the friend I gained in her. A big hug and a thank you to Bob Church for his generous help on many areas of the book, in particular the diet and enrichment chapters. What's a ferret book without the influences of Bob Church?

Thank you to a doll of a guy, Travis Livieri, for his devotion and work with black-footed ferrets and for lending his support to me. Thank you to the following fantastic veterinarians for reviewing and contributing to medical sections or issues: Dr. Bruce Williams (ECE and the infamous Poop Chart), Dr. Jerry Murray (heart disease, heartworms, and diet), Dr. Karen Purcell (descenting and diet), and Dr. Katrina Ramsell (DIM). Some of these wonderful vets took their precious time to review other parts of the book as well. Vickie McKimmey of Just a Business of Ferrets and Scarlett Gray of Scarlett's Happy Dookers, both judges with the American Ferret Association, spent a lot of time going through pictures to pick out the best color photos for the color insert. I thank them from the bottom of my heart! Speaking of photos, thank you to Jennifer Deming for your talent as a photographer. I was blessed to find you. You are nothing but a pleasure to work with — a true gem!

Many other individuals helped with this book, including Sukie Crandall with her wealth of knowledge, Bill Gruber, Renee Downs, Dr. John Lewington, Julie Fossa, and Marie Bartholdsson. Dr. June McNicholas was priceless when it came to sharing her thoughts on hybrids. And I'd still know nothing about angoras had it not been for Lisa Oestereich and Christine Matthis. A heartfelt thank you to each of you. Special thanks to Dr. Valerie Staton for sharing her expertise on ferret introductions and aggression. Her grasp of ferret behavior is amazing! Finally, a special thank you to Rebecca Stout, aka Wolfy, who jumped through hoops to get me information on deaf ferrets and to update her Web site in anticipation of it being published in *Ferrets For Dummies, 2nd Edition.* She's a champ! Editors Mike Lewis, Josh Dials, and Natalie Harris of Wiley have to be acknowledged for putting up with my mood swings and difficult moments. There were many others who helped make the second edition possible, and to all of them I extend a heartfelt thank you!

Publisher's Acknowledgments

We're proud of this book; please send us your comments through our Dummies online registration form located at `www.dummies.com/register/`.

Some of the people who helped bring this book to market include the following:

Acquisitions, Editorial, and Media Development

Project Editor: Natalie Faye Harris

(Previous Edition: Tracy Barr)

Acquisitions Editor: Michael Lewis

(Previous Edition: Scott Prentzas)

Copy Editor: Josh Dials

(Previous Edition: Sandra Blackthorn)

Technical Editor: Susan Brown, DVM

(Previous Edition: Bob Church)

Editorial Manager: Christine Beck

Editorial Assistants: Erin Calligan Mooney, Joe Niesen, Leeann Harney, David Lutton

Cover and Interior Photos: Jennifer Deming — Photos with Flair

Cartoons: Rich Tennant (`www.the5thwave.com`)

Composition Services

Project Coordinator: Erin Smith

Layout and Graphics: Carl Byers, Stephanie D. Jumper, Christine Williams

Special Art: Barbara Frake

Anniversary Logo Design: Richard Pacifico

Proofreaders: Susan Moritz, Ethel M. Winslow

Indexer: Potomac Indexing, LLC

Publishing and Editorial for Consumer Dummies

> **Diane Graves Steele,** Vice President and Publisher, Consumer Dummies
>
> **Joyce Pepple,** Acquisitions Director, Consumer Dummies
>
> **Kristin A. Cocks,** Product Development Director, Consumer Dummies
>
> **Michael Spring,** Vice President and Publisher, Travel
>
> **Kelly Regan,** Editorial Director, Travel

Publishing for Technology Dummies

> **Andy Cummings,** Vice President and Publisher, Dummies Technology/General User

Composition Services

> **Gerry Fahey,** Vice President of Production Services
>
> **Debbie Stailey,** Director of Composition Services

Contents at a Glance

Foreword xxi

Introduction 1

Part I: Is a Ferret Right for You? 7
Chapter 1: What You Need to Know About Ferrets.................................9
Chapter 2: Understanding What Ferrets Are (And Aren't)........................21
Chapter 3: Ferrets and the Law: Licensing and Other Issues 39

Part II: Finding Your Ferret and Hanging Up the Welcome Hammock 45
Chapter 4: On the Tail of a New Carpet Shark (Um, Ferret)....................47
Chapter 5: Home Sweet Home: Preparing Your Ferret's Quarters 63
Chapter 6: Ferret-Proofing Your Home 89
Chapter 7: Introducing Fuzzy to His New Family 97

Part III: Basic Ferret Care and Feeding 115
Chapter 8: Filling Your Ferret's Belly 117
Chapter 9: Cleaning Time: Not All Ferret Fun and Games.....................143
Chapter 10: Enrichment: Yours and Your Ferret's 161
Chapter 11: Have Ferret, May Travel 181

Part IV: Tackling Your Ferret's Health Issues and Treatments..191
Chapter 12: Setting Up Your Ferret's Health Plan: Vets and First-Aid Kits.............193
Chapter 13: Helping Your Hurt Ferret: First-Aid Basics.....................209
Chapter 14: Ferreting Out Ferret Pests 233
Chapter 15: Handling Viruses, Infections, and Other Conditions and Illnesses.....243
Chapter 16: Finding and Treating the Big C and Other Lumps.................275
Chapter 17: Saying Goodbye When the Time Comes 287

Part V: Ferret Psychology 101: Behavior and Training..299
Chapter 18: Understanding What Fuzzy Is Trying to Tell You 301
Chapter 19: Putting Your Ferret through Basic Training: Easy as 1-2-3? 313
Chapter 20: Dealing with the Behaviorally Challenged Ferret................319

Part VI: Breeding Ferrets: The Facts, Fallacies, and Plain Ol' Hard Work 329

Chapter 21: Should You Breed Your Ferret? Looking at the Big Picture 331
Chapter 22: Unmasking the Details of Ferret Love 337
Chapter 23: From Birth to Bundle of Energy: Walking a Fuzzy's Timeline 349

Part VII: The Part of Tens 355

Chapter 24: Ten Common Ferret Myths and Misconceptions 357
Chapter 25: Ten Recipes Your Ferret Will Love 363

Index 373

Table of Contents

Foreword..*xxi*

Introduction *1*

About This Book...2
Conventions Used in This Book 2
What You're Not to Read 2
Foolish Assumptions 3
How This Book Is Organized..3
    Part I: Is a Ferret Right for You?....................................4
    Part II: Finding Your Ferret and Hanging Up
      the Welcome Hammock 4
    Part III: Basic Ferret Care and Feeding...............................4
    Part IV: Tackling Your Ferret's Health Issues and Treatments 4
    Part V: Ferret Psychology 101: Behavior and Training....................5
    Part VI: Breeding Ferrets: The Facts, Fallacies,
      and Plain ol' Hard Work 5
    Part VII: The Part of Tens 5
Icons Used in This Book...5
Where to Go from Here..6

Part 1: Is a Ferret Right for You? *7*

Chapter 1: What You Need to Know About Ferrets **9**

First Question: What Is a Ferret?...10
Giving the Ferret a Physical: Examining Fuzzy Characteristics 11
    Looking at the life span of a fuzzy.......................................11
    In this corner, weighing in at 12
    Getting to the point about claws and teeth 13
    Making sense of senses 14
Exercise and Time Considerations — Yours and Your Fuzzy's 14
Taking a Whiff of the Odor Factor...15
    To descent or not to descent? 16
    Controlling your fuzzy's odor 16
Getting the Dish on Financial Matters 17
Extreme Cage Makeover: Providing the Space They Need 18
Facing the Challenges of Ferret-Proofing Your Home.........................18
Ferrets and Kids 19

Ferrets and Other Household Pets 19
Leaping over the Legal Hurdles...20

Chapter 2: Understanding What Ferrets Are (And Aren't) **21**

Yes, Ferrets Are Domesticated 22
Getting to Know Fuzzies in the Past and Present 23
    Ferrets throughout history 23
    Ferrets have always had a knack for meeting man's needs 24
    Ferrets catching on 24
Spotlighting the Sport of Ferreting 25
Exploring the Hot Topic of Ferret Hybrids 26
    The pros of and arguments for ferret hybridization.......................27
    The cons of hybridization 28
Picturing the Physical Appearance of the Domestic Ferret.....................29
    The spectrum of fuzzy colors 29
    Fuzzy color patterns 31
Not Just Another Color: The Black-Footed Ferret.....................................32
    The one, true North American ferret! 33
    Are black-footed ferrets really that different?...................................33
    Habitat (or is that prairie dog?) destruction 34
    The Black-Footed Ferret Recovery Plan 35

Chapter 3: Ferrets and the Law: Licensing and Other Issues **39**

"A License? But He Can't Even Reach the Pedals!" 39
Ferret-Free Zones and Why They Exist 40
    What's it gonna be? Wild, domestic, or exotic?..................................41
    Feral ferrets in my neighborhood?...42
    Should people fear rabies?..43
Knowing the Law and the Consequences of Breaking It 43

**Part II: Finding Your Ferret and Hanging Up
the Welcome Hammock**..**45**

Chapter 4: On the Tail of a New Carpet Shark (Um, Ferret) **47**

Ferret Shopping 101 48
Are You in the Market for a New or Used Ferret? 49
    Starting off with a kit..49
    Adopting an older ferret 50
Should You Pre-Order Blue or Pink Bedding (Get a Boy or Girl)?............51
Pitting Altered versus Whole Furballs...51
    Boys will be boys...52
    Girls will be girls...52
"You Want How Many Ferrets?"..53

Where to Find Your Ferret..56
   Perusing pet shops...56
   Picking out private breeders...58
   Adopting from a ferret shelter 59
   Checking the classified ads 61
   Rescuing the wayward weasel: Stray ferrets 61

Chapter 5: Home Sweet Home: Preparing Your Ferret's Quarters . . .63
Setting Up Fuzzy's Cage...63
   Size matters: Picking the proper cage 64
   Fuzzy blueprints: Making sure the design is right 64
   A home within a home: Finding a place inside for the cage 68
   A room with a view: Finding a place outside for the cage 69
Making Your Ferret's Bed 71
Setting Your Ferret's Table..71
   Serving your ferret's food with a sturdy dish 74
   Hydrating your ferret with a water bottle....................76
Designing Your Ferret's Bathroom 78
   Choosing the right litter box for your ferret................79
   Picking out the perfect litter 81
Acquiring Accessories and Other Stuff Fuzzy Needs 82
   Fluffing up extra snoozing sites...................................83
   Ferret toys galore! 84
   Leashes and harnesses for your ferret.........................85
   Finding a good travel taxi 87

Chapter 6: Ferret-Proofing Your Home 89
Inspecting Your Home for Ferret Hazards............................89
   Laundry room 90
   Kitchen..91
   Moldings, baseboards, and under cabinets..................91
   Windows and doors 91
   Floor vents and air returns 92
   Plants 92
   Heights 92
   Electrical cords...93
   Reclining chairs, rockers, and foldout couches 93
   Fireplaces 93
   Mattresses, couches, and chairs 93
   Toilets, bathtubs, and buckets 94
   Cabinets..94
   Trash cans 95
Changing Some of Your Home Habits 95
Getting a Vet..96

Chapter 7: Introducing Fuzzy to His New Family 97

Ferrets as Social Animals 98
You and Your New Ferret: Making the Most of Your Friendship 98
Hold me gently, please..99
Letting fuzzy set up shop in his home.....................................100
The steps to successful bonding...101
Fuzzy Meets Fluffy and Fido 103
Heeeere kitty, kitty!..103
Nice puppy! 104
Ferrets and other small animals 106
Preparing Your Child for the Ferret 106
Pause the cartoons: What your child should know
beforehand 106
Fuzzy, meet Junior: Making the introduction............................107
Fuzzy Meets Fuzzy: Adding Another Ferret to Your Family..................108
Meeting on neutral ground...109
Messing with their sniffers...110
Forcing a relationship..110
Easing your fuzzy into the business 111
Heading Off Stranger Danger 112

Part III: Basic Ferret Care and Feeding *115*

Chapter 8: Filling Your Ferret's Belly 117

Water, Water, Everywhere 118
Ferrets as Diners 118
Feeding the Traditional Commercial Diet 119
Wet or dry food?...120
Setting a feeding schedule...122
Changing kibble diets 123
Serving Up an Alternative Diet 123
Getting to know the wild polecat's diet....................................125
Bellying up to a bone-filled diet...125
Choosing commercial raw or freeze-dried raw diets....................128
The evolutionary diet: Feeding your pet small animals
or insects 130
Exploring the alternative way of feeding....................................135
Supplementing Your Fuzzy's Diet...139
Omega-3 fatty acids...139
Omega-6 fatty acids...140
Savoring Treat Time!..140
Giving the good stuff...140
Avoiding the not-so-good stuff...141

Chapter 9: Cleaning Time: Not All Ferret Fun and Games **143**

Cleaning House for a Cozy Cage...143
    Doing your fuzzy's dishes...144
    Stripping his bed 145
    Scrubbing (or scooping) the toilet.....................................145
    Tearing down the house 146
    Getting the gunk off the toys...146
Scrub a Dub Fuzz: Navigating Bathtime..................................147
    One bath too many?...147
    Picking a shampoo 147
    Choosing the crime scene 148
    Doing the deed..149
Caring for Those Little Ears..152
    Gathering supplies 153
    Executing the ear clean 153
Nailing Down the Manicure..154
    Choosing your clipping method...155
    Performing the clip 156
Chewing On Chomper Maintenance..157
    Performing the dental checkup..157
    Brushing his teeth 159
Breaking Out the Hairbrush..160

Chapter 10: Enrichment: Yours and Your Ferret's **161**

Why Is Enrichment Necessary?..162
What Does Enrichment Do for Ferrets?....................................162
    Relieves boredom and stress...163
    Facilitates bonding...163
    Keeps their senses alive and well 163
    Helps to curb negative behaviors 164
    Keeps the flab at bay 164
    Encourages curiosity and creative problem solving 164
    Helps to keep bones, muscles, organs, and joints healthy..........165
    Improves heart health and overall circulation.............................165
    Makes humans smile and laugh...165
Understanding Your Ferret's Senses..166
    Hearing..166
    Smelling 166
    Tasting 166
    Seeing..167
    Touching..167
Recommended Enrichment Activities for You and Your Fuzzy............167
    Organizing your ferret's play areas...................................168
    Movement and physical-exercise activities 169

Social-development activities 169
Food-related activities 170
Training exercises 170
Using novel objects in activities..............................174
Finding Your Own Enrichment at Ferret Clubs....................175
Participating in Regional Shows, Club Shows, and Competitions 175
So, you want to show your fuzzy?..............................176
Preparing to bring home the blue ribbon 176
Fun matches..178
Annual Ferret Symposiums 179
Internet Clubs and Lists 179
Ferret Mailing List (FML) 180
Ferret Health List (FHL)...180

Chapter 11: Have Ferret, May Travel **181**
Fuzzy Is Going on Vacation! 181
Checking ahead 182
Packing the necessities..182
On the Road or Flying High 183
Road trip! 183
Taking to the friendly skies 185
Going international 186
Leaving Your Furball in Good Hands 187
Let the interviews begin: Finding the perfect pet sitter 188
Away to camp: Boarding your ferret 190

Part IV: Tackling Your Ferret's Health Issues and Treatments **191**

Chapter 12: Setting Up Your Ferret's Health Plan: Vets and First-Aid Kits **193**
Selecting Your Ferret's Veterinarian 194
Interviewing potential vets 194
Going for a visit...195
Developing a good working. relationship....................196
Putting Your Vet to Work with Vaccinations and Checkups 198
Kits — the office visit..199
Adolescents and adults — the office visit....................200
Recognizing allergic reactions 201
Stocking Your Ferret First-Aid Kit 202
Ensuring Emergency Preparedness 205
The basic (quick) evacuation kit..............................206
Collecting and evacuating your fuzzy........................206
The deluxe (and orderly) evacuation kit....................207

Chapter 13: Helping Your Hurt Ferret: First-Aid Basics **209**

Behaviors You Usually Don't Need to Worry About 210
   Shivering..210
   Itching and scratching 210
   Yawning...211
   Excessive sleeping...211
   Sneezing, hiccuping, and coughing...212
   Butt dragging 212
   Drinking urine 213
Pain Management and Care 213
   Determining if your ferret is in pain.......................................214
   Caring for a ferret in pain 214
Setting Up Fuzzy's Home Hospital Room..216
Feeding the Sick or Debilitated Ferret..217
   The Assist Feed Recipe: Better than Mom's chicken soup 217
   The feeding method: Just as effective as the airplane
      into the mouth 219
Handling Actual Emergencies..220
   Shock...220
   Dehydration 221
   Bleeding 222
   Vomiting 224
   Diarrhea (and other fecal issues)...224
   Seizures...226
   Heatstroke 227
   Hypothermia 228
   Eye injuries 229
   Fractures or spinal injuries 230
   Poisoning 230
   Animal bites 231
   Electric shock 231
   Burns..232

Chapter 14: Ferreting Out Ferret Pests **233**

Booting External Critters That Go Bite in the Night 233
   Fleas 234
   Ticks 238
   Cuterebra flies...238
   Ear mites..239
   Sarcoptic mange (scabies)...240
Battling the Internal Bugaboos That Threaten Your Fuzzy 240
   Intestinal worms..241
   Giardia...241
   Coccidia (coccidiosis) 242

Chapter 15: Handling Viruses, Infections, and Other Conditions and Illnesses **243**

   Gastrointestinal (GI) Diseases 244
      Epizootic Catarrhal Enteritis (ECE).........................244
      Intestinal and stomach blockages............................247
      Helicobacter Mustelae (H. mustelae) Infection............248
      Eosinophilic Gastroenteritis 250
      Megaesophagus 251
   Dental Problems 252
      Faulty teeth 252
      The dreaded dental disease...................................254
   Heart Disease...256
      Dilated cardiomyopathy..256
      Heartworms...258
      What extra care you can give your ferret...................260
   Influenza (The "Flu")...260
   Urinary Tract Problems...263
      Bladder or urinary tract infections 263
      Prostate problems 264
      Stones and blockages 264
   Eye Problems 264
   Aleutian Disease Virus (ADV)..266
      Clinical signs 267
      Diagnosis and prognosis 268
      Treatment 268
   Canine Distemper..269
   Enlarged Spleen (Splenomegaly)....................................270
   Hairballs 271
   Rabies 271
   Ulcers 272
      Signs 273
      Diagnosis 274
      Treatment 274

Chapter 16: Finding and Treating the Big C and Other Lumps **275**

   Adrenal Gland Disease..275
      Making the diagnosis 277
      Treating the disease...278
   Insulinoma...280
      Making the diagnosis 281
      Treating the disease...281
   Lymphosarcoma (Lymphoma)..282
      Making the diagnosis 283
      Treating the disease...283
   Chordomas...283

Itchy Growths: Skin Tumors 284
    Mast cell tumors 284
    Basal cell tumors 286
    Sebaceous cell tumors 286

Chapter 17: Saying Goodbye When the Time Comes **287**
    Letting Go of Your Family Member 288
    Learning from Fuzzy's Death with a Postmortem 289
    Selecting Fuzzy's Final Burrowing Place 290
        Choosing cremation 291
        Proceeding to a pet cemetery....................................292
        Opting for a backyard burial....................................292
    Grieving for Your Lost Fuzzy 293
        Know you're not alone..294
        Face the feelings 295
        Give yourself time 295
        Help others deal with their loss 295
    Helping a Surviving Ferret Cope 296

Part V: Ferret Psychology 101:
Behavior and Training **299**

Chapter 18: Understanding What Fuzzy Is Trying to Tell You **301**
    Say What? Speaking Ferret-ese..301
        The dook..302
        The screech..302
        The bark..303
        The hiss 303
    You Make Me Feel Like Dancin'! Interpreting Your Ferret's Jig 303
        The dance of joy 303
        The war dance 305
    Decoding Your Ferret's Body Language 305
        The frizz look 306
        The alligator roll and wrestlemania 306
        The treasure hunt 307
        The chase is on 307
        Fuzzy stalking..308
        Tail wagging..308
    "Why Does My Ferret Do That?" Understanding
    Other Fuzzy Behaviors 308
        Digging to China 308
        Ferret fixations..309
        The movers are here 310
        A felon on your hands?..310

The zig-zag...311
Butt scooting...311
Coveting thy hidey-hole..........................312
Scoping out boundaries...........................312

Chapter 19: Putting Your Ferret through Basic Training: Easy as 1-2-3? **313**

Just Say NO to Biting 313
This Way to the Bathroom 315
Harnessing Your Fuzzy for a Walk 316
Getting fuzzy used to a harness 317
Following basic rules when you're out and about 318

Chapter 20: Dealing with the Behaviorally Challenged Ferret **319**

Understanding Your Dracula in Fuzzy's Clothing..........319
I'm having growing pains..................320
Nobody told me not to bite...............321
I'm in pain, darn it! 321
I'm a manly or bully ferret.................321
I'm facing a lot of change right now....322
Biting always worked before!.............322
I'm still fighting back.........................322
Some other reasons for my biting.....323
Socializing Your Biting Beast 323
Getting a grip 324
Getting unstuck...................................324
Taming the critter...............................326

Part VI: Breeding Ferrets: The Facts, Fallacies, and Plain Ol' Hard Work................................**329**

Chapter 21: Should You Breed Your Ferret? Looking at the Big Picture **331**

What It Takes to Be a Responsible Breeder...............332
Deep pockets 332
The emotional stake............................333
Time to care 334
Willingness to find out what you don't know 335
Avoiding a Need for More Shelters 335

Chapter 22: Unmasking the Details of Ferret Love **337**

Fine-Tuning the Organs 338
The boy (hob)......................................338
The girl (jill) 339
Making a love connection: Enter Neanderthal ferret..............339

What Happens If Your Unaltered Ferret Isn't Bred?..................................341
Mothering the Mom-to-Be 341
    Strange craving? Keeping mom nourished 342
    Providing a maternity ward..343
Heading Off to the Delivery Room 344
    The typical delivery 345
    The difficult delivery..346
Some Problems You May Face after Birth...346
    A difficult mother 347
    A mother incapable of nursing 347
    Calling on the foster mom 348

**Chapter 23: From Birth to Bundle of Energy:
Walking a Fuzzy's Timeline** **349**
    Fuzzy Infancy: Birth to 3 Weeks..349
    Furball Toddlerhood: 3 to 6 Weeks 351
    The Terrible Fuzzy Twos: 6 to 10 Weeks 352
    Adolescence Already? 10 to 15 Weeks..353

Part VII: The Part of Tens..................................355

Chapter 24: Ten Common Ferret Myths and Misconceptions **357**
    Ferrets Are Rodents 357
    Ferrets Are Wild, Dangerous Animals...358
    Feral Ferrets Will Take Over!..358
    Ferrets Are Vicious Biters 359
    Ferrets Pose a Serious Rabies Risk 359
    A Ferret's Stink Will Never Go Away 359
    Ferrets Can Catch the Common Cold 360
    Ferrets Were Domesticated in Egypt 360
    Ferrets Sleep 20+ Hours per Day 361
    Ferrets Need to Have Food Available at All Times...........................361

Chapter 25: Ten Recipes Your Ferret Will Love **363**
    Bob's Chicken Gravy..364
    Bob's Chicken Ferretisee..366
    Foster's Tuna Shake 366
    Bear's Jerky...367
    Stella's Super Soup...368
    Tui's Chewies...368
    Carnivore Stew 369
    Mickey's Meatloaf..370
    Clyde's Seaside Chunks 370
    Bluto's BARF 371

Index..373

Foreword

*W*hen I graduated from veterinary school and started my career in 1976 I didn't know anyone who kept a ferret for a pet much less had I ever seen one other than in pictures. My only experience with them was in an undergraduate ethology class where I watched a 30-minute video of the behavior of the European polecat, and I wrote a paper on the subject. I had seen and taken care of just about every other kind of "nontraditional" pet in my life, but a real live ferret was yet to be seen.

I saw my first pet ferret patient in 1978, at the small animal practice where I was employed in the Chicago suburbs. By 1980, I started a strictly exotic animal veterinary practice, and gradually these funny, wiggly little critters called ferrets entered my life in gradually increasing numbers, and the fascination began. There were few veterinarians I knew of at the time whos knew much about ferrets; even my colleagues in the United Kingdom, where ferrets had been used for centuries, knew very little about the diseases I was seeing here in the United States. James Fox's first edition of his book *Biology and Diseases of the Ferret* would not be published until 1988, so we had little science-based reference material on which to rely.

In 1982, I was asked to give a talk to the Chicago Veterinary Medical Association to a small group of veterinarians who were interested in exotic pets. I spent one afternoon at the Purdue University Veterinary School Library gleaning all I could about these little beasties. I read and copied every article, every chapter in a book, and every other publication I could find on ferrets, and I did it all in one afternoon! Remember there was no Internet to turn to back then; one had to go to the library and search through books and archived articles. I prepared for the talk, gathered a few photos, and made as extensive an outline as I could for a handout, a grand total of six pages long. Thinking I would be speaking to maybe 5 people, I walked into the room and there were 30 people waiting to hear all about ferrets! Everyone was hungry for knowledge, and they thought I had it!

After getting over my stage fright, I proceeded to give my talk, and by the end of that evening I was transformed into the local veterinary "ferret expert." Ferrets started coming into my practice in larger and larger numbers as they were referred by other veterinarians in the area. I got phone calls asking for consultations from veterinarians from all over the country. Over the next decade the percentage of ferrets in our practice grew from about 2 percent to 20 percent! Ferrets were fascinating, and their popularity as a pet was increasing rapidly. Caregivers and veterinarians wanted to know how to manage them.

I was so taken with these little guys that I got the first FERRET license plates for my car in Illinois in 1980, and in 1987, I cofounded the Greater Chicago

Ferret Association (GCFA) with Janice Miller to help ferret owners come together and share and learn more about ferrets. The GCFA had the first free-standing all-ferret shelter in the country, which has by now had several thousand ferrets pass through its portals. For the next two decades I spoke to numerous veterinary organizations and wrote in a number of veterinary texts about ferret husbandry and disease. I have personally cared for many fabulous ferrets of my own, starting with Guido, who was a stray a client found and gave me in 1982. He was a great teacher and a wonderful friend, and I will be forever grateful to him for helping me to understand the mystique, the wonder, and the comedy of this marvelous little creature.

So now, more than 30 years after I started my veterinary career, if I went to a veterinary school library to read everything I could about ferrets, it would easily take a week, not the mere afternoon it took me back in 1982. Just reading the information available on the Internet about ferrets would takes days in itself! Ferret caregivers and veterinarians from all over the world have contributed to a huge body of knowledge that continues to grow about this fascinating little critter. Much of it is good, but there still remains a lot of misinformation as well.

Considering how much information, both good and bad, is out there to wade through, Kim Schilling has done a phenomenal job sifting through it and putting it all together in this comprehensive book, *Ferrets For Dummies, 2nd Edition.* This is the second edition of the book, and it has been expanded greatly from the first with additional topics and lots of updates to the information in the first book. I have had the honor and pleasure of being Kim's Technical Editor on this book, and she has made my job very easy because she has taken hundreds of hours of her time in researching each topic thoroughly and then interpreting and condensing the information into a very readable format. Her attention to detail is phenomenal, and she has left no stone unturned when it comes to delving into ferret topics! Kim has a fabulous sense of humor, and it shows in her writing, making it a real pleasure to read this book. There is hardly a topic she has not touched on, even some of the more difficult or controversial ones, making this book a real gem for anyone wanting to learn how to care for our ferret friends.

It's fantastic to be able to have one book that so thoroughly covers all the ferret topics one could possibly imagine. Looking back 30 years to the time when we had little information about these important pets, I am so pleased to know we have such a gold mine as *Ferrets For Dummies, 2nd Edition,* available today.

I would recommend *Ferrets For Dummies, 2nd Edition,* without hesitation to anyone wanting to learn everything there is to know about caring for a ferret. This book is a must-have for the shelves of veterinarians, ferret rescue organizations, and any ferret caregiver. Even if you don't have a ferret but are interested in learning about them, this book is a fun and informative read.

Enjoy.

Susan A. Brown, DVM

Introduction

●●

*N*umerous people have told me that a true love for animals may be genetically predisposed. Maybe this is true. Or maybe some animals just tug at our heartstrings a little harder than others. I believe both statements to apply to me. Although my love for animals may be termed "genetics" by the white-coated scientists in those sterile laboratories, I prefer to call what was passed on to me a blessing. I knew the moment my eyes locked onto a bouncing, chattering ferret that I'd been hooked by something mysteriously fascinating. Each one of my ferrets has provided me with much happiness and joy over the years. Even though all my ferrets, young and old, share in common the ability to make me break out in laughter with their habitual silliness, each one is a unique little fuzzball. And they continuously amaze me with their intelligence and social play.

Ferrets are fun and mischievous. They're cunning looters. They can steal *and* break your heart. They come in all sorts of colors and sizes. Ferrets can get into the littlest cracks and holes, both in your home and in your soul. They're bound to make you break out in uncontrollable laughter at least once a day. They steal any chance they can to dance and dook and chatter about. And when they're through amazing you with their antics, most ferrets love nothing more than to curl up somewhere warm with you and snooze the rest of the day away.

Sound like the perfect pet? Not necessarily. As a shelter director, my motto is "Not all animals make good pets for people, and not all people make good parents for pets." No two households, people, or lifestyles are the same. Although ferrets can bring you plenty of joy, they also can be quite challenging at times.

That's why I wrote this book about these amazing creatures. If you don't yet have a ferret, this book can help you decide whether a fuzzy is for you. And if you already have a ferret, this book can help you give him the best possible care. To boot, this book offers practical health and medical information. And everything from cover to cover is in cut-to-the-chase format — only what you need to know, in good ol' plain English.

About This Book

You have plenty to discover — and a lot of responsibility to take on — when you decide to adopt a ferret. Pet ownership isn't something to take lightly. You should always make a lifetime commitment when deciding to bring any pet into your home. This book helps you gain better insight into what's required so that you can make the right choices for your lifestyle.

This book doesn't require a read from cover to cover (of course, you can read it that way if you want to). Instead, this book is a reference guide. If you have a particular topic you want to research, you can turn right to the chapter that covers the topic.

Each chapter is divided into sections, and each section contains pieces of info about some part of ferret keeping — things like this:

- ✔ Is a ferret the right pet for you?
- ✔ How do I pick a healthy ferret?
- ✔ What steps do I take to ferret-proof my home?
- ✔ How do I set up my ferret's cage?
- ✔ What medical conditions require a vet's care?

Conventions Used in This Book

Ferrets For Dummies, 2nd Edition, makes information easy to find and use. To guide you through the information and instructions in this book, I've used certain conventions:

- ✔ *Italics* note emphasis and highlight new words or terms that I define.
- ✔ **Boldfaced** text indicates the action part of numbered steps or identifies keywords in bulleted lists.
- ✔ Monofont sets apart Web sites and e-mail addresses.

What You're Not to Read

You don't actually *have* to read anything in this book. I'm confident you won't be able to resist turning the pages, but I won't test you on anything. I just want you to know that if you're in a hurry, you can skip over text marked by the Technical Stuff icon (see the section "Icons Used in This Book" if you want to know more about that). You also can skip over the gray text boxes (known as "sidebars"), because they don't contain critical ferret-owning information.

Foolish Assumptions

In writing *Ferrets For Dummies,* 2nd Edition, I made some assumptions about my readers:

- You're one of the thousands and thousands of people out there who has a nagging child or spouse who whines daily about wanting to own a ferret. Or maybe you've had your emotions kidnapped by a ferret, and you want to make sure that a ferret is the pet for you before you adopt him.

- Perhaps you're one of those lucky folks who already owns a ferret, and you want to know how to properly care for him.

- You may be a volunteer or employee at a ferret shelter, humane society, veterinarian clinic, or pet shop. You've been given (or have volunteered for) the task of ferret-keeper, and you want to know about caring for these fantastic furballs.

- You may be a "seasoned" ferret owner who's soon to discover that this book covers topics that you can't find in other ferret books, such as behavior challenges, alternative diet, and saying goodbye.

- You may be one of the many who realize the growing need for — and importance of — enrichment in the lives of our ferrets and value the extensive information provided by this book on enrichment.

- You may be a veterinarian who wants to know as much about the ferrets you treat — including basic history — as you do about the people who bring them in.

Whatever made you pick up this book, hold onto your hat, because you're in for the thrill of a lifetime!

How This Book Is Organized

To help you find the information you're looking for, I divide this book into seven parts. Each part includes several chapters relating to a specific topic on ferrets. Find the part that suits you and jump right in!

Part I: Is a Ferret Right for You?

Part I is probably the most important part for people who are in the "considering" stage. Ferrets aren't cats — and they certainly aren't dogs. And heaven knows they're not for everyone! This part tells you what you can expect from a ferret and what a ferret will expect (and need) from you. And for people who are absolutely set on becoming a ferret human, you need to check out this part to brush up on the legalities of owning a ferret where you live.

Part II: Finding Your Ferret and Hanging Up the Welcome Hammock

So many ferrets, so little time! This part gives you detailed steps on what to look for in a new ferret and how to find the right one for you. Young or old? Single, pair, or trio? Shelter, breeder, or pet shop? And after you decide on the right ferret, you have other important stuff to do before he comes home, like setting up his cage properly and getting all the necessary ferret supplies. Finally, this part gives you solid tips on interacting with your new ferret and safely introducing him to other family members.

Part III: Basic Ferret Care and Feeding

No time to rest, because you have some more decisions to make. What kinds of foods and treats are good for your ferret? How do you keep him from getting bored? This part gives you suggestions for how to be creative and stay safe in the ferret kitchen and on the ferret playground. But having a ferret isn't all fun and games, so you also find out how and when to clean up your ferret and his cage. Finally, this part has great tips and guidance that can help you make decisions about whether to travel (and how to travel) with your ferret.

Part IV: Tackling Your Ferret's Health Issues and Treatments

From stocking the must-have first-aid kit, to knowing how to give first aid, to explaining more serious ferret health issues, this part covers all aspects of ferret healthcare — right down to knowing when to say goodbye to your dearly loved ferret. In addition, this part helps you find the best vet for your ferret and gives you a basic overview of common illnesses and diseases so you'll know when you need to head off to the vet's office.

Part V: Ferret Psychology 101: Behavior and Training

So, you think your ferret is crazy? You want to know what your ferret is saying? And what does he mean when he moves in all directions at one time? This part clues you in to ferret communication and behavior. Knowing a little more about your ferret will help you with basic training such as nip training, litter-box training, and leash and harness training. Getting instructions on dealing with the behaviorally challenged ferret is just as important, so this part dives into that topic as well.

Part VI: Breeding Ferrets: The Facts, Fallacies, and Plain ol' Hard Work

This part offers a brief introduction to ferret reproduction and growth, from the breeding pair to the birth to preparing kits for their new homes. It touches on medical issues related to breeding and explains what's required to be a responsible breeder. But most importantly, this part gets you to think about the whole breeding picture. Why breed? What are the problems associated with breeding? Do you have what it takes to breed, or are you just creating more need for ferret shelters?

Part VII: The Part of Tens

I've saved some of the best information for last! Thinking of trying an alternative diet? Here you can read about some great recipes to try at home. Want to know about some common myths and misconceptions so you can know the real facts and educate others? I have you covered.

Icons Used in This Book

To help you navigate this book full of great information, I include icons that point out helpful hints, fun facts, and things you'd be wise to keep in mind. In a nutshell, the icons do the following:

This icon provides tidbits of info that can make your life as a ferret mom or dad a little easier. Many of these tips were discovered by people, including myself, who learned some ferret-owning facts the hard way.

This icon points out interesting and sometimes technical ferret facts — some of which I stumbled upon while researching for this book. Not all this stuff makes for good dinner conversation, but you're never too old to learn. Consider this information interesting but nonessential.

Don't glaze over the information accompanying this icon. Paying attention to what's here can save your ferret's life or prevent injury and illness — perhaps even major vet bills.

The paragraph(s) accompanying this icon points out important stuff that you should store in an easily accessed part of your brain.

This icon highlights terms that may be new to you and that you may encounter or need to know in the future as a ferret owner.

Where to Go from Here

If you're thinking about getting a ferret, or you want to know how to get a healthy one, start at the beginning with Parts I and II. If you already have a ferret, you can delve into whatever chapter you want, hopping around as issues or problems arise, or as time permits.

Bottom line? Enjoy this book as it was meant to be enjoyed. Remember: People learn new things every day about ferrets. And the best teachers are our ferrets themselves. Don't be afraid to ask questions from the experts, such as your vet. Doing so is well worth the time, and it makes ferret parenting a much more pleasant experience. Besides, asking is the only way you can learn.

Part I

Is a Ferret Right for You?

The 5th Wave   By Rich Tennant

"I think a ferret would be a perfect pet for you, what with all the weasels you've dated."

In this part . . .

*E*very animal has a beast within that takes a little get-ting used to. This goes for humans, too. Because you're reading this book, I can safely assume that you're thinking of adding a ferret to your family. The world, it seems, has been bombarded with dogs and cats, and maybe you've decided you want a more exciting pet to spice up your life.

What's wrong with a ferret? Maybe nothing at all. A ferret may be the perfect pet for you. Or perhaps you should reconsider your decision to get a fuzzy. The answer to the question "Can't we all just get along?" is never cut and dry. It's important to know what you'll be dealing with before you bring home any pet. And this part helps you sort out exactly what you're dealing with so you know what a ferret is all about and whether adopting one is right for you. I also discuss whether you're even allowed to own a fuzzy, which depends on the laws in your city and state.

Chapter 1

What You Need to Know About Ferrets

In This Chapter

▶ Reviewing the description of a ferret

▶ Listing the basic ferret info, from color to odor

▶ Understanding the fuzzy's exercise needs

▶ Addressing the financial and legal matters that ferrets bring

▶ Incorporating the ferret into your home

▶ Introducing your fuzzy to other kids and pets

*T*o the undiscerning eye, she looks a little rat-like. But she acts and moves more like a cat. Sometimes, she fools you and becomes quite dog-like. She resembles some animals you see roaming your backyard or other curious critters featured on a nature television show. And at some point, you'll witness some people in a pet store pointing at a cage full of them, inquiring, "Good heavens, what in the world are those? Opossums?" I think not!

The lovable animal I refer to is the ferret, of course. She belongs to a colorful clan of creatures and often gets mistaken for different animals. In this chapter, I tell you all about the ferret's vast family, his close and distant relatives, and his interesting history. (And for you technical readers, I throw in all sorts of Latin lingo that may confuse even the professionals out there.)

And before you actually run out and get your new family member, you must consider all the things your ferret will require of you — space, safety, and so on — so I cover these things here as well. After all, how can you promise to be a good mom or dad to your fuzzy if you don't even know what goes into good ferret parenting? Taking an honest look at the requirements can mean the difference between living happily with a new family member and taking on a major, unwelcome chore.

Speaking ferret Latin

The ferret's scientific name as of press time, preferred mostly by North-American scientists, is *Mustela putorius furo*. This name exists because of the beliefs concerning the function and nature of the ferret. For those of you who don't speak ferret Latin, *Mustela* means "weasel" or "mouse killer." *Putorius* is derived from the Latin word *putoris*, meaning "stench," and *furo* is derived from the Latin word *furis*, meaning "thief." The word *ferret* itself is derived from the Latin word *furonem*, which also means "thief." Put all this together and you have one little "stinky mouse-killing thief." Although the historical ferret may have lived up to this dubious title, today's ferret is more often than not a cuddly little furball. For all practical purposes, I fondly refer to my ferrets as *Ferretus majorus pleasorus* in the comfort of my nonscientific home!

Some scientists who agree with me are now challenging the beliefs about ferrets — particularly some of the DNA evidence, as used in some paternity tests. The white coats doing most of the ancestral and DNA research are Europeans who prefer to call the ferret *Mustela furo*. Currently, several papers exist that support *Mustela furo*. The scientific name of our domestic ferret may very well change in the near future.

First Question: What Is a Ferret?

Although ferrets may look rodent-like with their long, pointed snouts and ticklish whiskers (see Figure 1-1), they're not rodents at all. Ferrets come from the order *Carnivora,* which simply means "meat or flesh eating." This order encompasses a huge group of animals, from Fifi the common lap dog to the mighty African lion. Within the order Carnivora, ferrets belong to the family *Mustelidae,* which they proudly share with such bold critters as the badger, wolverine, pine marten, and sea otter. Included in that family are both domesticated ferrets and ferret-like wild animals such as the weasel, European polecat, steppe polecat, black-footed ferret, and mink.

The word *ferret* is appropriately derived from the Latin word *Furonem,* which means "thief." As a new ferret owner, you'll quickly realize just how thieving your new family member can be. As cute as this endearing trait may be at times, it has its downsides. It once took me over a day to find all the contents of my purse, which I foolishly left open in the presence of roving ferrets.

Many ferret owners call their pets a variety of nicknames. Some of the names that I use throughout this book are fuzzy, carpet shark, snorkeler, furball, and fuzzbutt. I know that many more terms of endearment exist out there. Don't get confused!

Figure 1-1:
They may look like rodents, but ferrets are actually carnivores.

Giving the Ferret a Physical: Examining Fuzzy Characteristics

Before you bring a new fuzzy home or in the early stages of your ferret parenthood, you need to become familiar a ferret's physical inventory. When I say physical, I pretty much mean all the general stuff regarding a ferret's physical characteristics, from his paws and claws to his weight and remarkable (and not-so-remarkable) senses.

Take a look at Figure 1-2 if you really want to get down to the bones, literally, of examining a ferret's physical makeup! For information on ferret coats and colors, see Chapter 2.

In the following sections, I introduce you to the physical characteristics of the ferret. My version of a ferret physical also covers other tidbits you should know, like color combos and life span, because knowing how to accessorize your fuzzy and how long you'll be caring for him is important.

Looking at the life span of a fuzzy

The average life span of a well-cared-for ferret is between 6 to 8 years, but I've heard many stories of ferrets that have lived for up to 9 or 10 years, barring any unforeseen mishaps. My belief is that a ferret's environment — his caging, disease, stress, diet, and so on — plays a role in his short lifespan. As ferret owners discover more and are taught more about the ferret, they'll undoubtedly be able to increase the expected lifespan significantly.

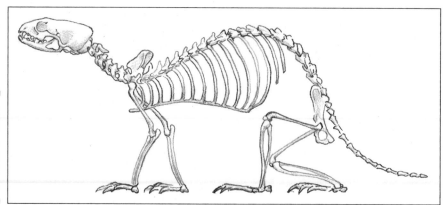

Figure 1-2:
A ferret's
skeleton,
displaying
the ferret's
long spine.

For now, though, you can only do your best to make your ferret's quality of life top-notch. At 1 year old, your fuzzy is considered full grown. At 3 to 4, he's considered middle-aged, and at 5 to 6 years of age, he's considered a geriatric, or an old fert! At this time, she may begin to slowly lose weight and start encountering debilitating illnesses. This is when things get tough and you're faced with difficult choices (see Chapter 17 for advice on saying good-bye to your fuzzy).

As heartbreaking as it is, ferrets are prone to many diseases and may be genetically or medically flawed. Like most companion pets, whose life spans are short compared to humans, ferrets' lives are compacted into only 6 to 8 oh-so-short years. The average human has 65 to 70 years to experience what a ferret experiences in under a decade. The ferret is an amazing trooper with a tremendous fight for life, and you can certainly do your part to help. See Chapters 15 and 16 for more on the conditions that can afflict your fuzzy and for tips on how to care for him.

In this corner, weighing in at . . .

A carpet shark's size makes him an ideal pet for both the apartment dweller and the homeowner. As is the case with some mammal species, unneutered male ferrets typically measure up to two times larger than females — called *sexual dimorphism*. There is a notable weight difference in the head and torso, where the male is wider and less dainty.

A typical altered female ferret weighs between a slim ⅔ths of a pound (0.3 kg) and a whopping 2½ pounds (1.1 kg) — and that's a big girl. Neutered males normally weigh 2 to 3½ pounds (0.9 to 1.6 kg), and unaltered males may weigh in at 4 to 6 pounds (1.8 to 2.7 kg) or more. In tape-measure terms, without the tail, female ferrets are between 13 and 14 inches (33 and 35.5 cm) long, and males generally measure between 15 and 16 inches (38 and 40.6 cm). A ferret's tail is 3 to 4 inches (7.6 to 10 cm) long. See Figure 1-3.

Ferrets are kind of like humans in that they tend to bulk up in the winter. Sometimes ferrets gain 40 percent of their weight at this time of the year and then lose it in the spring (as do humans, right?). This isn't always the rule, though; some ferrets always seem skinny, and others are belly draggers all year round. Could it have something to do with health and/or exercise? Better check it out. (Parts III and IV of this book cover various issues related to exercise and health.)

Getting to the point about claws and teeth

On each of a ferret's soft paws is a set of five nonretractable claws designed for digging and grasping. Nature designed the claws to stay there for a ferret's benefit and survival, so you should never remove them. Frequent clipping, about every 7–10 days, is recommended (see Chapter 9 for more on grooming tips and Chapter 6 for more on ferret-proofing your home).

Declawing your ferret is a big, fat no-no. For a fuzzball, declawing is a painful, mutilating surgery with way more risks than benefits. Ferrets need their claws for digging, grasping, walking, and playing. The base of the claw gives the ferret's foot added strength to support his weight. Removing the claws causes foot problems and/or pain when walking. If you think you'll be too lazy to clip your ferret's nails, you must recognize that a ferret isn't the pet for you.

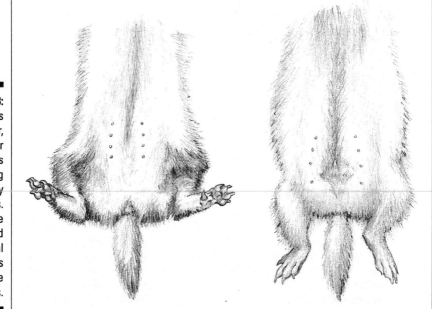

Figure 1-3:
Male ferrets are bulkier, with their penises resembling belly buttons. Females are smaller and have vulval openings near the anus.

Like all carnivores (see the first section in this chapter), ferrets have large canine teeth that can be rather intimidating. A ferret's teeth usually hang lower than his lip flap and are in full view. Although any animal with a mouth can and will bite under certain circumstances, I've found the biting ferret to be the exception rather than the rule. Most ferrets use their canine teeth to show off to their friends and to eat. When a ferret nips, she does it out of fear or play. An occasional warning nip may be a sign of the ferret's disapproval of one thing or another. (See Chapter 3 for more about the laws governing ferret bites.)

Make no doubt about it, the bite of a disgruntled ferret is painful and can draw blood. Take measures to make sure bites don't happen, and unless medically warranted for your ferret's health, don't alter his canine teeth; leave them right where they belong.

Making sense of senses

A ferret's senses vary in degree of acuteness (see Chapter 10 for more on ferret senses). Like human infants, a ferret's eyesight isn't that well-developed, and his ability to distinguish color is limited. A ferret can only see some reds and blues. Make no mistake about it, though: Even the most restricted ferret can and will find any object he wasn't intended to find (and his stubby little legs will help him steal the objects back to his hidey-hole). In a sense, all ferrets have sticky fingers: If they find it, it belongs to them. If they want it, it's theirs. You get the idea.

A ferret's sense of smell is far superior to a human's, and his little paw pads are more sensitive to the touch. Also, a fuzzy's sense of hearing is remarkable. If you open a bag of raisins from across your house, for example, be assured that your ferret will hear the bag opening and come a-begging. So, remember to whisper when discussing sensitive issues such as altering or going on vacation.

Have I mentioned that ferrets have another sense? They seem to understand us humans. Scary!

Exercise and Time Considerations — Yours and Your Fuzzy's

When determining whether a ferret is the perfect pet for you, get introspective and look at your lifestyle. Ferrets are interactive and intelligent pets that need a lot of attention. If you want a pet that you can keep in a cage and look at every once in a while, you must accept that a ferret isn't for you. Fish are good when left in their cages. Ferrets are exploratory characters that aim to please their humans. Okay, they really aim to please themselves, but they tickle us pink in the process.

Ferrets need a lot of exercise and attention to be happy and healthy. Plan on spending no less than four hours a day playing in a safe, stimulating, enriched, ferret-proof environment. If you leave a fuzzy in a cage or unattended too often, it actually leads to boredom and stress, which can in turn lead to serious health issues. Trust me, it will do you a world of good to get down on the floor with your ferret and let out your inner fuzzy. (For more information about enriching your ferret's life, check out Chapter 10.)

 If you don't think you can provide your ferret with the proper amount of exercise and attention, and that's your only ferret hang-up, perhaps you should consider adopting two ferrets. Ferrets live to play and they play to live, so if you can't be an interactive human all the time, get your fuzzy a playmate. Besides, although one furball is intensely amusing, two (or more) are downright hysterical. In fact, I recommend getting two or three no matter what (see Chapter 4 for more on this advice).

If you let him, a healthy caged ferret will sleep 18 to 20 hours a day. Does this make these ferrets nocturnal or diurnal? Neither. I think they should get a category all to themselves. How about ferturnal? Most weasels are considered nocturnal, although they may change their sleeping patterns depending on habitat, competition, and food availability. Like their polecat relatives, healthy, free-roaming ferrets with little cage time should sleep only 15 to 18 hours a day. Strive to make your ferrets as active as possible.

Ferrets tend to be *crepuscular,* which means they usually pep up and come out at dusk and dawn, similar to deer. However, ferrets change their activity levels to meet their humans' schedules. For example, if you're a night owl and sleep all day, your ferrets will be night owls too. Just as weasels will adapt to best suit their survival needs, ferrets can be diurnal, nocturnal, or crepuscular. What sleeping patterns your ferret adopts is up to you! (For tips on your ferret's cage and bedding for sleep time, see Chapter 5.)

Taking a Whiff of the Odor Factor

All ferrets come equipped with a really "neat" scenting mechanism. Located just outside the ferret's anus on both sides are anal sacs filled with foul-smelling fluid. All carnivores have these sacs, including the beloved canine. A ferret's system is quite different from the human scenting mechanism, though, which is more often than not triggered by disagreeable food or the simple desire to offend. When excited, overstimulated, scared, or angry, your ferret will, without aim, discharge his secret weapon. But the ferret's odor, although intentionally disturbing, rapidly dispels — just like yours! The following sections deal with a couple issues you face when playing the odor factor.

To descent or not to descent?

The majority of ferrets I've run across have been descented at a very early age — before they reach the pet trade. In other words, vets have removed their anal glands. Most ferrets are commercially raised in fuzzy farms where neutering and descenting occur before the fuzzies can be shipped out. As a new owner, you have no real way to tell whether a ferret has been descented, however. The moment of truth comes at the moment of nasal impact.

Personally I don't recommend descenting ferrets. I find it an unnecessary and potentially harmful procedure. However, some ferret owners can't or don't want to tolerate the rare "poof" of odor expelled from the undescented ferret. Finding a vet who's performed this procedure before may be a challenge, but most experienced ferret vets may be willing to take on the challenge and should do just fine. Don't be surprised if you find that this surgery doesn't cut down on the odor as much as you thought it would. The anal glands are not the problem! Ferrets are musky critters with oil glands in their skin. And unneutered ferrets are extremely smelly.

If you should happen upon a ferret with full scent capabilities in your search for a pet, take note, though: Descenting isn't necessary for living happily with a ferret. In fact, descenting is a North-American practice and is illegal in many European countries that consider it unethical. The ferret's scent glands may be an important behavioral and social tool. Perhaps they use scent as a means of identifying one ferret from another or determining the health status of another ferret. Scent may also indicate where a ferret is in its breeding cycle.

Unless medically necessitated, I suggest that you leave your ferret be and pay more heed to his emotional state so you can control the odor. Some people actually like the smell. I find myself neutral to it. Those of you who have roommates will surely agree that ferret odor is more often the lesser of the two evils.

Controlling your fuzzy's odor

The ferret's odor is unique and requires regular maintenance for odor control. You need to change his oil and rotate his tires every 3,000 miles, so to speak. Frequently changing his litter and bedding is the best way to control odor (see Chapter 9).

Bathing your ferret often results in a stinkier fuzzy because his oil glands go into overdrive to replace the oils you washed down the drain. I only bathe my ferrets a few times a year, and that seems plenty.

An expert's opinion on descenting

"Ferret farms descent ferrets in the mistaken belief that it decreases the odor of these musky pets. In fact, it is completely unnecessary for odor control. Unfortunately for the ferrets, descenting can lead to lifetime complications including draining tracts, chronic abscesses, pain, and/or incontinence. As a veterinarian and ferret owner, I cannot recommend this as a routine procedure for any reason," says ferret expert Dr. Karen Purcell, author of *Essentials of Ferrets: A Guide for Practitioners* (AAHA Press) and relief veterinarian in New England.

There's always some odor involved with ferrets. Even the most well-cared-for ferret will have a slight musky smell. On average, the odor is no worse than a dog's smell; however, people's tolerances for smell are different. Obviously, if you let your ferret go for very long periods without a bath or if you become too lax with changing his litter box and bedding, his smell will become stronger.

Getting the Dish on Financial Matters

Ferrets are expensive pets. Whether you purchase your baby at a pet store, adopt her from a shelter, or have a neighbor leave her on your doorstep (see Chapter 4), you need to fork over not only emotion but also money. Investing in a ferret family member has many intangible rewards, but you must be willing to put out the cash when necessary to keep her safe and sound. The following list outlines the expenses you'll incur after adopting your fuzzy:

- ✔ **Basic accessories:** This category includes such things as cages, toys, bedding, bowls, litter boxes, treats, and so on.

- ✔ **Food:** Ferrets need high-quality ferret food, which is more costly than low-quality food. And the more ferrets you have, the more they'll eat. Are you willing to pay more for a high-quality food to keep your ferrets as healthy as possible? (See Chapter 8 for more on feeding your ferret.)

- ✔ **Neutering or spaying:** Your new baby may or may not be altered, but unless you plan on breeding, which I caution you to think twice about, get him altered as soon as possible. Besides being the responsible thing to do, it'll cut down on the odor.

- ✔ **Annual vet trips:** Besides regular checkups (see Chapter 12), your ferret should receive annual rabies and distemper vaccinations, as well as heartworm preventives (vaccinations may be required by law; see Chapter 3).

As your ferret ages, the chances of him developing an illness or disease increases. Often, this means more frequent trips to the vet for special tests and/or medication. You owe it to any pet you have to provide quality medical care at all times.

The dollars can add up. Think about starting a pet fund, in which you put aside a few dollars each week in case an emergency comes up and you fall a little short financially. Also, pet insurance is becoming more and more popular among ferret owners. Do your research (starting with your veterinarian) to see whether insurance is an avenue to pursue. Either way, do yourself a favor and put aside some funds if you can.

Extreme Cage Makeover: Providing the Space They Need

You shouldn't bring a ferret to your home before you've completely and adequately set up his house for his arrival. Even though ferrets make great pets for both the house and apartment, you shouldn't compromise one luxury: His cage should be roomy, and you should make adequate room for it. (See Chapter 5 for more on creating a ferret cage.)

If your only available space is a wall that's supporting the world's largest beer-bottle collection, you should consider parting with the bottles or packing them up. Even if you could squeeze in both the ferret and the beer bottles, doing so wouldn't be a good idea. Your carpet shark could knock them over and break them, or your thief could manage to drag a bottle or two back to his secret hidey-hole!

Facing the Challenges of Ferret-Proofing Your Home

Ferrets are trouble magnets. From digging up the plants and carpeting, to stealing your stuff, to terrorizing the cats and dogs — if something can be messed with, a ferret will mess with it.

I compare this vigorous playtime madness to a human toddler on a double espresso. To combat the madness and protect your ferret, you need to ferret-proof your home — or at least the areas the little bugger has access to. It may be as simple as moving the houseplants, or it may be as involved as boarding up the cracks and crevices under your cabinets. Nature designed the ferret to search out your ferret-proofing failures. Therefore, ferret-proofing is a continuous activity as your curious fuzzy finds more and more flaws.

If you even question whether something is unsafe, it's probably unsafe. Otherwise, you wouldn't give it a second thought. Expect the impossible, prepare for the worst, and hope for the best. What actually happens will probably be somewhere in between. For tips on how to make your home safe for your ferret, head to Chapter 6

Ferrets and Kids

Ferrets can make good pets for single people living in apartments and for families in homes. I don't like to stereotype human children as a whole by saying this pet or that pet isn't good with kids. Usually, it's the other way around. Many kids aren't good around certain types of pets, although many are great. I was taking care of pets before I was even 10 years old, and I did so with great pleasure and responsibility. I didn't mind getting scratched or bitten, and I didn't mind the cage cleaning. I was an exception to most kids.

Ferrets can be playfully nippy and squirmy, and they require a lot of attention and care. Most young children can and will activate the hyper switch in ferrets. And don't be fooled if your kid promises to be 100-percent responsible for his new ferret. You must evaluate your family members honestly before bringing a ferret home and expect that you'll be the main caretaker. See Chapter 7 for more on this topic.

Ferrets and Other Household Pets

All animals have unique personalities, so to assume that one pet will get along with another is to be overly optimistic — an attitude that could lead to heartbreak. Multi-species interaction is a complex issue. I simply can't guarantee that your new fuzzy will get along with your other pets.

Certain breeds of dogs are bred to hunt small animals, which the ferret is. And ferrets are bred as predators and may find birds, hamsters, and even small kittens as the perfect prey. Cats and ferrets often get along well, but you can't force a relationship that isn't there.

Having said all that, I don't see a reason why a ferret couldn't peacefully cohabitate in most homes if the owners use common sense. The key is to know your animals and their limits. Provide meticulous supervision at all times. When you introduce your pets, you may have to conclude that mixing the species just won't work in your home; be prepared to offer your ferret a safe place to adequately play away from all your other pets. (See Chapter 7 for more on introducing your ferret to other animals.)

Leaping over the Legal Hurdles

You must be aware of the legal aspects of owning a ferret. Before you consider the time, cost, adjustment, and olfactory aspects of ferret parenthood, do some digging to be sure that ferrets are legal where you live. What licenses may you need? What restrictions does your local government place on pet owners?

It's truly heartbreaking to lose a ferret to legal snags after investing so much time and love. Fortunately, I haven't experienced this pain firsthand, but I do shed tears when I read the emotional testimonies of people who've lost legal battles and ultimately their beloved fuzzies. For more information about the legal issues that govern owning a ferret, head to Chapter 3.

Chapter 2

Understanding What Ferrets Are (And Aren't)

In This Chapter

▶ Acquainting yourself with your lovable domestic ferret

▶ Perusing the historical timeline of the ferret

▶ Taking a look at the sport of ferreting

▶ Going green (not really) with ferret hybrids

▶ Reviewing the domestic ferret's appearance

▶ Examining the plight and the rebirth of the black-footed ferret

*I*t's important to discuss domestication when it comes to ferrets; the issue is at the center of a ferret's identity. Some people hold the mistaken belief that ferrets are wild animals, but that couldn't be further from the truth. Lumping them in with wild animals for regulatory purposes is, in my opinion, a crime (for more, see Chapter 3). In reality, ferrets are domesticated polecats, which means they're descendants of wild polecats that were domesticated by humans. This chapter will teach you about what it means to be domesticated and why ferrets are domesticated. It's really quite interesting.

You also discover in this chapter that ferrets are endearing critters that come in a multitude of colors and patterns, which I explain in detail. But ferret types don't end at colors. In your search for a ferret you may come across an angora or even a ferret-polecat hybrid, so this chapter prepares you a little for that unusual and exciting encounter. But you're not likely to encounter the ferret's rare and extremely endangered cousin, the black-footed ferret. So I'll introduce you to him here. You'll get to know about his plight and the heroic efforts of a group of people to reintroduce him back into the wild.

This chapter also burrows through the past and takes you into the present, taking note of historical ferret sightings — some of which are more like hallucinations. You find out why people prized the beloved ferret so much in the first place, and that common folk weren't the only ones who enjoyed the company of weasels. You also get a brief lesson on the art of ferreting, as well as a stern lecture on why your ferret should hunt only within the safety of your home.

Yes, Ferrets Are Domesticated

Domestication is a long process in which people selectively breed wild animals in captivity for human benefit. There are three main criteria for domestication:

✔ **Humans select the animals to be bred; the animals can't select mates themselves.**

In the case of unaltered pet ferrets, their breeding is under complete control of humans. People not only pair up the ferrets, but also can and sometimes do tell them when and when not to breed by using light cycles. They can take ferrets out of season by using vasectomized males or drugs so that they can't reproduce. Humans can even have ferrets produce multiple litters per year or prevent them from having any litters in a year.

✔ **The animal experiences some type of genetic change that reflects the human selection and distinguishes it from its wild counterparts.**

Domestication has caused profound changes to ferret behavior:

• Domesticated ferrets by nature don't fear humans.

• They demonstrate prolonged litter behaviors toward other ferrets, which allows them to be housed with other ferrets.

• They demonstrate play behavior into late adulthood.

Will the ferret's real daddy please stand up?

A huge amount of mystery and controversy surrounds our little ferret friends' history — perhaps because all polecat groups are very closely related and can interbreed successfully (that is, they can produce viable hybrids). Nobody really knows how the ferret is related to the rest of the polecats, except that it *is* a domesticated polecat, and the European polecat *(Mustela putorius)* and the steppe polecat *(Mustela eversmanni)* may be involved. The most commonly accepted among several theories points toward the European polecat as having the most likely claim to ferret ancestry.

Although scientists have found little archeological evidence to support this idea, genetically speaking, today's ferret and the entire polecat group Subgenera Putorius (*Mustela eversmanni, Mustela putorius,* and *Mustela nigripes*) are practically twins. The most likely conclusion is that the domestic ferret is a polecat hybrid. But even a seemingly insignificant genetic discrepancy can mean the difference between a horse and a zebra or a dog and a coyote.

So, the studies move forward. However, it's quite possible that we may never know the real ancestry in our lifetime or in any other lifetime. For your purposes, all you truly need to know is that you're dealing with a unique little creature — more affectionate than ferocious, and so easy to fall in love with.

In addition to behavioral changes, the domesticated ferret features extreme changes to fur color when compared to wild polecats. Ferrets can be bred for a multitude of colors and patterns, and albinism occurs frequently.

✔ **Humans derive some benefit from the domestication of the animal.**

People domesticated ferrets to be mousers because they wanted a polecat that could hunt mice and be predictably tame toward humans. By the end of the domestication process, that's exactly what they had. In the past and still today, people used ferrets in the sport of ferreting to hunt rabbits. Ferret domestication has also benefited humans in the areas of fur production, experimental science, and, of course, companionship.

Some domestication scientists would add a fourth bullet indicating tameness as a criterion, but not all domesticated animals are tame, which I can attest to as a keeper of wild animals. And some wild animals are tame, so tameness is relative.

Getting to Know Fuzzies in the Past and Present

Domesticated ferrets have been around for about 2,500 years and have stolen the hearts of such people as Queen Elizabeth I and comedian Dick Smothers. They were avid sailors during the American Revolutionary war, and they've been skilled hunters from the time of domestication until now. It seems their talents abound. Since domesticating ferrets, people have found many uses for this wonderful animal, though it wasn't until several decades ago that the ferret actually started catching on as a lovable pet.

Ferrets throughout history

Tracking the ferret's timeline is both factually difficult and headache inducing. Many sources cite the people of Egypt as the original domesticators of ferrets, but we have no proof that this theory is true. Egyptian hieroglyphics portray images of weasel-like creatures, but several animals can fit the description — the mongoose being one of them. Prior to the domestication of the cat, the mongoose held the high esteem of snake catcher and keeper of the house in Egypt — and does so still today. Experts can logically conclude that these hieroglyphics don't show ferrets at all, but rather another animal native to the land. After all, you haven't seen reports of ferret mummies being discovered in Egypt, have you? And the Egyptians seemingly mummified everything! Additionally, the hieroglyphics date back almost 500 years prior to the domestication of the cat, which happened about 4,000 years ago.

The first known written reference to an animal likely to be the domesticated ferret popped up around 400 BC and was penned by the Greek satirical writer Aristophanes (448–385 BC). Later, in 350 BC, the Greek naturalist and philosopher Aristotle (384–322 BC) penned another reference. A ferret supposedly made an appearance in the Bible, but it turned out to be a mistake in translation. The word in question, translated correctly, means "small crawling things"; in modern day translations, it means "gecko."

Experts estimate that the ferret was introduced to North America a little more than 300 years ago. But only recently (in about the past 30 years) have most pet owners discovered the ferret's "fetching" personality.

Ferrets have always had a knack for meeting man's needs

Earlier civilizations must have found the ferret to be quite the efficient exterminator, because Caesar Augustus received a request around 60 BC to sail several ferrets to the Balearic Islands to control the rabbit population. And ferrets are no strangers to the seas; during the American Revolutionary War, several ferrets would roam the ships at sea to patrol for rodents. In fact, one ship was named after a ferret: In an 1823 newspaper article, a U.S. schooner, *The Ferret,* was reported to be chasing (capturing) pirates. People also used the small, flexible critters to navigate wire, cable, and tools through small openings and tunnels.

You can find many more documented reports on the use of ferrets to control pests and hunt small game. Supposedly, two of the greatest ferret keepers were German Emperor Frederick II (1194–1250) and Genghis Khan (1167–1227), ruler of the Mongol empire. The hunting of small game is called *ferreting* — a word still used today, both literally and figuratively (see the upcoming ferreting section for more on the topic).

Ferrets catching on

Ferrets have tunneled their way into the lives of many historical figures — from Caesar Augustus, who was asked for the working ferrets' services to rid an island of rabbits, to Queen Elizabeth I, who had a portrait done with one of her royal fuzzies. Ferrets have been frequent subjects of famous artists, such as Leonardo da Vinci. Other famous ferret humans include comedian Dick Smothers and actor Dave Foley. Ferrets have even weaseled into the theater, play roles in such movies as *Kindergarten Cop, Garfield, Tale of Two Kitties, Starship Troopers, Star Trek: The Next Generation,* and *Beastmaster,* to mention just a few.

Ferrets have made brief appearances on some television shows. For instance, Dr. Wendy Winsted and her ferrets Melinda and McGuinn made a guest appearance on what was then called *Late Night with David Letterman.* They (the ferrets) performed the roll-over trick for a lap of milk and a bite of a stagehand's roast beef sandwich.

Ferrets also are a common source of punch lines and jokes. Take, for example, the television series *M*A*S*H.* Major Frank Burns was often referred to as "ferret face." I'm not sure where the insult lies, though. And David Letterman has frequently used the ferret in his Top Ten lists. I suppose I can see some humor in it. After all, I have some very weasely friends. They know who they are!

Spotlighting the Sport of Ferreting

The sport of *ferreting* — hunting small game with ferrets — probably developed hand in hand with the domestication of the ferret. The ferret keeper, or *ferret-meister* (similar to a wisenheimer), would release a couple ferrets near rabbit burrows and send them in to find the game. Like today's pointers and other gun dogs, working ferrets wore bells placed on their collars so their keepers could track them. The ferret's job wasn't to hunt; it was simply supposed to chase the rabbit or other game out of its burrow. Often, the fleeing animal became entangled in nets that keepers used to prevent escape. The hunter then killed the prey with a club or gun or used dogs or hawks to catch the game.

Sometimes, a ferret would stay in the hole, eat its share of the catch, and then go to sleep! The aggravated keeper would have to send in another ferret tethered to a line to locate and awaken the stuffed, sleepy ferret. The keeper would then follow the line and dig out the ferrets and what was left of the carcass. Another option was to cover up all the exit holes except for one, set a mink trap, and hope the thieving ferret would be caught by morning.

Ferret keepers were sometimes poachers. The poachers would hide the ferret in his pants and take the fuzzy out at night to hunt. Poachers were possibly the first large-scale pet ferret owners. This makes sense if you consider that a poacher would typically spend more time bonding with and socializing his ferrets to reduce the risk of getting caught. As ferreting became more popular and the ferret gained respect, highly educated people took up the sport, and most people kept their ferrets in conditions far superior to what most people at that time experienced.

Many people in Australia and Europe still enjoy the sport of ferreting (see Figure 2-1); however, it's illegal in the United States and Canada.

Figure 2-1:
Here's a
working
ferret
teamed up
with a
human
hunter.

I don't advise trying your hand at the sport of ferreting for many reasons:

✔ It's illegal.

✔ Your ferret can get lost, maybe even for good.

✔ You may expose your ferret to a disease.

✔ It's cold, dark, and scary in those rabbit burrows (to me, anyway).

✔ Your ferret would prefer to be cuddled up with you in a safe, warm house.

✔ Your ferret can drown in water-filled burrows.

✔ Hey, what did a rabbit ever do to you?

Although traditional ferreting is illegal in the United States, fuzzies remain quite the charmers and are beloved snatchers of our small worldly possessions.

Exploring the Hot Topic of Ferret Hybrids

The subject of ferret hybrids is a hotly debated topic in many ferret circles. Very simply put, a *hybrid* is a cross between a domestic animal and its wild counterpart — in this case, a ferret and a polecat. A hybrid can have just a smidge of wild blood or a whole lot of it, depending on the breeding. In the same mold, behavioral and physical traits are diluted or concentrated, depending on the breeding.

What kind of pet does the average ferret hybrid make? Is the result a ferret or a polecat? Some say the animal is neither, claiming it's a confused critter stuck in the middle, belonging neither in the wild nor in captivity, thus the ethical and moral dilemma. The fuzzy is neither wild nor domesticated. Other people disagree, saying that the confusion lies between the handler and the animal. They argue that properly socialized hybrids — especially those with low polecat content — can be content, happy, and playful in captivity.

So, what are the benefits of hybridization? Why do people do it (and who does it)? And what are the cons? The following sections break down the issue.

The pros of and arguments for ferret hybridization

You must examine what it is that makes people attracted to the ferret hybrid in the first place. Do they honestly believe that a hybrid is a good household pet? Do people just desire a little piece of the wild? Is it fair? Experienced owners can't emphasize enough that ferret hybrids definitely aren't for the inexperienced or uneducated. Other than just wanting a piece of the wild in your living room, what's the benefit to breeding and owning hybrids? Some argue that if done responsibly and correctly, hybrid breeding can enhance existing ferret bloodlines and make ferrets healthier, hardier, and sounder by introducing polecat blood into the mix. Responsible and educated owners love their hybrids and seem to understand them quite well.

Having had a ferret hybrid, I can attest to the fact that they're not for beginners. In fact, mine was a rescue that came from an inexperienced person who didn't do her research before purchasing this beautiful animal. She didn't properly socialize him, and she had the bites to prove it. I sit on the fence with this issue and tend to lean towards advising people not to get hybrids as pets. They're too difficult to work with, especially high-percentage hybrids, and it's just not fair to the animal. A small percentage of people out there can properly handle ferret hybrids and keep them the way they need to be kept. I also believe there are some breeders out there that can knowledgeably use polecats to enhance the ferret species as a whole. Do all breeders know how to do this? No. Ferreting out the good people is difficult, so I remain skeptical of all who breed ferret hybrids and want to own them as pets. Ferret owners must think long and hard before making such a decision to keep these often misunderstood and easily mishandled beauties.

A hybrid ferret certainly has some benefits:

> ✔ A hybrid is a beautiful animal. They often bear beautiful, dark markings and have stocky, muscular bodies (see the following section for more on ferret appearances).

✔ Hybrids have much better eyesight than non-hybrids, and they rely more on eyesight than domesticated ferrets do.

✔ They have extraordinary physical capabilities.

✔ They are very dominant and independent in most situations.

Owners of hybrids also report that they require a rigorous enrichment routine due to their higher energy and curiosity levels. Hybrids are intelligent buggers that map and survey their areas much more quickly than ferrets, which also causes them to become bored more easily. And when hybrids are done exploring down low, they climb to the higher levels and explore!

Putting a hybrid in the hands of an uneducated owner often leads to an abused, isolated animal and a frustrated, possibly injured owner. You simply can't treat a hybrid like a ferret. For example, you can't scruff them (grab them by the hair on the neck). And you can't pass them around to your friends! Exhibiting dominance over a hybrid is a no-no. Successful interaction comes when you reach a mutual understanding and level of respect. Knowing how to read the hybrid's body language and respond appropriately is key as well (see Chapter 18 for more on ferret body language). See the following section for a rundown of the cons of hybridization.

The cons of hybridization

Most ferret-polecat offspring — especially those with a high percentage of polecat blood — display the characteristics of the wild polecat, which certainly isn't favorable in a captive environment. Hybrids, in general, display the following characteristics:

✔ They're shy and fearful of humans.

✔ They're less social and less willing to live in groups.

✔ They typically don't make good working ferrets (where ferreting is legal, they won't enter unfamiliar holes or burrows like domesticated ferrets do).

✔ They frighten easily, are cautious, and hide at the slightest new sound or sight.

✔ They don't tolerate new people or being held, and they're quick to bite if they feel uncomfortable.

✔ They don't tolerate being caged very well; they need a lot of room to roam and explore on a daily basis. Ferret-proofing can be quite challenging, and the result is that hybrids are very accident-prone in a household.

✔ Their mentality makes them more challenging; they're more emotional, sensitive, and higher strung than the non-hybrid.

What type of people should consider owning a hybrid? Should anyone? Here's what Dr. June McNicholas, BSc PhD, says about the topic: "It's taken centuries of selective breeding to produce the sociable, gregarious, outgoing domestic ferret from the shy, solitary and largely unmanageable polecat. So why try to reintroduce the very qualities that it's taken so long to remove?"

Although Dr. McNicholas is ethically against the breeding of hybrid ferrets, she says, "For those people who decide to explore the options, I would say that the common sense rules apply when selecting a [hybrid] kit. Is it healthy? Is it happy to be handled by its owner and by you? Is it full of curiosity and confidence, and ready to explore its surroundings? If so, fine. It may not be a hybrid at all! If so, what are you prepared to pay?" And I dare say that she isn't just speaking in regards to financial price.

Picturing the Physical Appearance of the Domestic Ferret

Ferrets — those long, slender beauties — come in a variety of colors and patterns. Colors range from the easily recognized albino with her white fur and pink eyes, to the dark-eyed white (DEW) with her white coat and dark eyes, to the darker sables and all shades in between. As if colors weren't enough, ferrets also come in color patterns, which have to do with color concentrations or placement of white markings. Eye colors, mask shapes, and even nose colorings play roles in how your ferret may be classified. Color, however, should be the last factor in picking out your new ferret.

Ferret people are coming up with more and more definitions of coat colors and patterns all the time (maybe just to confuse the general public!), but many basic colors and patterns are defined for you. I present these in the sections that follow.

The spectrum of fuzzy colors

Every ferret has a color, and in that color is a pattern. Some colors and patterns change from season to season, and others will stay the same. Personally, when it comes to colors, I go by The American Ferret Association Standards. So, unless you bought a neon ferret, your fuzzy will most likely fall into one of the following categories that most ferret enthusiasts seem to agree on. (**Note:** These colors are show standards, so most ferrets won't match 100 percent.) Refer to the color photos in the middle of this book to see some of these ferret colors in their full glory!

Groups of ferret experts argue over the names of shades of sables and silvers. You may find that one group calls one shade a fancy name and another group calls it something different. No matter how many color names the experts come up with, some ferrets will be lighter or darker than what their definitions specify. So, it seems the definitions may never end.

- **Albino:** Resulting from a lack of pigment in the skin and eyes, albino ferrets range from a creamy white to a preferred snow-white color — both on the guardhairs and undercoat. All albinos have light- to medium-pink eyes, with ruby being preferred, and pink noses.

- **Black:** The black ferret is absolutely stunning. His guardhairs are truly black in color. His undercoat is white or has a light golden cast, and his eyes are black or near black, with a nose to match. A speckled black nose also is acceptable.

- **Black sable:** This ferret is such a dark brown that he actually appears black. He has a white or cream undercoat that barely shows through the dark guardhairs. His eyes should be dark brown to near black, with a nose to match. A heavily mottled (marbled), blackish brown nose is acceptable as well.

- **Champagne:** This ferret is a light to medium tan or a diluted chocolate. His undercoat is white to creamy in color, and his eyes are light to dark burgundy. Like the chocolate, the champagne ferret's nose should be pink, with or without the brown/beige "T" outline.

- **Chocolate:** The chocolate ferret's coat is another shade variation of sable, but in a tasty shade of milk-chocolate brown. The ferret's undercoat has a golden cast to it or is white. His eyes are almost always brown but can be dark burgundy as well. The chocolate's nose is pink, with or without the brown "T" outline; it can also be beige or brick in color.

- **Cinnamon:** The cinnamon's coat is a very beautiful shade of light reddish brown. His undercoat has a golden cast to it or is white. The ferret's eyes are light to medium burgundy. His nose may be pink, but a pinkish/beige nose with a brick colored "T" outline (or completely brick-colored nose) is preferred. However, many experts argue that true red cinnamons don't exist any longer.

- **Dark-eyed white (DEW):** This category is one of my favorites. These beauties resemble albinos because of their white or creamy coats and pink noses. The exception is their eye color, which is a dark burgundy. The DEW pattern has 10 percent or less colored guardhairs in the form of a stripe, colored tail, spots, or a sprinkling throughout the coat.

The DEW ferret and DEW pattern are prone to deafness. *Waardensburg Syndrome* is a ferret condition that genetically links the white fur on the head to deafness (similar to the condition of deafness in many blue-eyed white cats). In addition to dark-eyed whites, pandas and shetlands/blazes (other ferret pattern types; see the following section) are often prone to deafness, though this isn't always the case. ***Note:*** Deaf ferrets make fine pets if you take extra care to properly train them and be careful not to startle them.

✔ **Sable:** This ferret color is probably the most common. The guardhairs are a rich, deep brown, and they're evenly and densely dispersed. The undercoat on the neck, back, and belly is white or cream colored. The eyes are brown or close to black, and the nose is light or dappled brown. The nose may also have a brown "T" outline.

Guardhairs are the stiffer, longer, and more prominent pieces of fur that cover the shorter and softer undercoat. Guardhairs provide the ferret's coloration or camouflage and aid in waterproofing the fur. The undercoat also act as insulation.

Fuzzy color patterns

Ferret *patterns* are used to describe color concentrations and white markings on the ferret's body. With patterns, the main discriminating factors are the legs and tail, or *points,* and how the point color or mask shape (see below) relates to the rest of the body color. The following list presents the most commonly recognized ferret patterns. Flip to the color photos in the center of this book to see what some of these look like!

✔ **Blaze:** These ferrets usually have smudges or rings of color around their eyes rather than masks. Small masks are acceptable, but full masks are not. A white blaze extends from the face up over the head and hopefully down the ferret's neck to the shoulders. All four of his feet have mitts or white tips; sometimes his knees are also white. Bibs, white or mottled bellies, and roaning may also be present. He should have ruby or brown eyes, and his nose should be pink (with or without a lighter outline).

✔ **Mitts:** Ferrets with mitts look like their paws have been dipped in white marshmallow fluff. They also have white bibs. A mitt's colors and patterns should be appropriate for his standards. The eyes should be a varying shade of burgundy, and the color standard should determine nose color. Knee patches and a tail tip may or may not be present.

✔ **Panda:** Ferrets of any color that have white heads, necks, and throats. Some pandas have "rings" around their eyes, which is acceptable; all pandas should have four white mitts (or paws). Bibs and knee patches (yes, ferrets have knees) may be present, as well as a white tip on the tail. His eyes should be a shade of burgundy, and his nose should be pink (with or without a lighter outline).

✔ **Roan:** This ferret almost has an even mixture of colored and white guardhairs. Typically, you want to see 50 to 60 percent colored and 40 to 50 percent white hairs. The color and pattern will determine the mask he needs to wear, along with his nose. For instance, a black roan mitt can have a hood or regular mask.

✔ **Siamese or point:** These are ferrets of any color that have much darker points than body color. His mask is shaped like a thin letter V. Champagne versions of this ferret may have no mask (see the previous section for more on colors). The nose should be light in color, such as pink or beige, or have a "T" outline.

✔ **Solid:** The solid ferret is slightly more concentrated in color than the standard ferret — ideally, 100 percent of the guardhairs will be colored. This means that you can't distinguish his points from the rest of his body, because the ferret's outer coat is solid in color. He should have a full T-bar mask and a nose color appropriate for his coat color (see the previous section).

✔ **Standards:** This ferret pattern is perhaps the most common. The percentage of colored guardhairs should be approximately 90 to 100 compared to the white guardhairs present. The body appears lighter in color than the points (the legs and tail), which makes the points easily distinguishable from the rest of the body. Standards should have nose colors appropriate for their body colors standard and full or T-bar masks.

Hey! Where did my "silver" and "silver mitt" go? The silver, according to The American Ferret Association, is considered a "black roan." And you guessed it: The silver mitt is now the "black roan mitt."

Not Just Another Color: The Black-Footed Ferret

The black-footed ferret, known as *Mustela nigripes,* is a small, carnivorous predator that lives in the wild and weighs between 1.5 and 2.5 pounds (0.7–1.1 kg) — approximately the same size as the mink and our domesticated fuzzy, or slightly larger than the weasel. In captivity, he may live as long as nine years, two to three times longer than expected in the wild. See Figure 2-2 to see what a black-footed ferret looks like. Compare it to Figure 1-1 in Chapter 1 to see how different the black-footed ferret looks from the domestic ferret. Refer also to the photo in the color insert.

The black-footed ferret arrived in North America as an efficient predator, but it was in North America that he evolved into the specialized predator of prairie dogs. The black-footed ferret is known to be the only native North-American ferret and is the smallest of the polecats.

The black-footed ferret is considered by most to be one of the rarest mammals in the United States and perhaps the entire world. What has caused such a skilled hunter and cousin to our domestic ferret to earn such a title? It's no doubt that the plight of the black-footed ferret was caused both directly and indirectly by the human race. Sadly, his future remains uncertain.

Figure 2-2:
A black-footed ferret.

This section describes the physical traits of the black-footed ferret and how our domestic ferret stands up in comparison. Here you also find an overview on how the black-footed ferret compares to our domestic ferret, where the black-footed ferret came from, where he's been, and where he's heading.

The one, true North American ferret!

The black-footed ferret adapted in North America long before the ferret was even domesticated. A close relative of the Siberian polecat, *mustela eversmanii,* the ancestral black-footed ferret is thought to have come from northeast Asia, crossing at the point now known as the Bering Strait, between Russia and Alaska. The actual time period he scampered into North America remains uncertain. The estimates date as far back as 1 million years ago to as recent as 100,000 years ago.

Are black-footed ferrets really that different?

Black-footed ferrets and our domesticated fuzzies share many similar physical features, body size, and behaviors. Skeletally speaking, they're almost identical. Small differences appear in the skull. The domestic ferret has a shorter and more-rounded head and a slightly smaller nose. The domestic ferret's smaller ears give it an appearance of having a more pointed snout than the black-footed ferret. Both have strong front paws for digging and burrowing. The black-footed ferret has a more tubular tail unlike the tapered tail of the domestic ferret. It also has noticeably larger nocturnal eyes and broader ears needed for extra keen senses, along with a noticeably longer neck than the domestic ferret.

The black-footed ferret's nose is almost always solid black. He also always has the distinctive black feet, legs, and tip of tail. While our domestic ferrets can vary a great deal in color, shade, and pattern, only limited variations in shade of body color exist in the black-footed ferret. Always present is a white, cream, or buff full bib and a saddle of brown on his back. The saddle area is filled in with dark-tipped guard hairs that are lighter towards the roots of the hairs. Fur generally becomes lighter in shade towards and on the belly. All areas of brown can vary from light medium to dark depending on season and individual animal. Also very prominent on the black-footed ferret and almost all polecats is a white spot just above the top inner corner of each eye.

Habitat (or is that prairie dog?) destruction

The black-footed ferret's range was as vast as the prairie dog's. They thrived only where prairie dogs thrived, covering over 700 million acres. From southern Canada to northern Mexico, the prairie dog colonies were the life source for the black-footed ferret. Making up 90 percent of the black-footed ferret's diet, the prairie dog also furnished essential burrows, which were vital in providing shelter to the black-footed ferret. These burrows were safe havens that kept out the extreme weather and protected the black-footed ferret from predators. The burrows were also convenient places to whelp and rear offspring safely.

So with the essential presence of millions of prairie dogs inhabiting the territories, what could possibly push the black-footed ferret to the edge of extinction?

The most devastating human actions leading to the demise of the black-footed ferret weren't against the ferret at all but, rather, its food source — the prairie dog. Prairie dog colonies were viewed by local residents with extreme abomination for many reasons. Ranchers complained that the colonies competed with the local livestock for vital food. Agriculturists argued that they destroyed the land. As frequent carriers of sylvatic plague, introduced to North America by none other than the human animal, prairie dogs were also considered extreme health risks to nearby humans.

Prairie dogs knew as well as people where the best living environment was. The locals didn't want their peaceful neighbors, and with the help of the U.S. government, that lead to rapid decimation of prairie dog populations.

The most reckless attack on the prairie dog came in the form of mass poisoning. Cans of cyanide gas were tossed into the burrows, or strychnine pellets were left disguised as treats. Contaminated carcasses were often eaten, which killed unaware diners, including black-footed ferrets, wolves, and eagles to name a few. Other animals inhabiting the burrows fell victim to these cruel assaults as well. The prairie dogs that survived the various strikes lost their habitat to land-clearing machines such as the bulldozer.

Experts estimate that up to 99 percent of the once-vast prairie dog range remains cleared of these peaceful critters, leaving only a few million acres with surviving colonies. In fact, legal poisoning and shooting of prairie dogs continues to this day.

With the black-footed ferret's food source practically decimated, its demise rapidly grew closer. In 1960, people realized that the black-footed ferret population might be in danger, but by then it was too late. By the mid-1960s, the first in-depth studies began to indicate how grim the future looked for the black-footed ferret. In 1967, the black-footed ferret became legally protected — only 116 years after being given its official scientific name in 1851 by John James Audubon and John Bachman. And in 1973, the black-footed ferret was one of the first animals to be placed on the current Endangered Species List.

The last wild black-footed ferret was initially thought to have been seen in 1974, but a small group was discovered in Wyoming in 1981 after a dog presented an unusual and unfortunately dead animal to its bewildered human. The newly discovered colony flourished and reached almost 130 animals. However, the population was destroyed by 1985. Turns out that 50 percent of the prairie dog population feeding this hopeful Wyoming ferret colony tested positive for the rodent-decimating sylvatic plague, known to humans as bubonic plague, killing both prairie dogs and ferrets.

Even more tragic was the fact that canine distemper, 100 percent fatal to black-footed ferrets, swept through the fragile group. This was as big a factor in wiping out the black-footed ferret as was plague. The race was then on to capture the remaining wild black-footed ferrets. There we were! Only eighteen ferrets were left in 1987. They stood on the brink of extinction again. Between 1985 and 1987, the very last 18 black-footed ferrets were rescued. The last-known wild ferret was taken alive in February 1987 in Wyoming — that is, before the reintroduction of the critters began taking place.

The Black-Footed Ferret Recovery Plan

The monumental goal of the Black-Footed Ferret Recovery Plan, developed and approved by the U.S. Fish and Wildlife Service in 1988, is to establish no less than ten geographically separate populations of wild, self-sustaining black-footed ferrets. This plan calls for the establishment of 1,500 breeding wild black-footed ferrets in order for the species to be removed from the endangered species list.

With the dedicated help of member organizations of The Black-Footed Ferret Recovery Implementation Team (BFFRIT), created in 1996, this goal is slowly being recognized. These organizations work with the U.S. Fish and Wildlife Service and act as advisory teams. According to their Web site, www.black footedferret.org: "Through a team effort, the agencies and partners involved on the Black-footed Ferret Recovery Implementation Team will promote strategic public awareness, understanding, and support, resulting in the successful recovery of the black-footed ferret and the conservation of the ecosystem upon which it depends."

Once thought to be extinct in 1980, more than 5,000 have been produced in captivity since 1987. Responsible for this are: Louisville Zoo, Toronto Zoo, The National Zoo, The Phoenix Zoo, Cheyenne Mountain Zoo, and The National Black-Footed Ferret Conservation Center. More than 2,500 have been released into the wild since 1991. Approximately 700 exist today. The people responsible for the Recovery Program have gained a greater understanding of captive breeding and have even begun to use such means as artificial insemination (AI). Maybe that number will double or even triple in another 25 years.

Captive breeding

Only since 1991 have attempts been made to reintroduce this species into the wild through captive-breeding efforts. In the beginning, these efforts were met with sobering obstacles. From the limited gene pool of only 18 captive black-footed ferrets, to the inability to successfully rehabilitate captive-reared juveniles into the wild, to the lack of habitat for release, the future looked grim for the black-footed ferret.

Today things are looking up because much has been learned about raising black-footed ferrets in captivity. Although black-footed ferrets retain some instincts, such as killing and eating prairie dogs, burrowing, and recognizing and avoiding predators, those instincts aren't as sharp as they would be had they been born in the wild. After all, they've been in captivity for 20 years!

For this reason, captive-born kits are now sent to survival boot camp for a month and a half to learn how to survive in the wild. Living in semi-natural, but protected, communities, the ferrets are allowed to sharpen their skills by interacting with live prairie dogs and living in real burrows. Preconditioning routines and procedures such as these have increased the survival rate of captive-born kits released into the wild threefold. Additionally, some sites have even been successful at transferring wild ferrets from one site to another, which is important for maintaining genetic distribution.

Progress being made

In the beginning years, only three states participated in releases: Wyoming, South Dakota, and Montana. Today things are quite different. In the U.S., there are now 10 different black-footed ferret reintroduction sites located in six different states: Arizona, Colorado, Utah, South Dakota, Wyoming, and Montana. Mexico also participates in the reintroduction project. Currently Kansas and Canada are being pursued as possible sites, and the list is growing. The sites must be located where significant prairie dog towns still exist, so this means mainly federal, state, and tribal lands.

Hurdles in recovery

Nothing worth doing is ever easy. Some things are in man's control, while other things aren't. Although significant progress has been made in The Black-Footed Ferret Recovery Plan, several challenges still remain. Unfortunately, all must be conquered in order to win the battle of the black-footed ferret.

- **Political:** This is perhaps the biggest and longest-standing threat facing the black-footed ferret. It's not even against the ferret itself, but rather against its food source — the prairie dog. The biggest myth is that livestock suffer broken legs from stepping in prairie dog burrows. The fact is, cows aren't that stupid.

  People also don't want their livestock competing for grassland. There are even state laws that mandate you eradicate prairie dogs from your land. The county will do it if you don't and then send you a bill later! Political pressure still exists to poison prairie dogs even on America's public lands. No prairie dogs. No food. No ferrets.

- **Biological:** Black-footed ferrets are highly susceptible to both plague and also canine distemper. With the exception of South Dakota, which has never had plague, all states have had outbreaks in prairie dogs. The Recovery Program is currently experimenting with a human plague vaccine to protect the black-footed ferret. Each ferret caught is given a series of two shots over a two week period. Although this vaccinates the ferrets, it doesn't help the prairie dogs. So, they hope to come up with an oral vaccine to mass vaccinate the prairie dogs.

- **Economic:** This hurdle comes up almost everywhere help is needed. There simply isn't enough money to keep people in place to do what's needed. Finding more sites to put ferrets on also takes money, and raising money takes money. Without funding, the Recovery Program is doomed.

✔ **Social:** Public awareness and education are missing components to the recovery program. How can anyone help a program they don't understand or even know about? Most people don't even know what a black-footed ferret even is. Says Travis Livieri of Prairie Wildlife Research, "Wolves and grizzlies are two of the most widely recognized and celebrated endangered species, but nowhere as near as endangered as black-footed ferrets." The people responsible for the Recovery Program need to do more public outreach. They need to view education as being as important as the recovery process itself.

Black-footed ferrets are one of the most recoverable species on the endangered species list. They're the "panda" of the prairie. The prairie dog is the keystone of the prairie. By preserving the prairie dog ecosystem, we're not only saving the black-footed ferret, we're also saving the swift fox, burrowing owl, ferruginous hawks, and mountain plover. They're all directly linked to prairie dogs. Bison and antelope also thrive in the prairie dog ecosystem. You can make a difference in saving these animals.

Although the government recognizes that the survival of the black-footed ferret depends directly on the survival of prairie dog colonies, the government continues to support the mass killing of prairie dogs. It's possible that because the black-footed ferret is a specialized hunter and hasn't adapted to an alternate diet, people may soon lose these beautiful critters forever.

So, what can you do? First, you can learn about the prairie — what it is and its history. Did you know that you own a part of the prairie? It doesn't matter where you live! Find out which zoos have black-footed ferrets, and visit one of these magnificent creatures. Write to or call your local conservation office to find out how you can become directly involved in the fight to save your local prairies. And if you live in a state where prairie dogs reside, step forward and take action. Find out what you can do to help protect the prairie dog's future. And don't forget, you can go to www.blackfootedferret.org and cyber adopt a black-footed ferret today!

Chapter 3

Ferrets and the Law: Licensing and Other Issues

In This Chapter

▶ Addressing licensing issues

▶ Examining the existence and purpose of ferret-free zones

▶ Familiarizing yourself with ferret law

Some of you may be just beginning to develop a mild adoration of fuzzies; others have a fully developed love for the creatures that have melted the hearts of millions. The point is you care for the little critters, so it may surprise you to learn that ferrets actually are illegal in some cities and in some states as a whole. Places where ferrets aren't welcome or are downright illegal are called *ferret-free zones*. Likewise, *ferret-friendly zones* are places where ferrets are safe from the politicians and other ferret haters. The classification of your living area depends on how your local government categorizes the ferret.

This chapter explains how you can find out whether having a fuzzy is legal where you live. Obviously, you should obtain this information before you take a ferret into your heart and home. You may be surprised to find out that you may even need a license for your ferret, so I talk about that too. I also show you the rationale behind outlawing these critters, and I present the ramifications of being caught red-handed with a fugitive furball.

"A License? But He Can't Even Reach the Pedals!"

Some cities and states require that owners obtain licenses or permits for their ferrets. A license can be free (such as in my state of Illinois), or it can cost as much as $100 per year. In some places, fees are per ferret, so be sure you double-check the rules for your area by first calling your state's department of natural resources or fish and game department (whatever the state department is called). Next check with the county animal regulations, and finally your township. To get a license for your ferret, if even needed at all, you must follow the procedures provided by your governing entity.

Some permits are just useless pieces of paper, but not all permits come free of strings. For example, some require that you don't have children under a certain age in your household if you want to bring home a ferret, and some require proof of vaccinations and/or neutering/spaying.

Some states and cities don't regulate ferret ownership at all; however, that doesn't mean they look upon ferrets as welcome guests. Where ferret tolerance is low, confiscations or fines may be imposed routinely or randomly. Unfortunately, some cities are very confused; they say that permits are necessary to breed and/or sell ferrets but that it's illegal to own them. Huh? It can seem at times to be a conspiracy on the part of a few against the many ferret lovers. This is something we must deal with; all you can do is arm yourself with information, and jump through the necessary hoops.

Ferret-Free Zones and Why They Exist

Although the United States Department of Agriculture classifies ferrets as domesticated critters, some rogue state agencies still insist that domestic ferrets are wild animals. Others say that ferrets aren't wild animals but rather exotic animals. Still others believe that ferrets are domesticated but hold firmly to the idea that they're dangerous. Well, I'm here to tell you, without a doubt, the ferret is domesticated. But because many states regulate wild and exotic animals, and these states lump in the poor ferret where it just doesn't belong, ferrets end up getting regulated or discriminated against.

For instance, California and Hawaii are the states that continue to outlaw ferrets (many military bases all over the country also ban furballs). However, just because your state lists ferrets as legal doesn't mean your city does. Many major and some smaller cities remain in the dark ages as ferret-free zones. (Check out the section "Knowing the Law and the Consequences of Breaking It" to find out where to get this information.) While the lovable ferret continues to get wrapped up in bureaucracy, dedicated ferret freedom fighters continue to do their best to mow down misconceptions in the hopes of protecting and legalizing ferrets everywhere.

You may wonder how ferrets — these captivating bundles of energy and joy — can be such a source of controversy. It all lies in the myths and misconceptions department, as the following sections explain.

Californians unite!

One thing "ferret people" have in common is their devotion to their beloved pet ferrets, and Californians are no different. Being illegal in their state means simply that they have to fight harder for their rights and the rights of their fuzzies. Several organizations have sprouted up over the years to help change the regulations in California; two especially are worth noting due to their diligence in challenging the government to get ferret ownership legalized:

✔ **Ferrets Anonymous** (www.ferrets anonymous.com) is a nonprofit grass-roots organization made up of California ferret enthusiasts who are working to promote awareness of the domestic ferret in conjunction with their efforts toward ferret legalization. Ferrets Anonymous publishes *The FerretPaw Print,* a bi-monthly newsletter with legalization updates and informative articles. Ferrets Anonymous has Chapters located all over California, so you're bound to find a Chapter nearby if you live in that state.

✔ **The Northern California Ferret Alliance** (www.ncferretalliance.org) is another educational organization active in ferret's rights. I'll let its Web site speak for the organization: "The Northern California Ferret Alliance is a nonprofit organization dedicated to the domestic ferret and the people who love them. The NCFA provides education to the local community regarding ferret care, health concerns and current legalization issues, support and social events for local ferret enthusiasts as well as fund raising for ferret rescue organizations."

Another Web site that contains great information is that of the organization Californians for Ferret Legalization. Although the organization itself is now defunct, its Web site remains up and running. This site contains more information than any other in terms of the legal issues ferrets and their owners face in California. Visit the site at www.ferretnews.org.

What's it gonna be? Wild, domestic, or exotic?

Perhaps the biggest misconception about ferrets is that they're wild or non-domesticated animals — no different from the neighborhood skunks and raccoons. The truth is that ferrets are domesticated animals and have been for thousands of years. Ferrets depend on their humans for survival, so how can certain governments classify them as wildlife? The answer probably lies in how scientists named them way back when.

Depending on your school of belief, the ferret is either a species all to itself *(Mustela furo)* or a descendant of the wild European polecat *(Mustela putorius furo).* The ferret is "scientifically" known by the latter distinction, which is the legal glitch that many governments have used to classify fuzzies as wildlife. Many labels come with being classified as "wildlife" — people believe wildlife to be dangerous, unpredictable, and a disease risk. Most cities and states deem wildlife illegal to keep or require special permits in situations of ownership.

The scientific name of the fuzzy isn't the only thing standing in your way in many places:

✔ Some people consider ferrets to be wild because they look so much like their cousins: the minks, weasels, and polecats. But just because you may look like a famous athlete doesn't make you part of his team, right?

✔ One of the world's most endangered wildlife species, the black-footed ferret, happens to have "ferret" in its name, though it is wild and our ferret isn't.

Feral ferrets in my neighborhood?

Perhaps the most outrageous misconception about owning ferrets — or unfounded paranoia, actually — is the fear that pet ferrets will escape, unite in the wild, form large feral (wild) colonies, and develop their own organized crime rings. Okay, maybe I'm exaggerating a bit. But some governmental suits actually believe the part about the development of feral colonies. These politicians preach the idea that these colonies of roving feral ferrets will destroy native wildlife and livestock.

Here are some reasons why the feral-ferret scenario is very unlikely:

✔ Ferrets are domestic animals (see the previous section), and they rely on humans for survival.

✔ The majority of ferrets entering the pet trade are spayed or neutered.

✔ Ferrets are indoor pets and escape is unlikely.

Many species of domestic animals are capable of going feral, but for a colony to form, their environment has to be just perfect for them, and they have to have the necessary skills. In particular,

✔ There must be several feral breeders around to make more animals.

✔ There must be an open environmental niche.

North America has few open niches left for small predatory mammals such as the ferret. The niches are already filled with more competitive mustelids (a ferret's cousins), such as the American mink and the long-tailed weasel.

✔ The animal must know how to escape from predators and find food.

These are just a few of the many reasons why the likelihood of ferrets taking over your environment is very small.

Should people fear rabies?

Zero reports have been made of a ferret transmitting rabies to a human, and only a handful of cases of ferrets carrying rabies have ever been documented. In fact, dogs and cats are at much greater risk of being exposed to rabies, thus putting you at greater risk. The following points should further solidify your argument to others (and to yourself) that rabies isn't a significant risk in ferrets:

- ✔ Ferrets have little opportunity to come in contact with rabies-infected animals in the first place.

- ✔ Infected ferrets are thought to carry dumb rabies and die quickly after becoming infected. (To compare dumb rabies with furious rabies, see Chapter 15.)

- ✔ Researchers are in the early stages of investigating the hypothesis that ferrets don't even pass the rabies virus through their saliva.

An approved rabies vaccine is available for ferrets to alleviate the fear of the disease being present. Part of being a responsible ferret owner is having your lovable fuzzball vaccinated on a yearly basis (see Chapter 12). Most cities and states recognize the rabies vaccine developed for the ferret as being protective against rabies, so for your sake and your ferret's, keep proof of her vaccinations on hand. A bite from your ferret without proof of rabies vaccination can cost her her life.

Knowing the Law and the Consequences of Breaking It

Ferret ownership isn't legal or tolerated everywhere. You need to check with an appropriate and knowledgeable agency before you bring home a fuzzy to get the exact details pertaining to ferret ownership where you live. Doing so can save your ferret's life. A good way to find out whether your ferret is welcome in your city or living area is to call your local Fish and Game Department, Department of Conservation, or Wildlife Department.

Another good source of information is your local humane society, because it's the society's business to know the local laws pertaining to all animals. But perhaps the best source of ferret law is your local ferret club or shelter, if your area has one. This is probably the safest source that will give you the most accurate information. After all, ferret people have the most invested in keeping their ferrets safe. Finally, check with your veterinarian. He has probably been treating ferrets and should know the general laws pertaining to them.

Please, please *don't* rely solely on the advice or opinion of a pet-shop employee or breeder when it comes to ferret law. Even if these folks know your local laws, they may not be forthcoming in providing accurate information to potential buyers. This isn't true of all pet-shop employees or breeders, but why risk it? If you must ask one of these sources, be sure to get a second and third opinion.

So, say you get caught red-handed breaking your local ferret laws. So what?

First of all, the danger to your little fuzzy is great. Some ferret-free zones won't hesitate to remove your furry family member from her safe, secure home for good. If your ferret is lucky, she may get shipped to a shelter in a ferret-friendly zone where her life can begin anew. If she's unlucky, though, her life will abruptly end — all because of your carelessness and unfortunate misconceptions. Confiscation of your fuzzy is basically inevitable, but you may also get slapped with fines. Some fines are pretty hefty — like $2,000 per ferret offense.

Part II
Finding Your Ferret and Hanging Up the Welcome Hammock

The 5th Wave · By Rich Tennant

"Did I mention how much this type of ferret likes to burrow?"

In this part . . .

So, you're getting more serious about living happily with a fuzzball, but you don't know where to start. Where do you shop for ferrets? How do you know whether you're adopting a healthy one? What exactly are ferret accessories, anyway? What are the do's and don'ts when making out a shopping list?

In this part, I help you answer those questions and share everything you need to know to both find your ferret and set up her home. This part also lets you know what you need to do to prepare for her arrival and get your house ready: things like ferret-proofing, finding a vet, and, finally, introducing your new baby to her new family. In a nutshell, this part deals with finding your ferret and preparing for her arrival.

Chapter 4

On the Tail of a New Carpet Shark (Um, Ferret)

In This Chapter

▶ Studying the basics of ferret shopping

▶ Deciding between a baby or an older fuzzy

▶ Choosing a male or female ferret

▶ Examining the differences between altered and whole fuzzies

▶ Filling your home with multiple furballs

▶ Picking from the variety of pet sellers you can find

Most people who want a ferret as a new family member have an image of what the perfect ferret is. Friendly, sweet, loving, playful, adventurous — those are just a few of the characteristics ferret lovers dream about. But when it actually comes down to choosing a ferret for your home, friendly, sweet, and all the other adjectives get you only so far. You also need to think in terms of health, gender, and even age. And when you have all those characteristics figured out, you should consider whether you want to get more than one!

This chapter helps you choose the perfect ferret for your home and your family. I explain what the normal and ideal traits are and warn about some characteristics to avoid. Some sections talk about the differences in genders and ages. You may be surprised by what you discover in this chapter! When you have an idea of what type of ferret you're looking for, you can start to look in the right places to seek out your dream fuzzball. You have several options to consider, all with pros and cons, and I cover them later in the chapter.

Ferret Shopping 101

If you're new to ferret ownership (welcome to the club!), it's important to choose a healthy ferret with a pleasant personality to bring into your home. Only someone more experienced in ferret care should have the confidence to care for a ferret that needs special attention. The following list presents some tips to keep in mind when shopping for your new fuzzy friend:

- Her fur should be soft, shiny, and full. She should have no patches of missing fur.

- Her eyes should be clear and bright. No discharge should be coming from the eyes, ears, or nose.

- Her underside should be clean and healthy looking. Look for signs of diarrhea or bloating, which can be evidence of parasites or illness.

- The ideal ferret is inquisitive when you approach; she doesn't cower or run to a hiding place. She should be jumpy and playful.

Don't view nipping in a young ferret as a warning sign. Nipping is normal for a youngster. However, you should avoid a ferret that bites aggressively out of fear. You should be able to recognize the difference. Problem ferrets hang on when they bite and draw blood.

- Color should be your last deciding factor because many coat colors and patterns have a tendency to change and lighten over time.

Many wonderful breeder ferrets, pet-store ferrets, and shelter ferrets need good homes. Some of these ferrets require special attention; most do not. For information on finding your perfect ferret, see the section "Where to Find Your Ferret" later in this chapter.

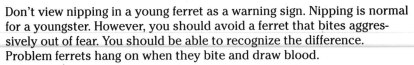

"But I felt so sorry for her . . ."

I can't tell you how many people bring animals to shelters, ferrets included, because they didn't think long enough about their decisions to take on such a responsibility. I always ask people why they acquired their pets in the first place when they come to our shelter (I'm the curious type), and many say that they felt sorry for the animals. Getting a pet out of sympathy rarely leads to a win-win situation. Caring for an animal you know inside and out and have prepared for is difficult enough; taking on an animal that you know little about or that has underlying problems can lead to frustration, anger, and a sense of hopelessness.

Are You in the Market for a New or Used Ferret?

The decision you make about how old you want your ferret to be should be based on your experience and lifestyle. Some people automatically think that they should start off with baby ferrets; they have many reasons, some of which just don't make sense. The thought that you must begin with a baby so that she'll bond with you doesn't hold true in the ferret world. Most adult ferrets adapt well to change and will love you no matter how long you've had them. Other people like to use the "I want little Johnny and the ferret to grow up together" reasoning.

The fact is, both adult and baby ferrets make good pets. The following sections help you make your decision.

Starting off with a kit

Baby ferrets, or *kits,* are absolutely adorable and hard to resist. They're delightfully bouncy and mischievous, with a seemingly endless supply of energy. Adults have their fair share of spunk, but kits are just a tad bit more energetic than their adult counterparts.

If you have small children, I recommend that a kit not be your first choice. If you're alone or have only one or two other adults in your household, and you have a lot of extra attention to give, a kit may be just what you're looking for.

If you don't have small children, here are some things to know about kits before you purchase one:

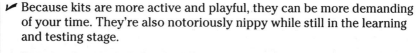

- Because kits are more active and playful, they can be more demanding of your time. They're also notoriously nippy while still in the learning and testing stage.

    Biting isn't cute and shouldn't be encouraged through play. It can get out of hand and become a behavior issue if you don't deal with it immediately. To find out how to deal with biting, see Chapter 20.

- You'll need to train and socialize a kit. You'll be the one who has to teach a kit what is and isn't acceptable.

- You'll need to make sure that a kit has all her baby shots. Medically speaking, a baby fuzzy should already have received her first distemper shot by the time she goes home with you. She may need up to four shots, depending on how old she is and what medicine she's already received (see Chapter 12 for details).

Adopting an older ferret

Adult ferrets make wonderful pets. You don't have to purchase a ferret as a baby to get her to bond with you. An adult ferret will love you and display all the charisma and energy you could hope for. Unfortunately, thousands of wonderful adult ferrets wait patiently in shelters for homes simply because people believe that older ferrets are damaged in some way. Some people even dare to think that the adults aren't as cute as kits. I beg to differ! Almost all the ferrets I've owned have been hand-me-down adults. And each one, with a unique personality, melted my heart right away.

Families with smaller children, people looking for cuddlers, or even those of you who believe in rescuing before purchasing would make excellent homes for older ferrets. If this sounds like you and you're thinking about adopting an older ferret, keep the following points in mind:

- ✔ Because the life span of a ferret is relatively short (averaging 6 to 8 years), you may have less time to spend with an older or adult ferret. This isn't always the case, though. I've lost young ferrets to disease and had some of my older adoptees live years beyond the normal expectancy. The average life span is just something you may want to think about.

- ✔ Generally speaking, older ferrets seem to be more relaxed with themselves and wiser to their surroundings, but they're still inquisitive and mischievous. Unless they fall ill, most adults are wildly amusing and playful. Some can get into just as much, if not more, trouble than their young counterparts! Adult ferrets just seem to have had the edge taken off.

- ✔ Adult ferrets can be more set in their ways. Behavior difficulties, if they exist, can be more challenging to correct. Some adult ferrets have been neglected or abused, so they may need a little more understanding and patience. On the other hand, adults that have been treated well (and even many neglected and abused ferrets) adapt well to new environments and have little or no difficulty bonding with their new humans.

The majority of older ferrets have had at least one other caretaker. Most are already trained to use the litter box (see Chapter 19) and have been taught that nipping is unacceptable. However, adult ferrets that haven't been properly socialized may bite out of fear. If you decide that an older ferret is right for your home, take the time to play and socialize with the ferrets you consider for adoption. It won't take long to determine if any special needs exist, and then you must decide if you're capable of handling those needs.

Should You Pre-Order Blue or Pink Bedding (Get a Boy or Girl)?

A decision you have to make when looking to adopt a ferret is whether you want a male or female. This should be a minor role in your decision, because health and personality are the number one factors!

Females are called either *jills* (unspayed) or *sprites* (spayed). Males are called either *hobs* (unneutered) or *gibs* (neutered).

Females typically are smaller and daintier than males. As boy ferrets mature, they tend to become more cuddly and couch-potato-ish. Females tend to remain more squirmish, as though they'd rather be anywhere else than in your loving grasp. I hate to hold fast to this stereotype, however, because I've had some females that were quite the opposite. Sometimes, all it takes to get a ferret — particularly a girl — to settle down is a bit of human intervention, such as rubbing her ear or another "grooming" gesture (see Chapter 9).

Unless they're very sick or old, all ferrets are amusing bundles of energy with a propensity to please and make trouble, regardless of gender.

Pitting Altered versus Whole Furballs

Most ferrets that enter the pet trade come from mass ferret producers, so more than likely your ferret will already be neutered or spayed, negating a choice on your part. Sometimes the only way to know for sure is by a tattoo in the ear, though not all breeders tattoo their ferrets.

In the female ferret, spaying is a medical necessity. Unlike some mammals that go into heat for short periods of time, the female ferret stays in heat until she's bred. The unending heat cycle more often than not leads to a life-threatening condition called *aplastic anemia*. Spaying your ferret can save her life. In the male ferret, neutering is more of a behavioral necessity. It lessens aggression toward other male ferrets and urine marking on the ground (which also dramatically decreases the odor of boys).

Aplastic anemia is a condition caused by high levels of the hormone estrogen, which is produced when the ferret is in heat. A high level of estrogen suppresses the production of vital red and white blood cells in the bone marrow. As the disease advances, this suppression becomes irreversible. Secondary bacterial infections occur due to the lack of white blood cells to fight infection. The ferret's blood can't clot properly, so bleeding becomes a problem.

Severe anemia sets in and an insidious death follows. Signs can be seen in ferrets that have been in heat for a month, and they can remain in heat for up to 6 months if unbred. How long it takes for aplastic anemia to kill a ferret depends on many variables.

If you plan to adopt a whole, or unaltered, ferret, you should have the altering procedure done by the time the fuzzy is 6 months old, unless you're planning to breed her. Commercial breeders alter their babies as young as 6 weeks old. Some people, however, suggest that males be altered as late as 12 months and females as late as 9 months so that they can reach full growth. Personally, I wait until 6 months for both the males and females.

Very few differences exist between altered male and altered female ferrets. In fact, every altered ferret I've ever met had his or her own unique personality that was unrelated to gender or age. All ferrets are amusing, hyper to various degrees, and easy to please, as long as you meet their needs. The following sections dig deeper into the behavior and characteristics of male and female ferrets and how they relate to sexual maturation.

Boys will be boys

You can identify your male as whole if his testicles begin to drop (appear) and his odor becomes stronger as the breeding period approaches. Like many animals, from the prairie dog to the moose elk, unneutered ferrets enter a period of breeding when all they can think about is passing on their superior genetic makeup. For ferrets, this breeding cycle may start in the spring and last six months, all the way until fall.

During the breeding season, males on the prowl can become aggressive toward other whole male ferrets. During this period, a boy's weight also can fluctuate a great deal; he usually loses weight while staying preoccupied with the girls. Some males even become depressed or anxious if they fail to find the girls of their dreams for nights of unbridled romance.

For their own safety and the safety of cagemates, you should house unaltered males separately during mating season if you're not using them for breeding. But I suggest that you do them and yourself a favor and neuter.

Girls will be girls

Females, although less intent on finding the hobs of their dreams, enter a period of heat if left unaltered. You can easily tell whether your ferret is in heat because her vulva (genitals) swells a great deal from the increase in hormones.

If you're faced with a female fuzzy in heat, your vet may choose to administer a hormone shot to bring her out of heat before spaying her. Or the vet may breed her to a vasectomized male to fake her out of heat before spaying her. Spaying your female while she's in heat is possible, but it's considered dangerous due to the risk of hemorrhaging.

Swelling of the vulva can also be a sign of an incomplete or partial spay. Altering ferrets at a very young age can result in this rare surgical error. Unfortunately, a swollen vulva also is a common symptom of adrenal problems in a female ferret. Don't overlook a swollen vulva. If you have a ferret with this symptom, take a visit to an experienced ferret veterinarian; he'll yield the answers you need in order to proceed with the proper course of action.

"You Want How Many Ferrets?"

Perhaps you've already thought about what type of ferret you want, what gender you'd like, what kind of great cage you can make for your fuzzy, and so on; one question you may not have thought about, though, is how many ferrets to get, probably because you just assume that you'll get one. One ferret can be happy and content in a cage as long as she gets plenty of playtime out of the cage every day. However, if you have a busy schedule and your ferret won't get out of the cage as often as she should, you may want to consider getting two or three ferrets.

I advise all ferret owners to have at least two fuzzies. If you're already caring for one ferret, housing two ferrets won't be that much different. In fact, having three is about the same! Now that I think of it, three is probably a perfect ferret number (see the nearby sidebar for more). I used to think that one could never have too many ferrets. Experience has led me to change my mind. Groups of ferrets shouldn't exceed what a normal litter size would be — and the average litter size is five to eight kits. The bigger the group, the more stress created. If you'd like to adopt more than eight ferrets, you should consider breaking them up into groups.

Most altered ferrets will get along with other altered ferrets with little or no problem (see the previous section for more on altering your ferret). Sure, they'll go through their share of aggressive squabbles and fighting for hierarchy, but they'll eventually develop a bond. Even though ferrets have a deep-rooted solitary instinct, they'll come to view other ferrets as littermates and play and bop around accordingly (see Figure 4-1). As usual, there are exceptions to the rule, so you'll have to intervene when introductions and living situations go sour (see Chapter 7 for more on dealing with ferret introductions and living situations).

Figure 4-1:
Ferrets
make good
companions
for each
other and
usually
play well
together.

Ferrets aren't territorial to the extent that dogs are, but they are territorial critters by nature. In the wild, polecats mark territories and chase off other polecats of the same gender. In a cage, ferrets have little microterritories and squabble over seemingly insignificant things. Although multiple ferrets usually share just about everything, from the water bottle to the litter box to the sock stolen right off your foot, they do make claims to certain things (such as a section on their beds).

Statistically speaking, it's easiest to introduce one gender to the opposite gender. (And all introductions should be made with altered ferrets, unless you want to have many more.) There tends to be more acceptance if you go this route. Introducing an altered boy to an altered boy also has a high success rate. Surprisingly, a female ferret generally has the most difficulty accepting another female ferret. Keep this in mind when considering adopting multiple ferrets. You can't make any predictions, however.

If you already have one ferret and are considering adding another, do so with some caution:

✔ Introduce new furballs in neutral territories with neutral toys, just to be sure there are no bad feelings off the bat. See Chapter 7 on introductions.

✔ An older ferret may not find the antics and energy of a kit or an adolescent as amusing as you do. On the other hand, a younger ferret may be just what the doctor ordered for the sometimes lazy and depressed carpet shark, assuming no serious illness is going on.

Three's a good company

I've heard many tales of a ferret becoming severely depressed when her long-term cage-mate died. The best thing to do for a grieving ferret, in my opinion, is to get her another ferret as soon as possible. This is where adopting three ferrets comes in handy. Having three means the loss of one ferret won't leave another ferret completely alone, and you'll have time to bring another ferret into your life and the lives of the surviving ferrets at your own pace. But that's just my opinion, and some people think I'm nuts! Ferret lovers often wonder how they started with three ferrets and quickly end up with seven or more. That, my friends, is called *ferret math*. It's what ferret lovers blame for the mysterious additions and multiplications of ferrets. It just happens!

✔ It's not unusual for the more dominant ferret to act a little bullyish and make the first tackle. They may screech at each other with humped backs and roll each other for a moment or two. Tails may get puffed like pipe cleaners or bottle brushes. One may take all the toys and stockpile them in a guarded corner or hidey-hole. These aren't unusual acts associated with introductions.

✔ Watch for the warning signs of true aggression, like ongoing screeching and puffed tails. There should be little to no screeching, and tails should return to normal size within 10 minutes of the initial meeting. If one or both ferrets is doing more biting and screaming than playing after 5 or 10 minutes, call it a day and try again later.

It's unusual to have one ferret kill another, but occasionally you'll come across an oddball that just simply hates other ferrets and makes an honest effort to injure the other. These guys should remain single. One ferret drawing blood or literally scaring the poop out of another ferret indicates a serious problem, and a mismatch has likely occurred.

A *solitary ferret* is a ferret that has reverted back to normal adult polecat behavior in terms of accepting other ferrets. In other words, she wants to live alone! Face it, ferrets are individuals, and a small percentage just won't tolerate being with other ferrets. If you have such a fuzzy, you'll have to keep her separate from the others.

The bottom line is this: One ferret is amusing; two or more ferrets are a stitch. In and out of the cage, multiple ferrets wrestle and tumble together. They chatter and screech and fuss about. They steal each other's treasures and then collapse together in a cuddly pile until one decides to start the routine over again. If you're even questioning how many fuzzies to bring home, get at least two!

More than just the cold shoulder

Here's some advice from Animal Behaviorist Dr. Valerie Staton: "Sometimes it's the new ferret that is being aggressive, not the current residents. When this happens you are likely dealing with fear aggression, not territorial or dominance aggression. Make sure that the new ferret feels safe in her surroundings and has scouted out a safe hiding place before making the introduction. Also, try not to start an introduction when the ferrets are wound up and excited. Sleepy ferrets are less likely to make sudden moves that might startle a nervous newcomer."

Where to Find Your Ferret

You can adopt or purchase a ferret from many places and from many people. Where you go depends on your priorities, what you're looking for, and how far you're willing to go to get your ferret (to the ends of the earth, no doubt!). Pet shops and breeders are the places to go for kits, though shelters and private individuals may have them at times. Shelters and private individuals will have your adults, but pet shops and breeders may often have adults up for sale on occasion as well. To minimize the pains of introductions and quarantining, if you opt for bringing home more than one ferret, consider getting them from the same source. Almost all the sources I mention will offer multiples for sale or adoption. The following sections present the many different locales where little fuzzies are waiting for you as you read.

No matter where they come from, most ferrets are very adaptable to new people and new environments. If you're generous with your time, patience, love, and ferret-friendly treats, you'll have a friend for life.

Perusing pet shops

Perhaps the most commonly thought of source for buying a ferret is the local pet shop. The goal of a pet shop is to sell to customers, not to make your life with a ferret harmonious, so you need to do your homework on the ferret and research your local pet shop before buying a new carpet shark. The following list presents some things to think about if you plan to get your ferret from a pet shop:

- Pet shops are convenient, but your choice can be limited, because they usually only have a few commercially bred kits (baby ferrets) at any given time.

- The majority of the kits come from mass producers (ferret farms). Occasionally, a pet shop will buy kits from a local breeder. You may even find an older fuzzy that wasn't bought as a kit or whose previous owner returned her.

Ferrets that originate from mass ferret producers tend to be a little smaller. Many private breeders put out larger and bulkier fuzzbutts. If size is important to you, you need to know where your potential youngsters came from.

- You may or may not get a health guarantee with your purchase of a ferret from a pet shop.

I suggest that you request a written health guarantee; if the pet shop refuses, look elsewhere for your ferret. Reputable pet shops usually sell healthy animals and therefore should be more than willing to offer written health guarantees.

- Pet shops may be more expensive than many shelters. The expense may be well worth it if your ferret is in top health and has a great personality to match!

- In good pet shops, workers play with the kits frequently to ensure proper socialization, and members of the staff have been trained extensively in the care of the animals they sell.

In bad pet shops, staff members leave kits in their cages until potential buyers ask to see them. This practice can lead to poor socialization at a critical point in the ferrets' lives. In these bad pet shops, employees may be unknowledgeable in the care of specific animals, which causes them to recite misinformation to unknowing customers, and the shops won't offer solid after-sale support.

You need to find out whether the pet shop you're considering is one of the good ones; keep the following bits of advice in mind:

- Don't purchase a ferret on your first visit. Make several visits to see how the staff truly cares for the animals.

- Pet shops should be clean and tidy, as should the animal cages that house the potential pets. The animals should look and act healthy and have clean food and water.

- Employees should be knowledgeable about the animals customers inquire about, or they should be willing to seek out the correct answers to questions. They should be sensitive to your concerns regarding ferrets without displaying the "sell sell sell" attitude.

I suggest that you see if the pet shop has printed educational materials about ferrets — for example, the pros and cons of having one, the guidelines to determining if a ferret is suitable for you, and information on general care. You can get and look over this information ahead of time to test the employees' level of knowledge about the pets they sell.

> ✔ Try to find people who have purchased animals from your local shop and get their opinions. You also can check with the Better Business Bureau for prior complaints about the shop or call your local Humane Society to ask about the shop.

Picking out private breeders

A logical and common place to find a ferret for adoption is a private breeder — a private breeder can be an individual with a single breeding pair of ferrets or a fancy ferretry with up to a dozen breeding pairs. The biggest typically don't produce more than a dozen or so litters a year. Like pet shops, you can find good breeders and bad breeders. Locating a reputable breeder can be difficult because few private ferret breeders are out there. You can expect to pay two to three times more for a private-breeder ferret than a pet-store ferret.

A good source for finding ferret breeders is a small-pet magazine — particularly a ferret-specific magazine, such as *Ferrets* magazine (www.ferretsmagazine.com). This wonderful magazine not only offers readers up-to-date ferret information on a bimonthly basis, but also advertises breeders and provides other ferret-related resources. You also can use word of mouth in the ferret community; other people may be able to point you toward respected breeders. Additionally, the Internet provides a wealth of information on ferret breeders and their ferretries. This latter option is a great starting place in your search for a private breeder.

People breed ferrets for several reasons, and you must keep them in mind when trying to find a breeder. Some breed for money and profit; others breed because they love fuzzies; and for some, it's a combination of both. A good breeder will be very honest and up front with you about the responsibility of having a ferret as a pet.

Although a good breeder should be pleasant and easy to talk with, you may end up feeling like you're the one being quizzed. This can be a very good thing. A breeder who's too eager to part with kits may be raising ferrets only for the profit and not for the well being of the ferrets or the buyers.

Here are some more ways you can find out whether a breeder is reputable and a ferret lover:

> ✔ Try to get references from people who've bought kits from the breeder.
>
> ✔ If geographically feasible, travel to see the breeder's facility to get a sense of how the ferrets are kept.
>
> ✔ Ask the breeder about his motivation for breeding ferrets. A good breeder may say that he's breeding ferrets to improve the species.

My, what big ferrets you have!

Private breeders often produce bigger ferrets than commercial ferret breeders or pet shops, usually because private breeders don't neuter/spay their babies early. Hormones play a role in growth . . . well, let me clarify this a bit. Early neutering causes males to be smaller due to lack of estrogen. However, this same lack of estrogen due to early neutering actually causes females to be *larger*. Most commercially bred ferret babies are altered at 6 weeks after birth.

Ferrets from private breeders usually are altered at the new owners' expense and discretion. A reputable breeder will discuss your options with you.

> ✔ Ask the breeder about vaccination and vet schedules and any illnesses he has encountered with the ferret. Make sure, if you purchase a kit, that you get a written health guarantee from the breeder. An adoption (or purchase) contract should be available for you to see ahead of time.

> ✔ A good breeder will offer after-sales support. Ask if the breeder is willing to chat with you when you call with a question regarding your newly purchased baby.

> ✔ Ask about what happens if the ferret doesn't work out for you. Will the breeder take the ferret back? A responsible breeder will do this.

Note: A good breeder may have only one or two pairs of breeding ferrets, or he may have many more. Although you certainly don't want inbred ferrets, the amount of breeding pairs doesn't tell you if he does or doesn't practice good breeding.

A good look at the animals in stock will tell you more about the breeding practices of a private breeder than anything else. A good breeder, regardless of the number of ferrets he has, will have humane conditions, active and alert ferrets, and intensely curious kits.

When you find a good, honest, reputable breeder, you may have to wait for the next litter to arrive. Some breeders will allow you to special-order certain coat colors or patterns.

Adopting from a ferret shelter

Perhaps the most overlooked location for adopting a wonderful pet ferret is a ferret shelter. At a shelter, you can find ferrets of all colors, patterns, and personalities. Some are youngsters that proved too energetic for their uneducated owners. Others are past their life expectancies and need gentle and loving homes for their final months. Some have been abused and/or neglected and require experienced, patient ferret homes. Others have been well cared for until their surrender. Many shelter fuzzies have special needs, such as daily medications or special feedings.

If these things sound good to you, a shelter may be the perfect place for you to look. The number of ferrets that wind up in shelters is overwhelming. No matter what type of ferret you're looking for, a shelter is bound to have her. Adopting a ferret from a shelter is a great way to support the ferret cause. Want an extra perk? An adoption may mean a membership to the shelter's ferret club (if it has one). Membership could include newsletters, ferret shows, holiday parties, and fundraisers. So, along with adding a wonderful new family member, you get the chance to meet other furball fanatics and make a connection to a lifelong support group.

If you're considering getting your ferret from a shelter, heed the following information:

- ✔ Shelters rely on ferret adoptions for financial assistance and to make room for incoming fuzzies. Many shelters have no less than 60 ferrets at any given time. Adoption fees at shelters usually are lower; they vary depending on the age and health of the ferret being adopted.

- ✔ Most people work in the business of ferret rescuing and sheltering only because of their undying devotion to ferrets, so you don't have to worry about greedy or negative motives.

- ✔ Expect shelter operators to conduct friendly yet thorough interviews with potential adopters. That's good and necessary in the shelter business. The job of the shelter folks is to put their ferrets into lifelong, loving homes. They want to find the best families for these homeless fuzzies.

- ✔ Many shelters may have certain restrictions or requirements that breeders and pet shops may not have. For instance, almost all shelters require that the owners return the ferrets to the shelters if the relationships don't work out. Some have age restrictions on young children. Others want proof from landlords that ferrets are allowed. And still others require the entire family to be present for the adoption process. Every shelter has its own process.

- ✔ Most ferret shelters have veterinarians who work closely with them to monitor the health of the ferrets in their care. Some shelters have blood work performed on older fuzzies just for peace of mind.

A ferret you're considering adopting from a shelter should already be vaccinated before you bring her home, and a general physical has to have ruled out most illnesses.

- ✔ Most ferret shelter staff members are eager to extend after-adoption support — when they aren't up to their elbows in work! After your adoption, you're bound to make friends with the shelter workers, which means a lifetime of support and continuing knowledge.

Are you starting to look for that perfect shelter ferret but don't know where to go? Start surfing the Web to research nearby ferret shelters. Here are a couple great places to start:

    www.ferretcentral.org
    www.supportourshelters.org/SOS-ShelterList.html

Both sites keep up-to-date lists of ferret shelters around the world.

Checking the classified ads

The newspaper classified ads or the bulletin boards at veterinary clinics or pet shops are more wonderful sources for ferrets in need of homes. If you live in a larger city (one where owning a ferret is legal; see Chapter 3), it isn't uncommon to come across posted signs or ads for ferrets that need new homes. Sometimes, the sellers will be willing to part with cages and supplies as part of their fees.

Most often, the ferrets being sold through ads are older. The good news is that a previous owner can provide a wealth of background information on a particular ferret, which you may not be able to get when adopting through other avenues. If you're hoping to adopt from a private individual who can provide as much background information as possible on your new ferret, adopting through an ad may be for you.

In these situations, you're most likely not going to get the niceties such as pre-purchase vet visits or health guarantees. The ferret(s) will come "as is," and "as is" frequently comes with the cage and all supplies. The adoption fee usually is worth that alone. The ferrets themselves should be outwardly healthy and have good temperaments.

Buyer beware: Like a pet shop, a private seller's ultimate goal may be getting rid of the ferret and getting cash in hand as soon as possible. Many sellers, though, are kind animal lovers who just want their fuzzies to go to more appropriate homes and want to recuperate some of their initial investments.

Rescuing the wayward weasel: Stray ferrets

Unfortunately, some people will find stray ferrets that are lost or have been abandoned by their previous caretakers. Always be cautious with a found ferret because you don't know what she's been through. She's likely scared and hungry and probably is very confused. She doesn't know if your intentions are good or bad, and she may bite out of fear or defense.

Ferrets are susceptible to rabies, so take this into consideration and take proper precautions if you find a stray ferret. The first thing you should do is protect yourself from being bitten and take the ferret to the vet for a complete checkup. Remember that the ferret doesn't need to have bite wounds for it to have been exposed to the virus. Next, follow the proper quarantine procedures for a minimum of two weeks, housing the ferret in her own cage several rooms away from your other ferrets, feeding and cleaning her last, and wearing a different shirt over your clothes while handling that ferret.

Handle the ferret very cautiously, because if you're bitten, she'll need to be quarantined at the vet for a minimum of ten days, as required by most states for your own safety. Some states still require that the ferret be euthanized and be tested for rabies because her vaccination status is unknown.

If you find a lost ferret, you should make every attempt to find her home because someone may be grieving the loss of this little furball. Place an ad in your local paper and post notes on bulletin boards at pet shops, veterinary clinics, and other high-traffic areas. Many large newspapers allow you to place lost-and-found ads free of charge for up to one week. Be sure to leave out some specific identifying information in the ad so that the real owner can prove his or her ownership.

Nowadays, microchipping domestic pets has become common procedure. A microchip can help you rescue a lost animal by tying the unique chip number to the owner. If you find a stray ferret, take the animal to your local veterinarian to have her scanned for a chip.

If the weeks go by and you don't find her home, you may decide that you want to keep her. Be sure to quarantine her before introducing her to your other fuzzies. She may be sick or have fleas. A trip to the vet with your newly found friend is a must. If you don't find her home and you can't keep her, don't abandon the little fuzzy. You can contact many excellent ferret shelters that would be more than happy to find your friend a proper home. You can also place an ad for the many ferret fanatics out there who may reply quickly to the chance to adopt a new pet.

The majority of dog/cat shelters accept ferrets, but many kill the ferrets instead of going to the trouble of finding them good homes. Don't take a found ferret to your local animal shelter, no matter how good its intentions may seem. Contact a good ferret shelter that will take her in and find a good home for her, or take her into your own home.

Some people mistakenly identify minks and long-tailed weasels as ferrets. I've gone out on more than my fair share of stray ferret calls where I've come home with minks. Although these wild animals are awfully cute, minks can pack a powerful bite and shouldn't be approached. Be sure the critter you're "rescuing" is indeed a ferret!

Chapter 5

Home Sweet Home: Preparing Your Ferret's Quarters

In This Chapter

▶ Getting your ferret's house ready

▶ Organizing fuzzy's bedroom and bathroom

▶ Picking a food dish and water bowl

▶ Adding all sorts of accessories that you and your ferret will love

*B*efore you bring your new ferret home, you should be completely prepared for his arrival. If you're all set for your new bundle of joy before he arrives, you'll spend less time "ferreting" for forgotten items and more time bonding with your baby.

This chapter presents the must-haves for your ferret to live comfortably and safely in your home, as well as the accessories that will enrich his quality of life. You find everything you need to know about ferret accommodations: from the house and furniture to the bathroom accessories and wardrobe. If you already have a ferret and all the necessary accommodations, please read this chapter anyway to make sure you haven't forgotten something. With so many things to think about, overlooking an item or two is easy.

Setting Up Fuzzy's Cage

Preparing the cage is where true fuzzball lovers often show their fanatical yet creative sides. Cages range from simple, single-level ranches to multilevel mansions with guesthouses. The cage you choose depends on your taste and what you can afford, both financially and spatially. The effort in choosing is worth it, though. After all, your ferret has to stay in his house when he's not out playing, so you should work on creating as stimulating an environment as possible. The following sections cover the necessary cage considerations, from size to location.

Ferrets are carnivores. You should house ferrets only with other ferrets or by themselves. Although most pet ferrets don't recognize small animals as food, they may play small animals and birds to death. Many ferrets, though, have a strong predatory urge. I've known people who've lost rats, mice, sugar gliders, birds, and guinea pigs to pet ferrets. If you insist on interaction between your ferret and other animals, supervise them closely and cautiously.

Size matters: Picking the proper cage

The cage for one or two ferrets should be at least 3 feet wide x 2 feet deep x 2 feet high. This size is the absolute minimum. For households with more ferrets, I suggest going to multilevel cages (see Figure 5-1). As with most pets, the bigger the cage, the better. Whatever size you choose, be sure your fuzzy's cage has enough space for a playroom, kitchen, bedroom, bathroom, and, of course, your baby. You wouldn't want to eat, sleep, and play in your toilet, and neither would your ferret.

Fuzzy blueprints: Making sure the design is right

Many, many types of pet cages are more than adequate for your ferret. Due to the complexity of the ferret's housing needs, though, ferret owners really should consider bringing in the custom ferret cage. This can be a cage special made by professionals or built with your own bare hands if you have the skills and talent. I recommend two things, however. First, make sure the doors are big enough so that you can put a larger litter box or even a nest box in the cage. And, if you do include larger doors, make sure you attach extra door latches to prevent gaps and escapes. (For more on nest boxes, see the sidebar "Bob Church's simple steps to saving fuzzy's sanity" later in this chapter.)

Pick up a ferret magazine and see how creative ferret humans can be with cage designs. Construct a cage on your own, or with professionals, that fits all your ferret's needs. I present the keys to a good cage in the following list, and I go into greater detail in the sections that follow:

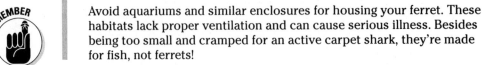

- ✔ **Ample size:** The floor space should be roomy to allow for ample playing and comfortable snoozing.
- ✔ **Good ventilation:** Poor ventilation combined with stinky, damp patches of urine and stool can lead to illness and disease.

Avoid aquariums and similar enclosures for housing your ferret. These habitats lack proper ventilation and can cause serious illness. Besides being too small and cramped for an active carpet shark, they're made for fish, not ferrets!

Figure 5-1:
Snap bolts
can keep
your ferret
safely
confined
when you
can't
supervise
him.

✔ **Small openings between wire and secure doors:** Ferrets are master escape artists. They'll try to stick their heads into or through any opening they can get their snouts into. They can and will push open doors with their heads.

Severe injury or even strangulation can occur in an unsuitable cage. Make sure that your cage design features no large openings and that, if necessary, snap bolts reinforce the doors on the cage (*snap bolts* are the snaps at the end of a dog leash; see Figure 5-1).

✔ **Sturdiness and easy access for cleaning:** Certain ferret cages come with pull-out trays to catch the litter and food crumbs that fall to the bottom. If you're lucky, you'll find or build a cage that has a built-in metal litter box that pulls out.

I found a company called Corner Creek Acres, which is located in Ottumwa, Iowa. The folks there build beautiful, spacious cages for incredibly reasonable prices. They ship, too. The company offers many designs but will custom-build any cage to your specifications. These cages are among the best cages I've come across for small critters such as ferrets. You can contact the company by calling 641-684-7122.

Materials

Perhaps the best types of ferret cages are made of sturdy galvanized wire. I prefer the black vinyl-coated wire because it's not only decorative but also easier on your ferret's feet. If the cage's floor is made of wire, be sure the little squares are no bigger than ¼ inch x ¼ inch. Ferrets have little feet, and spaced wire can be hard on their sensitive pads. And you certainly don't want anything wide enough for your ferret's feet to fall through.

A company I love is Kritter Koncepts in Cambridge, WI. It makes custom black vinyl-coated wire cages that are both attractive and affordable. You can reach Kritter Koncepts at 608-423-3124, or you can view its Web site at www.kritterkoncepts.net.

You should consider covering a wire-bottom cage with as much soft material as possible to prevent sore or injured feet. Here are some options you can consider:

✔ You can cut a piece of carpeting and fit it into the bottom of the cage. If you use carpeting, you must take it out and wash it thoroughly or replace it as necessary. Dirty bedding usually accounts for most ferret odor, so your nose will tell you when the time has come!

You need to supervise ferrets with carpeted cages. They love to dig at the fibers, and some ferrets find the fibers simply delicious, which can be dangerous. Also, be aware that your ferret can snag its claws on carpet fibers and other fabrics, which may cause him to become trapped or injured. Keeping his nails trimmed will help (see Chapter 9), but it won't necessarily prevent this problem.

✔ You can use a fitted piece of linoleum flooring or Plexiglas to cover the floor. I like the linoleum because it's flexible and the easiest surface to clean.

Cages made of wood are impossible to completely sanitize, because the material is porous and easily absorbs urine. Your ferret may chew and ingest the wood, or damage to the teeth may occur. And certain treated woods can contain harmful chemicals. Three strikes, you're out! Likewise, certain metal surfaces may contain lead and zinc (which is just as toxic as lead; most cages no longer have lead, but the galvanizing process may still include zinc); when ingested, these materials can be harmful to your ferret. Do your cage research before you dish out the money to save yourself a pile of trouble in the end.

One story or multilevel?

Although a single-level cage will do the job, it just doesn't seem appropriate for the captive lifestyle of a ferret (see the chapters in Part I for basics on the ferret lifestyle and Part V for more on ferret psychology). Ferrets are active and inquisitive. And as ground dwellers, they love to burrow under piles of stuff. But they also enjoy racing up and down the ramps in a multilevel cage like the one in Figure 5-2. Multilevels also add more opportunity for you to attach cage accessories that are almost as important as the cage itself (see the later section "Acquiring Accessories and Other Stuff Fuzzy Needs").

Here are some factors to consider when creating/purchasing a multilevel cage:

- ✔ The ramps in a multilevel should be made of wire because solid ramps act more like slides than ladders.
- ✔ Multilevel cages should have multiple doors to access the different levels.
- ✔ You should consider adding a litter box to the upper level.
- ✔ At some point during the routine cleaning process, you'll have to reach into the far corners of all levels of the cage, so be sure you can access them.
- ✔ You should provide snap bolts at the doorway gaps for extra security.

Leave the single level cages for the hospital cages or for those ferrets that may be injured or too old to navigate ramps safely.

Figure 5-2:
Most ferrets greatly appreciate multilevel cages.

A home within a home: Finding a place inside for the cage

Placement of his cage is vital to the health and happiness of your ferret. If you can, place the cage where he can see you several times a day. It should be a quiet, comfortable place, conducive to snoozing when necessary, but it shouldn't be so far out of the way that the fuzzy's forgotten in your daily routine. Some ferret lovers actually dedicate entire rooms to ferrets and their cages. When I kept my ferrets in my home, my cages were connected by colorful tubes. I never knew which ferret would be sleeping in which cage! Sometimes, as many as eight were piled snuggly onto one hammock, although I had four to five hammocks throughout my maze of cages.

Here are some other pointers and reminders on indoor cage placement:

- ✔ **Extreme blowing air can cause your ferret to get sick.** Drafts, or air movement itself, don't make people or animals sick. Cold air blowing continuously on the cage isn't good; however, cool air is fine. Also, hot air blowing continuously on the cage isn't good. Extremes are the problem, not the air movement itself.

    Putting a cage near an outflow vent of an air conditioner or furnace is bad because of the dust and debris that may be blown out during the first few seconds. This can cause respiratory irritation or infection. It may also cause eye irritations.

- ✔ **High humidity without good ventilation will cause distress.** Basements and small, poorly ventilated rooms often are damp and great breeding grounds for bacteria. If you must house your ferrets in a high-moisture area, use a dehumidifier.

- ✔ **Too much light will interfere with sleep cycles.** It's important to have a cage site that can be darkened at night. Erratic photoperiods and long light cycles can be a health problem for ferrets, so they need to be able to have about 10 to 12 hours of complete darkness. (See Chapter 16 for info on adrenal gland disease.) Another option is some sort of light-eliminating covering over the cage for part of the day.

- ✔ **Loud noise will stress your ferret and interfere with the sleep cycle.** Avoid placing the cage next to televisions or stereo speakers. The loud noise is very disturbing and if used at night can interfere with the normal sleep cycle.

- ✔ **Place the cage on tile if at all possible, and pull the cage at least 6 inches from the wall.** A ferret's toilet habits can get sloppy, and you'll most definitely be cleaning both the floor and wall surrounding the cage routinely. You may want to consider putting up a large piece of acrylic glass to cover the wall closest to the cage. If you absolutely must put the cage on carpeting, invest in more acrylic glass or place a large piece of linoleum under the cage. Ferrets love to scoot up into the corners of their cages and poop out the sides!

Heading off cage stress

Cage stress is often associated with a ferret's inability to escape to a safe place. You can identify a ferret suffering from cage stress by watching his behavior. Some signs may include the following:

✔ Constant pacing back and forth

✔ Gnawing on the cage bars (which can ultimately result in canine tooth fractures)

✔ Scratching incessantly at a corner of the cage

✔ Sores on his head and face from trying to push his way out of his confines

✔ Destruction in the cage, including the tipping of bowls and litter boxes, more so than "normal"

It's imperative that your fuzzy have somewhere dark and warm to hide and get away from all that's going on around him. You can use piles of fluffy bedding or a snooze sack, for example.

Providing safety and security helps prevent cage stress. If you have a particularly nervous ferret (see Part V of this book for more on ferret psychology), you can cover part of his cage with a sheet or large towel.

Wooden parrot nest boxes can make great hidey-holes and sleeping spots for ferrets. In addition, a nest box can make for a fun climbing experience. Insert a few cuddly pieces of bedding into the box, and place the box into the cage or your ferret's play area. Watch for wood chewing. If you notice a lot of wear and tear, replace the box or scrap the idea altogether. Also, wood is porous and difficult to clean. Ferrets generally don't poop or pee where they sleep, but the young, sick, or disabled may be the exceptions to that rule. Check parrot nest boxes frequently for soiling and throw them out if they do become dirty. The urine will also eventually release ammonia, which is unhealthy for a ferret to breath.

A room with a view: Finding a place outside for the cage

As more and more people recognize the importance of natural lighting for ferrets, ferrets have been moving outside to experience Mother Nature first hand. Housing your ferret outside is a complicated issue that needs a great deal of consideration on your part, in addition to extreme diligence to health and safety. Not only does your cage have to be completely escape-proof and at least partially covered, but your ferrets also need heartworm protection. And cage placement is one of the most critical aspects of keeping ferrets successfully outside.

I keep my ferrets outside, and they come in for personal playtime. They thrive outdoors, but I pay close attention to their needs, checking on them two or more times a day. I also have more than one ferret, so they can cuddle when it's cool out. Outdoor housing isn't for the lazy or the scatter-brained caretaker. Here are some tips on outdoor cage placement:

✔ **Extreme cold and cold wind can kill.** Below-freezing weather exposure without a heated sleeping area, or exposure to freezing wind, can kill your ferret. Placement of the cage in the sun during the winter months is totally acceptable. You can cover one side of the cage for shade but place the nest box in the sun. Additionally, you need more than bedding to keep him warm. Nest boxes packed with straw will work. Avoid cloth, because it can get moist and freeze. Cloth also is a poor insulator. Move food, water, and litter boxes close to the nest box so that he'll come out to eat, drink, and go potty. Also, use a heated water bowl. You can purchase one online so your ferret won't snorkel during cold months. The best protection, though, is considering housing him indoors during the extreme winter months.

✔ **More dangerous than the cold is the heat of the sun and high humidity.** Although ferrets enjoy the warmth that sunlight provides, direct sunlight with no relief can be deadly. Ferrets can get heatstroke or heat exhaustion if kept in hot places, even for just a short time. A temp of 80 degrees Fahrenheit or higher — especially with high humidity — is dangerous for your ferret. Be sure you shade a large part of the cage at all times so the fuzzy can escape the sun's hot rays. Place your cage under the comforting shade of trees if you have them. And be sure the nest box is always in the shade. Also, consider adding a litter box filled with water as a nice pool. Placement of cages on hot decks is ill-advised. Again, you should consider moving your ferret indoors when the weather becomes extreme.

✔ **Fenced yards are optimal.** Keeping your ferret's cage shaded in a fenced yard will keep predators such as foxes, coyotes, and dogs from getting to your ferret. It will also keep your curious neighbors out, thus keeping your ferret safe.

Some people think keeping ferrets outdoors is abusive. If done properly, it can be very healthy for your ferrets. With the exception of talking briefly about building an outdoor supervised play area for ferret enrichment (see Chapter 10), this edition of *Ferrets For Dummies* doesn't go into the specifics of constructing permanent outdoor enclosures, due to the complexity of the topic. However, I can recommend a phenomenal book that discusses this subject in great detail and length to anyone serious about outdoor housing. It's called *Ferret Husbandry, Medicine and Surgery,* 2nd Edition, by John H. Lewington (Saunders/Elsevier Limited). Even if you keep your ferret outside for only a few months a year, the book is well worth owning.

Of course, there are some places that you should just flat out avoid putting your ferrets:

✔ **Garages:** These are full of danger. Besides being devoid of healthy natural lighting, many garages can get overly hot in the summer and lack necessary ventilation. Most people keep chemicals in garages, including gasoline, that give off harmful fumes. And cars coming in and going out certainly add to the dangerous pollution.

> ✔ **A deck:** These heat up like a stove. Have you ever tried to walk barefoot across a hot wooden deck in the summer? It's like walking across hot coals. A cage placed on a deck in the summer will roast in the hot sun, even if it's covered.

Making Your Ferret's Bed

Ferrets absolutely love to tunnel and nestle in their bedding, so knowing what and what not to use is important. Whether you cover the cage bottom is up to you (see the earlier section "Materials"), but be sure to fill bedroom areas with plenty of old T-shirts, sweatshirts, pillowcases, or towels. You want to provide good snoozing sites and hiding places for your ferret. One neat piece of bedding is simple to make: Simply snip off the legs of an old pair of pants or blue jeans. You can also buy custom ferret snooze sacks and fabric tunnels at any major pet supply store or online ferret supply store, but if you're handy with a sewing machine, you can easily make them. These accessories are attractive and cozy.

You should wash all bedding regularly to aid in reducing odors. Keep a clean, fresh supply of bedding on hand to use when you're washing the dirty stuff.

Inspect your ferret's bedding routinely. Some carpet sharks find cloth an irresistible delicacy and chew holes in the fabric. These ferrets shouldn't have cloth. The danger comes from the ferret actually swallowing chunks of cloth. You'll find that certain ferrets need stronger types of fabric, such as denim, to prevent "cloth grazing." Small holes also pose a danger when your ferret is playing or digging around to get comfortable. He's apt to poke his head through a hole, and if he twists and turns just right, he may find himself trapped, and strangulation may occur. So toss the holey stuff. Finally, raggedy fibers and materials like terry cloth can catch on long claws, so toss the raggedy stuff and avoid fabrics like terry cloth.

Setting Your Ferret's Table

Picking out your ferret's food and water supplies doesn't have to be as tedious as picking out good china as a newlywed. However, not all food and water dishes will live up to your ferret's high standards, and he may put them through a battery of destruction tests before you can finally settle on the best feeding tools. Ferrets are extremely cunning little buggers. The average ferret can master even the most ferret-proof dish — meaning almost all dishes can be flung about the cage, tipped over, chewed up, pooped in, dug out, or slept in. You need to find the best possible dish and attempt to outsmart your ferret by adding a few clever accessories to keep the food and water clean and in their dishes. Remember, it's all in the presentation! The following sections show you the way.

Bob Church's simple steps to saving fuzzy's sanity

Besides enrichment (see Chapter 10), a ferret's need for security is perhaps his most overlooked necessity. People think of ferrets as gregarious creatures that need little alone time. The fact is, however, a ferret needs a place to call his own — a place to defend, if necessary, against the onslaught of other ferrets. A lack of privacy and self-protection is a leading cause of stress in ferrets. A nest box, which makes for a great bed and climbing area, is the perfect solution to this problem.

You can build a nest box for your fuzzy on your own. And if you think building a nest box would be too expensive and time consuming, ferret friend and enthusiast Bob Church makes it too easy for you to refuse! It should cost you only five or six dollars per nest box.

Pick out the following tools:

✔ Black marker

✔ Hobby knife with a #11 blade

And purchase the following materials:

✔ One Rubbermaid Duratote storage box — four gallon size (about $4.00)

✔ One PVC flush downspout — 2 x 3 x 4 inch size (about $1.50)

Rubbermaid and generic totes are inexpensive, and you can find them in most department and hardware stores. They're easy to clean and disinfect, are durable, and provide the darkness necessary to make an adequate nest box. Remember! A ferret needs complete darkness! These totes are strong but can be easily cut. They're attractive and functional both inside and outside of the cage, but you must properly measure if you plan to use the tote inside the cage. The PVC fittings are smooth and rounded, ensuring that your ferret doesn't rub himself and get chaffed. Males can't hook themselves on edges, and the PVC is easy to clean.

But it may be challenging to find the PVC fitting, which is probably mysteriously hidden somewhere in your local hardware or home-improvement store. Just tell an employee, as if you know what you're talking about, that you're looking for "a PVC 2" x 3" x 4" flush downspout that's the adapter fitting that attaches a 4" round pipe to a 2" x 3" rectangular downspout." The opening of the fitting should be just large enough for the biggest ferret to squeeze through but small enough for a little one to defend. The worker should happily lead you through a maze of unidentifiable stuff to this perplexing fitting. Memorize this spot and hope that the store doesn't rearrange before the next time you come looking to build a nest box.

Rubbermaid probably didn't know it at the time, but it designed its tote to be a nest box for ferrets! The recessed panel on the narrow side of the tote is a perfect location for the PVC fitting. Just follow these steps to create your fuzzy's nest box, and refer to the figure as needed to see how you're doing:

1. **Place the rectangular part of the fitting flush onto the storage box, and trace around the outer edge with your black marker.**

   You can put the fitting high or low, but putting it higher up makes it easier for your ferret to defend. On the other hand, if your ferret has hind-end weakness or is older, you may want to put the fitting on the lower end.

2. **Because you want the PVC fitting to fit tightly into the tote, don't cut along the line you just traced; instead, carefully cut just inside the line (figure a).**

   Round the corners instead of making them 90-degree angles to keep the plastic from tearing when you actually insert the PVC fitting. You're almost there! You should now have a gaping hole in the narrow side of the tote box. You put the fitting in this hole, but first you must make the plastic a little more supple so that you can easily insert the fitting.

3. **Fill your tub or sink with hot water, and immerse the cut end of the tote into the water.**

Let the plastic soak for a few minutes. The heat of the water will soften the plastic, but not for long, so you have to act fast and carefully.

4. **While the plastic is still soft, push the rectangular part of the fitting through the hole (figure b).**

   The fit will be tight, so you'll need to give the fitting a firm push. The plastic will slowly give way and reform around the fitting to create a secure connection. When the fitting is in place, your hard work is done. Just add some soft, warm bedding (figure d), pop on the storage box's lid, and let your ferret (figure c) do the rest!

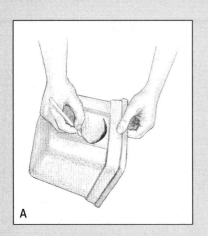

A

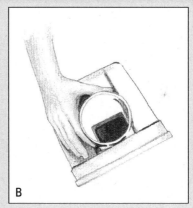

B

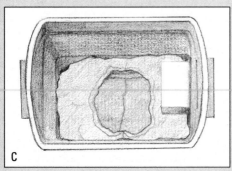

C

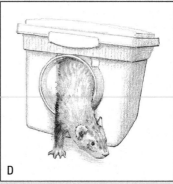

D

Serving your ferret's food with a sturdy dish

Pet dishes come in just about every size, shape, color, and texture. Their makers guarantee amazing things, such as non-tippable, indestructible, and easy to clean. And for the average pet, these claims are true. But a ferret sees a challenge in all that surrounds him, and a simple food dish is no exception. You need to choose the dish that best suits your ferret's needs. Remembering a few things may make your purchase easier and more successful. In the following sections, I prepare you for the food challenge that lies ahead and give you some bowl options.

Stay away from food dish materials such as flimsy plastic and unglazed pottery or ceramic. Stick with stainless steel, thick plastic, or heavily glazed ceramic.

Fuzzy feeding challenges

Your ferret is bound to find the one weakness of the bowl you purchase for him. Bowls are gnawed on, tipped, and tossed. They're buried in bedding and even in litter boxes. Almost any bowl, attached or detached, is subject to becoming a sleeping area. Unless you buy an itty-bitty bowl or have a ferret the size of a housecat, you'll just have to be amused with this enchanting trait.

Less amusing is how many ferrets love to dig their food out of their bowls. This is another trait you must learn to live with. If your ferret cage has multiple levels (see the earlier section "Setting Up Fuzzy's Cage"), you can place the food dish anywhere on the top level or put it away from the corners on the lower levels (ferrets like to poop in corners). You should discard contaminated food immediately. Likewise, a poopy food dish is an unsanitary food dish; wash it right away.

Attachable bowls

You can fasten small metal C-clamps from a hardware store around the bowl, hanger, and side of the cage to prevent dish tragedy (see Figure 5-3). Although attachable bowls don't prevent digging, they do work to prevent tipping and catapulting. You can also drill a couple of holes in a sturdy plastic dish and fasten it to the sides of the cage with cable ties or even thin wire.

Another option is a wire dish hanger that simply hangs over the wire of the cage. If you choose this option, grab your pliers and bend the holder until it can't be lifted off the wire. Oftentimes, this type of holder falls prey to the "flip and tip" method of kill. With only the top fastened to the cage, the ferret can lift the bottom and fling the food out of the cage. A simple garbage tie or piece of wire can secure the bottom of the hanger to the cage, too.

Even attachable bowls have flaws. Not all are ferret-proof as far as becoming detached. The round stainless-steel bowls that fit snugly into an attached round wire hanger are great until the fit becomes just a tad loose. Being the predator he is, your ferret will sense the minute weakness of the dish. With a push and a shove of his back feet, a ferret lying on his back can easily flip the dish right out of its holder and into a soiled litter box. Quality ferret food certainly isn't cheap, so choose carefully the manner in which you present it to your ferret.

Weighted bowls

Unless your ferret is Hercules (and he may very well be), a heavily weighted dish or one made of a heavy material (such as thick ceramic) helps minimize the distance he can catapult the dish across his cage. If you can't fasten your ferret's bowl to the side of his cage, get the heaviest bowl possible — preferably one that's wider at the base to make it more difficult to tip over.

Always place heavy ceramic bowls on the lowest level of the cage. On higher levels, these bowls can be quite dangerous if they're pushed off and tumble onto a fuzzy below.

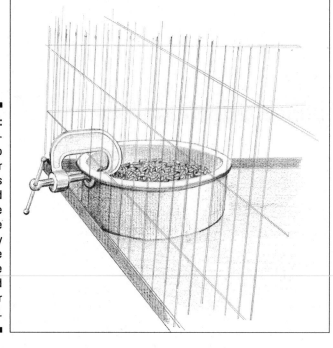

Figure 5-3:
Use a C-clamp to secure your ferret's bowl, and you'll come to believe that they were made with the frenzied ferret owner in mind.

Plastic bowls

If you're determined to buy a plastic food dish, make sure you purchase the heavy-duty type. The less porous the composition of the bowl, the more sanitary and easier to clean it is. Avoid lightweight plastic. It's easily damaged, and as a result of constant scratching and gnawing, small grooves and holes, which can be difficult to see, accumulate and harbor harmful bacteria.

To fully sanitize a plastic dish, you need to dip it into boiling water for about 5 minutes. You can also sanitize the bowl with a 30:1 water to bleach solution and let it soak for 20 minutes. Remember to wash it and rinse it well after soaking.

Hydrating your ferret with a water bottle

Up until now, I've said little about water dishes, and I have a simple explanation as to why: Most ferret owners don't put their ferrets' drinking water into bowls. Ferrets love to play in water, and they view water dishes as mini-pools.

The water bottle is perhaps one of the greatest *and* least appreciated inventions made available to pet owners. You can easily clean it, it doesn't tip over, and it provides uncontaminated water throughout the day. The last point is very important, because providing a constant supply of clean, fresh water is essential to your ferret's well being. ***Note:*** Water bottles work best when you fill them at least halfway, so keep this in mind when feeding and watering.

Bottle sizes vary, from those suitable for a mouse to those large enough for dogs and cats. A bottle that's too small yields little water and empties quickly. One that's too large, such as those designed for dogs, can be difficult for a ferret to operate because it requires a much harder push. Fortunately, bottle makers have taken some of the thought out of the process by making several specifically for ferrets. If you can't find a bottle at a pet supply shop, a guinea pig or rabbit water bottle is appropriate.

Picking out a bottle is just the first step. You also must attach the bottle to fuzzy's cage and train him to use it. Find out how in the sections that follow.

An older or weaker ferret, or even a ferret with bad or sensitive teeth, may find it very difficult to drink from a water bottle. He would prefer to become dehydrated rather than take an uncomfortable or painful drink. Ferrets like this are exceptions to the rule; provide them with water bowls rather than water bottles.

Attaching the bottle to the cage

Ferret water bottles are designed to mount on the outside of the cage (see Figure 5-4). Bottles hung on the inside of the cage are fair game; most ferrets will quickly seize and dismantle them. Also, outside mounting is convenient for you, because you have easy access to the bottle, which you should change daily.

Figure 5-4: Water bottles should be secured from outside the cage.

As with anything your ferret sees, if his water bottle isn't firmly attached, you'll find it on the floor the next time you check his cage. And you'll have him staring pitifully out at you with his "What took you so long to get here?" look.

A water bottle doesn't work too well if your fuzzy can't reach it. I've seen many people place their pets' water bottles way too high or way too low without even thinking about it. Position the bottle at a comfortable height so that your ferret doesn't have to strain himself by reaching too high or crouching too low to snatch a drink. Also, keep in mind the number of ferrets residing in the cage. If you have three or more in one cage, consider adding another bottle. For multilevel cages, providing water bottles on the top and bottom levels is a good idea.

Training fuzzy to use his water bottle

When training a newcomer to use the water bottle, place a shallow dish of water just beneath the bottle until the water bottle level indicates that the ferret is using it. Taking away his water bowl prematurely can lead to dehydration. Also, you should separate a ferret that's still learning to use a water bottle until you know that he's drinking from it. It won't do him any good if other ferrets are drinking from the bottle and you assume he is, too.

Most animals quickly discover that water flows from the tube when the stainless steel ball is gently pushed in. I have even witnessed my ingenious ferrets holding the ball in with a toenail to allow for more water to flow out.

Keeping the water bottle filled and the cage clean can be temporarily tedious, but it's well worth the effort in the end. Just through curiosity, most ferrets figure out the workings of the water bottle and do so without risking dangerous dehydration, illness, and possible death.

Designing Your Ferret's Bathroom

Ferrets are naturally clean animals that can and should be trained to use a kitty litter box. Therefore, you need to equip your ferret's castle with a suitable bathroom. Believe it or not, you have some things to consider before running out and buying the first plastic cat box you see. The first thing is the size of the cage door through which you plan on shoving the litter box (this is where custom cages with built-in, pull-out litter pans can be convenient; see the earlier section "Setting Up Fuzzy's Cage"). In most instances, you won't have a problem, but be sure to double-check the size of your door. I've had many brilliant ideas foiled due to the width of the cage door! There are some very big housecats out there and some very big litter boxes.

You also need to consider the size of the cage and of your ferret family. Your ferret's cage should have at least one litter box, but large cages and cages with several ferrets should contain a minimum of two boxes. You'll find that corners are coveted spots for pooping, and a corner is the best place for a litter box. Keep that in mind when shopping for cages, as well.

Never, ever use plastic litter-box liners in any ferret litter box. Your ferret will tear them to shreds, and ingesting this material can cause serious blockage.

Choosing the right litter box for your ferret

The type of pooper(s) you have determines the most suitable litter box for you. His age and health status make a difference, too (see Part IV for more on health issues). Here are some things to think about:

- Ferrets who aim high (those, for example, who scoot their butts up to the corners and aim for the peaks of the poop hills) need litter boxes with high sides. Ferrets that don't much care where they go (the ones, for example, who enter the box and squat down to do their business as soon as all four feet are in) are probably okay with a low-sided litter box.

- As ferrets age, they may lose mobility in their hind legs, which can make getting into litter boxes more difficult. The same holds true for the sick or injured guys. Invest in a low-sided box for a debilitated fuzzball, even if he has a temporary condition.

- Baby ferrets are full of energy, and they can and will get into almost anything. If your ferret is too small to get into a litter box, it may be too soon to be training him to use it.

- If you have a super-duper big cage, a covered litter box may be feasible. Perhaps you need a combination of both a low-sided box, which may do well on the bottom level (see Figure 5-5), and a high-sided box, which you can put on a top level if it fits, or vice versa. Also available are smaller triangular boxes that fit only in the corner of the cage. They sit low in the front and very high in the back. However, most ferrets prefer to use litter boxes that they can get all four feet in.

Finding the right litter box for your ferret may be a crapshoot at first. If you're a good observer, you can figure out what your ferret's litter-box needs are. On the other hand, I'm a good observer, and I have ferrets that make me move the boxes all around. I think they do it just to keep me on my toes!

Plastic litter boxes

Your ferret will most likely have a durable, plastic kitty litter box that comes from a pet shop or pet supply store. These are inexpensive and easy to replace when they become worn out. Also, they come in many shapes and sizes to fit your ferret's cage and needs. You may also find a particular color that fits your choice of decorating.

What about those plastic boxes with rims around the top to help keep the litter in the box? Some people like this feature. I find the rim to be an ineffective weapon against talented litter pitchers, which most ferrets pride themselves in being. Additionally, most rims aren't fitted well enough to the litter boxes and become just another object tossed about the cage.

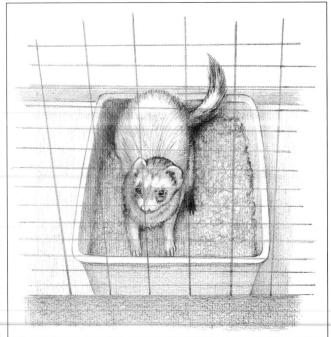

Figure 5-5:
A ferret in a low-sided litter box at the bottom of the cage.

Slide-in metal litter boxes

Some ferret cages have built-in metal slide-in/pull-out litter boxes. Just open the little door and pull out the box for easy cleaning. This type of box fits snugly into its own space, which eliminates the need to secure it. This may sound perfect, but it has its own problems. My ferrets drag their bedding into it, so I've inserted a short Plexiglas barrier to prevent this. Perhaps the worst thing about this type of box is that after a year or so — depending on the amount of urine it receives — the bottom of the metal pan slowly corrodes, which leads to holes.

Here are a few things you can do to prevent the corroding, or at least delay it:

- ✔ You can line the bottom and ½ inch of the sides with contact paper. The contact paper is okay, but it doesn't last very long and eventually peels or cracks when you clean it.

- ✔ You can cut a fitted piece of linoleum and place it on the bottom of the pan. This fix works fairly well, but you must remove the linoleum regularly for cleaning when urine leaks under it.

- ✔ Another solution I've heard of is that you can spray the bottom of the metal pan with a safe coating, such as cooking spray, in between cleanings. You also can paint the bottom with a nontoxic paint or coating, such as Teflon.

Most metal pans are longer than a typical plastic litter box. However, I put a plastic litter box on my ferrets' favorite side of the metal box, and I fill the space that's left over with litter. So, my large metal box is divided into two, and the unprotected side gets little use — except for when I fail to clean the box as often as I should. This solution may seem to defeat the purpose of the built-in metal box, but the kitty litter box still fits in snugly, pulls out with the metal box, and isn't tossed about the cage.

Picking out the perfect litter

Don't think that the cheap, generic litter you can force a cat to use will do for your ferret. In most cases, cats are cleaner about their toilet habits. They go into the box, do their duty, politely cover it up, and exit quickly to be sure that no one saw who issued that smell. Ferrets are different. They dig and burrow in their litter. They toss it about as they roughhouse with each other or a favorite toy. Some drag their bedding into the litter box and go to sleep. A litter box is to most ferrets what a sandbox is to a creative child. Therefore, picking litter for your ferret requires more than simply picking up the cheapest litter in the kitty aisle of your grocery store.

The litter you choose for your fuzzball should be absorbent and as free of dust as possible. Also, get bigger pieces because litter gets stuck in the strangest of places and can cause illness. The following list presents the options for your litter-snorkeling fuzzy:

- **Pelleted litters:** I prefer pelleted litter to the other types of litters available, and many consider it the best litter for ferrets. It exists in many forms on the pet market. Most are made from plant fibers or recycled newspaper. For the most part, pelleted litters rate high on the absorbency scale. Some of these litters are even considered digestible in case of accidental or intentional ingestion. Most varieties are fairly dust-free and free of perfumes, and they're difficult for a ferret to shove up his tiny nose. Although no litter is completely safe from the throws of ferret paws, pelleted litter is heavier and bigger, making it a little harder to toss overboard.

- **Wood stove pellets:** Made of compressed wood chips, wood stove pellets are rapidly becoming a favorite litter among ferret owners, right up there with pelleted litters. Wood stove pellets are inexpensive and do a great job of controlling odor. You can find this product at major home-improvement centers and many other stores.

- **Clay litter:** Clay litter is very popular among both cat and ferret fanciers. It's cheap, abundant, fairly absorbent, and you can find it anywhere, even the grocery store. Most clay litters, however — even the ones that claim to be 99-percent dust-free — produce a ton of dust. Just because you can't see it when it settles after the initial pour doesn't mean the dust isn't there. Regular playing, digging, and walking on the litter upsets the dust.

Respiratory problems can develop over a period of time if your ferret inhales too much dust. Bits of clay litter (along with scoopable litter) easily find ways into a ferret's ears, eyes, nose, and mouth. Also, clay (and scoopable) litters can stick between a little ferret's toes, not to mention cling to his little butt when he scoots it across the litter after going. Additionally, because ferrets burrow through litter and sit in it, clay litter coats their hair and dries it out as well as attracting more dirt to the coat.

✔ **Scoopable litter:** Scoopable litter is another popular choice. The absorbency of high-quality scoopable litter is excellent, making it convenient and easy to clean. It may have a pretty smell (before use, of course) or it may be odorless. Many, but not all, scoopable litters can be flushed right down the toilet along with the poop and urine. However, scoopable litter is incredibly dusty. The consistency is as fine as sand, making it easier to inhale and ingest. This is one I don't recommend for ferrets.

You must take extra caution with newly bathed or wet ferrets. Like dogs, ferrets go bonkers after baths. They roll around and wipe themselves across every surface available, including the litter box. Water + scoopable litter = cement. It dries quickly and can be very tedious to clean. Your ferret's eyes, ears, nose, mouth, toes, and behind can be subject to scoopable-litter impaction.

✔ **Corncob litter:** Although it's decorative to some degree, my experience with corncob litter says that you're just asking for trouble. First off, this litter is so light and airy that most of it is out of the litter box in no time. It isn't very absorbent, and it molds quickly; and mold can lead to respiratory disease. And many ferrets just can't resist nibbling on it a little, which can lead to a bowel impaction. Perhaps the only good thing I can say about corncob litter is that it isn't dusty.

✔ **Newspaper:** You may find that a plain sheet of newspaper or shredded newspaper works well for your ferret's litter. Although it isn't pretty, newspaper is cheap and does the job. Litter material is the only reason I subscribe to my local newspaper!

Acquiring Accessories and Other Stuff Fuzzy Needs

Ferrets are curious, active, and intelligent creatures. Picking out a suitable cage and throwing in the basic necessities isn't enough to make your fuzzy comfortable and happy. A ferret needs stimulation. You can add some extras to his cage, his playtime, and his life for his amusement and yours. Have a little fun and regularly rearrange his townhouse. Doing so also makes the cage look neater in your home. In the following sections, I introduce the accessories you can add to your ferret's cage and the accessories you can use to travel around with your fuzzy.

Fluffing up extra snoozing sites

No ferret's home is complete without at least one hanging hammock (see Figure 5-6). Hammocks come in all shapes and sizes. You can purchase one from a pet store or make one yourself. A hammock should be made from soft yet durable fabric and have hooks or clasps on all four corners to attach it to the top of the cage. Your fuzzy's hammock should be located near a shelf or ramp so he has safe, easy access to it.

Figure 5-6: A typical ferret hammock that can be hung inside the cage.

Some hammocks look more like hanging sleeping bags. Your ferret can choose to sleep right on top of it or snuggle between the two layers of fabric. I've had some ferrets who liked to squish inside a hammock with another pile of ferrets heaped on top of them. It reminds me of circus clowns crammed in a VW Bug (just when you think it can't possibly hold anymore . . .).

You need to provide warm, dark places for your ferret to hide out and sleep in. Ferrets need to burrow and feel safe. You can utilize nest boxes for optimal stress control. A general rule is that the number of nest boxes should equal the number of ferrets plus one. If you don't give your fuzzy security, he'll likely suffer cage stress.

Because tunneling is a ferret's favorite extracurricular activity, you may want to hang some plastic tubes in your fuzzy's cage. Ferrets enjoy running through them and even curling up for a nap. The tubes are easy to clean and colorful, so they brighten up the cage area. You can find them in major pet supply stores or online ferret supply stores. They're made specifically for ferrets.

Ferret toys galore!

Ferrets are materialistic critters with an eye for valuables. Although you probably won't be able to prevent the thieving of some of your prized possessions, you can provide your ferret with his own valued toys. In addition to providing entertainment, toys help to satisfy your ferret's natural instinct to hoard food. But you need to know what toys are safe and what toys are bad ideas.

Good toys

Your ferret should be able to enjoy an assortment of toys both in the cage and out. Try to keep up with his level of intelligence and curiosity, and provide him with as much excitement as possible. Here are some toys you can use:

- ✔ Hard rubber balls (maybe even one with a bell safely inside)
- ✔ Cat toys that are made of hard plastic
- ✔ Tennis balls and racquetballs
- ✔ Paper bags and cardboard boxes
- ✔ Human infant toys, such as plastic keys and rattles and terry-cloth-covered squeaky things
- ✔ Large ferret balls — the kind that have holes in them for entering and exiting
- ✔ Fun tunneling toys like PVC piping, clothes-dryer hoses, and ferret tubes
- ✔ The best ferret toy ever: you!

Ferrets love noisy toys, so find some safe toys that have bells inside or that squeak. You can hang some toys in his cage for extra fun — large, dangling parrot toys work well. Squeaky toys, though, should never be left unsupervised in the cage or in the play area, because they can be chewed. Instead, use them for one-on-one enrichment (see Chapter 10).

You need to inspect toys routinely. Throw away any toys that have stuffing pulled out, and pay close attention to squeaky toys, because ferrets have been known to pull out the squeakers and ingest them.

Toys to avoid

Exercise caution when purchasing playthings for your fuzzball. Most of the toys in the market are designed for dogs and cats. Ferrets love to chew and gnaw and destroy the stuff they covet so fiercely. However, their bodies don't process the junk in quite the same manner as dogs and cats' bodies do. If your fuzzy eats something he shouldn't, you'll find occasional bits of foreign gunk, such as rubber or plastic, in his poop. More often, what doesn't choke him usually finds a nice place to settle in his stomach or intestine and causes just enough damage to warrant immediate medical attention — not to mention extreme panic for you. A best-case scenario: You can give a major dose of kitty or ferret hairball remedy (½ tablespoon) to help push it on through. A bad-case scenario: Fuzzy has to have surgery to remove the blockage. And the most awful scenario of all: Death that could've been prevented.

Here are some things you don't want to use as ferret toys:

- Any toy made of latex or soft, flexible rubber/plastic, including unsupervised squeaky toys
- Anything with small pieces that your ferret can chew off and swallow
- Objects small enough that your ferret can get his head stuck in them
- Toys that show signs of ferret wear and tear

Your ferret will try to pilfer through your belongings and come up with a few toys you've obviously forgotten about, including socks, shoes, car keys, lipstick, and various other sundries. If you're a smoker, watch your cigarettes, too. Ferrets find them wonderfully fascinating, but they're not only toxic, but also can cause obstructions. You also should avoid bedding that contains foam rubber or stuffing.

Ferret owners should monitor their ferrets when it comes to playing with certain toys. For example, I don't include plastic bags in the "toys to avoid" list, mainly because ferrets love them! They make great enrichment toys. You do need to monitor their use, though. Don't leave the bags in the cage or unattended with your ferret. Bags and other potentially dangerous items can make great play items if you're diligent at watching and supervising the play. That's not to say, however, that all toys are safe even with proper monitoring. Some objects are flat out dangerous. Use common sense.

Leashes and harnesses for your ferret

Ferrets can learn to be walked on leashes, provided that they have comfortably fitting harnesses. Leashes and harnesses are especially important if you plan on taking your ferret outside for romps or when you have guests over who want to get to know your fuzzbutt. You can purchase many types of harnesses, but the long, slender body of the ferret makes him a difficult fit. You should choose a harness made specifically for ferrets — one that's H-shaped across the back and that fastens around the neck and belly (see Figure 5-7).

Just like a puppy, your ferret will resist the sudden restraint on his freedom. He'll twist and turn and play tug of war as though he's truly claustrophobic. He'll do the typical alligator roll and fake a horrible torture. Believe me — he'll

Not cuckoo about collars

Some people put collars on their ferrets with little success; others do so with good results. I suppose it depends on the ferret's personality and his ability to tolerate a collar. A ferret's head isn't much wider than the neck it's attached to. I find it next to impossible to keep a collar on for long, including those "designed specifically for ferrets." A collar is a collar. It's all round, and it's no match for a ferret who wants to eliminate it. Collars become coveted objects for the hidey-hole, though. They also get caught on things — especially if they have bells on them. This may cause entrapment or strangulation. Use a collar with caution. You'll never catch one of my guys wearing one!

get over it. As long as you can squeeze your finger under the harness, you can be sure that it isn't too tight. Ferrets are master escape artists. Any looser and your ferret will be free in no time. Be patient and persistent with your teachings and reward him for good behavior. Unless you use the harness only when taking him to the vet, he'll eventually associate it with playtime. (For more tips on getting him used to the harness, see Chapter 19.)

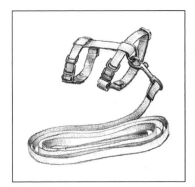

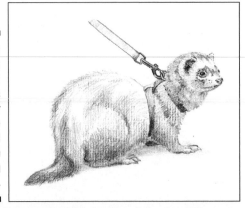

Figure 5-7:
Leashes and harnesses keep your ferret safe outside and when meeting people.

Finding a good travel taxi

A travel taxi is probably one of the first accessories you'll want to purchase after you have your ferret's cage set up. After all, your baby needs to arrive home safely. Ferrets are neat, and it's fun to show them off, but a vehicle isn't a safe place to showcase your fuzzy. He can get stuck under the seat and under a pedal. He can obstruct your view by cruising on the dashboard. All this stuff can cause an accident, and an unrestrained fuzzy is too vulnerable to come out of a serious accident in one piece.

Consider the following when looking for an appropriate travel taxi:

✔ A simple, small, plastic cat carrier can comfortably accommodate a couple of ferrets for short trips to the vet or to grandmother's house. The carrier should contain a soft towel or other type of bedding for comfort and snoozing. Most carriers are designed for adequate ventilation, so that shouldn't be much of a worry.

✔ Avoid folding cardboard carriers that shelters or pet shops may send you home with. It doesn't take long for a ferret to figure his way out of one by scratching or chewing. Cardboard carriers also can't be properly sanitized. You don't want to have ferret pee leak through the bottom of a cardboard carrier and onto your car seat.

✔ Carriers that open like suitcases are okay for short trips, but for longer trips, a carrier with a wire-grated, front-opening door (see Figure 5-8) is more appropriate. Larger carriers of the same type (made for small or medium-sized dogs) are appropriate for temporarily housing ferrets on trips, because one can hold a small litter box in addition to the ferrets and their bedding.

As much as I hate to admit this, not everyone enjoys ferrets as much as I do. When traveling to the vet or other places, keep your ferret contained in case you run across one of these oddball people. My vet doesn't like it when I come waltzing in with a 10-foot snake draped around my neck. It scares the poodle owners! So I bring snakes to the vet in reptile carriers. Your pet carrier (minus the snake) is the safest place for your furball anyway. Strangers poking at him may be too much stimulation for your little guy, and he may nip out of fear or excitement. Unless you're in a comfortable and ferret-friendly environment, keep your fuzzy safe in his carrier.

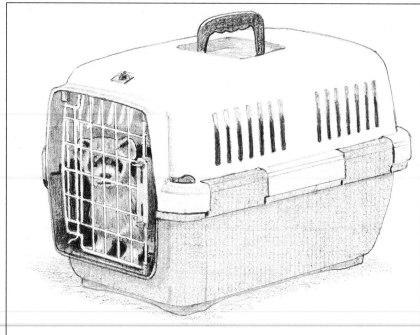

Figure 5-8:
Pet carriers
should be
securely
built with
narrow bars
to keep the
ferret from
escaping.

Chapter 6

Ferret-Proofing Your Home

In This Chapter

▶ Taking care of trouble spots in your home to make it ferret-friendly

▶ Altering your habits to prevent a tragedy

▶ Finding a qualified vet

*A*t first, your home is a scary yet stimulating jungle to a tiny ferret, and she'll be chomping at the bit to find or cause trouble. And believe me, if she's able to find or cause trouble, she certainly will. Carpet sharks are notorious explorers and excavators. They like to push and pull and carry and toss every little household item they can. They can fit into the tiniest of tiny places and manage their way to the highest of spots. And they all put their leaping skills to the greatest challenge. Whoever came up with the phrase "Curiosity killed the cat" obviously hadn't been exposed to ferrets. Curiosity, although one of the ferret's most amusing qualities, can be her worst enemy.

Therefore, from the time your new fuzzy first walks into her new home, the environment should be ferret-proofed. In this chapter, you find out how to get your house ready for your new arrival. I also explain what habits you can change to keep your ferret safe and let you know how to cross off your next important priority: finding a good vet for your fuzzy.

Inspecting Your Home for Ferret Hazards

With the possible exception of a single closed-off room (a rubber-padded cell?) with no furniture, holes, or floor vents, most areas in a home can't be completely ferret-proofed. You have to be satisfied with doing your absolute best to minimize the possibilities of ferret tragedies. Like the parent of a toddler, you must keep your pet out of harm's way. However, unlike a human toddler, a ferret will rarely scream out for you when she hurts herself or gets wedged somewhere. Your fuzzbutt depends on you to remain vigilant at all times when she's out of her cage.

The following list outlines some general guidelines for ferret-proofing your home:

- ✔ **Put up security gates to keep ferrets from danger zones.** Don't settle for easily climbed children's gates; those are just neat obstacles for a ferret to scale and master like a ladder. You may have to build something at least 3 feet high out of wood, Plexiglas, or another material that ferrets can't easily climb.

- ✔ **Be careful what you leave lying around your home.** Any object is fair game to a ferret. Some dangerous items include pen caps, rubber bands, cotton balls and cotton swabs, coins, latex/vinyl/rubbery things, sponges, plastic bags, jewelry, foam rubber, latex rubber, polyester stuffing, dried vegetables, and bandages.

- ✔ **Don't store chemicals, such as cleaners or antifreeze, in accessible places.** Ferrets can knock the containers over, causing spills, and ingest poisonous chemicals. At the very least, they'll want to lick the containers just for a taste and may ingest chemical residue.

- ✔ **Put your medications out of reach.** You may be aware that prescription meds can be extremely dangerous and toxic to your ferret, but you may not know that many over-the-counter medications, such as Tylenol, can be as deadly as rat poison to your ferret.

- ✔ **Don't forget that ferrets can jump.** You should ferret-proof anything less than 30 inches off the ground or that your ferret can reach by climbing.

Some people leave their ferrets out of their cages to go unsupervised all day. I believe only an experienced ferret owner can pull this off without too many hitches. A person confident enough to leave a ferret unsupervised knows the ferret inside and out and knows the ways of ferret-proofing.

You get the idea. Think and prepare as though you have a toddler exploring your environment. Everything a toddler touches ends up in his mouth. A ferret isn't that different. The following sections lead you through ferret-proofing the different areas of your home and point out dangers that you may not have thought about. The bits of wisdom in these sections are made possible by all the close calls, injuries, and fatalities experienced by thousands of ferret lovers all over the country, including myself. Learn from our mistakes!

Laundry room

Utility/laundry rooms often are loaded with dangerous items, and they're practically impossible to ferret-proof, so you should keep these rooms off-limits altogether. Your ferret may decide to chew on the dryer vent hose and tunnel right out through to the scary outside. Even worse, your fuzzy could quickly crawl up into the clothes dryer to take a nap beneath all those soft clothes, especially when they're warm. You may not see her go in, and it will be too late when you do find her.

Kitchen

Block off your kitchen from curious ferrets if you can. You want to keep your fuzzy away from all those dangerous appliances in the kitchen. Here are a few of the ways your fuzzy can get hurt in the kitchen:

- ✔ Refrigerators and other appliances have fans that can abruptly turn on and injure or kill your ferret.

- ✔ Ingested fiberglass insulation can cause blockages or severe illness.

- ✔ Stoves have pilot lights that can cause severe burns.

- ✔ All appliances have electrical cords that can cause electrocution when chewed on.

- ✔ Your ferret can get severely wedged inside a space in an appliance and suffocate before you get the chance to rescue her.

- ✔ If you're like I am, you keep your bottom kitchen cabinets filled with cleaners that are poisonous if swallowed by your ferret.

I've known ferrets to climb into dishwashers, refrigerators, and freezers when no one's looking. You can imagine the worst-case scenarios! Ferrets are adventure seekers, and they'll try anything once. But sometimes once is all the chance they'll ever get.

Moldings, baseboards, and under cabinets

Get on your belly and make sure that all the moldings and baseboards in your home are intact and complete all around the rooms. You don't want any mystery spaces. Double-check with your hands beneath the cabinets to make sure that your ferret can't get up into the cabinets from under the ledges. Home builders often seem to skimp in this area.

Also check for holes that lead into walls or to the great outdoors. Any hole wider than one inch is a potential hidey-hole or danger zone. Board all these holes up. If a hole is less than one inch wide, decide whether your ferret can widen it with her teeth or claws. After all, drywall and similar materials are no match for a fuzzy's weapons.

Windows and doors

To prevent escapes and falls from high places, double-check the safety of your windows, doors, and screens. Make sure your screens are securely fastened and your doors are shut tight while your fuzzy is prowling. Also, you probably shouldn't open any accessible window when your ferret is out and about. An exposed screen, likewise, isn't very hard to tear open or pull out with teeth or claws.

How big are the gaps between the bottoms of your doors and the floor? More than one inch? Better lower them to prevent your ferret from scooting under or getting stuck. Don't underestimate the average furball!

It won't take long for your ferret to realize that she has the strength and smarts to open some doors and windows. You can use snap bolts to keep her safely inside your home (see Chapter 5).

Floor vents and air returns

Your ferret may be able to pull off your floor vents and air returns if they aren't secure. I know my floor vent grates just lay loosely on top of the holes they cover (for decoration, I guess). After a ferret gets into a vent, she can tunnel through the house and get stuck somewhere or fall to a place where she can't get out.

Try to securely fasten any loose grates with small pieces of Velcro. It's effective, and you can hide the strips from view.

Floor fans can be dangerous to your fuzzy. A moving fan blade can remove a toe, paw, or tail tip (or worse). If the blade protector on your fan (the cage covering the fan) is broken, your ferret may decide to explore and end up in deep trouble. Don't use fans near your free-roaming ferret.

Plants

Your ferret will try to taste all your plants, and some plants are poisonous when eaten. She'll also promptly remove every trace of dirt from the pot, because ferrets are excellent diggers. The problem is, some dirt contains harmful bacteria or chemicals from fertilizers or pesticides.

Heights

Look around you. Everything in your home is a potential stepstool, ladder, or launching pad, including your fuzzy's townhouse (see Chapter 5 for more on fuzzy cages). You may need to move or block certain items to prevent your ferret from getting too high up. Pay close attention to how accessible your stairwells, curtain rods, and countertops are. A significant fall almost always injures a ferret, and sometimes it can be fatal.

Electrical cords

Ooooh, electrical cords seem like yummy chew toys to the grazing ferret. In the eyes of pet owners, though, electrical cords are electrocutioners and fire starters. Try applying bitter- or sour-tasting spray (available at most pet stores) on the cords to deter the ferret's gnawing urge. Another simple solution is to wrap electrical cords in aluminum foil. Most ferrets don't enjoy chewing on foil. However, the best solution is to keep all electrical cords completely out of your ferret's reach or to enclose them in special cable or cord moldings, available at home improvement stores.

Reclining chairs, rockers, and foldout couches

Many furniture items can be death traps. It's easy to plop down into a rocker or recliner and forget the danger of crushing your romping ferret in between the moving parts. I suggest that you don't use reclining chairs, rockers, or foldouts when your ferret is out playing or that you keep them out of your ferret's play-designated space. I, for instance, make everyone sit on the floor when my fuzzies are out and about!

Fireplaces

Nothing can match a walk on the wild side for your fuzzy, and fireplaces have it all: wood, dirt, and sometimes even rocks. If you want to keep your ferret and house soot-free, make your fireplace off-limits to snorkeling ferrets. You can invest in a heavy-duty fireplace grill that ferrets can't climb and that you can push flush against the fireplace. I went another route and installed glass doors on our fireplace.

Mattresses, couches, and chairs

Ferrets can easily crawl beneath most couches and chairs or the cushions on them, and they'll be tempted to do so. Mattresses are just as alluring. Those places make good hidey-holes, and the fabric beneath the furniture is awfully enticing. The danger is that you can squish your ferret between the cushions or under the chair if you unknowingly sit on her.

Many ferrets are tempted to dig and chew and tear at the underside fabric of furniture, often creating holes. Besides being detrimental to the furniture, chewing holes often allows furballs to find the stuffing that's revealed behind the protective fabric cloth. The same goes for mattresses. Ferrets love to chew on soft, foamy, rubbery things. If your ferret ingests the foam or other stuffing, intestinal blockage can occur.

Some ferret people prefer to use futons rather than traditional couches and chairs. Or, when the time comes to replace their furniture, ferret people choose to buy couches and chairs that are flush against the floor so their ferrets can't get under them. If these aren't viable options for you, you can turn your chairs and couches over and try to staple some heavy-duty cloth to the bottoms to keep your ferret out. Remember to staple close together so she can't get in between the staples.

Most ferret owners don't need to go to such extremes if they keep a close eye on their fuzzies during play time and inspect their furniture routinely for signs of destruction. And look before you sit!

Toilets, bathtubs, and buckets

Supervised recreational swimming can be fun for some fuzzies, but even the most athletic ferret risks drowning after a while. To prevent accidents, keep the lids down on toilets and keep bathroom doors closed when you have bathtubs full of water. Buckets of water or other liquids can also pose a drowning threat. Even if your ferret doesn't drown, she may become violently ill if she swims in a chemical of some sort.

Many bathmats and area rugs have rubber backings to prevent slippage. Unfortunately, these backings are delicious and sometimes deadly to fuzzies. Even the little rubber tips on door stops can block your ferret's intestinal tract when ingested. Watch for signs of interest in these items. You can easily pick up bathmats and rugs during playtime, and if necessary, you can remove the baseboard doorstops and replace them with stops that fasten to the tops of doors.

Cabinets

A ferret is quick to discover that she can easily pry open accessible cabinet doors. I don't recommend using most child latches as a solution. Most child latches are designed so that you have to slip your hand in and release the latches to open the cabinets. And if you can slip your hand in, the cabinet opens just enough for your ferret to come on in or get her head caught.

However, certain child latches are designed to work just fine. For example, one uses a magnet to release the latch on the inside of the cabinet door.

Supervise your ferret when she's playing around cabinets, and be sure that they don't contain dangerous chemicals or small ingestible objects. Also, make sure that your low cabinets don't have holes that can lead to other awaiting dangers. For example, I have one cabinet that has a poorly fitted pipe coming through the bottom of it. I can see right down to the basement!

Trash cans

Garbage cans are simply irresistible to roving ferrets. Think of all the disgusting and dangerous items you throw away on a daily basis. Would you want a fuzzy kiss from a ferret that just had her nose in all that?

Keep all your garbage cans out of your fuzzy's reach when she's out. If she has access, she'll tip them over or find a way into them. Depending on what's in the trash, your ferret's curiosity could kill her or make her terribly ill. And who's to say you won't accidentally throw out your fuzzy with the trash if she climbs in and curls up for a snooze with a stinky banana peel? Fix your cans with sturdy lids and keep them completely out of your ferret's reach.

So, you can't put all your trash cans up high or fasten them tightly with sturdy lids. Tired of fishing trash out of hidey-holes? Exasperated at the thought of sweeping up half-dried coffee grounds for the third time this week? Try weighing down your garbage can. Place about five pounds of sand or smooth round pebbles in the bottom so your fuzzy can't tip the can!

Changing Some of Your Home Habits

Those of you with children may remember those selfish days when you could do anything your own way without needing to take others into consideration. Those of you without children may be there now! For every potential ferret owner: You can kiss your selfish days goodbye. Well, maybe the adjustment isn't as drastic as that, but you need to be prepared to adjust your habits and daily routine. Your furball is depending on you for survival.

The following list presents some actions you should make part of your daily fuzzy-owning routine:

✔ **Watch where you step, and don't carry stuff that blocks your vision.** A ferret's favorite place to be and snooze is under things: carpets and rugs (hence the nickname "carpet sharks"), clothing, pet beds, you name it.

Shuffle your feet when walking if you have to. Ferrets are quick and quiet. They can be underfoot in a flash. Tread lightly, for a ferret is bound to be close at foot.

✔ **Check the clothes dryer and washer thoroughly before operating them.** Also check carefully before you toss a load of clothes into the washer. Ferrets aren't bulky and heavy like bricks. You'll hardly notice if your fuzzy has burrowed into your dirty underwear (assuming you're not wearing them at the time).

✔ **Don't plop lazily onto the couch or chair.** If your fuzzy isn't under the furniture, she may be under the cushions. Also, the moving parts in a reclining chair or sofa can injure or kill your ferret.

✔ **Don't leave small objects lying around.** Stealing is an endearing but sometimes deadly ferret trait. If your fuzzy doesn't eat or chew a small object up, she may hide it — and hide it well. You may not find your stolen objects for a very long time. This is particularly annoying if the item your fuzzy steals is valuable.

✔ **Don't open or close doors quickly.** You may startle or, worse, accidentally injure your ferret. The same goes for cabinets, drawers, refrigerators, freezers, washers, dryers, and dishwashers.

Getting a Vet

Every ferret has different medical needs, and not all veterinarians are trained equally when it comes to the health and well being of ferrets. Although ferrets are the third most popular carnivorous pet in America — topped only by dogs and cats — they're far less popular in the vet's office. Some vets just don't like ferrets; others get hung up on the common misconceptions people have about fuzzies.

It's important to seek out a veterinarian who's comfortable and experienced with ferret medicine before you bring a new fuzzy into your home. You want to ensure that your ferret will have the best routine medical care available. More importantly, you won't jeopardize your pet's life while doing the panic shuffle if an emergency arises. You'll have done your research, and you'll know who to call.

To find out what to look for in a veterinarian and what questions to ask before you enlist his or her services, head to the chapters in Part IV.

Chapter 7

Introducing Fuzzy to His New Family

In This Chapter

▶ Assessing your fuzzy's social tendencies

▶ Helping your new pet adjust to his new environment

▶ Making all your pet introductions

▶ Showing your kids how to safely interact with the ferret

▶ Joining fuzzy and fuzzy for the start of a beautiful friendship

▶ Controlling your ferret around strangers

*B*ringing home a new ferret often means that you must face the delicate issue of introducing your new family member to your existing family members. It may not be as easy as you think. Take, for example, your domestic kitty that's used to being king or queen of the roost. An arrogant ruler, no doubt. Your cat will be dethroned, as will your spouse or any other member of the household, when your new ferret takes his spot by your side.

Knowing how to interact safely with your fuzzy on a one-to-one basis in his new surroundings is imperative, and this chapter tells you how. This chapter also offers insight into the social aspect of ferrets. These creatures aren't all they appear to be; they're even more wonderful than I can put on paper. That said, I discuss sticky subjects such as how to teach your kids to be safe and appropriate around fuzzbutts. Finally, I explain how to introduce your fuzzy to Fido and Fluffy, as well as to those neighbors who just have to stick their noses in your business.

You should quarantine any new ferret you bring into your home for at least two weeks until you know for sure he isn't sick. Although he may look healthy when you bring him home, he may be harboring parasites or transmittable illnesses. Some serious ferret illnesses will flare their ugly heads only during stressful times, like a sudden change of environment. To quarantine, find a comfortable cage for your new ferret and house him at least two rooms away from your existing clan. Always feed and clean your new ferret last and remember to wash your hands thoroughly between handling ferrets. Wear another shirt over your clothing when handling your new ferret and leave it in the new ferret's room when you leave or go back and forth between ferret rooms. Most importantly, remind all members of the household to follow the same rules, or else the quarantine isn't a quarantine at all. When the quarantine period is over, the introductions can begin!

Ferrets as Social Animals

Ferret-owning humans swear up and down that ferrets are incredibly social critters. The fact is, polecats, ferrets included, are solitary animals with territorial tendencies. They don't act like dogs, which seek out other dogs, form packs, and travel around in groups. If you were to release three ferrets of the same gender in your backyard, they would more than likely go in three separate directions. In the wild, polecats defend their territories fervently against polecats of the same gender. (Naturally, if a member of the opposite sex enters a polecat's territory, she's more than welcome to stay awhile.)

The need to be solitary and territorial is, for the most part, kept under control by our beloved domestic ferrets under normal circumstances. But make no mistake about it: Although they play with and tolerate each other to the delight of all onlookers, ferrets maintain little unspoken territories, and at times they squabble with trespassers or thieves. However, there's a reason that thousands of ferret owners coo to themselves as they watch their babies pile in big sleepy heaps at the end of the day. Ferrets, after proper introductions, will view other ferrets as littermates and play about accordingly. They'll wrestle and dance as though they're the best of buddies, and in many cases, they can be the best of buddies. The simple fact is that ferrets establish a hierarchy amongst themselves and stake out microterritories in their tiny domains. In this way, are they really that different from us?

You and Your New Ferret: Making the Most of Your Friendship

Most ferrets enjoy the companionship of humans. It probably won't take long before your new fuzzy sees you as the perfect playmate — assuming you're willing to play nicely with him. To get to that stage, you have to make your fuzzy comfortable in your arms and in his surroundings. Sometimes, it takes a little bit of patience and extra understanding before you begin to feel that your ferret has bonded with you.

Your body movements and tone of voice can influence his reactions to you. The age of your ferret and his history (some ferrets come with emotional baggage; see Chapter 20) also may determine how quickly he blends into your family.

Before you introduce your ferret to other family members, get to know him better and learn how to properly interact with him. The following sections show you how.

Hold me gently, please

In order to introduce your fuzzy to your family and to others, you need to become comfortable holding him — and he needs to be comfortable being held. Many healthy ferrets maintain the "I'd rather be anywhere than in your arms" position. In most cases, it has nothing to do with how you're actually holding the little guy (see Figure 7-1 for an example). There are always exceptions to the rule, though. I've run across many furballs who love to be held and cuddled. Usually, these guys are the older, more mature ferrets who have come to appreciate humans over the years.

To hold your ferret, support both his front and back legs in your arms (see Figure 7-1). Supporting his entire body is important. I can assure you that he'll try to move around quite a bit and probably try to crawl up your chest and onto your shoulder — maybe even onto your head! You can adjust his position, but remember not to squeeze his little body too tightly. You may find that sitting down and holding him on your lap works better for you. Use a treat such as Linatone or Ferretone to entice him into staying put.

If your ferret decides to nip you in protest of being held, don't reward the behavior by putting him down to play. You don't want to give in to his bad behavior, because he'll know what to do in the future when he wants down. Instead, if he nips, immediately tell him "No!" and place him in his cage. This way, your fuzzy will begin to associate biting with jail time (for more, see Chapter 19).

Scruffing, if done correctly, is a safe and painless way to hold a ferret when you need him to remain still for activities like trimming nails and cleaning ears. Simply grab the large, thick patch of skin behind his neck with your entire hand and lift him up. His hanging body should naturally remain still. You should support his bottom, especially if he's a heavy furball. However, note that the more support his bottom receives, the more he can move around. You should use scruffing mainly when more control is necessary for his safety or yours.

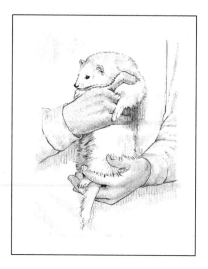

Figure 7-1:
Demonstrating proper ways to hold a ferret.

Letting fuzzy set up shop in his home

I always advise people to allow their ferrets to get used to their new cages before they introduce them to the wonders of their new surroundings (Chapter 5 gives the lowdown on cages). This practice gives your ferret the chance to soak in all the new smells, both good and bad (people can give off funny scents!). Your ferret has a unique personality that you need to become familiar with. Only time will allow this to happen. Ease your ferret into your routine slowly; better yet, let him slowly ease *you* into *his* routine.

For starters, keep his cage in a convenient location — one that won't allow your 100-pound dog to rattle the cage every time she runs by. The following list presents some more cage tips:

- Don't allow the cage to become a resting shelf for your curious cat until your ferret has become comfortable with having that particular cat around (see the upcoming section "Fuzzy Meets Fluffy and Fido").

- Instruct children and other family members to keep their fingers out of the cage until your ferret has become comfortable with all the humans around (see the section "Preparing Your Child for the Ferret").

- If you like, you can partially cover the cage until you all get to know each other.

After a day or two of letting your ferret settle into his new home, take him to a different safe place, such as a bathroom. Sit down alone with some toys and let your ferret explore you at his own pace. Move slowly and quietly, talking softly as you encourage him to play. Watch his body language to see how comfortable he is with you. Some fuzzies are more laid back and eager to accept the change in lifestyle. Others may maintain pipe-cleaner tails for hours until they become more relaxed. When you become comfortable with your ferret's temperament in his new environment, you can begin to give him more freedom. Let him roam first when the kids are at school and the other pets are confined to another area of the house and then move on from there.

The steps to successful bonding

Bonding with your ferret is an important part of establishing and maintaining a pet-loving, harmonious household. The rewards experienced as a result of properly bonding with your ferret will guarantee you a lifetime of love. The goal of bonding, after all, is to not only make life tolerable, but also to turn your ferret into a lap pet and you into a friend for life.

Establishing a bond isn't something that happens naturally or overnight. It takes effort, time, and trust from both parties, and it's an ongoing process. Here are some activities you can engage in to help cement your bond with your ferret:

- **Playing:** Ferrets need frequent human interaction to remain happy, and you can provide this interaction and bond with your ferret by playing with him. Whether you get down on your belly and roll around with him or teach him new tricks, play is vital to your relationship. (See Chapter 10 for more information on play and enrichment.)

✔ **Holding:** One of the best ways to bond with your ferret is to carry him around with you (see the earlier section "Hold me gently, please? [Why a question mark?]" for more on this topic). You can carry your ferret the old-fashioned way by cradling him in your arms and taking him with you from room to room, or you can just plant yourselves on the couch and watch television. Time carrying your ferret around should be limited, with frequent "down time" rests in between so that your ferret doesn't become too stressed and so he can take potty breaks.

✔ **Grooming:** Grooming your ferret is a natural bonding tool. The activity mimics the way the ferret's mother and littermates would groom him in a familial environment. You should practice grooming rituals on a regular basis to enhance your bonding experience with your ferret; they'll help to soften even the most hardcore biter. (For more hygiene information, see Chapter 9.) The following are some grooming activities that promote bonding:

  • **Face rubbing and cleaning:** Gently hold your ferret's head, and using your thumb or thumb and forefinger, stroke his face. I usually use both hands to hold a ferret's head, and I stroke his face with my thumbs from his nose back to his ears. For the cleaning part, you can take a warm, damp washcloth and gently stroke the face fur in the same direction the fur goes (with the grain).

  • **Fur plucking:** Fur plucking is quite simple to do, but you must do it gently. Use your thumb and forefinger to gingerly tug on a tuft of fur on your ferret's head or neck. You also may tug on the fur located on his neck and belly; I've found these areas to be the most accepting, although you can pluck any part of your fuzzy's fur.

  • **A warm, damp washcloth rubdown:** This is one of the most effective grooming/bonding methods, but it takes a little practice and getting used to for both parties. All you need is a small, damp (not wet), warm washcloth. Starting at your ferret's face and working your way back, rub him with the washcloth. Move in the same direction his fur flows. You may need to rinse and warm your washcloth periodically.

    Don't forget his belly, his bottom, and his genitals! Remember, what you want to do is mock his mother's behavior. A washcloth rubdown is not only a great way to bond with your ferret, but also a good way to help keep him clean — at least a little.

All these bonding rituals are easy and can be done just about anywhere and at anytime — even while you're watching television. In addition to having a calming and soothing effect on the ferret, the grooming good for your own blood pressure!

Fuzzy Meets Fluffy and Fido

If you love ferrets (or are thinking of getting one so you can fall in love), chances are you already have other pets in your home. You'll probably be able to introduce your ferret to your dogs and cats with no problems, provided that you take the necessary steps to minimize the natural tension between them. Not all ferrets have the same temperament; likewise, all cats and dogs have unique personalities that influence pet-to-pet relationships. In addition, some breeds of dogs (generally speaking) aren't as good with ferrets as others.

As a rule, ferrets get along better with cats. Ferrets and dogs together present unique conflicts that you should monitor closely. In the following sections, I explain how you can introduce your ferret to both cats and dogs, and I briefly cover other small animals in case you have your own miniature zoo at home!

Heeeere kitty, kitty!

Ferrets and cats can make great companions, depending on their tempera-ments. I have three fat cats, and each one responds differently to my ferrets, and vice versa. Butch is usually neutral around my ferrets, often feeling too crabby to ferret around. Sometimes, though, he gets a wild hair up his heinie and waits patiently around the corner for a ferret to amble by so he can make a tackle. Old man Smokey has zero tolerance for ferret behavior. He either stays up high or throws haphazard swats toward any fuzzy that's curious enough to cop a sniff. He then runs away and hides. Snickers, the youngest of the clan, is always up for a good wrestle. He tolerates ferret antics and enjoys getting down and dirty with all the furballs. They bite each other, take turns chasing, and play hide and seek. Snickers, however, usually wears down the ferrets. Eventually they'll run away and seek solitude in a hidey-hole after an hour or two.

You can do your part to try to make all your pet relationships like the one Snickers (or even Butch) and my ferrets have. To smooth the feline-ferret introductions in your house, follow these steps, one cat at a time:

1. **After your ferret gets comfortable in his new surroundings (see the previous sections), allow kitty to move freely about the outside of the ferret's cage while fuzzy is inside.**

   Let them sniff each other, and watch how they react. You may see no reaction at all.

2. **Take your ferret out of his cage and hold him securely while both he and kitty explore each other.**

   New smells are intriguing to ferrets. Both he and the cat may have puffed tails.

3. **If all seems calm so far, put your ferret down and watch cautiously as the two interact.**

   If conflict arises, end the meeting and try again later. It may take a few meetings before everyone is completely comfortable.

Many people think that the ferret is the animal in the most danger during a cat-ferret encounter. My experience has been that most healthy adult ferrets can hold their own against cats and can even be more aggressive. Until you're sure that your ferret and cat can play nicely together, always supervise their games. Even after you become comfortable, supervision is a good idea.

Adult ferrets have been known to kill kittens, so never leave an adult ferret and a kitten unsupervised. Better yet, let your kitten develop into an arrogant adolescent before subjecting her to ferret torture. It's only fair!

Nice puppy!

The relationship between a dog and ferret can be a little more complicated than the bond between a cat and ferret. Although cats come in different breeds, they all have pretty similar characteristics and are similar in size. Dogs, on the other hand, can be itty-bitty or massive in size and can be bred for certain personality traits and job functions. You must take your dog's size and personality into consideration when introducing your ferret to her.

I've heard of many ferrets being killed by dogs, and the owners blame the dogs. The fault usually lies with the human who wasn't supervising the interaction or who didn't take into consideration the personality of the dog. It's your responsibility to keep your fuzzy safe and healthy; it's a dog's responsibility to be a dog.

Common dog/ferret characteristics

Although good dog-ferret relationships certainly do exist, I tend to mistrust most dogs around ferrets for several reasons:

- ✔ Some breeds of dogs, like Terriers, Spaniels, and Hounds, are bred to hunt ferret-size game, and they may find a ferret awfully tempting. Supervise your ferret with these dogs with extreme caution.

- ✔ Some dogs are very territorial. An otherwise laid-back, ferret-friendly pup may attack a ferret that ventures too close to her food, toys, or den. Keep your dog's stuff out of your ferret's territory, and watch for signs that your dog is getting possessive with other objects.

- ✔ A nursing dog can get extremely aggressive toward other animals when she's protecting her litter.

✔ Large or hyper dogs may inadvertently paw a ferret to death or injure his spine in an attempt to engage in play.

✔ Some dogs don't like little animals or young animals and are very freaky around them. My dog Ara was great with cats but was unpredictable around kittens.

✔ Some dogs do well with ferrets until a fuzzy nips or chases them. A ferret is bound to nip and chase during play. If your dog can dish it out but can't take it, don't allow her to play with a fuzzy at all.

✔ Some dogs just aren't good with other animals, including ferrets.

Of course, many exceptions exist, which is why you'll never know how an interaction will go until you try. Some nursing dogs allow ferrets to snuggle in with the rest of the litter. Some big dogs tiptoe gently around ferrets. Because every animal is an individual, you must decide how to allow your fuzzy to interact with your dog. Use common sense. If it feels or looks unsafe for your ferret, it probably is.

The Fuzzy-Fido introduction

Introducing a fuzzy and a dog should be almost the same as introducing a fuzzy and a cat. The main difference is that the process is slower. Just follow these steps:

1. **When your fuzzy is feeling settled in his new home (see the first section of this chapter), allow your dog to roam freely around and investigate your ferret's cage — with fuzzy in the cage and with you present.**

   Allow this type of interaction to take place for several days. Especially if you have a large dog, don't allow your dog alone with the cage. I have a friend who lost fuzzies to a large dog that tore apart the fuzzy cage in a matter of 15 unsupervised minutes.

2. **If the cage sniffing seems to be going well, take your ferret out and hold him securely; let your dog and ferret sniff each other.**

   You'll know things are going well if neither your dog nor you ferret is lunging at the other, or your ferret isn't cowering in the corner. If either is showing aggression, stop the introductions and try again the next day. Keep up the process until they become desensitized toward each other. This may take a month or more and may never work out at all.

3. **If the mutual smelling goes well, harness and leash your fuzzy and put him down on the ground with the dog in the room.**

   Ideally, your dog's tail should be wagging and he should smell the ferret. Your ferret may or may not be interested in sniffing back. He may dance with excitement or just ignore your dog. Watch your dog for warning signs such as hackles up, baring teeth, or stiffened body. Every play interaction between your dog and ferret will be different from here on out and should be supervised due to the unpredictable nature of both animals.

No matter how well a dog and ferret seem to get along, never leave them unsupervised. Be extra vigilant. Dogs can be funny critters, and I don't mean funny ha-ha. They're quick, and you may not be able to rescue your ferret if he needs help.

Ferrets and other small animals

Ferrets are predatory by nature. Allowing them to play with other small animals — such as rabbits, hamsters, birds, hedgehogs, guinea pigs, and lizards — is, in essence, messing with the laws of nature. As I mention in Chapter 8, most kibble-raised ferrets won't even recognize smaller animals as food. However, the quick movements made by small pets may trigger the predatory reaction in your fuzzbutt. Even if a small pet stays perfectly still, your ferret's curiosity can take over, and, like a dog pawing during play, your ferret may kill the small animal accidentally.

Yes, exceptions to this trend exist, but I wouldn't want to risk the life of a small pet just to see if my ferret falls into the exception category. As a general guideline, keep your ferret separated from any animal his cousins may prey on in the wild.

Preparing Your Child for the Ferret

Some adults think young, innocent kids automatically know what to do and what not to do around animals. Not so. You need to teach your child about interacting safely with animals. Although some youngsters may have more common sense than their adult counterparts, an adult is still responsible for keeping both the child and the pet safe. In the following sections, I let you know what your kid needs to know before the introduction, and I take you through the process of making the introduction.

Never allow any pet, ferret or otherwise, to interact unsupervised with a baby, toddler, or incapacitated person. Doing so is incredibly irresponsible. The human and the pet can get severely injured, particularly if the pet is a small animal such as a ferret.

Pause the cartoons: What your child should know beforehand

Children can activate the insanity button in even the calmest person or ferret. Fuzzies already are strung out on excess energy, and kids can easily manage to activate their overload switch. That's a given, and something you must deal with. Behavior aside, though, you must keep in mind that kids are smaller than adults. They're clumsier, and they have much higher pitched voices. These factors alone can make an already nervous ferret even more excited; when you combine the added hyperactivity a kid brings in, you can have double trouble.

Your job as a responsible adult and ferret-owning human is to teach your child what you know about ferrets in terms he or she will understand. When you're done explaining the following points to your kid, you can explain them again to any of his or her young friends who may also want to interact with your fuzzbutt:

- Many kids get frightened easily around animals, particularly when they get nipped or scratched. Explain to your child that ferrets are very active and playful.

- Stress to your child the importance of not running around or roughhousing where ferrets are loose. Give reasons why so she'll understand.

- Reinforce the importance of properly holding a fuzzy (see the section "Hold me gently, please? [Why a question mark?]"). Children have a tendency to squeeze things in order not to drop them. And they insist on holding things and then rapidly and without warning change their minds and let the objects or animals drop to the floor.

  Insisting that your child always holds the ferret while sitting down is a good idea. That way, even if your fuzzbutt squirms away, he won't end up plopping to the floor.

For safety reasons, always supervise children when they're interacting with your ferret until you feel confident that they know how to properly play.

Fuzzy, meet Junior: Making the introduction

Kids can be quite unpredictable around and in their interactions with animals. The introductions you make are very important in educating your child about animal safety. It's important to go slowly and explain things as you go along.

The first step in the introduction phase is to go over the rules I mention in the previous section. When your child fully understands what you're saying, go over the following to help ease your ferret safely and comfortably into your child's life:

1. **Because most children automatically shy away from being bitten or scratched, make sure your child wears long pants and long sleeves to prevent your ferret from clawing.** This way, the child will find handling the ferret easier and safer.

2. **Start off slowly by having your child sit on the floor in the same room with the ferret.** Allow the ferret to approach your child on his own terms, but keep him from climbing on your child. This is a good time to practice patience.

3. **If the ferret seems relaxed around your child, and your child hasn't gone into hyper mode, pick up your ferret and demonstrate the proper way to hold him.** Point out his sharp claws and teeth and explain why it's important to properly hold the ferret.

4. **With your child still sitting on the ground, place the ferret in the child's lap and allow the ferret to get used to being with a new person.** Encourage your child to gently pet the ferret.

5. **If the meeting is going well and everyone is still calm, place the ferret into your child's arms, again showing her the proper way to hold the ferret.** Make sure you keep your hands just below the ferret in case your child decides she no longer wants to hold him. If you feel comfortable with your child's comfort level, you can have her stand up and hold the ferret.

6. **If the you and your ferret both seem comfortable with how your child is handling the situation, demonstrate how to put the ferret back down.** At this time, you also can show your child how to properly pick up the ferret. Learning how to pick up your ferret and put him back down is just as important as learning how to hold him. Remind your child that she should never interact with the ferret without adult supervision.

With these simple guidelines, you should be able to determine how responsible your child will be with a ferret, and how your ferret will do with a child. Some kids and some ferrets take a little longer to get the hang of it. If this is the case with your loved ones, go slow! Never force a child or a pet to interact until both parties feel and act comfortable. Moving to the next step before your child and pet have mastered the prior step may lead to injuries.

Fuzzy Meets Fuzzy: Adding Another Ferret to Your Family

Introducing a new ferret to your other ferret pet(s) can be tricky business (and, remember, should only be done after the proper quarantining process). Like many other species of mammals, ferrets vie for top position. They do so through play wrestling and biting. Some ferrets are natural leaders; others are natural followers; and some would rather venture through life without ever encountering another ferret. You may not know which type you're bringing home until you see him spring into action.

Here are some bits of information to keep in mind when introducing your new ferret to his new family:

- ✔ Kits (very young ferrets) are perfect squeaky toys for older ferrets, although the kits rarely see it this way. Adult ferrets can be quite possessive of youngsters. They may try to drag them around and stuff them in hidey-holes while guarding aggressively against curious visitors.

- ✔ Newly introduced ferrets often display their frizzed tails for the first ten minutes or so. This behavior is normal. Pay particular attention when one ferret aggressively tackles another and performs an immediate alligator roll, because this behavior can signal trouble. A dominant ferret may take a lot longer to accept a new ferret and in some instances will act particularly aggressive.

  Sometimes, a frightened ferret screams and hisses as the more aggressive ferret tries to engage in play. Ferrets play rough, but if one fuzzy seems overly bullied or frightened, separate him and try introducing again later.

- ✔ Ferrets that have been isolated for a long period of time may feel particularly frightened at the sight of another fuzzy.

- ✔ Although ferrets are capable of severely injuring — and even killing — another ferret, it rarely happens. Of course, you should always end the meeting if blood is drawn, and you should always have a spare cage for the newcomer in case the introduction turns sour. Your quarantine cage is perfect for this.

Some signs will almost immediately tell you that the new relationship probably won't work out: Drawing blood, one ferret literally having the poop scared out of him, and persistent screaming, to name a few. It may take only a few minutes for a newcomer to be welcomed, or it may take hours, days, or even months. Some ferrets just won't, under any circumstances, coexist. Most ferrets eventually learn to get along with other ferrets, though. If your ferrets only display bottle-brush tails and keep coming back for more sniffs, they should become best buds in no time.

That being said, you can do certain things to encourage a successful introduction and relationship between fuzzies. I cover these actions in the sections that follow, as well as steps you can take to introduce multiple fuzzies.

Meeting on neutral ground

For your initial introduction, you should choose a ferret-proof room (see Chapter 6) that your established ferret hasn't yet explored. It should contain ferret toys, tubes and climbing furniture, as well as food and water. It should also contain secure nest boxes with small openings (see Chapter 5). Another neutral place can be in your yard, with all the ferrets harnessed and leashed.

When all parties are on site, place them together and watch cautiously to see how they react and interact. If the introduction is a rough one, place them in separate cages and try again later.

Messing with their sniffers

Ferrets have a tremendous sense of smell. They identify other ferrets and objects based on the unique scents they give off. The scent of a new ferret can be intimidating and provoke aggression or fear. So, you can take some actions to get their noses used to each other:

✔ Because a lot of disagreements arise from one ferret not liking another's special smell, making them smell alike can help to curtail fuzzy tension. Your ferrets are probably due for baths anyway, so break out the most fragrant (and safe) shampoo you can find and give them baths (if you want a more exotic smell, you can add a little vanilla extract to the bath; see Chapter 9 for more on cleaning). The boys will be busy feeling embarrassed at how girly they smell, and the girls will be busy walking with their heads held high. An established ferret will notice a newcomer, but everyone will smell pretty much the same at this point.

✔ You can clean all toys and bedding in your main fuzzy cage before lumping them in together. Also, don't forget to clean the cage and change the litter boxes. These tasks give your new ferret ample opportunity to get his scent in the cage at the same time as the others.

✔ You also can switch the cage bedding of the new ferret with the cage bedding of the established fuzzy, and vice versa. This way, they have no choice but to live with each other's stink. They'll either get used to each other or resent the other even more. Usually, they get used to each other. I use this tactic when introducing most animals to each other, from rabbits to foxes. Although it doesn't always work, it has a high success rate.

Forcing a relationship

Some ferret relationships require a little extra help to get going, to the point where it seems like you're forcing the relationship. Hey, no one said the intro would be easy! The following list presents a few more tips for helping your tough guys get through the initial bad times:

✔ **Carry the buggers around together.** They may be so busy wondering where they're going that they'll forget their hatred for each other — even if just for a moment. Carry your ferrets everywhere you go in the house. Hold them on your lap together. Make them watch television with you — together!

✔ **Stick the ferrets in a carrier together and take them to the vet for their shots and checkups.** Fear and anxiety have a bonding effect on both humans and animals. Your fuzzies can share the moment and hate you together.

✔ **Allow them to share a tasty treat off the same spoon at the same time.** You also can allow them to enjoy the irresistible licks of Linatone from the same bottle.

✔ **Bathe them together in the same tub at the same time.** They'll share a fear and anxiety similar to what they'll experience at the vet. Plus, the shared humiliation of the bath will lead to a bonding experience like no other.

✔ **Let them duke it out!** It may be time to stop babying them. Let them spend a few (3) days screeching, chasing, bullying, and fighting, but no longer than that! Most of the time, ferrets work out their differences if you let them. Use your common sense, but keep in mind that it usually looks and sounds worse than it really is.

Easing your fuzzy into the business

Sometimes nothing you try seems to work, especially when you have one or two ferrets that just seem unwilling to let a newcomer into the group. As frustrating as it may be, you should do everything you can to help ease the new guy into the family. Because ferrets have a hierarchy amongst themselves, it's important to get to know everyone one by one, starting with the most submissive ferret. The theory is that by the time the ferret has met the most dominant ferrets, he'll already have been accepted by the more submissive ferrets and have become part of the family:

1. **Introduce your new ferret to a safe, neutral room with plenty of hiding spots (see the earlier section "Meeting on neutral ground").**

   The first thing he'll do is make his rounds to get to know the place and the new scents. After he knows the territory, he'll familiarize himself with the toys and other items in the room. He'll then dance about in play and silliness, just like any healthy ferret should do. Before long, he'll become bored with his surroundings and look to you for more to do.

2. **Introduce your most submissive and docile opposite-sex ferret into the room. (If your new ferret is a boy, introduce a girl.)**

   Now that your new ferret's attention is off the room, he can focus on the newly introduced ferret. If all goes well, you should see a fair amount of sniffing, some silly dancing, and some play about the room.

3. **Introduce your next most docile and submissive opposite-sex ferret into the room.**

   Repeat this process with all ferrets of this characterization.

4. **When you run out of opposite-sex ferrets to introduce, bring in the most docile same-sex ferret.**

   Repeat this process as well.

5. **What should remain are the unintroduced ferrets that are your typical aggressors.**

   The idea is that your new ferret will be assimilated into the group and become more easily accepted by the more aggressive ferrets with the blessing of the others.

Although gender introductions can be unpredictable, boy ferret meeting girl ferret statistically has the best outcome. Boy ferret meeting boy ferret produces pretty good results, too. Girl ferret meeting girl ferret, on the other hand, can be more of a challenge.

If any of the previous steps fail at any point along the way, you should stop the introduction process and try again the next day. See the section "Messing with their sniffers" and bathe each of them right before starting the process again. Introduce Ferretone or another tasty treat when things start heating up and have them share a spoon. Take things you've learned in this chapter and incorporate them into this introduction process. Be creative. It may take several rounds of introductions or combinations of techniques. When all is said and done, there's no guarantee any introduction technique will work for your new ferret.

Heading Off Stranger Danger

Your new ferret may have several opportunities to encounter strangers when he enters your family and home. A meeting may take place at the vet's office or in the park during playtime (with you attached at the end of the leash, of course; see Chapter 5). It may be in your child's classroom during a show-and-tell or in your own home. You must realize that not everyone shares your fuzzy enthusiasm; some people will be taken aback at the quick display of curiosity shown by your ferret. Others may get annoyed at how bold your ferret can be as he tries to steal their possessions and mow through their hairdos. The good news is that you'll surely find people who are just like you and me. These people will be tickled pink at your ferret's charming personality.

Some ferrets are natural social butterflies; others quiver with nervousness when encountering new people or places. Use common sense; don't risk a stranger's health or your fuzzy's life if you already know that your ferret reacts badly to change or strangers. That said, here are some suggestions for dealing with strangers who come around your ferret:

✔ When allowing a stranger to touch your ferret for the first time, keep your ferret's head under control. Offer the stranger your ferret's bottom and back to pet in order to minimize any chance of biting.

✔ If you're entertaining guests at your home or if your kids have friends over, allow time for introductions; after the fuzzy curiosity has passed, it's best to keep your ferret caged. With so much else going on, supervising a roaming ferret becomes difficult. He can be mishandled or get injured with all the feet moving about.

✔ If the stranger will become a frequent visitor to your ferret, give her a brief education on the common behavior of ferrets and on the proper way to handle them. I can't stress the education factor enough. That, along with common sense, has allowed me to show off my fuzzies hundreds and hundreds of times with no tragedies to report.

Part III
Basic Ferret Care and Feeding

The 5th Wave   By Rich Tennant

©RICHTENNANT

"We keep her diet high in protein, high in nutrients, and high off the floor behind a locked door."

In this part . . .

Ferrets are complicated critters with complicated needs. This part deals with providing the basic necessities: how to keep your ferret and his cage clean, how to satisfy his nutritional requirements, how to provide the activities he needs to stay healthy and happy, and how to go traveling — with or without him.

Most people can keep a ferret alive, but keeping him healthy, happy, and sane is another matter. This part also takes caring for your ferret a couple steps further by delving into issues such as alternative diets and environmental enrichment for you and your fuzzy.

Chapter 8

Filling Your Ferret's Belly

· ·

In This Chapter

▶ Hydrating your fuzzy

▶ Scanning the dietary requirements for ferrets

▶ Giving your ferret a traditional dry or wet diet

▶ Supplying an alternative (natural) diet

▶ Adding supplements and treats to your fuzzy's diet

· ·

*P*roviding a suitable diet is essential for your ferret's good health, though feeding your fuzzy properly is easier said than done. The keys to a good diet are the proper amounts of

- ✔ Fat
- ✔ Meat-based protein
- ✔ Vitamins and minerals

So, what's the problem? Finding this perfect diet can be difficult and challenging for even an experienced fuzzy human.

That's why this chapter is extra-important. It covers the basic information you need to know about water — how much water to give and how often to give it — traditional diets, alternative diets, supplements, and treats. I also discuss the ferret's natural or evolutionary diet, a topic that in my opinion is important to know about in order to understand your ferret's nutritional needs. I even explain how to switch a ferret's diet if you find it necessary to do so; I hope I can convince some of you to do just that!

Just as important is that your ferret's diet be absent of, or have very minimal amounts of,

- ✔ Fruits
- ✔ Vegetables
- ✔ Starches
- ✔ Sugars

The wrong foods can lead to obesity, food-related illnesses, and a shortened life span. Just how big a part diet plays in terms of ferret diseases is still being researched, but experts know that it's big. We may all be surprised at what will eventually be discovered.

Water, Water, Everywhere

No living thing can live without water, but not all water is equal when it comes to hydrating your ferret. Some ferret owners prefer to use bottled or distilled water. However, experts strongly argue that distilled water lacks many important nutrients that pets need, so you may want to avoid distilled water all together. Unless your tap water tests positive for high levels of harmful chemicals, tap water should be sufficient to hydrate your ferret. Make sure that your ferret's water bottle is full at all times!

Ferrets as Diners

I think I can safely say that no one has come up with the perfect solution when it comes to the question of what people should feed their domestic ferrets. There are so many factors that come into play, from owner preference to food availability to ferret health. I can't give you a single right answer. But I do know a lot about ferrets' dietary quirks and feeding needs. The following list presents things all ferret owners should know about their ferrets; the more you know about your ferret, the better you'll be able to choose the right diet for her:

- ✔ Ferrets are *obligate carnivores,* meaning they meet virtually all their nutritional needs by eating meat-based (animal-based) foods. They must eat meat!

- ✔ Ferrets are *hypercarnivores,* meaning their anatomy, physiology, and behaviors are adapted to a strict carnivore lifestyle.

- ✔ Ferrets *olfactory imprint* on their foods, which means their food-odor preferences are generally established by 6 months of age and finalized by 8 to 12 months. At this point, the older they get, the less likely they'll be able to recognize the smell of a new food as being yummy.

- ✔ Ferrets aren't built to digest fiber. If you were to take a peek inside a ferret (not advised), you'd see that her large intestine is short and tubular and that the ferret lacks a cecum. The *cecum* is a blind pouch located at the junction where the small intestine ends and the large intestine begins; this is the place where fiber is bacterially digested (similar to the human appendix). Too much fiber in your ferret's belly leads to extra-squishy or mucousy poops.

✔ Ferrets may have a rapid GI transit time, depending on what food they consume. Food may pass in as little as 3 to 4 hours, which leaves little time to digest and absorb nutrients. In 6 hours, if fasted, the stomach usually is completely emptied. For this reason, feeding high-quality meat-based products and fat is even more important.

✔ Ferrets can't digest milk as adults because of low levels of lactase.

✔ Ferrets, because they're carnivores, have very simple gut flora (bacteria). Unlike in herbivores, fermentation isn't needed to extract the nutrients during the digestive process. Digestive additives such as *Lactobacillus*, found in yogurt, aren't important and won't help a ferret digest food.

✔ The ferret's teeth are designed for tearing and cutting, not for chewing.

This list is just the beginning. This chapter is full of dietary information that should help you sort out the questions in your head!

Feeding the Traditional Commercial Diet

Traditional commercial diet formulas for ferrets have improved over the past decades as people have gained more knowledge and understanding of the ferret. But when it comes to dietary needs, your ferret is still no different from her polecat cousins: Her food should contain *taurine* (which helps keep her eyes and heart healthy) and be composed of between 15 and 20 percent fat and no less than 32 to 40 percent meat-based protein. When it comes to kibble and wet food, ferret owners have many options:

✔ The pet industry has come out with several foods formulated just for ferrets. The majority of these commercial diet foods meet the protein/fat-level requirements, and some are considered among the best commercially available food choices for your ferret.

✔ Some high-quality dry kitten foods have the necessary taurine, fat, and protein contents, but many don't. Before you make dry kitten food a staple of your ferret's diet, make sure the brand you choose has the nutritional content your ferret needs.

✔ Dog food isn't a source of proper nutrition for your ferret. It's usually too low in protein and too high in grains and veggies. It also doesn't contain the taurine additive that your ferret needs for healthy eyes and heart. As an infrequent treat, though, dog food is fine.

Don't expect a pet shop clerk to know what's best for your ferret. Many are fairly educated about the animals they sell, but I've overheard one or two telling new ferret owners to feed canned dog food or only hamburger meat. I even heard one clerk tell a customer that ferrets are herbivores (plant eaters). Instead, read through the information in the following sections about what type of commercial diet to feed your ferret. In these sections, I discuss what wet and dry foods are and the pros and cons of feeding them to your ferret. I also talk about setting up a feeding schedule and what to do if you want to change from one diet to another. After you know the facts, you can get with your vet to go over your options.

Wet or dry food?

Some people like to stick with a dry food for their ferrets, and others prefer to feed their fuzzies moist food. Some people alternate between the diets, and some savvy ferret owners mix the dry and moist foods. I personally try to give my ferrets as much variety as possible. The following sections give you some things to think about when deciding what type of food is right for your furball.

Commercial dry (kibble)

Kibble is widely available, hygienically safe, economical, and convenient, making it the most popular dietary choice among ferret owners. Many dry kibble options are available. They come in the form of kitten or ferret food. Some are at the top of my list, and others would go right into my garbage can. Some "nutritionally complete" ferret diets are available, but no matter what, you need to choose only a high-quality ferret or kitten kibble for your furball.

Dissecting pet food labels

Pet food labels, even those from reputable manufacturers, can be and often are misleading. Unless the label says all the protein is from meat, you can be sure it isn't. The protein can come from other sources thrown into the recipe. The hair in a hairball is close to 100 percent protein. Fecal matter (trace amounts are allowed in by-products) also is made up of protein. Ick! So even if your ferret's food is 30 percent protein, how much of it actually comes from meat? Even if meat is listed as the top ingredient, that doesn't mean the meat is where all the protein comes from.

Most pet foods have meat or chicken by-products listed as a first ingredient. What the heck are meat and chicken by-products, anyway? Hold onto your lunch. By-products are leftover gunky animal bits that aren't fit for human consumption. They don't even qualify to be stuffed into a hot dog casing (that's really bad). By-products include such yummies as heads (chicken), skin, feet,

blood, guts, beaks, tendons, stomach contents, discarded organs, and fecal matter (trace amounts). Once in a while, by-products may include bits of less-than-fresh meat. The protein from by-products may not be easily digested by your pet ferret. The key is the quality and wholesomeness of the by-products.

Consumers don't even know why many additives are thrown into the pet food. Some say "to preserve freshness." Sure. Can you imagine? And did they remember to add all those essential vitamins, amino acids, and minerals that ferrets evolved eating? Some manufacturers may try their best to make up for it in some way, but how do we really know the job was accomplished? And ponder this: If a food was perfect, as each ad campaign suggests, why do the same manufacturers continuously release "new and improved" versions? This is evidence that the diet was NOT as complete as advertising suggested.

If you want to feed your ferret kibble, keep this in mind: Ideally, the first three ingredients should be meat products, and the kibble should contain no corn. The majority of kibble is poultry-based. Avoid products that contain dried bits of fruits or vegetables, which ferrets can't digest.

Ferrets can't chew kibble, so they swallow it in chunks; thus, it may not be digested properly, especially if the ferret has limited access to water. Ferrets must first hydrate kibble (guaranteed to less than 10 percent moisture) before proper digestion. And contrary to popular belief, dry kibble doesn't significantly help wear down the tartar buildup on a fuzzy's teeth. Hard kibble fed as a sole diet *does* cause tooth wear because it's very abrasive. Sprinkle a few drops of water or chicken broth over the hard food and microwave it briefly to help soften it up a little without making it the consistency of canned food. This minimizes damage to the teeth and improves digestibility.

This all sounds well and good, right? But dry kibble isn't all good for all ferrets. The following list outlines some cons of feeding your ferret kibble:

- ✔ Kibble isn't mentally stimulating and is monotonous in taste.

- ✔ The heat and processing of the kibble may make some of the protein less digestible.

  Kibble is an *extruded* diet. The ingredients are finely ground into a dough and then pushed or drawn through a "kibble-shaped" tube with heat and pressure. The dough is then cut and dried.

- ✔ Starches/carbohydrates are used in the formation of kibble to hold the shape. Most kibbles have around 20 to 30 percent digestible carbohydrates.

- ✔ The higher than needed levels of carbs in kibble may contribute to diseases such as insulinoma (see Chapter 16), gastroenteritis, and bladder stones.

Commercial canned

Canned pet food is widely available, hygienically safe, economical, and convenient, and is therefore another popular choice among ferret owners. When looking for a canned food, you should stick with a high-quality feline or ferret food. The main ingredients should be meat products, and the food should contain no additional grains or sweeteners.

Canned ferret food has some benefits that you should consider when making the diet decision:

- ✔ Canned foods are mentally stimulating.

- ✔ Because many meat proteins are available, the tastes in canned foods are varied.

- ✔ Canned foods are low in carbs and high in fat and protein.

Of course, canned foods have their cons, too:

- ✔ High-quality canned feline or ferret food is easier on the teeth in terms of wear, but it may lead to faster tartar buildup.

- ✔ Canned food lacks the nutrient density to be a ferret's sole food. Because it is about 70 percent water, ferrets need to eat a larger volume of canned food to get the same calories provided by dry food, which has only about a 1-percent moisture content. Ferrets' tummies are small, so they may not be able to get all their nutrient needs from canned food only.

Depending on the brand, it's rare that a canned food would be a nutritionally better food than dry kibble. It's also slightly more expensive than kibble and can cause stinkier poops. Canned food shouldn't be the only food in the ferret's diet, but it would make an excellent addition to any main course, especially when served alongside kibble.

Setting a feeding schedule

Ferret owners influence how often their ferrets need to eat, because ferrets adapt their eating cycles to what and when they're being fed. For example, if you're feeding your ferret a kibble that's high in carbs, blood/sugar fluctuations can drive your ferret to eat more often — perhaps as often as every 4 to 5 hours. An even poorer diet could drive her to eat every 3 to 4 hours. However, if you're feeding a diet that's high in fat and meat-based protein, you'll leave your ferret satisfied for much longer — perhaps as long as 8 to 10 hours.

Some people think that leaving food out all the time leads to ferret obesity. They must be thinking of us humans! Normally, ferrets aren't gluttons and consume only the amount of fat needed to get the energy to terrorize their households in their normal capacity. This is called *eating to meet caloric need,* which is possible only when the ferret is eating a nutritionally complete food. If the ferret's diet is of nutritionally poor quality, your fuzzy will develop a nutritional deficit and will instinctively eat more to make up for it. This is called *eating to meet nutritional need.* If the poor diet also happens to be loaded with carbs (calorie dense), eating it can result in an obese ferret.

If you think your ferret is getting chunky, take her to the vet to rule out an enlarged spleen or fluid in her abdominal cavity. Enlarged spleens are common causes of rapid weight gain.

Some ferrets get slightly wider with age, and some get wider in the winter. In general, obesity is rarely a serious problem in ferrets — especially if their diets are balanced.

Changing kibble diets

There are many reasons for needing or wanting to change your ferret's kibble diet. It can be a medical necessity. The food you're currently feeding may be discontinued. Or you may find something better out there for her. But it may be difficult to convince your ferret that she needs to change to the new type of food — especially if the fuzzy has been fed a different or improper diet before coming into your care. If this is the case, you need to switch the ferret over to the good stuff, despite any protest she may display. I've had some ferrets that would eat any type of cat, kitten, or ferret food, no matter what. On the other hand, I've had some that refused all food until I could figure out exactly what they'd been eating before coming into my care. This is a case of extreme olfactory imprinting (see the earlier section "Ferrets as Diners").

The best way to switch your ferret's food is to mix her previous food with the new food of choice. Start off by adding just a small amount of the new food to the old. It's important not to switch completely to the new food immediately. Such a drastic change can lead to an upset tummy, diarrhea, and a generally crabby ferret. Gradually increase the amount of new food you include and decrease the amount of old food; do so over the course of 10 to 14 days. This process usually works well and gives your fuzzy's system a chance to get used to the change.

If your ferret eats around the new food and devours the old, give her time and don't give up. The switch may take several days or even as long as several months, so patience and persistence are positive virtues. The health of your baby could depend on it.

If you own multiple ferrets and house them in the same cage, telling whether a ferret has taken to her new food can be difficult, because the ferrets eat from the same bowl. As the food level is quickly depleted, you may be unaware that your ferret is slowly starving, which can be extremely dangerous. Watch for any significant weight changes in all your fuzzies, particularly the newcomers. In fact, I recommend that you house a new ferret separately until you know for sure that she's eating what the rest of the gang is eating. This practice gives you the opportunity to monitor her food intake closely and prevent a possible slow starvation.

Serving Up an Alternative Diet

People have fed their ferrets man-made foods — mostly out of convenience or lack of anything else good to feed — since World War II. Recently, the ferret world has seen a growing movement to switch to more natural diets. A natural diet consists of feeding, among other things, meats, organs, and bones. Some people believe the only way to true pet health is to feed a diet that the animal evolved eating, and kibble certainly wasn't around 2,500 years ago, much less a century ago.

The following list presents what proponents of natural and evolutionary diets believe the benefits are:

- ✔ A natural or evolutionary diet ensures that your ferret is getting her essential nutrients. For example, those essential amino acids that the ferret can't produce herself are commonly found in the foods her wild relatives eat: rabbits, mice, rats, birds, frogs, lizards, and squirrels. Calcium is another example: Many man-made cat, kitten, or ferret foods lack quality bone meal, so ferrets are losing out on needed calcium.

- ✔ A healthy ferret on a varied and natural diet doesn't need to have food available at all times. The ferret's wild relatives eat only once or twice a day, sometimes even missing days when food is scarce.

- ✔ Many people who feed their fuzzies a more natural diet believe that the variation of food consistency (bone, skin, meat, and so on) helps to flush out the intestinal tract, causing the ferret to be less prone to hairballs and other obstructions. The diet also helps to even out nutrient needs that are currently unknown.

- ✔ The design of the ferret's jaw and teeth leaves her with limited chewing capability. Her teeth were designed for cutting meat and bone, but not all the time — at least not up to ten meals per day. Kibble can be as hard as or harder than bone, and its abrasiveness leads to wear on the teeth. A natural diet generally is easier on the teeth.

The following sections explain what I call a *natural diet* (raw or freeze-dried raw) and an evolutionary diet (small, whole prey). But first, you need to understand the polecat a little better. And you'll also learn about bones as part of the alternative diet. Finally, I explore the different ways you can feed the natural or evolutionary diet to your ferret.

Most mainstream veterinarians are adamantly opposed to feeding raw meat diets, whether they're homemade or commercially prepared, and list many valid reasons why. Other vets and many holistic vets swear by the raw diet and give their valid reasons why as well. And each group refutes the other's reasons. Both sides sound right and reasonable. The only thing they agree on is that care and diligence are needed in handling raw food.

Although it's unknown exactly how the nutrient composition will be changed, it's possible to cook the diet to eliminate the risk of passing along any bacteria or parasites to your ferret. You can braise, steam, or microwave the food. This is also a good way to get your ferret switched over to the raw diet if this is what you choose to feed. Offer the food completely cooked or even slightly cooked to help get your ferret's system used to the change. Gradually mix in raw food with the cooked before switching completely to raw. See the section "Exploring the alternative way of feeding" for more advice on diet conversion.

Getting to know the wild polecat's diet

If I were to undertake the task of designing the perfect man-made ferret food, the first thing I would do is research. I would want to know what animal(s) was the ferret's closest relative and what it naturally thrived on in the wild.

Ferrets are descended from wild polecats, and experts know that both ferrets and polecats are obligate carnivores (see the section "Ferrets as Diners"). So, what do polecats prey on and eat in the wild? Mice, rats, rabbits, frogs, other amphibians, invertebrates, voles, small snakes, birds, eggs, and even some fish. Polecats often eat the entire carcass of smaller prey, from the organs to the bones, sometimes leaving the intestinal tract by the wayside. They also consume the fur of smaller prey and the downy part of birds as they eat the bodies. This natural diet is extremely low in carbohydrates. Most prey-animal carbohydrates originate from the animals' glycogen and blood sugar, with some possibly coming from the intestinal tracts of the animals. The diet also is high in meat-based protein and low in fiber. Additionally, this type of diet typically doesn't lead to dental disease. Admittedly, some polecats do get the disease, but the rate in polecats is much lower. The various textures of natural prey foods actually serve to massage the ferret's gums and help wipe the teeth clean.

Ferrets, if given the opportunity at a young age, would follow in their ancestors' dietary footsteps. Just for kicks, compare the evolutionary ingredients to the current list of ingredients found in your ferret's kibble. Nowhere in the polecat's diet would you find corn grits, corn meal, wheat, soy flour, rice, raisin puree, banana juice, cane molasses, corn sugar, dried potato products . . . well, you get the idea. Those are just some of the ingredients you may find in ferret kibble. What are food manufacturers thinking when they formulate our ferrets' food? They certainly aren't thinking of the evolutionary dietary needs of the ferret. (For more on an evolutionary diet, see the section that focuses on the topic later in this chapter.)

Bellying up to a bone-filled diet

Bones contain an incredible amount of good stuff, with calcium being the most obvious nutritional content. Bone marrow itself is made up of tissues rich in protein and fat. Bone and marrow contain high amounts of fatty acids, fats, iron, and other vitamins essential to the health of carnivores. Most of this good stuff comes from the ends of the bones, which are softer and easily bitten, chewed, and swallowed. The placement of the good stuff is beneficial, because the ends are the parts ferrets are most interested in. They usually leave the rest if they can find something else to eat.

BARF at home

Bones and **R**aw **F**ood

Biologically **A**ppropriate **R**aw **F**ood

Feeding your ferret, or any pet, BARF is based on the belief that you can mimic its evolutionary diet by combining whole, raw, natural foods. The BARF diet, which includes meats, bones, non-meats, and numerous supplements, was formulated by Dr. Ian Billinghurst, who claimed that man-made kibble doesn't allow domestic animals to thrive like their wild ancestors do on a raw diet.

Proponents believe BARF

- Can lengthen lifespan
- Can prevent and even reverse illnesses/diseases in pets
- Improves the immune system
- Improves pets' performance
- Improves coat and body odor
- Eliminates the need for dental cleanings
- Is more balanced than commercial kibbles

Many people "BARF" their pets on their own, using recipes they've gotten off the Internet or simply ones they've concocted themselves. This isn't always safe. A homemade diet can be the best or the worst food you can feed your ferret! It's very difficult to get the right formula down; you could make your ferret sick by not having the right amount of this, that, or the other thing. Says veterinarian Susan Brown, "100% homemade diets — either raw, cooked, or a combination thereof — have been used successfully in some cases with individual animals. However, this requires real diligence to detail and having enough variety in the diet to cover all of the needs of the ferret, including trace vitamins and minerals. In addition, the owner has to prevent over-supplementation of various vitamins and minerals, because excessive amounts of some substances can be as great a health risk as not enough of these same substances. Currently there are quite a few quality diet choices for the small carnivore, and it is my recommendation that a ferret's diet should have a majority of its substance based on a commercial diet, whether it is a commercial raw, kibble, freeze-dried, or canned diet, or even better a combination of at least two of these forms."

Opponents of BARF believe

- The risk of transmitting bacteria and parasites to people and pets far outweighs the pros of feeding BARF. *E.coli* and *salmonella* are particularly of concern.
- The diet poses a particular risk to pet owners who formulate and mix the diets, especially people who are young, elderly, or immuno-compromised.
- The diet is more often than not nutritionally unsound and inconsistent.
- The use of whole bones can cause intestinal obstructions/perforations, dental fractures, and gastroenteritis.

If you like the idea of BARF, there are several commercially made raw and freeze-dried ferret diets available, which I'll talk about later. They may be easier and more convenient to feed, as well as closer to the nutritional balance you're looking for. I also talk more about the controversy of feeding raw meat.

Fact is, bones are wonderful sources of natural nutrition. If you think your ferret would benefit from the calcium and other nutrients in bones, you should try adding them to her diet.

Can feeding bones to your ferret cause harm? Certainly. On rare occasions, a splinter may cut the esophagus, causing internal bleeding. A bone fragment can even puncture the intestinal tract or stomach. But in my experience, these scenarios happen less frequently than a ferret choking on commercial food. Plus, the middle piece of a bone is the part that would most likely cause damage, and most ferrets eat off the ends of the bones only, leaving the middles for the garbage can.

If you're thinking of including bones in your ferret's diet, try these suggestions:

- Start off with something you know is too big to swallow and too hard to splinter, like a cooked ham bone or soup bone. The more marrow included, the better. You can see for yourself that this type of bone is too hard to bite in pieces and too big to be swallowed. Your fuzzy still gets the benefit of the marrow and a bonus toy for later.

- Some people feed their ferrets raw bones, but I suggest briefly boiling the bones first. Don't bake or microwave the bones, because you'll dry them out and make them splinter. Besides softening the bone a little, boiling eliminates any bacteria.

- Try feeding only the softer ends of long bones or backbones. People often offer boiled chicken or turkey bones.

Bob's Bone Broth

Check out this recipe if you want to get the good stuff out of the bone and incorporate it into your ferret's diet (for more recipes, see Chapter 25):

1. Place chicken bones on a cutting board. Cover with plastic wrap and then cover with a towel. Using a mallet, smash the bones into small pieces.

2. Remove the towel and plastic and scrape the bone mash into a cooking pot.

3. Add enough water to boil and simmer for about an hour.

4. Strain the bone fragments and throw them away.

5. You can now use the broth as a soup, to mix with dry food, or as a base for boiling pieces of chicken.

If you're worried about contamination, boil the bones. If you're worried about pokey parts, smash them down. You don't have to eliminate bones from a ferret's diet simply because of worry.

Choosing commercial raw or freeze-dried raw diets

Several pet food companies have developed commercially prepared raw or freeze-dried raw diets for ferrets or felines. These types of diets can be a great substitute for making the natural raw diet yourself. They're a little more expensive, but they're certainly more convenient and are likely to be more nutritionally complete than homemade natural diets.

The pros of this type of natural diet include the following:

✔ Some formulas are closer to the ferret's evolutionary diet, in terms of composition, than commercial canned food or kibble.

✔ The diet is meat- and fat-based and is low on carbs.

✔ Many of the nutrients are retained because this diet is unprocessed.

✔ The diet may lessen the signs of and even prevent some GI diseases.

✔ The diet is easy to feed, because the food usually comes in little medallions or freeze-dried chunks, which can be fed dry or reconstituted with water.

✔ A wide variety of meat proteins are available; and the tastes are varied, making it more mentally stimulating.

✔ Your ferret will have smaller and less frequent poops, because she'll digest more of the food.

✔ You'll need to feed your ferret less frequently because of the natural nature of the diet.

The commercial raw or freeze-dried raw diet can be fed alone, but would also make an excellent addition to a kibble diet, or you can alternate this type of diet with kibble.

The diet, however, does have its cons, which include the following:

✔ Composition can vary greatly from diet to diet.

✔ The diet is hygienically questionable for you; you must use excellent hygiene practices if you apply the diet.

✔ You risk the transmission of parasites or bacteria to ferrets through the feeding of raw meat.

✔ It may or may not be nutritionally balanced.

E. coli and salmonella

Both *E. coli* and *salmonella* are opportunistic little buggers that can live in the ferret's intestines without causing upset. Clinical signs range from mild gastroenteritis to more disconcerting signs such as tarry/bloody stools, anorexia, pale mucous membranes, severe dehydration, and even death. At minimum, treatment includes the appropriate antibiotics and fluid therapy. But the questions still left unanswered are how often are ferrets truly infected with debilitating E. coli or salmonella infections?

Let me first say people will always perceive some sort of risk when feeding food, especially raw. However, perceived risk is what you **think** the risk is **regardless** of what the **actual** risk is. Because of perceived risk, raw foods are under continuous scrutiny, which is rarely given to commercial foods.

Your immune system supplies the soldiers that guard the body against microbial intruders, such as the dreaded salmonella and E. coli. It's an adaptive system, so if you've never encountered an organism, you can get really sick and even die if suddenly exposed.

The same process is true when it comes to salmonella and E. coli. As strict carnivores, polecats come into contact with both organisms on a frequent basis. As a result, they have a natural immunity that helps protect them. This immunity could be genetic or acquired or a combination of both. However, some studies show that the immune system has to be "taught" to recognize the good from the bad. That's the basis of inoculations; you use a weakened, dead, or harmless variant to teach the immune system how to fight the living and dangerous invader.

There is no doubt that commercial raw foods are potentially contaminated with dozens of species of bacteria, any of which could result in disease or infection to the handler or consumer.

This danger is not limited to raw meats, poultry, or eggs, but **all** raw foods, including raw vegetables and fruit. Salmonella and E. coli are the most commonly mentioned bacteria when discussing raw diets, but little empirical evidence exists to equate the perceived risk of infection to the actual risk. Arguments that the presence of salmonella in ferret feces proves it's a danger cannot be properly assessed without a baseline for comparison. A lot of emphasis is made of the risks of salmonella and E. coli, whatever they are, but little or no research has been done in ferrets that show —one way or another— that the presence of the bacteria constitutes an actual threat to the ferret or healthy individuals within their environment.

The solution to feeding is a common sense approach to the problem. If you want to feed a kibble diet, then empty the dish of uneaten food each day, wash the dish in hot soapy water, and let it sit in the sun (or under a UV lamp) for an hour. Just because kibble is dry, it doesn't mean it can't be contaminated with salmonella and E. coli.

Likewise, if you want to feed a raw diet, keep in mind that you cannot predict if any food will be contaminated or not. If you're still uncomfortable feeding raw meat, it can be *briefly* seared with a propane torch (or on a hot barbeque) to kill surface bacteria without seriously harming interior nutrients. Or, it can be immersed in food-grade hydrogen peroxide to kill surface bacteria (many internet stores carry the product). Perhaps the best way to kill as many bacteria as possible is to immerse the food in boiling water for a minute or so; again, to kill surface bacteria. Both searing and boiling will cook the contaminated surfaces, killing the bacteria, but allow the relatively sterile interiors to remain mostly uncooked, leaving important nutrients intact.

This diet isn't recommended for use in homes with people who are immuno-compromised. You *can* cook this food by braising, microwaving, or steaming to make it safe. Chances are, you'll change the nutrient composition to some degree with cooking, but it isn't known to what degree.

The evolutionary diet: Feeding your pet small animals or insects

The *evolutionary diet* is simple. Essentially, you feed your ferret what she evolved eating. The polecat's diet is varied and includes, among other things, small mammals (rabbits, mature mice, weanling and older rats, and chicks), insects, amphibians, eggs, carrion invertebrates, and fish, with perhaps a tiny amount of fresh fruit to "season" the diet (fruit is only seasonally available). The evolutionary diet is about offering freedom of choice and variety, and promoting the consumption of many different natural foods. Mimicking the evolutionary diet in captivity can be quite a challenge, though. Makers or for-mulators of BARF (bones and raw food/biologically appropriate raw food) and raw/freeze-dried raw diets claim to do it. But nothing can beat the real thing.

Because the ferret can consume an evolutionary diet, grow, survive, and suc-cessfully reproduce, the diet actually meets AAFCO (Association of American Feed Control Officials) requirements, the same as commercial kibble. (An important implication of the AAFCO requirements is that all modern diets attempt to match the evolutionary diet, making it the standard.) Although the evolutionary diet hasn't been studied in detail, its obvious success implies that it meets all the polecat's nutritional requirements, known or unknown. Tables 8-1 and 8-2 cover the nutritional content in many common types of vertebrate prey and invertebrate prey.

Table 8-1	Nutritional Composition of Vertebrate Prey		
Mammal	*Dry Matter (DM) %*	*Crude Protein (CP) %*	*Crude Fat (CF) %*
Neonatal mouse	19.1	64.2	17.0
Juvenile mouse	18.2	44.2	30.1
Adult mouse	32.7	55.8	23.6
Neonatal rat	20.8	57.9	23.7
Juvenile rat	30.0	56.1	27.5

Mammal	Dry Matter (DM) %	Crude Protein (CP) %	Crude Fat (CF) %
Adult rat	33.9	61.8	32.6
Neonatal rabbit	15.4	72.1	13.0
Adult rabbit*	26.2	65.2	15.8
Day-old chick	25.6	64.9	22.4
Green frog	22.5	71.2	10.2
Anolis lizard	29.4	67.4	N/A

*Dressed carcass

Meat matters

Many people argue that cooked meat (or eggs) is the ideal choice for diet. Others fight diligently to prove that raw is the best. Still others say, "If you must feed meat, feed it in the form of human baby food." And, of course, when discussing meat, there's always the issue of live or dead and the pros and cons of doing either. Well done or rare?

It's common knowledge that cooking meat kills off any harmful bacteria that may cause illness to the unfortunate diner. Some people suggest that you rinse raw meat in food-grade hydrogen peroxide to make it safe for pets. If you're comfortable with those answers, stick with them. However, I don't see little barbecue pits scattered throughout the forests, nor do I see dead coyotes, foxes, hawks, or other predators on the sides of the roads (unless they're car casualties). Carnivores eat raw meat. That's a fact of life.

If you're still unsure about raw meat, cut off the outside layer of the meat. The inside meat is generally sterile and safe. Make sure that the meat is fresh. I have fed live, fresh-killed, and thawed frozen meat to a number of animals over the years and have never had an incident of illness resulting from raw meat. Many Europeans continue to feed their ferrets mostly rabbit, and they're among the biggest, healthiest, and most muscular ferrets around.

Although clean raw meat (okay, cooked meat, too) is a wonderful food for ferrets, it can't be the sole food. Wild polecats eat the whole animal — bones, organs, and all. Domestic ferrets need all the good nutrients that come from the rest of the prey animal, not just the muscle meat. They also need some tooth resistance, such as tendons, to help clean their teeth. The same goes for fish as a food source. It's good, but it shouldn't be the only food source.

Also, freezing may kill off some bacteria but doesn't generally kill off everything. And even if meat is cooked, post-cooking handling can seriously contaminate the food before it's even poured into your ferret's bowl. No feeding regime is without risk.

Table 8-2	Nutritional Composition of Invertebrate Prey		
Insect	*Dry Matter (DM)%*	*Crude Protein (CP) %*	*Crude Fat (CF) %*
Crickets	30.8	20.5	6.8
Mealworms	38.1	18.7	13.4
Waxworms	41.5	14.1	24.9
Superworms	42.1	19.7	17.7
Earthworms	16.4	10.5	1.6
Cockroaches	38.7	20.9	11.0

Pros (and procedures) of the evolutionary diet

Pros of feeding your ferret the evolutionary diet (small whole prey) include the following:

- ✔ It's the most nutritionally complete diet available.
- ✔ The ferret retains all the nutrients.
- ✔ The diet is mentally and behaviorally stimulating.
- ✔ It may lessen the signs of and even prevent some GI diseases.
- ✔ Produces smaller and less-frequent stools because of its high digestibility.
- ✔ You don't need to feed your ferret as frequently.

This whole idea of feeding your ferret an evolutionary diet can be confusing in the beginning — especially when you're trying to figure out this business of prey. What is it, where do you get it, and what precautions do you take? Start small — give mice, feeder goldfish, chicks, mealworms, or crickets (for the daring) — and you may find that these food items work out just fine for your ferret. Or you may decide to upgrade to other items such as rats, small rabbits, small frogs, or small lizards. Whatever you decide or whatever your ferret likes, you can find prey animals at reptile supply stores or even most pet shops. Nowadays, you can even choose from hundreds of online sources to have your fresh, frozen prey and live insects shipped to your doorstep.

For people who want to feed a whole animal to a carnivore, the question is always, "Should a carnivore be fed a live or dead animal?" Mostly, this is a choice that addresses the owner's personal beliefs. However, it may be illegal to feed a live animal to another animal where you live.

Bob Church on free choice feeding

"The advantage of allowing the ferret free choice is that they will naturally select those foods that 'fill the nutritional gaps.' The hypothesis is that animals, if given free choice, will naturally select foods that meet their caloric and nutritional needs. Feeding this type of diet is simpler than it first appears. For example, I use two cafeteria trays, each with 8 small bowls, to feed my ferrets. One bowl may have crickets, another with large mealworms, another with chopped beef or pork, one with night crawlers, one with chopped up boiled egg, another with goldfish — you get the idea. About half of the bowls are filled with frozen mice. Once or twice a month, a SMALL amount of fresh finely minced fruit is offered. All feed animals were purchased after humane killing, or (in the case of the worms and insects) frozen to preserve nutrients and to eliminate escape. To lower the risk of binge eating of extremely favored items, they are given by hand. To reduce risk of food caching, the dishes are removed with all remaining food after about an hour. Leftover foods such as insects or frozen animals can be refrigerated and reused. With experience, it is an easy task to judge how much or little food is appropriate to offer. Every few days, all leftover or thawed food is dumped into a blender and turned into a 'prey shake' that can be frozen for future use as a food supplement, treat, or food base for sick ferrets. I have very little waste, no spoilage of cached foods, and no sick ferrets."

My decision to feed pre-killed versus live rests on what type of carnivore I'm feeding and the experience of the predator. I feed my ferrets fresh-killed prey. Polecats, ferrets included, are by nature efficient and quick predators that normally kill with a lightning-fast bite to the back of the neck. But most domesticated ferrets don't recognize small animals as food. Some are quick to kill; others play with the food until it happens to die. And some ferrets could care less and lazily watch a potential snack waltz on by. For a ferret eating a more natural diet, I see no reason to offer live food unless she's a quick predator. That's my opinion. I don't like to see the prey animal suffer anymore than it has to.

The majority of animal supply stores will give you a choice of purchasing most prey items live, frozen, or fresh-killed. It's a personal choice; go with whatever you're most comfortable with and what your skills are. However, I caution you to never feed a live rat to your ferret for the same reason I never feed live rats to my snakes: A rat can inflict serious wounds during a scuffle with even an excellent predator. Also, you should feed chicks sparingly. Although they're good for treats here and there, chicks are very low in calcium.

Research the source of your prey foods! If the prey isn't healthy, it isn't healthy for your ferret. Does the supply store feed the prey quality foods? Are the animals free of parasites, bacteria, and nutritional diseases? How does the company kill the prey before shipping? How does it pack the prey for shipping? Does it offer guarantees? How long has it been in business?

An aggressive myth

Many people believe that feeding live animals (and some even believe raw meat) makes your ferret more aggressive. This simply isn't true. Domestic doesn't mean unnatural. It only means tame, made fit for domestic life, adapted or bred to live with and be of use to man. Humans are domestic. Does that mean we can't cater to our primal urges once in a while?

Take a good look at the average housecat. Some of these sweet, purring kitties can be killing machines, responsible for millions of wildlife deaths each year. While they can be quick killers, they more often than not kill slowly, often playing and toying with the victim before death. And yet, our housecats remain dear to our hearts, sharing our pillows at night and claiming us as their possessions in the morning by rubbing up against our legs. Why would a ferret be any different?

Many "reports" of aggression are usually easily explained with a bit of investigation. Many of the reports resulted from ratters or rabbiters who starved their ferrets to increase their hunter instincts. Many of these animals would have aggressively defended their meals, giving the illusion the meat made them aggressive. Also, meat was a favored food in those days of the milk and bread diet, making it something to defend. Ferrets were supposed to chase rabbits from the burrow, and when a rabbit was caught by a ferret, it was forcibly removed, increasing aggression.

All ferrets have a natural predatory instinct. It shows in the way they play with their toys as well as in how they interact with each other. Feeding your ferret what she would naturally eat in the wild won't unleash some fantasy wild beast inside. It only gives her an opportunity to experience and benefit from something more natural than what she's used to. In the end, she'll be the same lovable character, except maybe a little happier, healthier, and more energetic.

Cons of the evolutionary diet

The following list presents some cons of feeding the evolutionary diet (small whole prey):

- ✔ The practice is distasteful to some ferret owners.

- ✔ The diet can be expensive (although you can be economical and raise your own mice or rats for food).

- ✔ Some sources of animals aren't nutritional — they aren't free of parasites, bacterial infections, and nutritional disease. This is becoming less of a problem, however, because of active reptile-owning enthusiasts needing many of the same foods.

With so many feed-supply options available to you, you shouldn't offer your ferret an animal that's come from the wild. In fact, you may do way more harm than good. Many wild animals harbor parasites and bacteria that can be passed on to your ferret. Another thing to consider is poison/pesticides. Speaking from personal experience, I know of someone who lost a ferret when a wild mouse got into the cage. The ferret ate the mouse; unfortunately, the mouse had just eaten a load of poison that had been left out in the garage. Wild animals can pick up pesticides on the grass, bushes, trees, and even on driveways. Always get your prey from a reputable company or raise it yourself.

As distasteful as this diet may be for some ferret owners, it's important that you fully educate yourself on every diet that's available to your ferret. Diet is such an important part of your ferret's well-being. I'd be negligent to leave out this important choice.

Exploring the alternative way of feeding

Perhaps the previous information in this section has sold you on a raw or evolutionary diet, but you're wondering how exactly to feed it to your ferret. After all, raw or live food may be a little messier than kibble. You'll certainly have to stay on top of the hygiene aspect of the feeding. And diligence will need to be at the top of your priority list. How you feed, though, depends on your ferret's manners and preferences and your setup.

Some ferrets have nice manners and eat over their bowls; I don't know any of them, though. Many are hoarders who cache their food for snacks at a later date. And some may pick up their food and drop it a foot or two away from their bowls and eat it there. It's likely that most ferrets will behave differently each time they eat — especially if their diets consist of something they particularly like. Keep these thoughts in mind when developing a feeding routine for your ferret.

The following sections detail how you can convert your ferret to the natural diet and how you can cater your feedings to ferrets that roam free and ferrets that dwell in a cage.

The most important part of feeding your ferret a natural diet full of raw foods is hygiene. Your health (and your family's) is your top priority:

- ✔ Wash your hands frequently, as well as your countertop and any utensils you use.
- ✔ Store the food according to manufacturer's instructions when applicable. Wash food bowls regularly and thoroughly.
- ✔ Mop the floors where a ferret eats.
- ✔ Wash ferret bedding and wipe down cage surfaces with a mild bleach solution more frequently (see Chapter 9 for more).

Converting your ferret to the natural world

Ferrets, like their polecat cousins, are olfactory hunters, meaning that they follow their noses to the dinner table. Whatever a ferret has consistently eaten during the first six months of her life, she'll see as the preferred food in the future — called *olfactory imprinting*.

Getting a ferret to betray her nose after chowing on kibble for so long can be challenging. However, it's well worth the effort if you're a true believer in the natural diet and want to broaden your ferret's culinary horizons. Of course, the conversion should occur when your fuzzy is as young as possible, but you *can* teach old ferrets new tricks. However, not all ferrets can be brought around — particularly the older kids. Make sure that you give it your all before giving up, though. Here are a couple steps you can take to start the process:

1. **If you haven't already been feeding canned food, start introducing high-quality canned cat or kitten food to your ferret.** You can add the food in a separate bowl, but mixing it with dry food will force the ferret to taste it. Occasionally, you can switch to a high-quality canned dog food just for variety. The poopy smell gets worse with canned food, but the end result (oh crap, a pun) causes less-stinky poops.

2. **Invest in baby food.** Yep, you read that right. You can use meat baby food, from infant to toddler, as an enticement for your ferret to try a new food. The chicken variety works well. Rub some of it on the ferret's nose or front teeth if she won't readily accept it. She'll surely lick it off.

Don't expect a change overnight. Persistence and experimentation are the keys to converting your ferret to a more natural diet. All ferrets are different. Some take several days to convert. Others take a week or so. After you get your ferret used to the idea of eating different food, though, you can step up your efforts and include more natural/evolutionary foods. Here are some tips to follow:

✔ **Put aside some freezer space for frozen mice.** Some people feed pre-killed chicks rather than mice. You usually can purchase pre-killed mice or chicks at a pet store — particularly one that sells reptiles. Store the animals in the freezer and thaw them as needed. After your ferret learns that a mouse or chick is food, the occasional frozen treat is okay. During winter, carnivores eat frozen meat all the time. When your ferret discovers that the mouse or chick is tasty, she'll be hooked.

✔ **Experiment with poultry.** You can chop up small pieces of chicken, turkey, or other poultry (bones and all) and allow your ferret to get a taste. You can use either cooked or raw poultry, depending on your comfort level. If you don't want to make a special ferret meal, save a couple cut-up pieces after your next poultry dinner.

✔ **Become an organ donor.** Chicken, pork, and beef livers, as well as chicken and beef hearts, are great treats and are full of nutrition. Slice them up and offer the cuts to your fuzzy. Liver, by itself, is a great occasional meal.

✔ **Be creative with hamburger.** Perhaps you've had those days when you mix anything you can find in the cupboards or freezer with hamburger. My mother called it junk, but we ate it, and it actually tasted good most of the time. Cook up some beef and add ground bones or kibble. Form it in shapes like the kibble if you must. Just be creative.

✔ **Use natural juices.** Many people forget how tasty the juices from cooked meats can be. I always use the juices as gravy over dry food. Natural juices can be a great introduction to a new taste, either in a separate bowl or over a small amount of kibble.

✔ **Throw in some fishies.** Canned tuna in spring water is yummy to many ferrets. Try it. You also can try feeding other prepared fish, such as trout or salmon, cooked shellfish, shrimp, and crawdads. Feeder fish are yummy, too.

✔ **Don't forget the bugs.** Even my dogs and cats eat bugs! Earthworms, crickets, cockroaches, and mealworms are tasty treats for your ferret. Your fuzzy, when she gets used to the idea, will eat only the squishy, juicy parts and leave the rest for you!

You may find that one of your ferrets loves liver, while another prefers hamburger. Remember, the natural diet is about freedom of choice! Conversion may take a little patience on your part. And don't forget that these natural foods spoil quickly. Don't let any linger around your ferret's cage or eating area for too long. If the food is still there in 12 hours, get rid of it! If you have to, try something different later.

Ferret expert Bob Church's advice for natural diet conversion is to offer the food to a ferret three times a day for three days. Wait a week and again offer the food three times a day for three days. If the ferret still turns up its nose at the food, offer it as an occasional enrichment, pulling it off the dietary shelf (for more on enrichment, see Chapter 10). This advice is for animals that readily accept strange foods. You can use it to determine personal preference. And keep notes so you don't have to repeat the exercise at a later date.

When your ferret finally switches to a raw food or evolutionary diet, she'll be likely to try just about anything, which is important because you don't want to stick to just one food item in this diet. She still needs a combination of soft and hard foods. Besides, some of the foods I mention in this chapter aren't complete diets. The combination of the foods is what makes them so good for your fuzzy. So don't rule out kibble for good. The biggest piece of bad news about natural diets? Your friends will often stare into your refrigerator in terror!

Free-roaming ferrets

As a feeder of a raw, freeze-dried raw, or an evolutionary diet, it's up to you to reexamine and adjust your feeding habits and routines so that caching or other behaviors associated with free-roaming ferrets don't become hygiene problems in your home. Imagine the olfactory shock that will hit you three to four days after your beloved ferret has cached some raw meat or a mouse in a secret hidey-hole. And the biggest problem is that the hidey-hole remains top secret, and it's your job to sniff it out.

For beginners in the natural dieting world, I don't generally recommend feeding your ferret openly where she free roams, although many people do it with great success. The reason is simple: Some people aren't as hygiene-conscientious as they need to be when dealing with raw meat or prey animals. Although you may be fully aware of each and every hidey-hole your ferret has, meaning that you can retrieve uneaten foods at the end of the feeding (or day), you can't see the invisible trail left while the ferret was dragging the food there. Too many surfaces can become contaminated without you even knowing it.

I suggest you set up a "feeding playpen" — which is a small contained area that the ferret can't escape from — in a tiled room and feed your ferret in it. Let her have her fill for a couple hours or however long it takes. Some ferrets eat quickly. Some may take a while before showing interest in their meat or mice. That's the downside of putting a time limit on feeding. You want to give your ferret adequate time to eat her share, so get to know your ferret's eating habits.

The downside to the feeding playpen method is that you remove some of the enrichment aspects of the feeding. I like to encourage my ferrets to forage; I often hide their food, whether it's meat or mice or kibble, and they must sniff it out (for more on enrichment, see Chapter 10). If you get comfortable with your ferret's eating habits and your ability to handle raw meats and prey animals hygienically, you can begin to experiment with different feeding routines. You may find that feeding in an open area works better for you and your ferret. There's more than one way for this to work.

Caged ferrets

Yes, caged ferrets have to eat, too, and you have to be just as diligent when it comes to hygiene. A feeding playpen, which I describe in the previous section, works just as well for caged ferrets. Small rooms, such as bathrooms, work perfectly for feeding, also. Or you can simply feed the meat or prey animals in the upper level of your ferret's cage (see Chapter 5 for more on cage construction). Your ferret likely will pull the mice and meat down into her bedding. You simply shake out the bedding at the end of the feeding and put in fresh bedding. Some people just change the bedding on a daily basis. I find this to be an acceptable practice as long as you also wipe down and clean the cage on a regular basis to prevent an accumulation of harmful bacteria.

Your ferret's cage is a haven for bacteria, no matter what you do. She'll poop in her litter box and possibly outside of it, and then walk in it and trudge through the cage and bedding. Bacteria multiply on her kibble, which she'll drop into her bedding. She licks her behind and then licks her water bottle. Your ferret doesn't live a sanitary life, nor should she. The good news? Absence of immune-system-challenging microorganisms can actually be harmful to your ferret. Living in a sterile or super-clean environment may lead to immune problems later down the road. This is called the *hygiene hypothesis.* Google it!

Supplementing Your Fuzzy's Diet

A *supplement* is something you add to your ferret's diet to make up for what's lacking in her day to day feedings. If your healthy ferret is on a truly balanced and suitable diet, she doesn't really need supplements. Although supplements were a necessary part of a ferret's diet years ago, today most diets available to your ferret are better formulated, thus more balanced for a fuzzy. Often, giving supplements is more a matter of choice because a ferret enjoys the taste and sees them as treats.

The most common supplement is a fatty-acid oil supplement, which ferrets find pleasant. The right fatty-acid supplement can be just what the doctor ordered or your worst nightmare. This section explains what you need to know about omega-3 and omega-6 fatty acids, which are the most commonly found fatty acids in pet-store supplements. Most supplements list the ingredients as I've listed them.

Fatty acids have to be incorporated into the cell membranes, so it may take several weeks for their effects to show. In fact, you may not see changes for two to three months. If possible, experts recommend that you split the daily dose, giving a half dose each in two 12-hour increments. Your ferret will still get a full daily dose, just not at once.

Omega-3 fatty acids

Omega-3 fatty acids, in general, have some great properties. They may slow the spread of cancer, reduce inflammation, lower blood pressure, and prevent ventricular arrhythmias. In addition to alpha-linoleic acid (ALA), the ingredients are as follows:

- Eicosapentaenoic acid (EPA): Reduces inflammation in atopy, arthritis, autoimmune disease, seborrhea, and decreases cholesterol
- Docosahhexoenoic acid (DHA): Reduces inflammation in atopy

Omega-6 fatty acids

Most quality pet foods contain adequate amounts of omega-6 fatty acids. Rich sources of this fatty acid include cold-water fish oils and the seeds of some plants such as sunflowers, borages, pumpkins, soybean, and flax. In addition to dihomo-gamma-linolenic acid (DGLA), the following list presents the ingredients in the supplement and the benefits (or detriments) they bring:

- ✔ Linoleic acid (LA): Helps improve dry skin and a dull hair coat
- ✔ Gamma linolenic acid (GLA): Reduces inflammation in atopy and auto-immune disease
- ✔ Arachidonic acid (AA): Can *increase* inflammation

Savoring Treat Time!

Treats can be a vital part of your relationship with your ferret, as long as they're the right types and are given in moderation. Some fuzzies come to expect a favorite treat at a certain time of day or after performing a neat trick. They all beg for them no matter what. Of course, all ferrets deserve treats. But, before starting your ferret on treats, discuss doing so with your veterinarian. Some traditional treats can aggravate medical conditions such as insulinoma or chronic bowel disease. My goal is to get you away from traditional bad treats and onto healthy ones! Better safe than sorry. The following sections show you the way.

Next time you're shopping for your ferret's treats in the pet store, take a look at the ingredients. Do you see any meat in the lists? Many treats don't even contain meat, or if they do, the meat often is way down on the lists. What you find high on the list more often than not is sugar and even more sugar — maybe even some plant materials that aren't good for ferrets. Avoid these and stick to the meat-based treats.

Giving the good stuff

Here are some treats that you can offer your ferret in moderation (remember to feed these in very small pieces and very small amounts; even the good stuff can be harmful if overfed):

- ✔ **Eggs:** Hard-boiled, poached, raw, or scrambled. Egg yolks (cooked or raw) are very nutritious. Eggs are perfect protein treats. However, some people won't risk feeding raw eggs due to the possibility of germs or harmful bacteria. It's a personal choice.

✔ **Meat:** Cooked or raw meats are great treats. Special favorites are chicken livers and hearts. Beef and turkey pieces are good, also. If you have a dehydrator, you can make your own unseasoned turkey, salmon, beef, or chicken jerky to give as treats. You should avoid processed meats such as lunchmeat or salami, because they're full of salt and additives.

A great treat for a half-dozen ferrets is to open a large fish-oil capsule, pour the oil into a dish, cut up some raw chicken (no more than 1-square-inch pieces), and place the pieces in the oil. Heat the mix in the microwave until the chicken just starts to turn white. This may destroy some of the nutrients, but it makes a great occasional treat.

✔ **Insects:** Earthworms, crickets, cockroaches, and mealworms are tasty treats. Just about anything you'd feed reptiles or amphibians will make a great treat for a ferret.

✔ **Small prey animals:** Mice, chicks, frogs, lizards, and rats all are healthy treats or main diet choices for your ferret (see the section "The evolutionary diet: Feeding your pet small animals/insects").

✔ **Chicken baby food:** A single lick or two from a spoon or off your finger is a nice way to say "I love you" to your ferret, or "job well-done!" Most ferrets love the taste of the baby food. Remember, though, not to give too much as to spoil her regular meal.

✔ **Nonacidic, soft fruits:** Melon, banana, berries, and papaya are good ones. Okay, so this isn't at the top of the list, but I had to sneak one in for the sweet-tooths in the bunch. Give no more than one to two tiny pieces (½ teaspoon) of these fruits a couple times a week. Most fruits are high-sugar treats, so watch the insulinoma patients!

✔ **High-quality kibble:** Most ferrets view a piece of their regular kibble as a treat if you feed the kibble from your hand. If this works for your ferret, she not only gets a treat, but also isn't straying too far from her diet! This feeding method also is a good way to introduce a new food item.

I've found that ferrets see almost *any* type of cooking oil as a treat. Mine especially enjoy fish-oil treats, but they never turn down a bit of olive oil on the end of my finger. You can cut open a fish-oil capsule, which contains enough oil to "treat" a handful of ferrets. Like all supplements, you should do this infrequently. My rule is, if your ferret wants a lot, she shouldn't get it very often.

Avoiding the not-so-good stuff

There is such a thing as loving your ferret to death. Many dog and cat owners do so unknowingly with large amounts of treats and table scraps. Although some treats will be fine for your ferret if given in moderation, you should avoid some not-so-healthy treats altogether, no matter how much your ferret begs. When your ferret fills herself with junk, she decreases the amount of room she has for good food. The following list presents the not-so-good treats you should toss out of your ferret's diet:

- ✔ **Alcohol and other high-sugar drinks/foods:** Too much sugar is a bad thing for a ferret. And a drunk ferret can quickly become a dead ferret. (Besides, you must be 21 to legally drink.)

- ✔ **Coffee and tea products:** No caffeine, please. Like ferrets don't speed around enough.

- ✔ **Dried fruits, including raisins:** Sorry guys and gals! These and other high-sugar fruit treats are on the banned list!

- ✔ *Most* **commercial ferret treats:** Most are low in or absent of meat content but high in sugar. Check the labels carefully.

- ✔ **High-calorie/high-sugar supplements:** The major ingredient of Nutri-Cal (and similar products), for instance, is molasses, which if given to an insulinomic ferret when she isn't in the middle of a low-sugar incident can be unhealthy.

- ✔ **Cereals:** A good cereal treat must be low-salt and low-sugar, which most aren't. Two good ones are Cheerios and Kix. Other good ones are out there, too. No more than one to two pieces a day.

- ✔ **Veggies:** Vegetables may get lodged in the intestinal tract. Veggies also have little nutritional value for ferrets, and they come out the other end basically undigested if they make it that far.

- ✔ **Dairy products:** Many experts argue about lactose intolerance in ferrets. Some vets say it's prevalent, and others say it isn't. A single lick of milk probably won't harm most healthy ferrets. In fact, owners frequently use heavy cream (the real stuff) as a high-fat supplement to add weight on and boost energy in a debilitated ferret. And cheese contains very little lactose, so very small amounts are probably safe. Use your best judgment. If what you feed comes out the other end in smelly liquid form, your ferret probably is sensitive to lactose, but a little diarrhea from a small amount of dairy product won't harm her.

- ✔ **Seeds and nuts:** These things are indigestible and hard to pass, not to mention painful. They can cause blockages.

- ✔ **Chocolate:** Contains theobromide, which, in high doses, can be fatal in some pets (such as dogs). No one knows for sure if chocolate is as dangerous to ferrets. Milk chocolate is generally much safer. The big problem isn't the trace amounts of theobromide in the milk chocolate, it's the tons of sugar. Don't panic if your fuzzy accidentally happens on a tiny piece of chocolate, but don't use chocolate as a treat.

- ✔ **Salty foods:** Save the beer nuts for the bar. A small taste here or there, though, won't kill a ferret.

- ✔ **Fingers:** Just seeing if you're paying attention!

Chapter 9

Cleaning Time: Not All Ferret Fun and Games

In This Chapter

▶ Addressing the mess in fuzzy's cage

▶ Washing your furball

▶ Checking the ears and nails

▶ Performing the dental checkup

▶ Brushing your ferret's coat

*W*ouldn't you like to have a butler deliver your clean, happy ferret to you on the couch — and then get to work cleaning his cage and litter box — so you can just concentrate on the romping, playing, and cuddling parts? Okay, back to reality; most people don't have butlers, so they must face the routine chores of keeping ferrets. I'm talking about odor control, grooming, and general sanitation stuff here.

If you're anything like I am, you'll find it very satisfying to watch your gorgeous, clean, healthy ferret dash about with enthusiasm and then collapse in his unsoiled condo for a long nap. Besides giving you an opportunity to bond and discover possible health problems, cleaning and grooming are necessary for both your and your ferret's continued happiness and health.

In this chapter, I discuss the ins and outs of cleaning your fuzzy's cage, bedding, and dishes. I provide much-needed information on cleaning your fuzzy, too. Oh, cheer up. Into every life a little poop must fall!

Cleaning House for a Cozy Cage

When I say you need to regularly clean your fuzzy's house, I mean the entire house. What good is a sparkling cage if his bedding still has poop stuck in it or his toys are crusty from heaven knows what? Sometimes, people forget to do the whole overhaul. I admit it, I'm guilty at times. Just remember that you and your fuzzy will be happiest when the cleaning tornado hits the entire ferret condo. The following sections take you through the cleaning process for the cage, dishes, toys, bed, and toilet.

Doing your fuzzy's dishes

When I set out to clean my ferret's cage, I tackle food dishes and water bottles first, because I think one of the most important aspects of good husbandry is providing clean, fresh food and water at all times. Because pooping and peeing are frequent activities with ferrets, you're likely to find an occasional mess in the food dish or poop smeared on the side of it. If you notice this, or an unusually dirty bowl, take the dish out immediately and clean it thoroughly. If you ignore it, the poop/dirt won't go away. Trust me, I've tried. Otherwise, regular cleanings with soap and warm water every couple days usually are sufficient. You should have extra food dishes and water bottles on hand to swap with the dirty dishes that you'll be cleaning.

Maintenance on the dishes and bottles is simple. Soap and water should be adequate when coupled with a gentle scrubbing (with a bottlebrush, for instance). You also can use a mixture of vinegar and water or baking soda and water. The key to good husbandry is to scrub thoroughly to remove any particle or algae buildup. And don't neglect the tube and stainless steel balls on the water bottle. Keeping these things free of mineral deposits helps eliminate any leakage. Always remember to completely rinse before refilling.

A more effective cleaning solution is a mixture of warm water and a touch of bleach. At least once a week, clean all the dishes with the bleach and water solution (1:30). Unless you have bionic eyes, you can't see all the bacteria condos going up on your ferret's dishes. Come to terms with the fact that bacteria is there and wash frequently. Your ferret will thank you.

Properly rinsing dishes is just as important as cleaning the dishes. Although a trace amount of soap won't kill your ferret, it tastes pretty bad and can cause diarrhea. In addition, the residue attracts more dirt and bacteria. Bleach, on the other hand, can cause your ferret to become very ill. Take care when washing the dishes, and be sure to rinse well. As a safeguard, I wash with soap and water after I use bleach. After all, can anyone be too careful when dealing with their precious furballs?

Anything from a ferret cage may be contaminated with poop. Don't use the kitchen or kitchen sink when cleaning if at all possible because you can contaminate areas where you prepare food. Contamination can come with enteric bacteria like E. coli and salmonella from any pet contaminated items that you clean in a kitchen. Instead, use a bathroom sink, bathtub or laundry-room sink to do your cleaning. If the kitchen area is your only option, be sure to clean out the sink with a disinfectant and thoroughly clean any counter surfaces with disinfectant, such as Lysol or your bleach solution.

Stripping his bed

Your ferret's bedding can get pretty raunchy after a while. Because ferrets spend so much time running in and out of the litter box, chances are good that traces of poop and urine will make their way to your fuzzy's towels or other bedding. Particles of litter and food crumbs get mixed in there as well. Your fuzzy spends a lot of time snuggling and sleeping in his bedding, so thoroughly washing his bedding at least once a week is important.

Doing ferret laundry is no different from doing human laundry. I use laundry soap and hot water. Sometimes, I add a half-cup of bleach to the load. If you like this suggestion, make sure that the finished laundry doesn't have a strong bleach odor. If it does, another regular wash should fix the problem.

Before you toss in a load, though, consider the health of your washing machine. I always take bedding outside and thoroughly shake it out before throwing it in the washer. That way, I discard most of the loose litter and debris before washing the bedding. Look for little poopies that may be stuck to the bedding and pick them off. You don't want to throw debris into your washing machine. Trust me, there's nothing like wearing a "clean" shirt with a poop stain on it! Worse yet is having someone point it out to you.

Scrubbing (or scooping) the toilet

You should scoop litter boxes as often as you can, refilling them with litter as needed. Obviously, if you have many ferrets, it doesn't take long for the poop to start piling up. You'll notice the insides of the litter box getting pretty dirty after a short while, because most ferrets poop in the corners or at an edge. Some fuzzies hang their butts over the side, and the poop lands on the litter box edge.

Cleaning the litter box regularly helps reduce the number of accidents that happen outside the box, because most ferrets hate to get their feet dirty — unless they're playing outside in the dirt and sand.

You'll soon find out that cleaning the litter box can be a nasty undertaking. Use common sense when cleaning the waste. I take out all litter boxes and empty them completely into the garbage at least once a week. Use a rag or dish sponge (not the one from your kitchen) to scrub the bottom and sides of the litter box. Usually, soap and water are sufficient. At least twice a month, I use bleach water to clean the box. Don't forget to clean the C-clamps that hold the litter box to the cage (see Chapter 5), because they can get quite nasty, too.

Tearing down the house

Cleaning the cage can be the most time-consuming and tedious chore. You should clean the cage at least once every couple weeks. I suggest that if the weather is nice, you drag the entire cage outside and hose that sucker down with high-pressure water. The rest of the time, you need to get on your hands and knees and reach into the cage to get it clean. (For more on a ferret's cage, head to Chapter 5.) Here are the steps I take:

1. **Pull out any catch pans in the cage so you can change the newspaper or catch litter.**

2. **Sweep up the displaced litter and food particles from the flooring.**

    A little hand-held vacuum is perfect for this task.

3. **Spray the flooring with a pet-friendly cleaner and wipe it thoroughly, remembering to leave no residue behind.**

    You can find ferret-friendly cleaners in most pet stores. You're finished with the easy part!

4. **This step is the hard part: getting any solidified poop off the corners of the wire shelves.**

    I use rubber gloves and pull off the waste. What doesn't come off with the initial tug I push off with a long, metal stick (such as a shish-ka-bob skewer). You can also use a scouring pad, although the pad can be too abrasive and wear down any paint on the wire. A tool that works well is a nylon scrub pad — the kind you may use with a Teflon pan. It has a nylon mesh over a sponge. It doesn't ruin paint and it does a good job, after the cage has been wetted down, of getting crusty stuff off.

5. **After you clear off most of the poop, use a wet rag and thoroughly clean all the areas of the cage.**

    If you have short arms like I do or a cage that's difficult to reach into, you may find that you can't reach one or two far corners that always seem to have a small bit of poop residue. That's when hosing can be most effective.

6. **Now you're ready to reassemble the cage.**

Getting the gunk off the toys

Don't neglect the fuzzy's toys when you're cleaning his house — a mistake often made by us humans. Assume they're dirty every time you strip the cage, even if they look clean. The toys get dragged about the ferret's litter box and buried in his dirty bedding. Check them daily, as well, for obvious signs of being pooped or peed on. The cleaning method you use depends on the type of toy in question. You can safely throw most cloth toys in the wash with the rest of his bedding.

As for plastic toys, I simply soak them in bleach water or plain, warm water until I can easily scrub off all the grime. The important part is to always remember to thoroughly rinse the toys and leave no residue.

If you happen upon a toy buried beneath a pile of poop or in another messy situation, it's okay to just pitch it and buy your ferret a new toy. Some things are just too gross to clean. Plus, fuzzbutts deserve new toys as often as possible!

Scrub a Dub Fuzz: Navigating Bathtime

You have plenty to think about before bathing a smelly little ferret — such as choosing the right shampoo and knowing when and where to bathe him. Plus, not all ferrets like baths, so knowing what to do and what not to do can ease the anxiety both of you may be feeling. The following sections explain all the factors you must consider, and then I take you through the actual process of bathing your fuzzy.

One bath too many?

It's hard to believe that bathing a ferret may defeat the purpose — namely, making the fuzzy smell fresh — but it can be true. Bathing is important, but equally important is not washing your fuzzy too frequently. Bathing strips the skin and fur of their natural oils. The skin must work overtime to reproduce these oils to replace what you washed down the drain, making the smell worse initially. Excessive bathing also can lead to dry, flaky skin and coarse fur.

You'll probably notice initially that your ferret has a stronger smell than before the bath. Don't worry. The smell improves within a day or two.

Unless your ferret gets into something really nasty, don't bathe him more than once a month. I suggest bathing only a few times a year. Look at it this way: It gives the scratches on your arms ample time to heal before you bathe the furball again!

Picking a shampoo

The shampoo you use on your ferret should be very gentle, like baby shampoo. Don't use strong shampoos and regular dish soaps; they can lead to dry, itchy skin and brittle fur. Some over-the-counter pet shampoos work well, as long as the shampoo is safe for cats. Your vet may carry some good shampoos that are great for sensitive skin. There are also many ferret shampoos available on the market now. Dog shampoos often contain harsh chemicals that are safe for dogs but very harmful to ferrets.

What's with my ferret's tail acne?

Ferrets are prone to blackheads just like humans, although a ferret's usually show up on his tail. Often, hair loss and a reddish-brown, waxy film come with blackheads, which are caused by dirt and oil clogging their fuzzy pores. Although blackheads aren't too attractive, they're nothing to worry about. If you want to treat them, simply wash your fuzzy's tail every couple days (the tail only) with a shampoo that contains benzoyl peroxide or salicylic acid (which you can get from your vet). Gently scrub the tail with a washcloth and let the suds sit for a minute or two before rinsing.

Choose only shampoos that are ferret-safe. If you're unsure about a shampoo, stick with stuff that's made for cats, kittens, or ferrets. A tearless human baby shampoo also works well on ferrets.

If your ferret is unfortunate enough to have fleas, be sure to read Chapter 14 before picking a shampoo and bathing him.

Choosing the crime scene

Where's the best place to bathe your ferret? The bathtub is an obvious choice. Many people look at bath time as a great opportunity for the water-loving fuzzy to play in the bathtub. This is okay, but limit the free swim to before the water gets all soapy and yucky. The downside to bathing in the tub is that it's tough on the human back and knees.

Many ferrets get so excited at the thought of bathing (yeah, right) that they poop in the water, so you may have to do some cleanup right away!

Sinks also are great places to clean a smelly ferret. The water flow from a sink faucet is a little gentler, and your back and knees will thank you. Avoid the kitchen sink for hygiene reasons; choose either a bathroom or laundry-room sink. Pull-out hoses are good for easy rinsing.

Some people even let their fuzzies into the shower with them. Unless your ferret is comfortable with this method and manageable in the shower — or you shower with your clothes on — I urge you to take extra precaution. A naked human is an extra-vulnerable human!

Doing the deed

You need to do some preparatory work before you can begin the deed of bathing. First, you need some good supplies: an appropriate shampoo, plenty of clean, dry towels for both you and your ferret, and hip boots and goggles (for you). The water you prepare should be a temperature that's comfortable for a human child.

A ferret's body temperature is quite a bit higher than a human's (100–104°F). What feels warm to you may be a pinch too chilly for a ferret, causing fuzzy goosebumps. Keep the water warm, but always test it before wetting your ferret; you don't want to scald the little bugger.

Fill the tub, sink, or basin with the water — just deep enough to submerge the ferret's body while allowing his feet to touch the bottom. This gives the anxious fuzzy a little extra security, because being unable to feel solid ground beneath your feet can be a terrifying experience.

Now you're ready to bathe. But what if your ferret isn't? The following sections give you some tips for bathing a water-shy ferret and take you through the normal bathing process.

Bathing a reluctant ferret

When it comes to bath time, not all ferrets enjoy water like their otter cousins. Some act like housecats when they get the slightest bit of water on their paws. Others, fortunately, take to it with Olympic-like style. Oftentimes, a ferret's first few encounters with water will determine his attitude. Whether your ferret's disdain for baths is due to his personality or to post-traumatic stress disorder, your job as a ferret human is to make the bathing process as pleasurable as possible.

If you can convince your fuzzy to look at bath time as a treat and reward, your battle may not be as big. Keep in mind that bathing the resistant ferret will not hurt him unless you're too forceful. You may need to lightly scruff him (see Chapter 7) and allow his feet to touch the bottom of the sink or tub to support his weight. Here are some more tips:

1. **Allow him to play in the sink or tub for a moment without any water to get used to the crime scene.**

2. **Turn on the faucet just enough for a thin stream to come out, and allow your ferret to explore the water. Offer him a treat, such as a lick of meat baby food from a spoon, as a reward for being a good boy.**

3. **While he's still licking his chops, pick him up and put him under the warm stream of water. Offer him another lick of treat.**

4. **Slowly increase the flow of water until he's all wet.**

5. **Put your ferret down and offer him one more lick of treat. Continue onto the next section.**

Water anxiety, of course, magically disappears *after* bath time. I frequently find myself spending time racing to keep my ferrets out of full coffee cups, toilets, and the dogs' water bowls. Bath anxiety may just be a control thing. Who knows for sure?

Wax on, wax off

I start a ferret's bath by lathering his back, because that's the easiest place to pour the shampoo. You can also pour the shampoo on your hands and rub your hands together before lathering him up. From there, I spread the shampoo evenly across all parts of his body, including the top of his head. Be careful not to get any soap in his eyes and ears. Some shampoos sting like heck, and your ferret will be sure to hold a grudge for next time. If you do get soap in your ferret's eyes, flush his face gently with water, using a cupped hand.

A ferret with water-soaked fur is slightly heavier than a dry ferret, so take extra care to support his full weight during and after the bath. It can be tricky to lather up the rascal while he's trying to crawl up your arm. You almost need an extra set of hands — two to hold the ferret, one to pour the shampoo, and one to lather. Giving a bath is an art that's quickly mastered by the multi-ferreted human, though.

Keeping soap out of your ferret's mouth can be more challenging. Plenty of fuzzies seem to enjoy the taste of soap. Although this quirk may appear disgusting to some, I must defend the ferret by saying I also enjoyed the taste of soap when I was a child. Unlike me, though, a ferret won't outgrow the taste. A little bit of soap won't hurt him, but keep him from sneaking in a lick anyway because there's nothing nutritious in soap and too much can make him ill.

After you have his body lathered up, you can get ready to rinse. Rinsing thoroughly is as important as lathering. Besides drying out his fur and making him itchy, soap residue left on the fur attracts dirt and gunk, and you'll soon have a dirty ferret again. For this reason, I suggest that you drain the water basin and use fresh, warm water to rinse. You can use a cup to pour the water over your ferret, or you can hold the ferret under the faucet — as long as the water pressure isn't too hard (see Figure 9-1). I enjoy using a hose that attaches to the faucet. Some sinks already have built-in hoses.

Don't drown the poor bugger while rinsing. In other words, don't pour water directly over his head. Use your hand to scoop water onto his head and to act as a washcloth. Remember to rinse the hard-to-reach areas, like the armpits and throat. A well-rinsed furball is a squeaky-clean furball!

Before you rinse, test the water temperature. Water that's too hot scalds, and water that's too cold causes your ferret to scramble for cover.

Figure 9-1:
Lather your ferret's entire body before rinsing, being careful not to get soap in his eyes.

Drying out

If you think a dog makes a fuss after a bath, wait until you get a load of the ferret. Drying time is a major production, no doubt about it. For fuzzy, this is happy, hopping, dooking time — a time for puffed tails and sideways sashays. The ferret's main goal is to get as dry and as filthy as he possibly can in the shortest amount of time. This means he'll try to rub up against anything and everything he can, from the couch cushions to the dust bunnies behind the sofa — and that disgusting little spot you can't reach behind the toilet.

You want to prevent your fuzzbutt from undoing all your hard work, which means you must take it upon yourself to dry him or at least allow him to dry himself in a clean, safe place. First things first: Towel-dry him as best you can, making sure that you're gentle yet thorough in removing as much water as possible. Some people like to use warm towels to dry their ferrets. You can warm a towel in the clothes dryer or microwave, but make sure you don't let the towel get too hot.

A great place for drying time is a bathtub filled with dry towels. You can also use a bathroom (with drained tub and toilet lid down) or the play room. Wherever you decide to let your ferret dry, though, keep in mind that he'll want to go to the bathroom soon after his bath. If he poops on your towel setup, he'll probably try to step in it, roll in it, and fall asleep in it. Drying time should be a supervised time. Besides, you wouldn't want to miss the drama for the world!

Some ferrets allow owners to use a hair dryer. (If you use a little round brush, you can give your fuzzy a little extra poof — just kidding.) For this method, use the warm, not hot, setting and keep the dryer moving so you don't aim warm air at the same part of the body for too long, which can cause burns (and split ends). Also, keep the dryer at least 12 inches from the body to prevent burns.

If after drying your ferret is still damp, you need to put him in a place where he can finish drying off. The best spot is a warm place with no drafts. And unless his cage is clean, filled with clean towels, and temporarily has the litter box removed, that spot is out of the question.

Caring for Those Little Ears

A ferret's normal earwax is light or reddish brown. It should have very little, if any, odor to it. If it stinks, something is wrong. Some furballs need their ears cleaned more frequently than others. Some can go for long periods of time. Health, age, and season may determine how much wax your fuzzy produces, so be sure to consult with your vet and follow your nose to any possible problems. What your eyes may miss, your nose may discover. I, for one, use playtime as an opportunity to do a quick ear inspection.

Ear cleaning should be done no more frequently than once every two to three months. Cleaning more frequently will cause more earwax production. In fact, earwax is protective and shouldn't be removed unless it's excessive or your ferret is about to enter a ferret show (see Chapter 10). Not cleaning the ears won't cause ear mites, deafness, or infections. In fact, ear disease in ferrets is pretty uncommon with the exception of mites, which are parasites transmitted directly from one ferret to another.

The only thing to clean when you clean a ferret's ears is the outer part — go nowhere near the ear canal (the hole). You're more likely to cause damage by poking around in the ear and shoving the normal wax into the ear canal. The following sections go through the preparation and the execution.

Ear cleaning can be tough for a beginner, so I suggest you have your vet demonstrate the procedure once or twice until you feel comfortable with it. No matter how comfortable you become, though, your ferret will hate having his ears cleaned. If done too often or incorrectly, it may be painful and uncomfortable. Those cotton swabs may look tiny for your ears, but they seem like large wads of cotton to a ferret. The key to preventing injury due to panic is gentleness. If you don't think you can handle the ear-cleaning process, your vet should be more than happy to perform the procedure for a minimal fee.

Gathering supplies

To clean your ferret's ears, you definitely need some cotton swabs. Here are a couple other things you need to acquire before you begin:

- ✔ **A good liquid ear cleanser:** You can purchase this product from most pet supply stores or from your vet. Make sure that the solution is safe for cats and kittens, because that means it will be safe for your fuzzy, too.

- ✔ **A small dish:** Especially if you have a bunch of ears to clean, a small dish may be helpful. Pour a little ear-cleaning solution into the dish. You can dip the clean end of a cotton swab into the liquid instead of fumbling around to squirt some on the tip. Some people moisten the tips of several swabs before they begin. If you do, be sure you place them on a clean surface to prevent them from getting dirty.

Executing the ear clean

Find a quiet and comfortable place to clean your ferret's ears, and follow the steps in this list:

1. **Dip a clean cotton swab in the ear-cleaning solution.**

2. **Scruff or firmly hold your ferret (see Chapter 7).**

   Make sure that your ferret's bottom is supported when you're scruffing him, especially if he's a big guy. If he moves too much, you can lessen the bottom support a little until he settles down. You also can try getting a better hold of the scruff from the beginning.

3. **Using your scruffing hand, hold the tip of his ear between your fingers. With your other hand, use the moistened end of the swab to wipe the inside of your ferret's ear.**

Some experienced ferret humans feel comfortable scruffing their ferrets with one hand and using the other to clean the ears. I prefer to have a helper hold my ferret. My arms eventually get sore from all the holding (especially in my multi-ferret household), and I like to have one hand free to hold my fuzzy's ear when I'm maneuvering the cotton swab in the other.

Always use the moistened end of the cotton swab first. It loosens and scoops up a lot of the ear gunk. Starting off with the dry tip can be too abrasive on the ferret's sensitive ears.

4. **Using a circular motion, make contact with the inner walls and crevices of the ear to remove all the hidden gunk.**

Never push the cotton swab into your ferret's ear canal. You may damage his ear canal or pack the earwax deep into it, making it difficult to get out and hard for the ferret to hear.

A good guide is to make sure that you can see the tip of the swab.

5. **Repeat with your collection of moistened swabs until the tips come out with little or no ick on them.**

Some ears require a repeat of the process with two or three freshly moistened swabs.

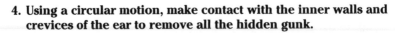

Never reuse a dirty swab, and never dip a used swab into the cleaning solution. Doing so contaminates the rest of the cleanser.

6. **Using the dry end of a swab, repeat the circular wiping process.**

Your ferret will probably squirm during the cleaning process. If you hit a particularly sensitive or itchy area, he may even jerk a leg back and forth like a dog does when you find a perfect scratching spot. However, this isn't a feel-good reaction. Be gentler and pull out the swab in case you're in too deep. Remember, you can have a lick of Linatone when you're finished as a treat for a job well done. Make sure that your ferret gets a taste, too!

Nailing Down the Manicure

The bottom line is this: Trimming his nails makes your ferret more comfortable. Fuzzies need their claws for many things, from walking and balance to climbing curtains and counter cruising. Overgrown nails can hurt the ferret, because long nails prevent his foot from resting flat on the ground. Trimming helps prevent the nails from splitting and getting caught on cage wires, carpeting, and bedding. Clipping your fuzzbutt's claws regularly also helps lessen the severity of human scratches and damage from digging.

You need to clip nails frequently because ferrets should never be declawed. A ferret's claws are non-retractable — like the claws on rabbits and dogs (cats have retractable claws) — so removing them would entail removing parts of his toes. Most veterinarians find this mutilating surgery too inhumane to perform, as do I.

The frequency of clipping varies from ferret to ferret, because nail-growth rates vary. Also, the amount and type of exercise you give your ferret factors in, because a lot of play may wear down his nails. On average, I find that I need to break out the nail trimmers every two to three weeks.

Now that you have the why and when down, you can get into the how. The following sections break down the clipping method you can use and how you can actually get the job done.

Choosing your clipping method

How you approach nail trimming depends on you and your ferret: You can use the scruff method, the distract method, or the sneak-attack method. The number of ferrets you have, your available time, the ferret's tolerance to nail clipping, and your ferret's distractibility are key factors in determining the method to use. The following list outlines these three methods:

- ✔ **The scruff method** is probably the quickest way to trim nails. It steadies your ferret, gives you a better grip, and lessens the chance of over-cutting. It generally calms the ferret (and you), so it's great for beginners who are getting used to the art of clipping.

   If your scruffed ferret moves around a lot while you're clipping, allow him to lick a treat, such as meat baby food, while you scruff him. You can clip his nails quickly and easily this way; however, this method *does* require two people.

- ✔ **The distract method** can take a little more time, but it's a nice way for you and your ferret to spend some quality time together. The method involves setting the fuzzy in your lap and placing a few drops of fatty acid supplement, or another tasty substance, on his belly. While he busies himself licking it off, you can dive in and clip before he has a chance to object. This method doesn't work with all ferrets, but it can be worth a try.

- ✔ **The sneak-attack method** is performed while your ferret is in a deep sleep. Depending on the quality of his sleep and your clipping talent, you may get all 20 nails clipped or just 1 or 2 before he wakes up.

No matter what clipping method you choose, you should give a treat to your fuzzy during or after the manicure. You want him to look forward to his clippings!

After you decide how you want to approach nail trimming, take a good look at your ferret's nails so you know what you're dealing with. Most fuzzy nails are long, curving, and dagger-like. Some fuzzies develop thicker nails as they age. The nails on the back paws are much shorter because they wear down more quickly, meaning they can be more difficult to clip. But unlike many dogs, whose nails are solid black, a ferret's nails are white. The *quick,* or vein, is easy to see, so you know exactly how much nail tip you can clip. So you have that going for you!

Performing the clip

To perform the clip, I use fingernail clippers designed for human babies. Regular-size human clippers work well, too. Some people like to use cat- or dog-nail clippers, but I find them too awkward to handle when clipping such tiny nails. You also have a hard time seeing what you're doing because of the shape of the clipper. Whatever clippers *you* find most comfortable, make sure that the blades are sharp before you clip. Dull blades can cause the nail walls to crush, leaving the edges rough. Also, make sure that the lighting in the room is adequate.

To trim your ferret's nails, follow these steps (you can use any of the clipping methods for these steps):

1. **Take your thumb and first finger and hold the paw close to the toes, with your thumb on the bottom of the paw.**

2. **Use the pressure of your thumb to spread the toes.**

   Doing so makes going from claw to claw easier.

3. **Clip as much of the white nail tip off each toe as you can, leaving some white after the quick (the interior of a ferret's nail; see a cross-section of a ferret nail in Figure 9-2).**

   Cutting into the quick is painful and causes the ferret to bleed. Because accidents happen (perhaps you weren't paying attention or your fuzzbutt suddenly moved), have some styptic powder or cornstarch on hand to stop any bleeding that may occur. Apply directly to the tip of the bleeding nail. If those materials aren't available, try dipping the bleeding nail into a bar of white soap, beeswax, or flour. You also can try running cold water over it. I suggest postponing the rest of the manicure until after your ferret has forgiven your dreadful deed.

   Even if the nail doesn't bleed, cutting too close to the quick can be painful, and your ferret will let you know. Take extra care with the back nails, because some have teeny-weeny nail tips. Look closely before clipping them. If the tips seem too short to clip, try filing them with a nail file, being careful not to scrape the fuzzy's sensitive paw pads.

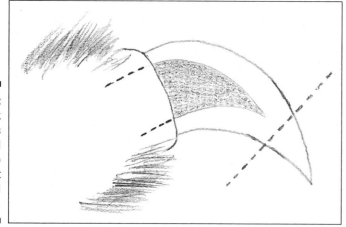

Figure 9-2:
The quick contains blood vessels, so be sure not to cut a nail too short.

If you let your ferret's nails grow for a long time between cuttings, the quicks will grow longer and longer into the nails, allowing you to cut off less and less of the nails. This isn't a good thing. Cutting frequently causes the quicks to regress back toward the paws so that you can cut a good amount of the nails off, giving your fuzzy more freedom and less of a chance of snagging.

Chewing On Chomper Maintenance

As a routine part of your ferret's grooming process, you should check out his teeth and gums. Tartar will build up on your ferret's teeth, regardless of his diet. In addition, neglected teeth can go bad and/or chip, leading to abscesses that can seriously affect his health. Aging ferrets have more dental problems than younger ones, so it's up to you to sink your teeth into this chore while your ferret is still young and chipper. Your fuzzy's future health and happiness depend on it.

All children resist brushing their teeth in the beginning, and a fuzzy is no different. The good news is, most ferrets get used to having their teeth cleaned if you do so regularly and gently. In the sections that follow, I show you how to perform a regular dental checkup, and I go through the process of brushing your fuzzy's teeth. Soon enough, you'll be a brushing wizard!

Performing the dental checkup

The dental checkup is easy with most ferrets, although it can be quite a challenge with more difficult patients. Most of my carpet sharks sit in my lap with minimal fidgeting and allow me to lift their gums for a peek. Others need to be scruffed gently while I perform the dental inspection (see Chapter 7).

I always like to have an extra pair of hands around so that I can concentrate on my findings. No matter how you handle the inspection, be gentle. Your ferret won't understand why you're poking around in his mouth, so take that into consideration.

You have two main things to look for when doing the dental checkup: the teeth and the gums.

With the exception of small traces of tartar buildup, if you see something out of the ordinary in your furball's mouth, contact your vet right away to schedule a visit. Dental problems can be serious enough to cause death. Non-dental problems that are located in the mouth are almost always signs of an underlying illness. Regardless of whether you have a dental emergency, your vet should perform yearly dental exams on your fuzzy and remove any excess tartar or decaying teeth.

Teeth

First, you should take a peek at all his teeth. The grayish or greenish discoloration you may see is *tartar,* which forms from plaque. Buildup happens at the same time and at the same rate on all the teeth. However, the ferret's tongue acts as sort of a windshield wiper, helping clear away the gunk on the lingual side, or "tongue side," of the teeth. Because the self-cleaning is less efficient on the outer side, tartar builds up faster on the buccal side, or "cheek side," of the teeth. And buildup occurs even faster in areas where folds and crevices exist, such as on the carnassials or back teeth.

The stuff you see on the teeth isn't necessarily the problem, though; even small amounts of buildup can signal under-the-gum disease. Although tartar doesn't cause gingivitis — which is characterized by red, inflamed gums — it may exacerbate the problem by injuring tissue and increasing the progression of gingivitis. Various stages of periodontal disease can follow gingivitis and are marked by the actual recession of the gum line, as well as bone loss. At this point, the ferret's teeth lose their support, loosen, and fall out. Diseased teeth can be painful, can lead to serious infection, and can cause the ferret to stop eating.

Without tooth cleaning and regular vet checkups, buildup (and problems) can increase as your ferret ages. A small amount of buildup is expected and not necessarily a cause for concern; however, it can become your ferret's enemy if not kept in check.

Gums

The gums should be smooth, moist, and a medium-pink color. Red, inflamed gums are a sign of gum disease, and your ferret should be treated immediately by your vet. If they appear very light in color (whitish/grayish/bluish), your ferret may be seriously ill, so a visit to your vet is a must. If you notice isolated swelling over one or two teeth, you can suspect a tooth abscess. If you dare, stick your nose up to his mouth and take a whiff. Conditions such as gum problems and ulcers result in a case of bad breath.

Ulcers on the gums or on the inside of the lip flap are a common sign of the disease *insulinoma*. These ulcers usually are whitish in color, and sometimes they ooze. Your ferret may point out these ulcers or other dental problems by pawing at his mouth. Other signs include drooling and a crusty bib. Although insulinoma isn't necessarily a dental problem, it is something to keep an eye out for as long as you have your eye in his mouth. (For more information on insulinoma, see Chapter 16.)

If you notice your ferret has bad breath at any time — not just during a checkup — you should call your vet to schedule an appointment. In addition to being a sign of mouth ulcers and gum problems, bad breath may be an indication of liver or kidney problems.

Brushing his teeth

After you perform an exam and find that everything is okay, what can you do to prevent any future dental problems? Brush his teeth! You can make cleaning your ferret's teeth a regular part of your grooming routine. All you have to do is invest in a cat toothbrush (don't use your spouse's) or a human infant toothbrush. You can purchase toothpaste designed for use on dogs or cats, although it seems that most ferrets find the taste disagreeable — even the meat flavored ones. It may be worth a try, though. You can also use Petromalt, which aids in preventing hairballs.

Never use adult human toothpaste to brush your ferret's teeth. The fluoride in adult human toothpaste is thought to be poisonous to fuzzies, and ferrets don't know the meaning of "rinse and spit." If you want to use human toothpaste, use toothpaste made especially for human toddlers.

To brush your ferret's teeth, follow these steps:

1. **Lift the gum and gently wipe his teeth with the toothbrush, using up and down and back and forth movements.**

2. **Gently go over his gums with the toothbrush after you finish the teeth.**

   Pay particular attention to cleaning his gum line (where the teeth disappear into the gums).

Patience and gentleness are the keys to successfully brushing your ferret's teeth. After all, you're not sanding down old paint. Some ferrets tolerate having their teeth brushed after a while, but others may have to be scruffed. Use the method that's the least stressful on you and your ferret.

Breaking Out the Hairbrush

Some people choose to brush their fuzzies' fur as they would a dog's or cat's. Other people skip this grooming step; maybe they're lazy or just find it unnecessary. There's no disadvantage to brushing as long as you use a soft brush and you're gentle, but brushing does have two main advantages:

- Helps to keep your ferret's coat clean and free of debris
- Removes loose fur — an especially important thing because fuzzies are prone to hairballs, and hairballs can be fatal

If you decide to brush your fuzzbutt, use a soft brush designed for kittens, rabbits, or other small mammals. These brushes generally are shorter bristled and just hard enough to remove loose fur without irritating sensitive skin. Stroke the brush in the same direction as the fur. Most furkids don't want to remain motionless for very long, so be aware that brushing can be a quick adventure. Some ferrets, however, enjoy this part of the grooming process and come to look forward to it.

Chapter 10

Enrichment: Yours and Your Ferret's

In This Chapter

▶ Understanding enrichment and its purpose

▶ Getting the scoop on a ferret's senses

▶ Developing your personal ferret enrichment program

▶ Hooking up with a ferret club

▶ Showing or competing with your ferret

▶ Reviewing ferret symposiums and Internet communities

Caring for your ferret means much more than providing her with fresh food and water. It's more than providing a roof over her head and cleaning up her poop, and it's even more than taking her for regular vet trips. Care goes way beyond that, which is where many pet owners fail in their responsibilities. Whether you own a dog, cat, bird, bunny, or ferret, your job is to keep your pet's life interesting and filled with enriching stimuli. In fact, her physical and psychological well-being depend on it!

Ferrets are as intelligent as small primates of the same body (and brain) size, which is proof that they need a lot of action-packed play and exploring time in a ferret-safe environment. Without a regular supply of stimulation, ferrets can become cage-crazy or depressed. Mentally, they can lose interest in their surroundings and their desire to explore or play. They may begin chewing on their cage bars and digging out their litter and food more frequently — basically, spending most of their time trying to find a way out of jail. Physically, they can become unfit and frequently will fall asleep on the hammock while watching reruns of old sitcoms. More importantly, the stress of having no enrichment can cause disease, such as ulcers, or make existing diseases worse.

This chapter is all about enrichment for both you and your ferret. I take the mystery out of the topic by further explaining what it is, why it's necessary, and what it does for ferrets. I try to give you enough information on ferret enrichment activities so that you can keep your ferret on her toes and even come up with your own enrichment ideas. I also guide you through some of the clubs, events, and resources available to you as a ferret owner. Take advantage of them. Here's to a happy and healthy life together!

Why Is Enrichment Necessary?

Like humans, ferrets possess an array of complex senses that need to be exercised on a daily basis. Imagine staring at the same wall for weeks on end. The sound of the same song playing over and over, which eventually becomes silent as you tune out the repetitiveness. Putting together the same puzzle so many times that you can do it in your sleep and you no longer enjoy the picture it creates. Your daily ration of macaroni and cheese squishing tastelessly in your mouth. You find some amusement in flinging it off your fork and watching it glob on the bare wall in front of you. The only smell filling your isolated room emanates from the toilet, which gets flushed every once in a while. Sound like torture? It is, and your ferret finds it excruciating as well. As a responsible ferret owner, your duty is to prevent your ferret from experiencing such depressing boredom. This presents quite a challenge to owners, because ferrets realize monotony in their surroundings rather quickly.

Humans tell our ferrets what and sometimes when to eat. We clean their cages and provide them with sleeping quarters. We introduce cagemates and take cagemates away. We medicate. We bathe. We groom. Humans are the ultimate ferret dictators, making most of their pets' life decisions for them. The basic goal of environmental enrichment is to get animals to interact with their environments, using their natural skills and behaviors, and to stimulate all their senses. You want to give your ferret something to think about, give her choices, and help her feel in control. Enrichment can also provide exercise, and it definitely relieves boredom.

What Does Enrichment Do for Ferrets?

What does enrichment do for ferrets? First of all, enrichment feels good! Enrichment can mean play! And what is play if not an activity that makes us feel good? This is a simple definition for an activity that utilizes a set of highly developed and often complicated skills. Dancing, chasing, dooking, hopping aimlessly in many directions at once . . . all are fun, and all feel wonderful! If play makes your ferret feel good, what's wrong with that? Enriching your ferret's life is certainly better than risking cage stress and boredom that can make her feel bad and adopt a negative outlook. But enrichment does even more than make you and your ferret feel good, as I explain the following sections.

Relieves boredom and stress

Boredom can be a major cause of stress for fuzzies. Ferrets are physically and emotionally sensitive to their surroundings. They need stimulation and enrichment to keep from getting bored. And boy, do they get bored easily!

Facilitates bonding

Although their natural tendency is to live a solitary life, ferrets are more likely than not to enjoy the company of other ferrets and humans — and even other types of pets. Through social enrichment, you can teach your ferret important social skills. Viewing each other much as they would littermates, ferrets brought together by adoption enjoy chasing each other and being chased. They rough and tumble and even steal from each other, testing their limits to the max. Sometimes, cats and dogs will partake in the ferret play as well, fostering camaraderie and trust between species.

Enrichment is extremely important when it comes to bonding with humans, too! Enrichment activities are the only true ways for your ferret to get to know you and for you to get to know your ferret. Enrichment will increase comfort levels, establish limits, build trust, and strengthen bonds. Even a timid or aggressive ferret will build up more confidence and trust through enrichment activities.

Bonding enrichments also can help parents solve the problem of how to get their children interested in ferrets. Children often persuade their parents to get a ferret but soon get bored with it, and the ferret languishes in a cage for long periods of time. Bonding enrichments can help tie a child to a ferret, which is great for all involved.

Keeps their senses alive and well

A ferret's every sense needs to be exercised routinely and equally to keep her sharp. Ferrets have an exceptional sense of smell; you'll frequently see your fuzzy with her nose to the ground as she sniffs out new and unusual things. Enrichment activities that call on this sense are great fun. Ferrets also benefit from games such as tag or pouncing, where they rely on their eyesight to hone in on victims. And what about touch, taste, and hearing? All very heightened senses that long to be tested. Keeping all this in mind, the possibilities for sensory enrichment are endless. (For more details on a ferret's senses, check out the section "Understanding Your Ferret's Senses.")

Helps to curb negative behaviors

Every ferret behavior is based on biological, medical, or psychological factors. A bored ferret can be a problematic ferret! So when you hear the term "cage crazy," you can assume it means just that! A few symptoms of cage craziness include

- Nipping or biting
- Gnawing on cage bars
- Fabric chewing
- Pacing

This acting out is her way of letting you know that she's unhappy. She's attempting to relieve some of the stress brought on by what's lacking in her life. This ferret needs some enrichment, stat!

Keeps the flab at bay

Lack of exercise or physical play contributes to chubbiness, whether you're talking about a human or a ferret. Physical enrichment activities burn calories and keep muscles toned and in shape. The ferret in its natural state is an extremely muscular critter, and you want to keep yours that way. Get your ferret out and exploring!

Encourages curiosity and creative problem solving

Enrichment is brain food! Enrichment not only increases the number of brain cells a ferret has, but also helps her brain recover from injury. Ferrets are both curious and adept problem-solvers. Providing enrichment will challenge your ferret by introducing new problems and encouraging the discovery of solutions.

Helps to keep bones, muscles, organs, and joints healthy

Physical enrichment improves joint and ligament performance, builds muscle, and increases strength. It also helps your ferret to build endurance when you're chasing her to retrieve your belongings! When humans exercise regularly, they preserve bone mass and increase bone density, because bones respond to mechanical stress by adding more bone tissue. It's likely your ferret gains benefits in this same way. Muscles and organs are exercised during physical enrichment and fed oxygen-rich blood, making them stronger and less prone to damage and infection. As they say, use them or lose them!

Improves heart health and overall circulation

Exercise and play gets a ferret's heart beating faster, thus facilitating rapid transportation of oxygen-rich blood and nutrients to all organs and areas of the body. As your ferret exercises, she engages in deep, rhythmic breathing, which assists her lungs in developing greater capacity and allows her to take in sufficient oxygen to nourish her cells. This is called *cardiovascular fitness.*

Enrichment play can also increase the size of her tiny blood vessels and improve the efficiency of the blood-delivery system. Physical play not only conditions the heart and lungs to work more efficiently during play, but also helps them work more efficiently during rest.

Makes humans smile and laugh

Ferrets are the ultimate in play therapy! It's hard not to find ferret antics worthy of giggles and smiles. All humans need to put aside time to laugh and have fun. Interacting with your ferret is a quick fix that rapidly dissipates anxiety, even if momentarily. It's a known fact that interacting with a pet in a positive way can reduce overall stress levels and lower blood pressure. And if that isn't a good enough reason to play with your ferret, how about the fact that she also giggles and smiles watching silly humans play along? You *and* your ferret will benefit from having fun!

Understanding Your Ferret's Senses

The pads on a ferret's paws are extremely sensitive. His face and nose are ticklish. His whiskers dance at the slightest sensation. His taste buds long to be awakened and stimulated with new tastes. Ferrets have an acute sense of hearing. They can hear a bag of treats being opened from across the house! That's right! Ferret senses are alive and well just like yours and mine. Understanding each sense will allow you to help your ferret live an enriching life. This section will teach you about the ferret's five senses. Every enrichment activity you implement will involve one or more of these senses. The more senses you stimulate, the better the enrichment.

Hearing

Ferrets have hearing that's at least comparable to a dog, meaning that it's excellent and highly developed. Reports indicate they can even hear frequencies as low as elephants can. Ferrets hear best in the range of 8 to 12 kilohertz (kHz). You can safely assume that your ferret can hear below and above the human ability.

Smelling

A foot of mud isn't enough to keep an innocent frog safe from a ferret, because the ferret's sense of smell is exceptionally strong. Her nose is so sensitive that she can likely sniff out water, which helps to explain how blind ferrets have little difficulty making their way to water bottles.

Unfortunately, a ferret's keen sense of smell can also be a disadvantage. The ferret's sense of smell causes her extreme *olfactory imprinting* — when a ferret "imprints" on food items by the age of 6 months old. This means that if she hasn't been exposed to the food by that age, she doesn't recognize it as food. When young, a ferret's smell cells that aren't exposed to specific types of odor wither away and die. Afterwards, because the ferret can't smell the food, she simply doesn't recognize it as something good to eat. (For more on this phenomenon, see the following section.)

Tasting

Experts and ferret owners don't know much about the ferret's sense of taste, but because it's closely tied to the sense of smell, they assume that ferrets also have a highly developed sense of taste. You'll certainly find that your ferret favors some tastes over others.

Because taste and smell are so closely tied together, you should expose a young ferret to as many food items as possible while she's young. That way, her smell cells will be more diversified and she'll be able to recognize more items as food when she grows into adulthood. This will allow you to provide a varied, free-choice diet and will give her a healthier life through adulthood (see Chapter 8).

Seeing

A common misconception is that the ferret's eyesight is exceptionally poor. Although the resolution (the ability to see fine detail) of a ferret's vision isn't as fine as a human's, and a ferret probably only sees limited colors — living in a world of grays, for instance — ferret vision isn't all that bad for a species that has adapted to see in the dark. Much of what's considered bad vision is probably an adaptation to living in cages, making ferrets appear more near-sighted than they actually are.

Touching

Ferrets have evolved to live in a dark, subterranean world. Consequently, they have a large number of specialized hairs sensitive to touch found around their mouths, on their necks, and even on their forearms! These special hairs illuminate the way so they can move through dark areas with no light.

A ferret's foot pads also are very sensitive to touch; they have small hairs that probably help the ferret find her way in the dark. The hairs may reduce sound as well, helping her evade predators and sneak up on prey.

Recommended Enrichment Activities for You and Your Fuzzy

Many activities will allow you to have safe, enriching fun with your ferret — as long as you're fun-loving, creative, and well-prepared. In the following sections, I cover some of the enrichment possibilities for you. First, I give you pointers on setting up appropriate areas for your activities, and then I tell you about the activities themselves. The enrichment activities I present stimulate any of the ferret's five senses: smell, vision, touch, taste, and hearing.

A ferret's toy chest can quickly become full of all sorts of toys and miscellaneous objects. To keep it together, you can come up with a simple storage system that works for you. You can manage toys and enrichment items by storing them in size-appropriate bins or ferret-proof plastic containers. You can label the bins according to toy type, manner of enrichment (hearing, smelling, tasting, touching, or seeing), or even by weekly rotation. It also helps to keep one labeled bin aside to hold all items that need to be cleaned (for more on cleaning toys, see Chapter 9).

Organizing your ferret's play areas

A ferret's outdoor play area is essentially an enclosed, ferret-proofed place where she can run and play — a place that's safe from escape or predation from other animals. It should have all the following items for enrichment purposes:

- ✔ Soil for digging
- ✔ Water for splashing
- ✔ Objects for climbing
- ✔ Novel items for exploration
- ✔ Tubes for running
- ✔ Dens for hiding and sleeping

Of paramount importance is ferret-proofing. Unless you're absolutely certain your ferret can't escape and that a predator can't get in, you shouldn't leave the ferret alone when outdoors.

You must remember that ferrets are excellent diggers and can dig themselves out of most play areas. They're also excellent climbers, so you must confine any climbing opportunities to the middle of the play area with no chance for escape. (People like using wood climbing tools, because wood is difficult to climb.) Many people will line the bottoms of their outdoor play areas with wire and cover them with dirt to prevent digging escape. Other people choose to dig out the perimeter of the play areas and bury cement cinder blocks two to three feet deep in the ground. This option certainly stops the ferret from digging out, or at least gives you time to fill in the holes after they get that deep. You can always continue putting the cinder blocks above ground and then build a structure on them. The design of the play area is your choice, but it must be escape-proof and predation-proof.

A ferret's indoor play area is usually a room designated for the ferret. It may be just for the ferret, or it may be a common living area. It should be well ferret-proofed, and preferably tiled (see Chapter 6 on ferret-proofing). You can bring a little of the outdoors inside by providing a dirt dig box, a small pool of water, or a box of leaves, but the cleanup is obviously a little more involved.

Movement and physical-exercise activities

This section provides a couple specific enrichment activities that require physical exertion and movement. Other activities that fall under this category include play activities, leashed walks, wrestling, and anything that causes the ferret to work her muscles.

Dirt galore

Cater to your ferret's desire to dig by giving her a big bin of topsoil or play sand in her play area. Playtime may get messy, but it's well worth the effort! Just look at the smile on your fuzzy's face (behind the dirt moustache).

Hide some tiny treasures in the dirt or sand pit for extra enrichment, and let her dig away. And if your dig box is outside, consider burying some earthworms in there. If your ferret is daring, she may enjoy the worms as tasty treats.

Ferret cheerleading

Invest in some cheap, plastic, multi-colored pom-poms, which you can find in most party supply stores. (Black and white would be the best contrast!) Now you're ready to try the following exercises:

- ✔ Dance the poms above your ferret's head and watch her dance and jump up to catch them.
- ✔ Race them along the floor to get your ferret to chase them or even ride them.
- ✔ Wiggle the poms in your ferret's face and watch her go crazy!

You can lightly scent the poms with perfume or scented food oils for added enticement and enrichment. This meets visual, smelling, hearing, and touching enrichments, assuming you complete all the exercises in this activity.

Social-development activities

This section presents some enrichment activities that relate to the social needs and development of your ferret. Other common types of social enrichments include face washing, grooming, petting, feeding by hand, and cuddling. (For more on grooming routines, head to Chapter 9.)

The washcloth rubdown

The washcloth rubdown is one of the most effective grooming/bonding methods, but it takes a little practice. All you need is a small, damp (not wet), warm washcloth. Starting at your ferret's face and working your way back across her body, rub your ferret with the washcloth. Move in the direction of her fur. You may need to rinse and warm your washcloth again during the activity to keep it fresh. Don't forget her belly, and particularly her bottom and genitals.

What you're doing is mocking her mom's behavior. This enrichment activity is not only a great way to bond with your ferret, but also a good way to keep her clean.

Sack 'o ferret

A great social enrichment activity is to get a bonding pouch or a sack and place your ferret inside. Carry her around while you do household chores or just sit with her and watch television or read a book. I usually have one hand in the pouch so that I can stay in contact with a ferret and play with her. Most ferret sacks and pouches have convenient straps so that you can hang them around your neck or over your shoulder.

Food-related activities

Enrichment activities that exploit the ferret's desire to eat can include giving bits of "forbidden" foods, such as a single lick of ice cream; tastes of human food, such as a tiny piece of pot roast; or even something unfamiliar. Some examples of ferret-safe foods include meat-based baby food and the creative ferret recipes listed in Chapter 25.

One useful food-related activity is the *stink trail*. Take a small piece of meat and "dab" it on the floor, making a trail to a hiding place. Be creative and make the trail zig-zag or go around the leg of a table. You can even use perfume as the scent and go up the corner of a couch. Watch your ferret follow the scent trail to the end!

Just the smell or experience of investigating food is enriching to a ferret, so even if your ferret doesn't eat the food, it isn't a failure of the enrichment.

Training exercises

This section presents some enrichment activities that encourage the training of your ferret to perform certain behaviors; others discourage your fuzzy from certain activities. Mostly, these activities are tricks (do's) and trainings (don'ts) that stimulate all your ferret's senses and help you out in the process!

Some fuzzies are cautious and anxious creatures; don't traumatize your ferret by insisting that she learn a certain training exercise if that trick obviously bothers her. Other ferrets will learn trick after trick. They may even teach you a few while still leaving room to invent new tricks of their own. Fuzzies are individual characters with unique personalities. All are extremely intelligent,

Ferrets come in a variety of colors and patterns. The following photos display several other varieties. Shown here is a champagne mitt (MMF's Flavis aka Moose, owned by Joy Decker). See Chapter 2 for more on ferret colors,

Albino

Sable blaze (AFA Gold Champion
KC's Sharper Image of Shamalar,
owned by Gail Suzanne Burlaka)

Black roan (JBF's Cabana Boy,
owned by Vickie McKimmey)

Standard sable (Thunderstorm weasel, owned by Patricia Stauffer)

Champagne point (AFA Gold Champion NB's Seamus Finnegan of RN, owned by Ruth L. Heller, DMV)

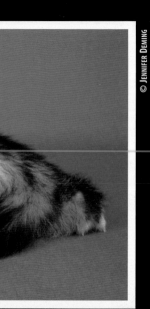

Black roan mitt (Bella, owned by Sarah Hamilton)

**Standard black sable
(Shady Hollows Fireworks aka
Batman, owned by Sally Heber)**

Black-eyed white

Black-eyed white with pattern

Black mitt (MMF's Fortunata aka Raini, owned by Cheryl Kern)

Standard chocolate (TH's Godiva Whisper of JBF, owned by Vickie McKimmey)

Standard champagne (SH's Juvenile Delinquent, owned by Emily Segall)

Sable mitt (Ricky, owned by Dee Gage)

Black-footed ferret, courtesy of the Louisville Zoo, Louisville, Kentucky. The black-footed ferret is native to the USA and shouldn't be confused with domesticated, pet ferrets. See Chapter 2 for more information.

It isn't unusual to see groups of ferrets — like Logan, Buffy, Monica, and Shelby here — nestled together for a nap.

An 8-week-old ferret being introduced to a 7-year-old Boxer. See Chapter 7 for more information on introducing ferrets to other pets.

Ferrets and children make fine friends, like Jared Deming and his ferret, Xavier. See Chapter 7 for the best ways to acclimate a ferret into your family.

Ferrets are sociable animals and enjoy playing together. It's a good idea to have more than one. (Savannah and Kevin, owned by Deb's Ferret Rescue & Boarding)

Exercising your ferret (or with your ferret!) is a great way to bond with him. Ferrets love to play! See Chapter 10 for tips on having fun with your ferret. (Xavier, owned by Jared Deming)

Though they are clean animals, the average ferret occasionally needs a bath. Chapter 9 tells you how to bathe and groom your ferret, and how to make the process easier for both of you. (Milton Millie, owned by Deb's Ferret Rescue & Boarding)

but some have less interest in learning pet tricks. Having your ferret act like a ferret should be delightful enough.

I beg your pardon?

The easiest trick to teach a ferret is to sit up and beg. The action comes naturally because ferrets often have to stand up high and peek for the things they want to pilfer. When your furball learns this trick, she may start running in front of you every chance she gets to beg for a treat, doggie-style. Teaching this trick requires that you have a favorite treat and a human hand — preferably attached to the rest of a human body:

1. **Sit on the floor with a treat in your hand or Linatone on your finger.**

2. **Reach straight away from your body and let your ferret sniff the treat so she knows that it's there.**

   You can even give her a tiny taste.

3. **Slowly raise your hand until she has to raise herself to reach the treat.**

   Don't let her rest her front paws on your lap or grab your hand. If she does, gently nudge her away or move farther from her and start over. The idea is to get her to do the trick without cheating.

4. **While she reaches up to get it, use the command you want to stick with, such as "Up," "Beg," or "Sit up."**

   Choose a simple word or phrase and be consistent with it.

When your ferret begins to associate the verbal command with the treat, start using only the hand motion to prompt the action. *Note:* Deaf ferrets can't read lips, but they can read body language and beg for treats just as frequently.

Scooter, I think your human is calling

Many people have taught their ferrets to come a-runnin' when they call their names. Teaching this trick is almost the same as conditioning ferrets to respond to a squeaky toy or another noise with a treat in mind. However, many people proclaim that each of their ferrets knows her name separately from the others and that some even recognize the names of their cagemates.

You have a few ways to teach your fuzzy her name and have her respond to it. Repetition and reward play the biggest roles. Here's one method that works well:

1. **During playtime, grab a treat and then call your ferret's name.**

   If she doesn't even notice that a noise came out of your mouth, make visual contact with her and call her name again.

2. **Crouch down and let her know that you have something good to show her, all while calling her name.**

3. **If she appears interested and comes toward you, reward the action with a small taste of the treat.**

4. **Move farther away and call her name again, repeating the process several times; soon, she should figure out that her name really means a treat.**

Treats are great motivators and help while you train your ferret. However, an unfit fuzzy won't come running when you call her name because she'll be a slug from all the yummy treats. Use verbal praise and lavish petting as alternate rewards for desired behavior. Doing so will keep your ferret healthier, and she may enjoy the surprise of the reward. You can also call your ferret's name and squeak her favorite toy at the same time. This combination usually gets a furball's attention, and she'll come running to investigate. Keep calling her name and using the toy as added motivation. After she masters the trick, use the squeaky toy less and less until you cut it out completely.

You can make the trick tougher by hiding from your ferret and then calling her. Ferrets are extremely intelligent creatures. If your ferret knows a positive reward is at the end of the voice rainbow, she'll listen for her name and come bouncing eagerly to greet you.

Jumping through hoops

Having your ferret jump through hoops is a relatively easy trick to teach. All you need is a small plastic hoop (or something similar) that measures about 1 foot in diameter. Here's one teaching method that works:

1. **Hold the hoop upright on the floor between you and your fuzzy.**

2. **Show her a treat to entice her through the hoop; when she starts walking through to get the treat, say "Jump" and then reward her when she passes through.**

   At this point, she has no clue what the heck you're talking about. She thinks you're nuts and just wants the treat. In time, though, she'll make the connection between the hoop, the command, and the treat.

3. **Gradually raise the hoop and try to entice her to jump through on command, using the treat during the early stages.**

You can get a ferret to jump through the hoop in several ways. Some ferrets will just jump through as you raise the hoop and say the command. Others will go under or around the hoop. If you have a difficult ferret, sit in a corner or narrow passageway to make it necessary for her to pass through the hoop. Always hold the treat up high so she has to look up and over the hoop rim to get to it. And don't forget to say "Jump" when the ferret passes through the hoop.

After your ferret masters walking through the hoop and learning the "Jump" command, you can try to place her on a slightly raised platform, like a pet carrier, and place the hoop in front of it off the ground. Raise the treat up high and say "Jump" as she hops through. This can help get your fuzzy airborne faster.

Several creative methods can teach this trick to your ferret. Tossing your ferret through the hoop and hollering "Jump," however, isn't a good way. Be gentle and creative, and pour on the praise for a job well done.

Roll over, Beethoven

A treat (such as a piece of cereal or piece of meat) can work wonders with teaching your ferret to roll over on command. Some fuzzies don't like to be placed on their backs and rolled over, so your ferret may give you a hard time at first. Not to worry; as usual, I know several ways to teach your fuzzy that have been successful in the past! Following is one method that works well:

1. **Hold a treat in your hand and allow your fuzzy to lick it.**

   The treat will distract her while you gently roll her over.

2. **While still holding the treat, move it in a circular motion over your ferret's head while you roll her over.**

   Many times at this point, a ferret's head will roll and her body will naturally follow as she tries to keep up with the treat.

3. **As she's rolling over — either on her own or with your gentle help — say "Over" or "Roll over."**

   Be consistent with the term you use.

In the beginning, you may have to roll over a stubborn fuzzy 100 percent of the way. Eventually, you can taper off to a three-quarter push, to a half push, to a slight nudge. Your fuzzy should need only the motivation of a treat and the command by the time she has learned what you want her to do. When she associates rolling over with treats and affection, you may find her running in front of you and rolling over to get attention, be picked up, or get a treat. It's quite amusing.

Using the circular hand motion is great for teaching deaf carpet sharks that can't hear commands. They simply roll over as you give them the hand signal.

Diving for treasures

The diving for treasures trick is pretty cool and fun to watch, but to pull it off you need a ferret that's comfortable with water and likes to snorkel around otter-style. Here's how you teach your ferret to dive for treasure:

1. **Find a treat that sinks and is easy to spot underwater.**

   A small piece of meat or a ½ of a blueberry is perfect for this trick.

2. **Get a large, empty litter box or something similar and fill it with water.**

3. **Place the treat in your open palm and rest your hand on the water's surface. Allow your ferret to grab the treat.**

4. **Repeat Step 3, but this time lower your hand just enough to soak the treat. Again, let your ferret grab it.**

5. **As your fuzzy gets used to this trick, lower your hand more and more until your ferret is (voluntarily) submerging her head in the water to get the treat.**

6. **When your fuzzy snorkeler becomes a pro at bobbing for goodies, toss the treat into the tub and watch her dive in.**

   If she doesn't dive on in, bring the treat up from the deep and show it to her in the palm of your hand. As she sticks her head in to get it, drop the treat to the bottom again. She should go directly to it and snarf it up.

Using novel objects in activities

A *novel object* is one that the ferret is unfamiliar with. Ferrets love unfamiliar objects and always seem to favor them over anything else. New smells are the most important characteristic, but ferrets also enjoy new textures, shapes, graphic designs, tastes, and locations. An empty box is a great starting point, for example. The box itself can be novel for a day; turning it upside down makes it novel once again. Cut a hole in the side to make it novel after your ferret loses interest. Filling it with cut grass increases the novelty greatly. You get the idea. The following sections present a couple more enrichment activities that feature novel objects.

The nice thing about novel objects is that you don't have to spend a lot of money on them or get fancy with them. Ferrets don't care. Be creative with simple, safe household objects. The aforementioned box works well. A bin filled with crumpled newspaper (the hearing/touching senses) or an old boot (smelling) is a novel object that costs next to nothing.

Crinkle tub

Fill a bin with crinkled balls of newspaper and place your ferret inside. You'll be tickled pink watching her bounce around and play in reaction to the crinkling sounds the paper makes. The more noise she can create, the more she'll dance. The paper also will feel new to her.

Checkerboard wall

Give your ferret something new and exciting to look at by creating a black and white checkerboard pattern for her cage or play area. You can use Plexiglas or wood for the wall. You can paint the checkerboard with non-toxic paint, or you can use tile or contact paper. It doesn't have to be fancy. Fasten or hang the board securely on the wall, low enough for the ferret to enjoy. You can even hang some toys from it. The idea is to give your ferret something sharply contrasting to look at (black and white works well).

Finding Your Own Enrichment at Ferret Clubs

Joining a ferret club is a great way to meet other ferret owners who share your love for ferrets. By staying in touch with ferret people, you can stay up to date with health issues and current events. You may even develop friendships that will last a lifetime! What could be better enrichment for you than that?

Ferret clubs exist all over the world, so you should be able to find one relatively close to home. Many clubs are associated with ferret shelters; others operate independently of shelters simply out of a love for ferrets. Many ferret clubs sponsor holiday parties with contests and games. Some even host ferret shows or fundraisers for ferret-related causes (see the following section for more on ferret shows).

Every dedicated ferret owner should consider joining a ferret club. For more information on joining a club in your area, check out the following resources:

- www.ferretcentral.org/orgs.html
- www.ferret.org/links/shelters.shtm

Participating in Regional Shows, Club Shows, and Competitions

Life with a ferret doesn't have to end at home! A whole ferret culture is out there, waiting to be explored. Many people view ferret ownership as a livelihood like no other. Some owners live and breathe ferrets, scheduling their activities around playtime and feedings. But when, you may wonder, do these owners get out to play? I'm glad you asked!

People love to show off their fuzzies, whether the pets are bare-furred or dressed up in silly costumes. Ferret shows and fun matches are held all over, and some are downright serious business. You can find out about ferret shows by doing Internet searches or checking with the American Ferret Association, which keeps an up-to-date listing of the major shows in the United States. You can receive contact information for all shows and get complete show packets with details on entering your ferret in classes and fun matches. The following sections break down your show options and cover fun matches and Ferret Symposiums.

So, you want to show your fuzzy?

The bottom line is this: Attending ferret shows, even as a spectator, is a great way to meet other fuzzy devotees and compare notes. You can swap stupid and silly stories, most of which are related to the bodily functions of ferrets. You can also learn about new medical treatments, get tips on overcoming behavioral problems, and find out the best ways to ferret-proof. Also, many vendors set up booths and sell ferret-related items at shows, ranging from food and ferret costumes to jewelry and other novelty items.

Of course, serious competition also exists. Rules, regulations, and standards vary from organization to organization. If you decide to show your ferret, know that she may be competing against generations of champions bred for show by private breeders.

Depending on the type of show and which organization is sponsoring it — such as The American Ferret Association (www.ferret.org) — you may have many entry classes to choose from (which I explain in the next section). And, depending on the show, points may be awarded to winners, just like with dog shows. To reach a certain level or tier in the show circuit, your ferret must obtain a certain number of points.

Naturally, looks aren't all that matter. Personality is a plus. Although points are awarded for clean ears, clean teeth, and a nice manicure, the most gorgeous, well-groomed ferret won't take home a ribbon if she bites the judge on the nose!

Preparing to bring home the blue ribbon

If you're set on showing your ferret, you need to consider several things. First up, what class will you enter?

- **Specialty classes** are for ferrets to be judged on color standards (see Chapter 2 for a list of ferret colors). Some shows have extra specialty classes for shelter ferrets, geriatric ferrets, and handicapped ferrets.

> ✔ **Championship classes** can be broken out by age, gender, and whether a ferret has been altered. Judges consider mainly body proportion, coat quality, and temperament. Champions may accrue points, making their babies more valuable in the future.

The most important part of showing your ferret is making sure she's up on her maintenance and manners, which includes the following (see Chapter 9 for grooming tips):

> ✔ **Temperament:** Your ferret should be well-socialized and easily handled. A biting ferret or a ferret that's overly nervous around strangers should be left at home, because a bite will almost always mean disqualification (see Chapter 19).

> ✔ **Nails:** You should trim your ferret's nails on a regular basis to keep the quick from growing too long with the nail. Preferably, you should clip your fuzzy's nails a couple days before the show so that they can smooth out, but don't clip them all the way down to the quick. Judges hate that. If you must clip them on the day of the show, make sure to use a nail file to round off the nails.

> ✔ **Ears:** You can clean her ears the night before or the day of the show, but be sure not to discolor the fur in and around the ears. There should be no noticeable earwax.

> ✔ **Teeth:** Dirty teeth will cost you points or a ribbon. Having gingivitis or red, inflamed gums also is a definite no-win situation! You should brush your ferret's teeth on a daily basis and take her to the vet for regular cleanings. A good brushing on the day of the show is warranted, but avoid scaling or scraping; you don't want to present a ferret with bleeding gums.

> And have a toothbrush on hand to get food out of her teeth at the last minute!

> ✔ **Coat:** Unless the show is during shedding season or your ferret has adrenal gland disease, her coat should be soft and luxurious. Over-bathing may leave her skin dry and flaky. A poor diet also will leave her coat in bad condition. You can bathe your ferret the night before or the day of the show, using a ferret shampoo or baby shampoo, as long as you haven't bathed her too recently. A teeny, weeny dab of Vaseline between the toes is great for dry skin, as well.

After you have a class and your ferret is ready to present, you need to get ready for the show. You need to remember to bring many things along on the trip. The following list runs through your supplies:

> ✔ Your show packet and confirmation

> ✔ Proof of up-to-date vaccinations — canine distemper and rabies vaccinations, specifically

Many shows also require proof that your ferret has tested negative for ADV (Aleutian's Disease). (For more on vaccinations and diseases, check out the chapters in Part IV.)

- A large cage, carrier, and/or playpen for her to be able to move about
- Extra food, water bowl, bottles of water, Linatone
- Camera
- Small litter box and litter, scooper, paper towels
- Bedding and hammock
- Plastic bags, wet wipes, two to three bath towels, sanitary wipes
- Leash and harness
- A grooming kit (including nail clippers, nail file, Q-tips, cotton balls, ear wash, tooth brush, hair brush, tissues, Vaseline, and coat-conditioner spray)
- Extra money for shopping (the vendors are awesome!)
- Your ferret!

Fun matches

Fun matches are a great way to have fun with ferrets and their nutty humans. *Fun matches* are light-hearted competitions held during shows and can often be entered the day of a show. A little non-beauty related competition is good for the soul. Fun match contests have nothing to do with how beautiful and well-behaved your ferret is. They have everything to do with creativity, personality, and skill. Sometimes, it's just fuzzy luck that wins out.

Fun match contests often include the following:

- **The yawning contest:** How many times can your ferret yawn in a set amount of time? The yawningest ferret wins.

  The first ferret competition I ever entered was a yawning contest, and my Cookie took the prize. She yawned 7 times in 60 seconds. I was so proud! Back then, you could scruff your ferret, which helped the yawns come on. Most contests now rely on natural yawns. I could win that contest, but none of my current ferrets could.

- **Tube racing:** The first ferret out the other side of her tube wins.

  Sometimes, you can use squeaky toys or stick your face through the exit hole to encourage your ferret through. I think my Nikki once curled up and went to sleep in a tube during a contest. We had to lift the tube and slide her out. Can't win 'em all!

- ✔ **The great paper bag escape:** Each ferret is placed into a large paper bag. The top of the bag is neatly folded down. The first ferret to escape wins the contest.

- ✔ **Silly pet tricks:** People come up with all sorts of silly ferret tricks, from rolling over to jumping through hoops. Ferrets perform their tricks in front of an audience and the audience favorite (judged by clapping) wins.

- ✔ **The costume contest:** Ferrets are dressed up in unique and often adorable costumes, from chefs and doctors to geisha girls and ballerinas. Also judged by the audience's clapping.

Annual Ferret Symposiums

In the fall of 2000, the very first Ferret Symposium was held in Toronto. Thanks to Randy Belair, president of the Ferret Aid Society in Toronto, the Ferret Symposium offered the North American ferret community its first ever chance to participate in an all-ferret educational weekend. Speakers included well-known ferret veterinarians, shelter workers, and ferret-knowledgeable individuals. Vendors kept shoppers busy, and the entertainment on hand encouraged people to gather and get to know each other. Randy's brainchild paved the way for other wonderful Ferret Symposiums that have since come and gone, and more are in the planning stages. Cities such as Las Vegas, St. Louis, Portland, and Atlanta have come to know the dedication and spirit of ferret owners.

Every dedicated ferret owner should consider attending a Ferret Symposium to learn about the latest health-care issues and medical treatments, as well as husbandry issues and other ferret-related topics. The speakers are phenomenal; the camaraderie is unbeatable; and the weekend is unforgettable. To learn more about upcoming Ferret Symposiums, visit The International Ferret Congress Web site at www.ferretcongress.org.

Internet Clubs and Lists

The Internet is home to a wealth of ferret information. Some of the information is outstanding. Some is okay. Some isn't so great. Weeding through the good, the bad, and the ugly can be difficult, and I'm no expert when it comes to surfing the Web. It can be a scary place, so be careful and choosy about what you want to believe.

Well-recognized Internet clubs and lists are great places to start when it comes to gathering online information about ferrets. Patiently observe what goes on there so you can quickly learn who's been around the block and who the respected authorities are. I mention two wonderful lists in the following sections that should get you off to a great start.

Ferret Mailing List (FML)

The Ferret Mailing List (FML) has been proudly running since 1987! It's a fantastic forum dedicated to the domestic or pet ferret. Any ferret-related topic is welcome, and anyone can join. Its 3,000+ member list includes pet owners, veterinarians, breeders, shelter managers, ferret-owner wannabes, and, of course, me! Moderated by superhuman Bill Gruber (also known as BIG) to keep posts on-topic and clean, the list is distributed in a digest-style format every morning and great information is posted daily. Currently, 15 years of archives are available by user-friendly searches.

To subscribe to the Ferret Mailing List, please e-mail `ferret-l-request@listserv.ferretmailinglist.org`. Include your name and the word "subscribe," or a note asking to subscribe.

Ferret Health List (FHL)

The Ferret Health List (FHL) is a phenomenal list founded by Christopher Bennett, a special person who thought it would be a great idea to have one place to gather to talk ferret health. His idea took off, and FHL's membership is steadily increasing. Today, his legacy is carried on by some other special people. Moderated by veterinarians and ferret-health-knowledgeable people, FHL's topics are limited to ferret health issues. Anyone can join the list, and posts are addressed frequently by vets or other people well-known in the ferret community.

To join this list, go to `pets.groups.yahoo.com/group/ferrethealth`. You must be signed up with Yahoo!, which is free.

Chapter 11

Have Ferret, May Travel

In This Chapter

▶ Preparing to take your fuzzy on vacation

▶ Reviewing your travel alternatives

▶ Exploring alternatives to taking fuzzy with you

Some people think a vacation gives them time away from the kids and pets. Others wouldn't dare leave their loved ones behind — human or ferret. For me, lugging my many fuzzbutts to my dream destination just doesn't seem feasible or relaxing. It's difficult enough taking a spouse along for the trip! (Of course, you can always decide to leave your spouse behind and take off with your fuzzies.)

This chapter deals specifically with the sensitive subject of travel decisions. Do you travel with your ferret or leave him behind in someone else's care? You should take certain things into consideration when making this decision; much of it depends on where you're going and for how long. The decision you make is personal, of course; but whatever you choose, this chapter has you covered.

Fuzzy Is Going on Vacation!

If you decide that your fuzzy deserves a vacation too, or if you just can't bear to leave him behind, you need to do some pre-trip investigating and preparing. Depending on how you want to travel and where you're traveling to, taking your ferret may be a somewhat simple task, or it may be a major ordeal. No matter what, the health and safety of your ferret should be your utmost concern.

Traveling, even comfortably, is very stressful on your fuzzy. If your ferret accompanies you in your travels, the trip should be as relaxing as possible for both of you. This means giving your fuzzy ample playtime and attention as usual — if not more. It also means providing a comfortable cage to live in while away from home. Don't keep him in a tiny carrier. After all, if the trip won't be a vacation for your ferret, too, you should leave him behind where he can at least have familiar surroundings (see the later section "Leaving Your Furball in Good Hands"). Also, provide plenty of favorite toys to keep him amused and preoccupied when he isn't sleeping. As an extra bonus for keeping him busy, he won't be dooking, "Are we there yet? Are we there yet?"

Checking ahead

Before you leave on your trip, you need to make sure that your fuzzy is welcome at your destination — especially if you'll be staying in a hotel. Sneaking a ferret into a ferret-free hotel may mean an extra charge for you or an expulsion, leaving you nowhere to go. Be smart. Likewise, don't show up on your Aunt Mary's doorstep with ferret in hand without getting permission first. A call from your car a mile from her house isn't what I have in mind, either. Being considerate of other people helps ensure that your ferret will be treated well on his vacation.

If you'll be staying at a hotel that allows ferrets (and other pets, for that matter), you may be required to pay a little extra for your room or put down a refundable deposit to cover possible damage. Hey, there's a reason why it's becoming more and more difficult to find pet-friendly hotels! Most hotels are afraid of the mess that some pets leave behind. Keep your hotel pet-friendly by cleaning up after your ferret before you leave. (See the following section for tips on what you need to bring to ensure a clean and healthy trip.)

Many people forget (or don't know) that their beloved fuzzies aren't welcome in all cities and states. If your destination is a ferret-free zone (see Chapter 3 for info on these places), leave your fuzzy behind. If you'll be passing through a ferret-free zone on the way to your destination, consider what may happen if you get pulled over for a traffic violation, get in a car accident, or if your ferret suddenly requires medical treatment. Although the odds of being discovered on a simple journey through a ferret-free zone are remote, check the ferret laws of the towns you'll be passing through just to be sure. The penalty can vary from a simple warning to the confiscation of your beloved pet. It's up to you to chance it or drive a different route. No matter the situation, though, keep a health certificate and proof of rabies vaccination on hand.

Packing the necessities

Traveling with your ferret will be relatively easy, as long as you pack the necessary items to make his journey (and yours) comfortable. Whether you'll be going across the state line or heading to the other side of the country, you need the following basic items:

- Your ferret's first-aid kit (see Chapter 12 for a list of what should go in this kit)

  Be sure to include an appropriate supply of medication that your ferret may need.

- Proof of current rabies vaccination and a current health certificate issued by your veterinarian

- A lasting supply of ferret food and a water bottle (see Chapter 8 for more on feeding your fuzzy)

- A pet carrier or travel cage to keep your ferret safe

  The bigger the travel cage, the better — especially if you're going on a long trip. If you must travel with a small carrier, bring along a decent-sized cage for the duration of the vacation. Don't keep your ferret cooped up.

- A harness and leash

- A litter box and litter

- Fluffy, snoozy bedding (don't forget to pack a change of bedding, too)

- Cleaning supplies to clean up after your ferret; wet wipes, plastic bags, and so on (see Chapter 9)

- Toys, toys, toys

Don't give your ferret any sedatives or tranquilizers of any sort while traveling. If you think your ferret must have a sedative, leave him at home or take one yourself and continue on with your travel plans!

On the Road or Flying High

We've come a long way since the horse and buggy! Getting to where you need to be has become much easier, whether you travel by plane, train, or automobile. Heck, you can even travel by ship, too! In this section, I talk about the most frequently used means of transportation — the scenic road trip and the zippy plane ride — so that you can make sure your ferret is comfortable and safe during his travels.

Road trip!

If you have the time (or if the thought of taking to the friendly skies makes you poof), you may decide to partake in a scenic road trip. Or perhaps the trip isn't long enough to warrant hopping on a plane. Although a road trip can be fun, you need to prepare for many things when driving with your ferret.

Road trip do's

When you decide to travel with your ferret (or children for that matter), you make a commitment to tend to his physical and emotional needs throughout the trip. This can be quite demanding. The following list presents some things you must do while on the road with your ferret:

- ✔ Do keep your ferret in his carrier or cage to prevent accidents when you're driving.

- ✔ Do make frequent rest stops and take the time to harness/leash your ferret for brisk walks. Also, resist the urge to let strangers handle your already stressed-out and excited fuzzy during stops. Stress is one of the conditions that can lead to unpredictable ferret behavior.

- ✔ Do keep a copy of your ferret's rabies vaccination certificate and medical records.

- ✔ Do offer your ferret water frequently during trips. A hanging water bottle or bowl in the carrier will continually drip or spill from the jostling.

- ✔ Do keep your car cool and well-ventilated.

- ✔ Do remember to medicate your ferret, if necessary, at scheduled times.

If you're crazy enough to take a long, hot, summer road trip in a vehicle without air conditioning, bring along a cooler with several two-liter plastic bottles of frozen water. Keep one of the frozen bottles wrapped in a towel and in your pet's travel carrier to keep him cool.

Ferrets are master escape artists. Take into consideration that your ferret may be able to get out of his cage or carrier in your vehicle. Also, a child or spouse may let him out without anyone knowing — a particularly scary situation if you drive with the windows down. And before slamming that car door shut, be sure your ferret is safe in his carrier where he belongs. In a car door versus ferret situation, the car door always wins.

Road trip don'ts

Driving with your ferret can be a challenge, and sometimes pets are the last thing on your mind. It's important to recognize the dangers associated with traveling with your ferret and be diligent in tending to his needs. You can prevent most accidents by using common sense or learning from others.

The following list presents some no no's for road trips with your fuzzy:

- ✔ Don't leave your ferret in the vehicle unattended when the temperature is extreme.

- ✔ Don't leave him in the vehicle overnight while you snooze comfortably in a motel.

- Don't leave your ferret in his carrier with his harness or collar on.

- Don't pack your ferret in the trunk. Besides being cruel, this treatment can kill him if the temperature is unstable or carbon monoxide leaks in.

- Don't fasten your caged ferret with the rest of your luggage on top of your vehicle. (You'd think common sense would prevail here . . .)

- Don't travel with a very sick, old, or pregnant ferret. The stress of traveling may jeopardize the already stressed fuzzy's health.

Taking to the friendly skies

Some extra requirements and considerations go along with traveling by air with your fuzzy. In addition to packing the necessary goods (see the earlier section "Packing the necessities"), you need to work on a couple pre-flight tasks:

- **Check with the airline to find out about any specific rules and regulations regarding traveling with pets.** Since 9/11, traveling with animals has become more restricted. Every airline is different. Most no longer allow in-cabin pets, for instance. Although each airline has its own set of rules about flying with pets, you can be sure of the following typical requirements (be sure to follow all rules, including any that I may not cover here):

  • You must make a prior reservation for your pet. Be sure to confirm the arrangement a couple days before takeoff. (*Note:* Airlines issue an additional charge for in-cabin travel — that is, the under-the-seat method — as opposed to cargo.)

    I advise pet owners to always try to take their pets with them in the cabin whenever possible. If you must fly your ferret via cargo, check with different airlines to see whether you can check in your ferret at the ticket counter; if not, you may have to make an additional stop at the cargo terminal. Try to choose an airline that allows checking at the ticket counter so you decrease the odds of your ferret being sent on a different flight.

  • Your vet must issue a health certificate no more than ten days before takeoff. The certificate indicates that your ferret is current on vaccinations and is healthy and fit for travel. (Keep proof of his current rabies vaccination on hand, too.)

  • You must provide an airline-approved carrier. If traveling in-cabin, your fuzzy's carrier must be small enough to fit beneath a seat. Also, your pet must remain in the carrier while on board. (Always call the airline to clarify what its definition of an "airline-approved" carrier is.)

For health reasons, USDA regulations stipulate that airlines can't transport most animals via cargo during extreme hot or cold conditions. If you must transport your ferret through cargo, be sure to take the expected temperature into consideration.

✔ **Prepare your fuzzy's carrier for the airline regulations.** Most airlines have guidelines to make sure that your pet's carrier is properly labeled for identification. At minimum, you should do the following:

- Attach a label to the carrier that clearly lists your name, address, and phone number, along with the same information for an alternate contact from home.

- Attach another carrier label that states "LIVE ANIMALS," with an up arrow for any directionally challenged cargo handlers. Many airlines will supply these stickers if you ask for them.

- Include information about your final destination — such as city/state, hotel name, and phone number — in case you need to be contacted about your lost pet.

You also should make some food available to your ferret during flight, and his carrier should contain comfortable bedding — fuzzy snoozy stuff.

Some airlines require that multiple pets travel in separate carriers. Three ferrets may require three carriers, which means more money for traveling. In-cabin traveling isn't possible with three carriers, unless you have two other family members traveling.

Always book nonstop flights whenever possible when traveling with a fuzzy — especially if your ferret won't be traveling in-cabin with you. A change of planes is an added stress, and you run the risk of losing your furball in the shuffle between flights. Nonstop flights also are shorter, thus minimizing the length of an already wearisome situation. If your fuzzy must change planes, find out what precautions the airline will take to ensure a safe and timely transfer.

Going international

Unless you plan to travel abroad for a very long period of time, I suggest you leave fuzzy at home. I've heard of many international trips that went smoothly, but also of several that were nightmares for everyone involved. Traveling abroad with a ferret — whether you're moving permanently or vacationing — *can* go quite smoothly, though, if you follow the guidelines of the airline (see the preceding section) and destination country. With regard to the latter, be sure to research the following:

✔ Does the destination country have a quarantine requirement?

✔ Does your fuzzy's health certificate need to be translated into the appropriate language?

✔ Does the destination country require that you obtain an import license?

✔ Do you need to mail or fax the proper paperwork prior to you leaving the country? (Always keep copies on you.)

✔ What's required to get through customs with your pet? (Usually, the proper documents get you right through.)

Most international flights have layovers before passengers continue on to their planned destinations. Almost all airlines allow passengers to visit their pets during layovers — if they've made prior arrangements. During this time, check on how your fuzzy is doing, and give him water, food, or any necessary medication.

Leaving Your Furball in Good Hands

You've decided to leave your fuzzy at home, in the care of capable handlers? Aaaaah, now this is a vacation! As much as I love fuzzies, I just have to get away from time to time, with no one to take care of but myself. Don't get me wrong, I always buckle with anxiety over finding the right person to watch my babies or the right place to take them to. And, of course, while I'm supposed to be relaxing on vacation, I'm wondering how all my kids are managing without me. Usually, when I get home, I must face the reality that some other people can play Fuzzy Mom just as well as I do. It's quite an ego smasher.

The following sections outline your two best options for ferret care in your stead: sitters and boarding centers. Here you find out how to make sure that you leave your fuzzy in good hands so you can relax (or get your business done, as the case may be).

No matter who takes care of your ferret while you're gone, make sure that you educate him or her on ferret basics — especially those considerations unique to your fuzzy. For example, you should provide the following information:

✔ The phone number where you can be reached and the name of the people you'll be staying with

✔ An emergency phone number (or two) of someone close to home, such as a friend or relative

✔ Your veterinarian's phone number and address, as well as the emergency clinic's phone number and address

✔ A copy of your fuzzy's medical records in case he needs to go somewhere for an emergency

✔ A copy of your ferret's rabies vaccination certificate or tag

✔ An adequate supply of necessary medication, as well as exact instructions on how to medicate your ferret

   Be sure to demonstrate the procedure (especially dosing) before you leave.

✔ A written description of your ferret and his personality (attach photos next to each description if you have multiple ferrets to be extra helpful), including any necessary do's and don'ts

✔ An adequate supply of food, along with precise written and demonstrated instructions on feeding (especially if you use a varied diet or you have a ferret that requires assisted feedings)

✔ Detailed instructions on how to clean up after your ferret, supervise safe playtime, and watch for signs of illness or injury

✔ A copy of *Ferrets For Dummies,* 2nd Edition!

When you leave your ferret in the hands of others, risk is involved. Nothing is foolproof. All you can really do is prepare your ferret's temporary caretaker as best you can. The more you educate, the better off everyone will be. More often than not, you'll arrive home to a happy, healthy ferret that's just darn glad to see you.

Let the interviews begin: Finding the perfect pet sitter

Many people scoff at the idea of paying strangers to come to their homes to visit with and care for their ferrets while they're away. But more and more people are choosing this option as reliable pet sitters gain experience and good reputations. Often, pet sitters come highly recommended by previous clients, veterinarians, friends, or neighbors. And pet sitters aren't just for vacationers anymore. Many people who work long hours choose pet sitters to assist in the routine care of their fuzzies.

If at all possible, pick a pet sitter who comes highly recommended by someone you trust. Request and carefully check the sitter's references. This person will have a key to your house and access to your belongings, not to mention the responsibility of the complete care of your fuzzy. Trustworthiness, reliability, and honesty are all musts.

Here are a few of the many questions you may consider asking a potential pet sitter:

- ✔ How long have you been pet sitting?
- ✔ Do you belong to an association?
- ✔ Do you charge per day? Per ferret? Per visit?
- ✔ Have you ever worked with ferrets? How long? How many clients?
- ✔ What do you know about ferrets? Do you like them?
- ✔ Who's your current veterinarian?
- ✔ What's your procedure in case of an emergency?
- ✔ Do you have a backup sitter in case of an emergency?
- ✔ How often do you come to the house?
- ✔ What do you do if the client runs out of food/supplies?
- ✔ Do you medicate ferrets? Are you knowledgeable/experienced in medicating?

Depending on how much you're willing to spend, your pet sitter can make a daily visit or stop by several times throughout the day. The sitter may clean daily, every other day, or however often you request. The arrangements usually are based on a fee schedule. Discuss your options with the pet sitter before you leave, and get everything in writing.

You may choose a trusted neighbor or friend to be your pet sitter. With all the animals at my home/shelter, it takes several people to come in on a daily basis to help with upkeep when I go away. I feel like I'm leaving a 100-page manual behind, but I always feel better if I know the people who will be coming into my home. Keep in mind: A paid pet sitter usually does a good job because his or her reputation relies on it; a friend usually does a good job because a friendship depends on it. On the other hand, having friends watch your pets can be tricky and awkward if you're not happy with the job they did. Each situation is different. Go with the option that makes you feel most comfortable and works best for your ferret.

Many pet sitters are more familiar with dogs, cats, and birds. It's up to you in some cases to educate the pet sitter on how to properly care for fuzzies. A good pet sitter should be willing to stop over once or twice before you leave to get acquainted with your fuzzbutt and his routine.

Away to camp: Boarding your ferret

If you can't find a reliable person to care for your fuzzy in your own home, you should board him while you're away. You have several boarding options:

- Some veterinarians board pets for a fee.
- Some ferret shelters will watch your ferret temporarily for a fee if you promise to pick him up within a designated period of time.
- A friend may agree to board a fuzzy houseguest temporarily.
- Some professional boarding facilities house animals other than dogs and cats.

If you choose an unfamiliar person or place to watch your fuzzy, get references and check them out. Visit the home, shelter, clinic, or boarding facility to evaluate its overall condition. Don't leave your ferret there unless you're completely comfortable and have checked the cages for safety and security.

Make sure you provide emergency numbers, explicit instructions, and so on before you leave. Also, you may face a few more hurdles if you board your ferret while you're gone:

- You may have to transport the ferret's condo to the home or facility.
- You'll have to provide your ferret's food because his diet is likely to be unique.
- You may be required to provide proof of current vaccinations or a health certificate.

  If the person or boarding facility doesn't require proof of current vaccinations or a health certificate, I'd avoid that person or facility altogether. If the person or place doesn't ask you for proof of your pet's health, it probably doesn't ask other boarders for proof, either.

- You may have to take the time to educate the caretaker on ferret-proofing and care so that he or she can go the extra mile while you're away. Many facilities aren't properly prepared to allow your ferret his daily freedom and exercise. Same goes for the homes of friends — unless you take the time to educate them.

If you send your ferret to a boarding facility, shelter, or animal clinic, you run the risk of your fuzzy catching a disease or an illness from another animal. A friend's home isn't always safe, either — especially if the home contains other ferrets or animals. Make sure that your ferret is up to date on his shots (see Chapter 12).

Part IV

Tackling Your Ferret's Health Issues and Treatments

The 5th Wave   By Rich Tennant

"Let me guess — the vet's analysis of the ferret's fleas showed them to be of the 100 percent fresh ground Colombian decaf variety."

In this part . . .

As a ferret owner, you need to prepare for minor (and major) catastrophes by having the best vet picked out and your first-aid kit stocked because every pet owner will face an emergency at one time or another. This part has you covered. In addition, I cover the most common diseases and illnesses ferrets face and explain what to look for and when you need to seek expert advice. This part also takes an in-depth look at knowing when to say goodbye to your ferret and covers the things to expect after she's gone. You have so much more to think about than you may realize.

Note: This part isn't meant to take the place of a veterinarian! Some of the chapters here merely guide you through administering basic first aid until your ferret can see the vet.

Chapter 12

Setting Up Your Ferret's Health Plan: Vets and First-Aid Kits

In This Chapter

▶ Choosing a good ferret vet

▶ Taking your fuzzy for routine checkups and preventative vaccines

▶ Filling your fuzzy first-aid kit with the essentials

▶ Preparing for emergencies

*H*ealth issues are inevitable for most creatures, and ferrets are no different. That's why you won't find many unemployed veterinarians! You can go through loads of trouble to safeguard your ferret, but something's bound to happen anyway. Some mishaps are preventable; others are not. Often, what has you running for the first-aid kit is an illness or an age-related problem. Here's the bottom line: If the situation is something you can learn from, soak up the lesson so you can prevent the episode from happening again.

All ferret owners need to arm themselves with certain information and tools for those "just-in-case" situations. That's what this chapter is all about. I discuss the process you should go through to select a qualified veterinarian for your fuzzy. Finding a good ferret vet at the very last, desperate moment can be difficult — if not life threatening — so start right away. Even if you aren't facing an emergency, your ferret still needs routine checkups and vaccinations to ensure good health, so I cover these topics as well. I list the items that need to go into your very own fuzzy first-aid kit. Trust me, it's better to have an unopened bottle of Betadine solution sit for ages than to get caught in a situation where you desperately need it but don't have it. Finally, I show you how to prepare for emergency situations so you can care for your ferret in her most pressing time of need.

I get phone calls all the time from people asking me for advice about their sick ferrets. Remember: I'm not a vet, nor do I claim to be. You shouldn't use this book in lieu of a visit to your vet. I purposely leave out dosage recommendations in this book because every ferret is different and every situation is different. You shouldn't diagnose your ferret, or give her prescription or over-the-counter meds, without a veterinarian consult. Also, providing first aid for your ferret doesn't mean you can forego a trip to the vet if the situation warrants it. Use your best judgment, and keep your ferret's health and happiness in mind at all times.

Selecting Your Ferret's Veterinarian

At some point, all responsible pet owners venture into a veterinarian's office. A vet handles your pet's routine care, answers questions about concerns you have, handles neuters/spays, and addresses any unforeseen emergencies. Your vet will become a part of your life, so knowing what to look for is important when searching for your ferret's doctor.

In your search for a vet, you'll encounter fancy, expensive veterinary facilities, modest, single-doctor practices, and many that fall in between. Don't judge a vet's abilities on looks alone. Rely on a vet's reputation, recommendations you receive, and your gut feelings.

In the following sections, I cover some questions you should ask potential vets and the importance of swinging by for a visit before entrusting your pet to a particular vet or clinic. And because your vet can and should be your ally in your ferret's care, I outline the ways you can develop a good working relationship with the doctor you choose.

Word of mouth is a wonderful way to find a good ferret vet. Talk to other ferret owners you know or who you can locate through your breeder or other acquaintances. Ask where they take their babies and what kind of care they receive. Call your local ferret shelter to see who people there recommend. With so many ferret-crazed people out there today, you're bound to find a good veterinarian! (Chapter 10 covers more ways to network with ferret owners.)

Interviewing potential vets

In your search for a vet, don't be afraid to ask questions. Questions are your best tools. A good, professional veterinarian and staff will recognize your valid concerns and won't hesitate to answer your questions as completely as possible.

Begin by calling a clinic and asking whoever answers the phone if the doctor treats ferrets. Some don't and will refer you elsewhere. When you find a candidate that does treat fuzzies, do a little more investigation by asking the person on the phone if he has time to answer some questions. Better yet, leave a message for the vet to call you back. Make a list of the following questions and, of course, revise them depending on who you're talking to:

- How long have you been practicing ferret medicine? How many ferrets do you encounter in a typical day or week?

- Does your facility stock vaccinations for ferrets, such as the USDA-approved rabies vaccine?

- Is your facility capable of properly housing ferrets that may need to be hospitalized? Can you handle overnight stays? Emergencies?

- What are your fees for routine care, such as checkups and vaccinations?

- Do you perform routine surgeries (such as spaying and neutering) on ferrets? Do you have experience with the more difficult surgeries, such as splenectomies, adrenal surgery, or other tumor removals?

- Can you handle and treat common diseases of the ferret?

- How do you stay up to date on the latest developments in ferret medicine and surgical techniques? What continuing education do you participate in?

Don't forget to be kind and courteous during the questioning, and always remember to thank the vet when you're through! The answers the vet and his staff give, and the general tone with which they give them, should give you a sense of whether this office is ferret-friendly. Do you feel comfortable with this doctor? If you don't, chances are your ferret won't either.

Going for a visit

After you talk to a vet who seems qualified and meets your criteria, pay the doctor a visit. You want to see if this doctor is all he appeared to be on the phone or as described by other clients. First appearances usually are a good indication of how the vet runs his practice:

- Are the office and treatment areas clean? Do they smell clean?

- Were you greeted in a friendly manner by the staff?

- Are the exam tables sanitized after each use?

- Do technicians and vets wash their hands after handling animals?

If you already have your fuzzy, you can assume that she's probably due for a checkup. Now's a great time to see the potential vet in action with your furball:

- ✔ Does the vet talk to your ferret in a calming way?

- ✔ Does he handle your ferret with care and show genuine concern for both you and your pet?

  It's very important that your new veterinarian listen to and acknowledge your concerns. You're the ferret's caregiver. If you've had her for some time, you know what's normal for your ferret. A vet who doesn't listen to you and learn from you may be too presumptuous to give your ferret the care that she needs — especially in emergency situations.

- ✔ Does he explain what's being done in a concise and clear manner?

- ✔ Does he answer your questions in an understandable fashion?

- ✔ Does he seem rushed and preoccupied with other goings-on in the clinic, or is he focused on your pet?

Have you found a knowledgeable and caring vet who works in a clean, efficient, and friendly office? Congrats! If not, keep searching until you find a vet who meets all your requirements.

A good vet will have a network of other professionals he can rely on for support with difficult or unfamiliar cases. The willingness to reach out for help and to learn from others is a positive trait and one that should be looked for in a vet as well.

Developing a good working relationship

It's important that you maintain a comfortable and efficient working relationship with your vet built on trust and respect. Your veterinarian, like you, should have your pet's well-being at the top of his priority list. No one knows your pet like you do, and your vet will count on you to tell him when your ferret isn't quite herself. I can't tell you how many times I've brought in an animal that looked fine but that had a "look" about her that told me she wasn't quite right. In those cases, routine tests always revealed ailments. Your second sense is what can link you and your veterinarian in your quest to keep fuzzy healthy.

Here are some things you can do to develop a working relationship with your vet and make your interactions friendlier and more efficient:

✔ **Keep accurate records.** Take the guesswork out of communicating with your vet. Write down how your ferret is acting when you think she's sick. Record what supportive care you've provided and how she's responded. List any medications and dosages you've administered and record any improvements or setbacks that you observe. And with all these observations, make sure you include times in hours and minutes.

✔ **Know your animal.** If you can't bring your pet in to the office yourself, make sure you give the person who can your fuzzy's basic information. Vets get frustrated when people can't answer basic questions about the animals they bring in. Create a basic information card for your ferret that explains how you feed and house her, how you handle her, how she normally acts, what her issues are, and so on. Best-case scenario: Bring in your fuzzy yourself.

✔ **Do what the vet tells you to do.** Give medications on time and at the correct dosages, and give them for as long as you're supposed to. Just as important, follow through with phone calls to the vet to give him progress reports.

✔ **Ask questions.** Your vet's job is to not only treat your ferret, but also to answer your questions. Write down any questions you have before you get there and be ready to take notes when the vet is talking to you. Never feel foolish for asking questions!

✔ **Stay educated, but don't be demanding.** You can do research on current health issues and be willing to learn what you can about your ferret's health. It's great to learn these things, but don't force what you learn on your vet, for multiple reasons:

   • Your vet may already know the information.

   • It shows a lack of trust and respect for your vet.

   • Your vet will find it hard to work with a demanding know-it-all.

   Instead, work as a team and offer up what you've learned. Seek your vet's professional opinion by asking how what you've learned can fit into your pet's diagnosis or treatment plan.

✔ **Be honest.** Relationships are built on honesty and trust. Here are some specific situations when truth will keep your relationship with your vet strong:

   • A vet doesn't want to hear "She was fine this morning" while looking at an animal that's obviously been in distress for days. Your vet depends on you to tell him everything that's going on. Your honesty may mean the difference between an accurate diagnosis and a misdiagnosis.

- • Be upfront from the start about your financial situation. Don't make your vet guess what you can and can't afford to do for your pet. The cost of care is a sensitive area for both sides, so just be honest.

- • Tell the truth about how you've followed through on treatment plans. If you didn't do what the vet told you to do, tell him so he doesn't assume that his plan doesn't work.

✔ **Respect boundaries.** Never have another vet call yours to provide help without your vet's prior knowledge and permission. It not only catches your vet off guard, but also shows a lack of trust in and respect for him.

✔ **Report problems you have at the vet's office.** If you should have a problem at a veterinary practice for any reason, report it to the proper staff member immediately. Voice your concerns respectfully and calmly, and be prepared to reach some sort of solution. Leaving the office angry or upset doesn't satisfy anyone or leave room for improvement. Vets want to clear up problems in their offices and prevent them from happening in the future.

✔ **Leave your personal issues at home.** The vet's exam room or waiting room is no place to start arguing over whether your pet's treatment is worth X amount of dollars. Nor is it the place to announce to your spouse that you want a divorce. Come alone or agree ahead of time to table any heated topics you want to discuss.

The bottom line: Keeping the lines of communication open will help your vet give your ferret the best care he possibly can.

Putting Your Vet to Work with Vaccinations and Checkups

I'm one of those people who thinks that no matter where or when you get a new pet, you should make a visit to the vet within a day or two of her homecoming and continue with regular checkups from that point on. If you take your fuzzy in for a checkup every year (every six months for ferrets 3 years and older), your vet will be able to rule out any illnesses and vaccinate your ferret if she's due. I'm an advocate of regular vaccinations for pets. Vaccinations for ferrets keep your fuzzy safe from disease. Without them, ferrets are highly susceptible to canine distemper. They may also contract the rabies virus.

This section covers ferret checkups and vaccinations. You find out what your vet does for your kit (baby ferret) or for your grown-up fuzzy, and I let you know how to watch for warning signals that your fuzzy is having an allergic reaction to a vaccine or other medicine.

I can't advise you one way or another when it comes to vaccinating your pet. The only person who can help you make vaccination decisions is your veterinarian. He should know how your fuzzy tolerated vaccinations in the past and how she'll likely tolerate them in the future. Discuss the pros and cons of vaccinating your ferret with your vet. Together, based on your fuzzy's history and future concerns, you can come up with a workable plan to keep your ferret safe.

Kits — the office visit

Baby ferrets (kits) receive some protective antibodies from their mothers, but these eventually start to wear away in stages as the kits age. Therefore, you must vaccinate your kit to counteract this gradual loss of protection. When you get your fuzzy, schedule an appointment to get her shots. Most farm-raised babies receive their first ferret-approved, modified live canine distemper shots at 4 to 6 weeks old. Private breeders usually give the first shots at 6 to 8 weeks.

Confer with your vet and avoid using a distemper vaccine that has anything other than canine distemper vaccine in it — canine hepatitis, leptospirosis, parainfluenza, and so on, for instance. Ferrets shouldn't get vaccinated for these diseases. The USDA ferret-approved vaccine is strictly canine distemper.

Distemper vaccine

Depending on your veterinarian, your ferret kit may be vaccinated for canine distemper — depending on its age at the time of the visit — according to different vaccine protocols (see Chapter 15 for more on canine distemper):

- ✔ One vet may want to vaccinate for canine distemper at 8, 11, and 14 weeks of age.
- ✔ Other vets prefer to vaccinate at 8, 12, and 16 weeks of age.
- ✔ Ferrets over 16 weeks of age with unknown or no vaccination history only need two distemper shots, given three to four weeks apart. At this age, the ferrets receive the same protection as the kits that receive the full series of distemper vaccinations.

Although uncommon, some ferrets have allergic reactions to the distemper booster (see the later section "Recognizing allergic reactions" for the signs). The allergic reaction may happen only once, or it may happen repeatedly. Some reactions can be life-threatening. If your ferret has a history of allergic reactions, your vet may pretreat her with an antihistamine to offset any reaction. If your ferret has a history of severe, life-threatening allergic reactions to the distemper vaccine, and she's strictly an indoor pet with no contact with strange ferrets, you may want to consider skipping the distemper vaccine.

Rabies vaccine

The USDA ferret-approved rabies vaccine is a killed vaccine and is labeled for use after the age of 12 weeks. Some vets wait until the ferret is 14 to 18 weeks old, just in case the fuzzy's birthday got recorded incorrectly somewhere along the way. The rabies vaccine will prevent your ferret from contracting rabies if she becomes exposed. Additionally, the proof of rabies vaccination likely will keep her out of boiling water should she bite or scratch someone (see Chapter 3). Without this proof, she may be quarantined or possibly lose her life. For this reason, you can't skip the rabies booster for any reason.

The timing of the rabies shot can be an issue for you, your vet, and your ferret. Many experts believe that a ferret should receive the rabies and distemper shots at least two weeks apart to prevent any potential allergic reactions. Keep that suggestion in mind when scheduling your ferret's vaccinations.

Overall kit checkup

In addition to the vaccines, your vet should set up an appointment to perform an overall checkup. The checkup should include testing your kit for internal parasites. To complete the tests, the vet requires a poop sample on your first visit. This sample also gives your vet an idea of how your ferret's digestive tract is performing.

An overall checkup should, at the very least, include these other elements as well:

- ✔ Weighing your fuzzy
- ✔ Listening to her heart and lungs
- ✔ Feeling her abdomen
- ✔ Checking her skin for external parasites and any abnormalities
- ✔ Checking her eyes, ears, and teeth

Adolescents and adults — the office visit

If you adopt an adult fuzzy, you don't need to make four or five trips to the vet like you would with a kit, but you do need to make at least two. Your ferret should receive a canine distemper shot along with her initial physical exam (see the previous section for explanations of these processes).

You should bring your ferret back about three weeks later for a second distemper shot as well as a rabies shot (assuming she's older than 3 months). Often, a vet will have you come in a third time for the rabies shot instead of giving it along with the final distemper shot to minimize the chance of a bad reaction. You can discuss this important option with your vet and come to a decision.

If you adopt an adult ferret with a questionable background, vaccinate her just in case. Better safe than sorry!

Checkups for adult ferrets are a little more complicated. In addition to performing annual exams like a ferret kit would receive, your vet should do some extra palpating (touchy-feely stuff) to rule out enlarged organs (particularly the spleen) or suspicious lumps. Middle-aged ferrets, or those 3 years and older, are at an increased risk for disease and should have routine exams every six months. Disease can spread rapidly, so early detection and intervention are imperative. It's also recommended that your vet test blood glucose every six months, so speak to him about this. Other blood testing and X-rays for heart disease and so on can be done on a yearly basis.

Don't forget to bring a morsel of poop to your fuzzy's physical exam; you'll make your vet's day, and he'll be able to rule out parasites.

During your initial appointments with the vet, broach the topic of the dreaded heartworm disease. If you're a responsible dog owner, you should already know about it. Just like dogs and cats, ferrets are susceptible to heartworm, a mosquito-delivered disease. Even if you don't take your ferret outside, she isn't bulletproof, because mosquitoes can get into your house. For more information on heartworm — including recognizing its symptoms and treating it — head to Chapter 15.

Recognizing allergic reactions

Ferrets can have a reaction to the vaccinations given by veterinarians. This allergic reaction, called *anaphylaxis,* almost always occurs within 30 minutes of the vaccination injection, but it can occur up to 24 hours later. Anaphylaxis isn't very common; it can present itself as either a slight reaction or, at worst, a life-threatening condition.

The first 24 hours after the vaccination is the most crucial period; after that, your fuzzy should be in the clear. You need to remain vigilant during the initial period as you watch for signs of a bad reaction. Here are the signs of anaphylaxis:

✔ Swelling around the eyes or nose

A tiny lump where the needle went in isn't a reaction; a tiny lump is very common.

✔ Vomiting

✔ Diarrhea (may be bloody)

✔ Seizures

✔ Lethargy

Usually, another sign should accompany the lethargy because a trip to the vet can be exhausting for your fuzzy.

✔ Pale mucous membranes (the tissue around the eyes or the gums)

A ferret that exhibits signs of anaphylaxis may not have a reaction to every single shot. Likewise, just because your ferret hasn't shown signs of anaphylaxis before doesn't mean that she never will.

I recommend that you wait around the clinic during the immediate waiting period (the first 30 minutes after the vaccine) just to be safe. It's important to immediately treat a fuzzy that's suffering from anaphylaxis. If you're already home when you notice the signs, pack right up and head back to the vet. On the way, keep your ferret warm (she may be experiencing the beginning signs of shock).

To treat anaphylaxis, your vet will most likely give your fuzzy an injection (yes, another one!) of an antihistamine and/or cortisone. Some vets also administer fluids. (*Note:* Some vets like to pretreat a ferret with a history of vaccination allergy with this medicine just to be on the safe side.) This course of action treats the allergic reaction and heads off the shock, which can be deadlier to your ferret than the allergic reaction itself.

Stocking Your Ferret First-Aid Kit

Perhaps you've already equipped your household with a first-aid kit for human use. A lot of what you put in your own first-aid kit also is useful for treating ferrets, but I recommend that you put together a first-aid kit strictly for your little fuzzy.

Always consult your vet before including (and using) any over-the-counter products, medications, or supplements in your fuzzy first-aid kit. Using some common items to treat your ferret may actually aggravate certain illnesses or diseases. Also, you need to get the proper dosage amounts from your vet for treatments. It's easy to overdose a ferret on medication.

Every ferret first-aid kit should include the following items (***Note:*** If you use something from the kit, be sure to replace it as soon as possible):

✔ **Emergency phone numbers:**

- Your veterinarian's number

- The number to a 24-hour emergency clinic

- The number for the National Animal Poison Control Center

    To reach the National Animal Poison Control Center, you can call 888-426-4435. This service costs $55 per case — credit cards only.

✔ **Health records (include the following for each of your ferrets):**

- General health records with a corresponding identification photo of the ferret

- Rabies certificates

- A list of prescription medications your ferret is currently taking

✔ **Foodstuffs:**

- Jars of meat baby food — chicken or lamb (for the sick kid)

- Light Karo syrup or Nutri-Cal (for a quick calorie boost)

- Pedialyte or Gatorade (to rehydrate a dehydrated ferret)

- A can of prescription feline A/D, which you can get from your vet (easily digested food for the sicky)

- Oxbow Carnivore Care (an excellent, complete supplement)

- Canola or olive oil (may help to move bad stuff through)

- Royal Canin canned diet (for sick ferrets needing good nutrition)

- Feline hairball laxative or preventive

All ferret owners should know about Carnivore Care, which is available from Oxbow Pet Products. This highly palatable nutritional supplement is made with easily digestible protein that's suitable for carnivores such as ferrets. The supplement offers complete nutrition to ferrets with reduced appetites. For more information on this product, head to the Web site www.oxbowhay.com; you can call 800-249-0366 to order it (you can't order online). You must provide your veterinarian's information when ordering this product (see Chapter 8 for more on diet).

I've listed many different meat sources for your first-aid kit, but you don't have to stock them all. You can stock one or stock all. It's a personal preference. You may want to start off by including them all in case you get a sick ferret that turns out to be a picky eater. But if you decide to stick with one, Carnivore Care is my first choice.

✔ **Cleaning solutions:**

- Betadine solution (for cleaning cuts)

- Nolvasan (for cleaning cuts)

  You can sometimes find this as an ear cleaner.

- Ear cleanser (for routine grooming)

- Eye wash/rinse (for flushing foreign bodies)

- Sterile saline solution (for flushing wounds)

✔ **Bandages and wraps:**

- Gauze pads

- Gauze wrap

- Washcloths

- Vet wrap (self-sticking variety — you can find this in drug stores in the bandage section)

- Adhesive bandage tape (cloth tape works the best)

✔ **Other health aids:**

- Styptic powder or beeswax (for bleeding nails)

- Antibiotic ointment (for soothing and protecting cuts and scrapes; Neosporin works well)

- Petroleum jelly (to help move a blockage and for lubricating a thermometer)

- Kaopectate or Pepto-Bismol (for diarrhea and soothing the tummy)

- Ferretone/Linatone (for mixing with medicine that tastes like you-know-what)

- Pediatric Liquid Benadryl (for counteracting allergic reactions; see the section "Recognizing allergic reactions")

Tylenol (acetaminophen) is extremely toxic to ferrets even in very low doses. The liver metabolizes the medicine, and it will send your ferret into liver failure quickly, eventually killing your fuzzy. Many over-the-counter medicines contain acetaminophen. Therefore, don't use any over-the-counter products without your vet's guidance and approval. You can prevent these types of fatal mistakes.

Bene-Bac is one of the most widely recommended items when it comes to ferret first-aid kits, because it's designed to replace beneficial bacteria in the digestive tract after illness or diarrhea. What you may not know, however, is that it doesn't work for obligate carnivores, such as ferrets. The bacteria contained in Bene-Bac is made for omnivores and some herbivores. Using Bene-Bac won't hurt your ferret, but it won't help, either; it only helps you feel better!

✔ **Miscellaneous items:**

- Heating pad (to help maintain a young or sick ferret's body temperature)
- Chemical heating pack (portable heat for the young or sick ferret)
- Nail clippers
- Eye droppers
- Tweezers (to remove foreign bodies)
- Cotton balls and cotton swabs
- Ice pack (to reduce swelling or slow down bleeding)
- Rubber or latex gloves
- Scissors
- Pen light (to help you see wounds and foreign bodies)
- Pill crusher
- Rectal thermometer

  The normal temperature for a ferret is about 102° Fahrenheit.

- Tongue depressors or popsicle sticks (for immobilizing injured limbs)
- Baby wipes (for general cleanup duties)

I also suggest that, whenever possible, you bring your first-aid kit to your ferret, as opposed to bringing your injured ferret to the first-aid kit. Make this easier by storing your first-aid supplies in a convenient and portable case. Fishing-tackle boxes and professional make-up boxes work great. You can also do a lot with Tupperware! Get one large bin and keep your supplies organized and labeled in smaller containers within that bin. Keep your first-aid case in a convenient and easy-to-reach location.

Ensuring Emergency Preparedness

Whether you've lived through them or have only heard about them, you know that real pet emergencies take place all the time. It seems like you hear more and more about disasters striking, leaving families and their pets with few options and nowhere to go. Disasters come in all shapes and sizes: floods, earthquakes, fires, hurricanes, tornadoes, and more.

Have you prepared your family and fuzzies to escape an emergency? Are you prepared to care for your pets during an emergency? Preparing for the collection and evacuation of your ferrets takes time, thought, and practice. Using the information in the following sections, you can take action and come up with a plan that best suits your situation.

The basic (quick) evacuation kit

The basic evacuation kit is for an emergency that allows for a small window of time to evacuate. Your only pet-related goal during a serious emergency is to get your ferret out quickly and safely. That's it. Anything else is just icing on the cake — and potentially dangerous icing at that.

The basic evacuation kit I suggest you put together is based on that one goal, making it quite simple. Here's what you need in this kit:

- A flashlight (in case the lights go out)
- A fabric bag (a thick pillowcase or something stronger to actually hold your ferrets in)
- A strong piece of rope (to tie the bag of ferrets shut; it should be about 2 feet)
- A small fire extinguisher (to put out any small fires you encounter)
- A police whistle, which you can purchase at an Army surplus store, or something equally loud and piercing (to call your ferrets)

The kit may seem too simple, but the purpose is to remain safe and get out fast. With this in mind, make sure you store the kit in a handy container and locate it in a convenient place.

Most ferret owners have more than one ferret. Actually, many have an abundance of ferrets! For every four ferrets you have, you need to pack one fabric bag and one piece of rope. In a true get-out-fast-or-else emergency, one bag may do fine for up to six or seven ferrets, but the strength of the bag may decrease with each ferret you put inside.

Collecting and evacuating your fuzzy

The number-one rule in an emergency is to stay calm, because you know your ferret won't. When an emergency strikes, pick up your ferret and toss her in a sack. When you're done with the sack, tie it off securely with the rope. When your ferret is safe and secure, leave the house. You've done your job.

If you have more than one fuzzy, an emergency situation is no time to worry about who gets along with whom. Pick up your ferrets and toss them in the sack. After you tie it off securely with the rope, get the heck out of there.

I'm in no way advocating that you should put your own life at risk to save the life of your pet. Trained professionals will come to the scene of an emergency to help you and your pet in times of crisis. Losing a pet is heartbreaking, but losing your life while trying to save a pet is catastrophic for many.

The deluxe (and orderly) evacuation kit

The basic evacuation kit is for a serious emergency that calls for quick action. The deluxe evacuation kit, on the other hand, is for an emergency that you know is coming, but that you have time to plan for. For example, a forest fire that's slowly making its way toward your home. Or a hurricane that's predicted to hit land in the next 24 hours. These are tragedies that you can prepare for with a little window of time. The deluxe kit is designed to be picked up and put in a car, taking up as little space as possible. Like the ferret first-aid kit and the basic evacuation kit (see earlier sections in this chapter), you should keep the deluxe kit in an area that's easily accessible and in a case that's ready to go.

In addition to the materials I mention for the basic kit, the deluxe kit should contain the following items; it may seem like a lot, but after you gather it up, you'll be done, and hopefully you'll never have to use the kit:

✔ **Foodstuffs:**

- Jars of chicken baby food
- At least a week's supply of your ferret's food, kept in a re-sealable container (swap out for fresh food regularly, if possible)
- Bottled water
- Pedialyte

✔ **A basic first-aid kit:**

- Betadine/iodine solution
- Gauze pads/wrap
- Adhesive tape
- Antibiotic cream/ointment
- Ferretone
- Heating pad or chemical heat packs

- Tweezers
- Cotton swabs
- Scissors
- Latex gloves
- Popsicle sticks
- Baby wipes
- Sanitizing gel
- Eye dropper
- A week's supply of medication (if necessary)

✔ **Restraint and identification:**

- Leash and harness with ID tag for each ferret
- Carrier or cage large enough for your ferret to move around in
- Copy of medical and up-to-date vaccination records
- Adoption/registration papers or other proof of ownership (including microchip number)
- Ferret identification card, which includes a recent photo, a written physical description (including tattoos and medical conditions), and a behavioral description
- An ID card with your name, address, phone number(s), and veterinarian's phone number
- Pre-planned emergency contact lists (veterinarians, family, and friends)
- Leather gloves (in case your ferret gets overly excited or scared and acts out in aggression)

✔ **Miscellaneous items:**

- Bedding (hammock, snooze sack)
- Hanging water bottle
- Non-tippable bowls
- Spoons
- Small garbage bags
- Dish soap
- Disposable litter tray
- Paper towels

Chapter 13

Helping Your Hurt Ferret: First-Aid Basics

In This Chapter

▶ Previewing a ferret's minor afflictions

▶ Acting in the event of an emergency

▶ Caring for your fuzzy in-house

▶ Arranging a room for your sick ferret

▶ Getting your sick ferret to eat

*Y*ou must face the facts: Your little ferret friend is (or will be) a trouble magnet. No matter how much you love him or how much money you spend on preventive care, your ferret will eventually test your first-aid knowledge and your ability to work under severe emotional duress. Even if you keep your ferret confined to a cage all day and night (Caution: The ferret patrol and I will hunt you down and pummel you if you do!), you'll still have a misfortune here or there. And even the sweetest, most innocent ferret may have a mishap through no fault of his own.

This chapter covers the process of providing immediate first aid. I discuss how to identify and fix an easy problem and how to control a difficult one until your fuzzy can receive care from a medical professional. I explain how you can manage your fuzzy's pain during injury or illness situations. And I go through the steps you can take during your ferret's recovery to keep him comfortable and nourished. (The other chapters in Part IV explain the serious diseases and illnesses you may come across and how you can treat them.)

Behaviors You Usually Don't Need to Worry About

You'll be happy to read that some funky ferret behaviors are normal. Like a grown man scratching his belly and dealing with indigestion after Thanksgiving dinner and then falling asleep during a football game, ferrets have a few peculiar behaviors that may startle you at first. Don't be alarmed. Many of the behaviors I list in the following sections often are harmless, and with the information here, you'll be prepared to deal with them and even predict their onset.

Shivering

Ferrets shiver for many reasons, but most of the reasons are simple and harmless. All ferrets shiver to raise their body temperature, which is necessary after sleeping more than half the day away! Shivering is a natural and effective temperature-raising method. Many also shiver when being scruffed. You may want to give a little bottom support to your shivering fuzzy in a scruffing situation (see Chapter 7). Frightened ferrets rarely shiver, but excited ferrets often do. If you suspect that your ferret's shivering is due to something other than these reasons, consult your veterinarian (for info on finding a qualified vet, refer to Chapter 12).

Itching and scratching

Ferrets are itchy critters, plain and simple. They'll sometimes awaken from a deep sleep just to feverishly scratch a sudden itch, and then they'll roll over and fall back to sleep. Or they'll stop in the middle of a mad dash across the room to scratch an itch. If you watch your ferret itch and scratch long enough, you'll begin to itch and scratch, too, because it makes most people paranoid about fleas. But scratching often is harmless and mainly annoying for the fuzzy.

If you do notice reddened areas, bumps, sores, or missing fur, explore your ferret's environment, such as his bedding and what it was last washed in. Consider that skin tends to dry out a little during the colder months. And although uncommon, fuzzies can have allergies. Sometimes, too much scratching can lead to raw spots that you may need to treat topically. If this is the case, see your vet. If you've ruled out fleas and no fur is missing, you can probably chalk up the scratching to a typical ferret quirk.

Yawning

Yawning is such a common ferret quirk that ferret enthusiasts have yawning contests (see Chapter 10)! I don't know why furkids yawn, but they do, and they do so frequently. Maybe it has something to do with how much sleep ferrets indulge in. Plus, scruffed ferrets are particularly vulnerable to yawning attacks. Although the effect of all the yawns seems nonexistent, people watching can be enticed into their own yawning attacks. I yawn as I write this!

Excessive sleeping

Sleeping excessively is common in ferrets, so don't take it as a sign that you're a complete bore. Sometimes, ferrets can sleep so hard that it appears they're in a coma or even dead. The fuzzies are warm and breathing, but they just won't wake up!

If you're a concerned mom or dad and insist on making sure that fuzzball is alive, you can try a few proven techniques. Start with the first and continue through the list:

1. **Lift him up and call his name loudly.**

2. **Give his back or belly a few good rubs, but don't shake him violently.**

3. **Scratch him between the ears.**

4. **Scruff (see Chapter 7) and wiggle him a bit if he still hasn't responded.**

5. **Put a dab of his favorite treat on his nose (see Chapter 8). The smell should get his little brain going; if not, he's probably sick.**

6. **As a last resort, you can rub a small amount of Nutri-Cal or Karo syrup on his gums.**

Usually, this deep sleep (referred to as SND [Sleeping Not Dead]) is normal. When the ferret finally raises an eyelid to inspect the rude gate-crasher, you can rest assured that he's okay. You can play with the fuzzy a bit if you still feel the need to reassure yourself. It's taken almost a full minute to wake up one or two of my guys on some occasions, and it still scares the beans out of me. If an SND situation occurs frequently with the same ferret, a trip to the vet may be a wise idea. (Chapter 10 discusses enrichment, which may lessen the amount of sleep your fuzzy needs, along with the proper diet [see Chapter 8].)

Although ferrets do sleep quite a bit, and some even enter the deep SND mode, be aware of sudden changes in your furkid's sleeping patterns. If he starts to sleep more often than usual, he may be giving you a sign of an underlying medical condition. Don't ignore sudden changes in behavior, because he may require immediate medical attention.

Sneezing, hiccuping, and coughing

With all the maladies fuzzies can get, you'd think sneezing, coughing, and hiccuping would be some more things to worry about. Not so. These conditions often are harmless and even useful for the fuzzy. Fuzzballs get around by sense of smell. If you watch closely, you'll see that your exploring ferret has his nose to the ground almost all the time. In the process, he's inhaling everything from dust bunnies to carpet fibers. He's bound to snort up bits and pieces of junk, and sneezing is the only way to clear his nose of it. When the sneezing attack is over, it's nose to the ground again.

Ferrets sometimes cough or hack as though they have something stuck in their throats. It's common and, more often than not, harmless. Coughing usually is a sign of a minor irritation to the throat or the reaction to a piece of kibble the fuzzy swallowed too quickly. If the coughing persists, though, contact your vet. Persistent coughing can also be a sign of several illnesses, including cardiomyopathy, so take note of how much coughing your fuzzy does and take him to see the vet. Better safe than sorry.

Hiccuping is a common and harmless fuzzy condition that results from the spasming of the ferret's diaphragm. In ferrets, hiccuping seems random and more of a bother to them than a condition to worry about. In humans, hiccuping often is a result of too much beer! Try giving your ferret a little lick of Ferretone or Nutri-Cal to try to shorten the duration of the hiccuping.

Butt dragging

The skid marks your ferret leaves behind after he uses the bathroom are more than pretty decorations. They're ferret proclamations! Ferrets like to use butt dragging to tell other animals, including humans, where they've been and what their territorial boundaries are. Although the butt dragging may not actually leave a visual trail, you can bet your bottom dollar that he's left a scent behind. Not to worry; you may not notice the smell at all, but other ferrets and animals will smell it loud and clear.

A suckler

Some fuzzies, as with many cats and kittens, find comfort in sucking on something soft — especially when they're falling asleep. (After all, their thumbs have sharp nails at the end.) This sucking behavior is common in animals that are separated from their mothers at an early age.

Some ferrets view the ears of other ferrets as pacifiers. If the recipient of the ear sucking doesn't mind, and his ear doesn't become raw and irritated, you can consider the sucking cute and not a problem. You should, however, offer an alternative, such as a safe baby toy.

Quick FAQS on healthy ferrets

Vets talk about the following ferret basics all the time, so get to know them to keep up with the conversation — at least a little:

✔ Normal body temperature: 100–103°F (37.8–39.4°C), with 101.9°F as the average

✔ Normal heart rate: 200 to 400 beats per minute

✔ Normal respiration: 33 to 36 breaths per minute

If your fuzzy's butt dragging seems unusually lengthy or if he does it more and more frequently, you can have your vet check him for parasites or other conditions that may be causing discomfort.

Because most ferrets in the United States are descented, they don't leave much of a scent, but they still display the behavior. These ferrets are primarily trying to leave anal gland scent, not feces. Still, the scent trail is there. After all, a butt's a butt.

Drinking urine

No one knows for sure why some adorable little fuzzies engage in the obnoxious practice of urine drinking. Maybe they just want to gross us humans out. It may be a sexual behavior. Some fuzzy experts believe that drinking urine is just another way for a thirsty ferret to consume liquid. If you want to curtail the activity, make sure that enough water is always available.

Honestly, although it seems disgusting to us, urine drinking is common for a ferret. It's a harmless act, unlike drinking too much beer, because urine is sterile, so ferrets aren't consuming a bunch of bacteria.

Pain Management and Care

Ferrets are quite the troopers! Their little bodies go through so much, and they put up a tremendous fight to live during even the most difficult of times. But ferrets, like so many other animals, are stoic creatures. They hide their pain in order to hide their "weaknesses," which would surely be death sentences in the wild. But if you know your ferret well (and make an effort to from the very first day you get him), you'll be able to tell that he's in pain, and there's no reason at all he needs to live that way.

Determining if your ferret is in pain

Couple the warning signs in the following list with your intimate knowledge of your fuzzy (or your fledgling knowledge) to tell if your ferret is in pain:

- **Facial expression:** Squinting, muscles twitching on the top of his head, tooth grinding, dull eyes

- **Appetite:** Reduced or absent appetite, dropping food from the mouth, difficulty swallowing, standing over food dish but not eating, selecting only soft foods

- **Posture:** Tucked abdomen, lying on side with no ability to get up, inability to stretch out or curl up

- **Activity:** Gait abnormalities (limping, holding limbs up, or dragging), restricted movement, trembling

- **Grooming:** Failure to groom himself, poor coat appearance, excessive licking or scratching

- **Self-awareness:** Protecting a body area, licking or chewing a body area

- **Vocalization:** Crying or moaning periodically, vocalizing when defecating, urinating, or moving

- **Attitude:** Unusual aggression, hiding more than usual, seeking comfort, bristling tail with depressed behavior, dull or uninterested attitude toward surroundings

- **Response to being touched:** Protective, vocalizing, escaping, biting

Some of the signs and behaviors in the previous list, while generally associated with pain, aren't solely indicators of pain. Some can be signs of other conditions. It all depends on your fuzzy. Pain can elicit extreme behaviors at opposite ends of the spectrum. Your ferret's pain may cause him to act unusually needy and seek comfort from you. Another ferret in pain may hide and isolate himself more than usual. No matter what, if any of the listed signs are present, you can assume that something abnormal is going on. A call and visit to your vet are warranted.

Caring for a ferret in pain

You have many options to manage your ferret's pain, and fortunately the list is growing. Managing pain will keep your ferret comfortable and help him recover from surgery, illness, or injury. Pain management during and after surgery or for an injury or chronic illness should always be a part of routine supportive care. Speak to your vet about it to set up a pain management regimen.

You'll know the pain management regimen you and your vet have chosen is working when the signs of pain begin to alleviate and your ferret starts to act more like himself. If, however, the signs continue or worsen, you need to contact your vet immediately to discuss a change of plans.

The following list presents some of the most common pain medications currently used on ferrets:

✔ **OPIOIDS:** Examples include buprenorphine, butorphanol, hydromorphone, and oxymorphone, and all are injections. These drugs are very effective for moderate to severe acute, post-surgical, or traumatic pain. They have a wide range of length of effectiveness, depending on which drug is used. Mild to profound sedation may accompany the treatment — the latter being a benefit if the pain is severe or a hindrance if you want to assess the level of pain. These drugs aren't good for chronic pain.

✔ **NSAIDs (Non-Steroidal Anti-Inflammatory Drugs):** Examples include meloxicam, carprofen, ketoprofen, ibuprofen, and aspirin. These oral medications have anti-inflammatory, pain-reducing, and fever-reducing properties. They can be effective for some types of acute and chronic pain. NSAIDs aren't recommended for ferrets that are pregnant, in shock, have stomach ulcers, or have kidney or liver disease. NSAIDs may also worsen gastritis.

✔ **Local anesthetics:** Examples include lidocaine and bupivicaine. Vets use these drugs during surgery at the incision site to help block localized pain. Local anesthetics are short-term pain killers administered by injection only.

Tylenol (acetaminophen) is extremely toxic to your ferret, even in very low doses. It's metabolized by the liver and will send your ferret reeling into liver failure quickly before killing him.

Many fuzzy owners and vets explore alternative pain-management techniques, such as the following:

✔ Acupuncture, which can be very effective at managing certain types of pain

✔ Chiropractic care, which is limited to managing pain of the musculoskeletal system

✔ Herbal/homeopathic care, which may reduce some pain and anxiety. (***Note:*** This option should be used only under the guidance of a veterinary professional who's familiar with the use of herbal/homeopathic medicine and its side effects.)

Use these options only under the direction and with the guidance of your trusted veterinarian (see Chapter 12).

Setting Up Fuzzy's Home Hospital Room

You can do non-medical things right at home to help alleviate anxiety and pain in your ferret. One of the most important parts of your ferret's treatment occurs during aftercare, which is where most of the problems begin and end. You can't become lax when your ferret needs special care that's critical to his health. Whether your ferret is injured, sick, recovering from surgery, or just plain elderly, you need to give special attention to the old and infirmed. Under the direction of your vet, you need to give medication exactly as prescribed, provide assisted feedings routinely, administer fluids when necessary, and so on.

And you have another critical step to take to get your ferret back to his old self: Make sure he has private space to which he can retreat:

- ✔ House him comfortably and in a quiet area.
- ✔ Be sure that no other ferrets, pets, or children can bother him.
- ✔ Keep his handling to a minimum, and keep it slow and easy.

Most post-surgical, critically ill, elderly, or injured ferrets have limited mobility or are prescribed restricted mobility by vets. The latter is for their safety while they heal and recover. Regardless of what your ferret's story is, he needs a hospital cage setup. Here's what you'll need:

- ✔ **One cage approximately 2.5'-wide x 2'-deep x 2'-tall**

  The cage should have easy access to move in and out and have a big enough spot for a small litter box. It can have a small ramp leading to a low shelf, but a single story is preferable (see Chapter 5).

- ✔ **One small litter box**
- ✔ **Litter or shredded newspaper (for ferrets with incisions)**
- ✔ **A water bottle or water bowl**

  Use a water bottle if your ferret is drinking on his own; a water bowl if he's too weak to use a bottle.

- ✔ **Food dish (if he's eating on his own)**
- ✔ **Plenty of fluffy bedding**
- ✔ **His favorite toys**

Your ferret needs to feel safe and comfortable, but you need to be able to check up on him often and provide him with the special one-on-one care he needs. The whole point of the hospital setup is to provide a safe recuperating spot for your ferret that's also convenient enough for you to do what you need to for your ferret. You also want to be able to get to your ferret quickly in case he's in distress. Therefore, forego putting any kind of nest box in the hospital cage. A nice pile of fluffy bedding is all that he needs for now.

To help with your fuzzy's need for security and sleep, cover the recovery cage with a towel or blanket. This will also help keep out drafts.

Feeding the Sick or Debilitated Ferret

Most ferret owners will, at some point, need to assist their ferrets when it comes to eating so that they continue to meet their nutritional and water-intake requirements (see Chapter 8). Your ferret may require supplemental feedings if he's sick or injured, old, has dental problems, or is recovering from surgery. No matter the reason, you need to follow through on assisted feeding four to six times a day if your fuzzy isn't eating on his own. The following sections give you the recipe so you can create a meal that will help heal or sustain your ferret and the method for feeding your needy fuzzy safely and effectively.

The Assist Feed Recipe: Better than Mom's chicken soup

You need to make a special food mixture to feed your sick or debilitated ferret. The recipe I present in this section has been called many silly names that have nothing to do with ferrets. For our purposes, I'll simply call the recipe the *Assist Feed Recipe* and hope it catches on. It's relatively simple to make. The only requirements are that the concoction must be soft, easy to digest, full of energy-boosting calories, healthy, and yummy enough to make your ferret forget about resisting it.

You have several options when it comes to making the Assist Feed Recipe. Susan Brown, DVM, and co-author of *Essentials of Ferrets: A Guide for Practitioners* (American Animal Hospital Association), offers the following "either or" suggestions:

1. **Mix up Carnivore Care as directed.**

   Highly digestible protein sources make Carnivore Care an ideal choice when providing nutrition to ferrets that aren't eating or need supplemental feedings. It's made by Oxbow Company and can be purchased from your vet or directly from the company. You should have a small supply of this in your ferret first-aid kit (see Chapter 12). If you don't, before you pick up the Carnivore Care, you can substitute your ferret's favorite high-quality kibble and grind it up, mixing it with water.

or

2. **Mix Carnivore Care with Ensure or Resource 2.0 rather than water to increase calories and palatability.**

   You may need to add a smidge of water to thin the mixture a little.

or

3. **Mix the Carnivore Care as directed and mix in canned Science Diet A/D (no more than 50 percent of the total volume) to increase the fat and flavor.**

or

4. **Mix the Carnivore Care as directed and add some meat baby food (no more than 25 percent of the total volume) to put in more fat and flavor.**

   Baby food is the *least* complete thing you can feed your ferret for the long term.

or

5. **Mix the Carnivore Care as directed and add an all-meat canned cat food (no more than 25 percent of the total volume) for more fat and flavor.**

If your ferret is extra picky, you can also try a 50/50 mixture of kibble and Carnivore Care. The key is to find a flavor that's palatable to your ferret so that he wants to eat the food. As long as your main ingredient (good high-quality protein, low-carb kibble, or Carnivore Care) is adequate, you can experiment with other ingredients.

Mix the batch up until it's smooth and creamy. If you're a fuzzy chef extraordinaire, your ferret will lick your concoction right from the spoon or bowl with little hesitation. If you're a disaster in the kitchen, you may have to use a feeding syringe to get the stuff into his mouth. Expect a little ptooeying in this case. And see the next section for suggestions on how best — and how often — to get the food down.

Susan Brown would like me to give you the following advice: "Any of these supplements, even A/D alone or baby food alone, is fine for the short term (one week or less) or supplementing a ferret that is also still eating some on his own. However, if you are feeding the ferret all of the food he's getting and it's going to be long term, I would always opt for Carnivore Care alone or in some combination. If the ferret is very thin, you can use combo #2 or #3 to beef him up. You can reduce the amount of Resource/Ensure or A/D if the ferret gets overweight and go back to just Carnivore Care alone."

Many published supplemental feeding recipes contain ingredients that aren't good for ferrets. Please stay away from the following items in particular:

✔ Sugary items (such as honey, corn syrup, maple syrup, or Nutri-Cal)

✔ Fruit (dried or otherwise)

✔ Grains

✔ Vegetables

If you think about it, your ferret can only fit so much into his stomach. You can't waste that space on low-calorie, hard-to-digest, non-dense foods. Your fuzzy should be eating quality high-calorie food. Additionally, high-sugar foods are tough on his pancreas and cause his blood-sugar levels to rise and fall rapidly. You don't want to add to your fuzzy's health problems!

The feeding method: Just as effective as the airplane into the mouth

The manner in which you feed your fuzzy his Assist Feed Recipe depends on his level of strength and willingness to eat:

✔ **If your ferret is strong enough** and finds the Assist Feed Recipe appetizing, you can present it to him in a shallow bowl or allow him to lick it one spoonful at a time. He may even prefer to lick the recipe off your finger. No matter what, don't just place him in a cage with the bowl and walk away. Watch him and make sure that he's doing more eating than spreading it around his cage or other area. Also, if he has cagemates, be aware that they'll probably try to get to the food before he gets his share.

✔ **If your ferret isn't strong enough** to feed himself, you'll have to feed him. If you do need to force feed, your first job is to take the word "force" out of your vocabulary. It's bad enough that the poor guy is sick. Don't make eating an unpleasant experience as well. (From here on out, I'll refer to this process as *assist feeding,* because that's really what you're doing.)

You can obtain a feeding syringe (it has no needle at the end) from your vet, or you can use an eyedropper (plastic, not glass) to assist feed your fuzzy. (**Note:** Eyedroppers can be a bit more time-consuming because they're smaller.) Suck up the formula into the syringe and squeeze a small amount into the corner of your ferret's mouth. He may crinkle up his nose and eyes with displeasure or surprise, but don't give up until you know he's had enough. Take the time to wipe his mouth and, if needed, your face, should the stuff go airborne during a violent ptooeying!

Way too often, fuzzy humans are in a hurry to feed their sick babies. Forcing large amounts of food into a ferret's mouth can cause him to aspirate or choke. Feed him slowly and in small amounts. Let him set the pace. It may just take him awhile to get used to your cooking!

Don't ever give up on a stubborn ferret that refuses to eat. Providing good nutrition and preventing dehydration are crucial to healing and/or prolonging the life of your ferret. You may end up with a ton of gunk on your body, but make sure that your sickie gets several cc's (3 to 4) of the good stuff four to six times a day. The feeding frequency can be less if he's eating a little on his own in between feedings.

Handling Actual Emergencies

Ferrets are tiny. They dehydrate quickly. They don't have very much blood, so they can't afford to lose much. Basically, fuzzies are stoic creatures, and unfortunately, they hide pain and illness too well. Sometimes, by the time you recognize a problem, it has become severe. The best prevention is to know your ferret's body language and behavior well. Your preparedness can save your furkid's life. And, unless the situation is as simple as a toenail cut too close to the quick, a visit to the vet as soon as possible is always a safe measure.

If your ferret is in pain or scared, he may bite. I can safely assume that your pet knows and trusts you. Your soft, reassuring voice may help comfort him and calm him down, but you should still exercise caution. (Head to Chapter 20 for tips on handling an aggressive ferret.)

Familiarize yourself with a nearby after-hours emergency hospital that's ferret-knowledgeable in case your ferret needs care when your veterinarian is unavailable.

In the following sections, I cover actual emergencies that you may encounter over the lifetime of your ferret. Some are common, such as dehydration and diarrhea, and others aren't so common, such as burns and electric shock. But these sections are designed to give you some basic information to prepare you for possible encounters with emergencies until you can get to the vet.

Shock

Shock is a common after-effect of traumatic injury or life-threatening illness, and it can cost your ferret his life. Shock is a serious medical emergency, and prevention and supportive therapy are essential. Check out the following list so you can recognize the big signs of shock:

- ✔ Rapid breathing
- ✔ Lethargy

- Shivering
- Fast heartbeat
- Pale nose, skin, and ears
- Skin that's cool to the touch
- Grey to bluish gums
- Unresponsiveness or extreme anxiety

Don't attempt to get a ferret in shock to eat or drink. Your fuzzy is having a hard time breathing, and his swallowing reflex just isn't there.

Get your fuzzy to the vet as soon as possible, trying to keep him warm on the way. Upon arrival, let your vet know what measures you've already taken and how your ferret has responded. Often, additional fluids given subcutaneously by the vet help speed the recovery. If your ferret is in shock due to blood loss, a blood transfusion from a healthy fuzzy can be lifesaving. It sounds extreme, but it has been done with great success.

Dehydration

Dehydration occurs because of abnormal fluid loss, which can happen if your ferret stops drinking or has severe or chronic diarrhea or vomiting. Except in cases where owners deny or restrict access to water or alter the water's taste, dehydration is almost always a sign of a serious underlying illness. Regardless of the cause, dehydration can be fatal if you don't address it immediately.

Some signs of dehydration include the following:

- Dry, tacky gums
- Low urine output
- Weakened state
- Difficulty opening his eyes all the way (constant squinting)
- Loss of sparkle or glossiness in his eyes

Not sure if one of these symptoms means your fuzzy is dehydrated? How can you find out for sure? Try this technique: Pull up on the skin on the back of your ferret's neck or shoulders to make a "tent." Does the skin stay in this tented position for a second or more after you let go, or does it snap back to its original elasticity? Dehydration causes the skin to stay pinched up for a while and not flatten. The longer it takes his skin to flatten out, the more dehydrated your ferret is.

Older ferrets or ferrets with adrenal gland disease lose a good amount of elasticity in their skin. In other words, their skin doesn't quickly snap back into place. Because of this, you may get a false result with the previous test, leading you to think your fuzzy is dehydrated. If your fuzzy is older or has adrenal gland disease, always look for the other signs of dehydration as well.

The immediate solution is to get fluids back into your ferret and get to your vet's office (or an emergency hospital) as soon as possible. By the time you determine your ferret is dehydrated, the situation has become an emergency and requires a trip to your vet. All supportive measures simply help stabilize your ferret until you can get him to professional help. To start, encourage your fuzzy to drink extra water. Some ferrets enjoy the fruity taste of drinks such as Pedialyte or Gatorade, and they get the added benefit of consuming extra electrolytes. Some people believe that warm chicken broth encourages drinking.

If your fuzzy refuses to drink at all, use a feeding syringe or an eyedropper to feed him the liquid. Hold your ferret in a normal standing position; don't tip him on his back. Be careful not to force too much liquid or squirt too quickly because he can choke.

Getting enough fluids into a dehydrated ferret is difficult. Often, a vet needs to administer extra fluids subcutaneously (under the skin) or intravenously (IV directly into the vein). Always take your ferret to the vet for treatment and so you can find out what's making your ferret ill in the first place. Treating the underlying illness often prevents future bouts of dehydration.

Bleeding

Fuzzies don't have very much blood in their bodies, so any wound that bleeds profusely requires immediate medical attention. The following sections show you how to begin treatment for common bleeding injuries; after you complete your initial treatment, all wounds or injuries should be looked at by a veterinarian as soon as possible, no matter the degree of the injury.

Bleeding from the ears, nose, mouth, rectum, or vaginal area is usually a sign of serious illness or injury. If you notice bleeding from one of these sources, visit your vet immediately or call a pet emergency hotline if your vet isn't available.

Treating injured nails

The most common source of ferret bleeding is a toenail that's cut too close to the quick (the pink, veined area of the nail). It's quite painful for your ferret; you'll hear him let out a series of small screeches to let you know that you screwed up. Here's how you can fix the mistake:

1. **Talk to him softly and hold him cautiously to inspect the damage (see Chapter 20 for tips on holding a potentially aggressive fuzzy).**

2. **Apply a small amount of styptic powder with your finger to the tip of the bleeding nail.**

3. **Press hard for a moment and then release your finger.**

4. **If the nail is still bleeding, repeat Steps 2 and 3.**

   Styptic powder burns, and you may tick off your ferret, so be careful. Get the powder off your finger quickly because it will burn you, too.

A painless alternative to styptic powder is beeswax. Some people suggest pressing the nail into a bar of white soap (preferably a mild one). Other owners use cornstarch or flour to stop nail bleeding. These remedies may take longer to work, but you won't put your ferret in any more pain.

Seek veterinary care as soon as possible if your fuzzy suffers more than just a closely clipped nail; otherwise, the area may become infected. If the nail has been torn off, don't use powder to treat the injury. Rather, immediately apply pressure to the top of the toe, not on the toe tip, and seek veterinary attention right away. The blood will eventually clot on its own. Torn claws may need to be removed completely and require stitches, but that's a worst-case scenario.

Treating cuts

A laceration on your fuzzy can be serious. Your ferret may need a more extensive exam, stitches, and/or antibiotics to treat the injury, but that should come immediately after you provide initial care to your fuzzy's boo-boo. Remember, ferrets don't have a lot of blood to lose, so act fast! Follow these steps:

1. **Gently wash the laceration with cold water.**

2. **Apply gentle but firm pressure on the wound.**

   Using something clean and dry is important — gauze or a clean washcloth, for instance.

3. **If possible, wrap the area with gauze and then use self-stick wrap to secure it to the wound.**

   Wrapping may not be possible, however, depending on where the wound is.

   Make sure that the wrap isn't too tight. Depending on the cause of the cut, your ferret may also be suffering from internal injuries that you can't see.

4. **Head to the vet if the laceration is wide, deep, or appears red or irritated.**

   A wound that won't stop bleeding needs immediate vet attention.

Vomiting

Vomiting can occur for several reasons, ranging from ingesting bad food, to an infection of the gastrointestinal (GI) tract, to an intestinal blockage. Keep a close eye on your vomiting ferret. Sometimes, a small piece of ingested material will come up with vomit, and then the vomiting will stop. But if your fuzzy vomits repeatedly and shows the following symptoms, he possibly has an intestinal blockage:

- Can't hold down his food
- Shows no interest in food
- Becomes depressed and lethargic

The only way to treat a blockage is to remove the object surgically. Not doing so may spell death for your ferret. Get to a vet as soon as possible!

Diarrhea (and other fecal issues)

Short bouts of infrequent diarrhea are quite common in ferrets. How can you tell if you're dealing with diarrhea? A ferret's normal stool is slightly soft but formed. Diarrhea is more liquid in form, and your ferret shows a higher frequency of pooping.

The cause of diarrhea can be very difficult to diagnose. The cause can be as simple as your ferret indulging in one too many treats (hey, we've all been there). Diarrhea can also be a sign of underlying diseases or illnesses or can result from changes in diet. An underlying condition may be easy to correct (influenza, for example) or difficult (eosinophilic gastroenteritis, for instance). But no matter what the cause, diarrhea can become life threatening because your fuzzy is losing precious fluids and not absorbing all his food. You need to get treatment immediately and get to the bottom of the cause.

Diarrhea is cause for alarm if it becomes serious and frequent (lasts for more than a day). If your fuzzy's diarrhea persists, take him and a sample of the poop to the vet immediately so she can rule out all the nasty things your fuzzy may have. The treatment may be as simple as daily doses of Kaopectate and electrolyte-replacing fluids, but let your vet decide. A professional can learn a lot just from looking at a ferret's poop! Table 13-1 goes through the many properties a sick fuzzy's poop can have and lists the possible conditions associated with them. Be on the lookout!

Table 13-1	Poop and Possible Related Conditions
Type of Poop	*Possible Malady*
Spaghetti-thin poop	Partial obstruction by a foreign body.
Green poop	A non-specific type of poop. The food possibly is moving too fast through the digestive tract, and the poop is green because the food isn't broken all the way down. Anything that causes rapid passage or diarrhea can cause green poop — disease, food changes, stress, ECE (see Chapter 16), and so on.
Bloody poop	Fresh, bright-red blood usually comes from the lower intestine or rectum. Large amounts of blood may indicate a massive hemorrhage from the entire length of the GI tract.
Seedy poop	A non-specific type of poop. Malabsorption or maldigestion is taking place, meaning that digestion or absorption isn't happening the way it should. The seedy material is undigested fat and starch complexes. Seedy or "birdseed" poop can accompany any disease that seriously affects the small intestine. Low-quality ferret diets that are high in plant protein as opposed to animal protein may cause seedy poop, because the ferrets can't digest all the plant protein and starches.
Black, tarry poop	Results from gastric bleeding or gastric ulcers. The black color comes from the digestion of the blood, which occurs in the stomach. Significant bleeding in the stomach must be present in order for the ferret's poop to turn black.

To check for lower GI blood in your ferret's poop to be sure, take a poop sample and put it in a piece of gauze. Soak the gauze in warm water. If blood is in the stool, the water will turn red, and you'll see the color against the white gauze.

In the case of treating severe diarrhea, your vet will request a complete history of your ferret in order to diagnose the cause. Be prepared to report the following:

- ✔ The age of the ferret
- ✔ How the ferret is living and with whom
- ✔ The extent and duration of his symptoms
- ✔ His diet
- ✔ Other significant information you can readily give

Your vet may also want to perform blood tests, X-rays, or biopsies of the intestinal tract to help hone in on a proper diagnosis. Your vet will likely treat your ferret immediately for dehydration and may provide additional nutritional support before moving on to a treatment based on the diagnosis and the severity of the condition.

Seizures

A *seizure* occurs when the electrical impulses in the ferret's brain misfire. It can last from seconds to a few minutes and is a very scary thing to witness. Some seizures can occur very quietly and go unnoticed, but the majority involve the involuntary thrashing about of the limbs in combination with any of the following:

- ✔ Loss of bladder/bowel control
- ✔ Salivating
- ✔ Vomiting
- ✔ Involuntary vocalizations

Seizures can be a sign of many different underlying conditions, from hypoglycemia (low blood sugar) to poisoning. They always merit a trip to the veterinarian's office immediately afterward, because you need to find the underlying cause and do everything you can to prevent future seizures.

I would only move a ferret if it's in a place that's dangerous. If he's already on the floor, leave him alone. In moving him, you may prolong the seizure or get yourself bitten. It's better to cover him with a light towel or washcloth to block out the light, which is a stimulus. Covering him may decrease the length of the seizure. Keep your fingers, pens, wallet, and any other objects away from your ferret's mouth when he's in the middle of the seizure and shoo away other ferrets and pets. If you have your wits about you, try to time the incident for future reference. (***Note:*** Neither people nor ferrets have the ability to swallow their tongues during a seizure. That's a myth.)

A ferret isn't in pain during a seizure, even if he's crying out. He's essentially unconscious and his body is going through involuntary muscle spasms. Don't try to hold your ferret down during a seizure. Restraining him can cause further injury — to him and to you. He may inadvertently and seriously bite you without even knowing what's going on around him. Because the jaws of a seizing animal/person clamp tightly shut, anything that gets in the way gets bitten severely. Also, restraining him is stimulating and may increase the length of the seizure.

In the end, you'll have a very wiped-out ferret. When your ferret's seizure ends, keep him calm, warm, and quiet. He'll be confused and shaken. To give him a needed boost to recovery, rub a little Karo syrup or honey on his gums. Repeat every five minutes until your fuzzy starts coming around. You can also offer him a little soft food, such as a high-protein canned food or meat baby food, to stabilize his blood sugar. If your ferret isn't feeling up to licking from a spoon or off a plate, offer the food from a feeding syringe. From start to finish, the ferret needs about 30 to 40 minutes to recover from the seizure, but get your ferret into the vet as soon as possible after the seizure ends.

Heatstroke

Ferrets are extremely susceptible to heatstroke — especially in temperatures above 80 degrees Fahrenheit. A heatstroke can quickly kill your ferret if you don't provide treatment immediately. Signs of heatstroke include

- ✔ Heavy panting
- ✔ Mucous coming from the nose or mouth
- ✔ Extreme lethargy or limpness
- ✔ Seizures
- ✔ Loss of consciousness

Your main objective is to lower the ferret's body temperature slowly. A gradual decrease in body temperature is necessary to prevent shock. (A rapid decrease in body temperature can be as deadly as heatstroke itself.) First, get the ferret out of the sun and heat and give him water to drink. If you have an electrolyte-replacing drink, such as Pedialyte or Gatorade, use it if your ferret will drink it.

If your ferret is unconscious, don't try to get any liquid or food into his mouth, because he can choke. Just keep him cool and provide first aid until you can get him to the vet.

After you remove fuzzy from the heat and get some fluids in him, you can slowly lower his body temperature in many different ways:

- ✔ Apply cool (not cold) water to body areas with less fur — the groin, lower stomach, and the feet, for example. You can place a wet washcloth on the key areas. The evaporation of the water on the skin cools the body and lowers his temperature.

- ✔ Place your fuzzy directly in shallow, room-temperature water, keeping his head and the top half of his body above water. Don't submerge him in cold water because the shock of doing so can kill him.

- ✔ Apply rubbing alcohol to his feet only, making sure not to miss his paw pads. You also can rub ice cubes on the ferret's feet.

✔ Place the ferret in front of a fan. This method isn't as effective as the others, but it's better than nothing in an emergency situation.

No matter how you think your ferret is weathering the situation and responding to your treatment, get him to the vet as soon as possible. Often, the vet will give a ferret additional fluids to make up for those lost during the heatstroke. She may also recommend additional medications or other home support.

Take extra precautions in the warmer months to prevent heatstroke. Don't leave your ferret in a closed-up, hot car. Keep your ferret and his carrier out of direct sunlight, and be sure to give him extra water. If you take your ferret outside during the very warm months, bring along a bottle or two of frozen water. Wrap the bottles in towels and keep them in the carrier or cage.

Hypothermia

Hypothermia is a potentially fatal condition where the body's temperature drops below the level required for normal functioning of the internal organs. Some animals are more prone to hypothermia than others: Very young and very old ferrets, small ferrets with short hair, ferrets with no shelter in cold weather, wet ferrets, and ferrets undergoing surgical procedures. Signs of hypothermia include

✔ Shivering (which often becomes violent)

✔ Cool skin or skin cold to the touch

✔ Slow, shallow breathing

✔ Lethargy

✔ Unresponsiveness

The hypothermic ferret needs immediate help from you to return his body temperature to normal. Depending on the duration and severity of the condition, tissue damage may already have occurred, so hypothermic ferrets should be warmed up very slowly. The following list presents some ways to accomplish this:

✔ Run dry towels through the dryer to warm them up, and then wrap your ferret in the warm towels.

A severely hypothermic ferret will be listless and unresponsive and therefore unable to move away from heat that you provide. Exercise extreme caution when you provide heat for a ferret so that you prevent burns. What feels warm to you may actually feel scorching to a ferret. Monitor the use of heat closely and keep watch over your ailing ferret to gauge his reactions.

✔ If your ferret is wet, use a hair dryer on the low setting to dry him and warm him up.

✔ Fill empty bottles, such as soda bottles, with warm water, wrap them in dish towels, and place them against your ferret's skin. The best placement is where your fuzzy has less fur, such as the armpit or the groin area. *Never* put an uncovered bottle against the ferret's skin; it may burn him.

✔ Warm a heating pad on the low setting, place a towel over it, lay your ferret on top of it, and then cover him with a warm towel.

Heating pads can be dangerous because they're the most common cause of overheating. Never leave your ferret unattended on a heating pad, and always keep checking the temperature of the pad and your ferret.

✔ Grab some sealable plastic baggies or socks and fill them with uncooked rice or lentils. Warm them in the microwave for one to two minutes, wrap them in a towel, and place them on areas with little fur.

When you come inside from extreme cold, it's hard to ignore how painful your fingers and toes are. Well, a severely hypothermic ferret may experience similar pain as his tissues warm up. As a result, he may bite or scratch at the areas and may even bite you in his time of discomfort. Be extra cautious when handling the fuzzy (see Chapter 20).

While your ferret is warming up, call your vet to discuss what else you should do. She may want to see your ferret for further examination. Additional veterinary care may include administering warm fluids intravenously and giving oxygen.

Lethargy and unresponsiveness also are common signs of hypoglycemia that goes along with insulinoma. It isn't uncommon for a hypoglycemic ferret to become hypothermic. If this situation happens with your fuzzy, take steps to warm him up, and if he's conscious and can swallow, give him a small amount of honey or sugar mixed with a little warm water. If he's unconscious, gently rub honey or sugar water on his gums. These actions may just save his life!

Eye injuries

Ferrets can get very rough when playing with each other, and they can get into a lot of trouble on their own. Eye injuries aren't beyond the ferret injury realm. If your ferret receives a scratch to an eye, flush out the eye with cool water or a saline solution. Any eye injury requires the attention of an experienced ferret vet, so waste no time after flushing the eye.

If you suspect that your fuzzy has foreign matter in his eye, such as litter or sand — which you can tell by a watery and squinty eye that lasts for more than an hour or so — don't apply pressure to the affected eye. Doing so can cause the particle to inflict further damage. Simply flush the eye and call your vet for instructions on how to proceed until you can get to the office.

Fractures or spinal injuries

Ferrets are extremely flexible and resilient, but occasionally bone injuries occur after a fall, after getting pounced on by a dog, or while getting folded up in a piece of furniture, for instance. If your ferret has a broken bone or an injured spine, he may be showing the following symptoms:

- ✔ Limping
- ✔ Showing resistance to moving
- ✔ Dragging a leg or holding one up

Sometimes, it's hard to recognize a break without an actual X-ray, so a trip to the vet is necessary. The best course of action is to keep your ferret immobile and quiet while you seek immediate medical attention. Don't try to fix anything on your own. Place your ferret in a small carrier and keep him warm during the trip.

If the injured body part is a paw, wrap it in a towel to steady the limb while you take the fuzzy to the vet. If you suspect his spine is injured, be extremely cautious. Spinal injuries can be devastating, if not fatal, so keep the ferret as still as possible in his small carrier. Wrap his body in a towel and get him to the vet immediately.

Poisoning

The world is a scary place for ferrets; even your home can be a source of harm. Most homes contain funky chemicals and cleaners, half of which humans don't remember storing. These chemicals and cleaners are poisonous to the little fuzzy. The most commonly encountered ferret poisons are rat poison and Tylenol. When your ferret finds and ingests these things, disaster ensues. Poisoning can also occur if you accidentally overdose your ferret on a prescribed medication.

Signs of poisoning include

- ✔ Vomiting
- ✔ Salivating
- ✔ Pawing at the mouth
- ✔ Diarrhea
- ✔ Lethargy
- ✔ Sudden weakness
- ✔ Seizures

✔ Unconsciousness

✔ An overturned chemical bottle or chewed up cleaner container (okay, so not a symptom, but definitely a warning signal)

If you suspect that your ferret has ingested something poisonous or has taken too much medicine, take him and the suspected substance to your vet immediately. Try to figure out how much he ingested and how long ago so you can tell the vet. Treatment depends on the ingested substance. It can range from induced vomiting to medication. Only your vet will know the proper course of action.

Keep the number to the National Animal Poison Control Center close at hand and make sure that your vet has it for reference. You can reach this nonprofit agency at 888-426-4435. The service costs $55 per case and accepts credit cards only.

Animal bites

People who own ferrets often have other animals in their homes. If you live in this type of home, you need to limit and monitor pet interactions closely to avoid bouts of aggression. If your ferret gets bitten by another household pet, wash his wound lightly with cold water and gently dab the area with hydrogen peroxide. If the wound is bleeding, apply pressure to slow the bleeding and get him to the vet immediately.

Cat bites are particularly dangerous to both people and ferrets due to the amount of bacteria in cat saliva. Often, cat bites require special antibiotics. If your kitty bites your fuzzy, make an extra-quick trip to the vet.

If a neighbor's pet, a stray, or a wild animal bites your ferret, take him to the vet right away. If you know the animal that bit your fuzzy, find out if it's up to date on its rabies vaccination first. Although the incidence is extremely low and unlikely, your ferret can contract rabies from an infected animal. Prevention is the key. Watch your ferret closely for changes in behavior and report them to the vet. (For information on rabies vaccine and prevention, see Chapter 12.)

Electric shock

An electric shock can be severe enough to kill your little fuzzy. Electric shock is usually the result of a fuzzy chewing on electrical cords, which is why you need to keep cords in your home far out of your ferret's reach (see Chapter 6 for info on ferret-proofing your house). Be aware that chewed cords can also cause a fire. Check your home regularly for and replace any frayed or bitten electrical cords.

There's very little you can do for a ferret that's experienced electric shock except keep him warm and quiet until you can get him to the veterinarian. If he's lucky enough to survive, you can be almost certain he'll suffer damage to his teeth, gums, and mouth. You and your vet will then proceed with the proper treatment program for his injuries. Trust me, prevention is much easier on both of you!

Burns

Sometimes carpet sharks get into things they shouldn't (actually, more often than sometimes). It isn't their fault; it's in their nature. One serious side effect of this curiosity, burns, occurs because owners aren't paying close enough attention and allow the fuzzies to venture into unsafe territory. Burns can come from getting too close to fireplaces, cigarettes, ovens, and even pilot lights. Bathing your ferret in extremely hot water can also scald him. If your ferret suffers a burn, immediately apply cold water directly to the burned area. And if you can, apply an ice pack for no more than five minutes. After this initial treatment, get your ferret to the vet immediately.

Chapter 14

Ferreting Out Ferret Pests

In This Chapter
▶ Eradicating external pests
▶ Zapping away internal bugs

Simply put, a *parasite* is an organism (or person) that feeds off another organism without giving anything back. You may even know one or two personally! Every living being is host to a parasite party or two — or maybe a hundred. Parasites come in all shapes and sizes. Some are internal, and some are external. Some are harmless and hardly noticeable; others can be quite damaging and difficult to miss.

This chapter deals specifically with external and internal pests that can bug the heck out of your fuzzy. I list these parasites and their warning signs and give you tips on keeping your fuzzy critter-free. I also shed some light on parasites, diseases, and germs that can affect both humans and their better halves, the carpet sharks.

Booting External Critters That Go Bite in the Night

They're ruthless and always hungry. Under a microscope, they look a bit like creepy prehistoric monsters. They're external parasites. Can anything be more annoying to the pet and pet owner than external parasites? Nothing that I know of. These incredibly sturdy little ectoparasites need little to survive, and unfortunately, you and your ferret can be hosts to these ungrateful diners. In the sections that follow, I introduce many common external parasites that you must combat, and I give you the ammunition to kick them off your and your fuzzy's dinner table — namely, your skin.

Fleas

Fleas are the most common external parasites seen on ferrets. They spend most of their time building flea resorts in your rugs and couches and in any other cozy place they can find. One such cozy place is in your fuzzy's coat. Ferrets are just as prone to flea infestations as Fidos and Tabbys. But before you can safely rid your domain of these blood-sucking pests and prevent them from turning your frisky ferret into an illing itchy, you need to know what kind of army you're dealing with:

- **Fleas are messy guests.** The act of feasting on your pet's warm blood triggers the female flea to lay thousands of eggs all over your home. Sometimes, you may observe a flea scurrying across its dinner table: your pet. More likely, you'll see only the end results of the flea's wild parties: the "flea dirt" left on the skin of your pet. This "dirt" is actually flea waste, which looks like tiny specks of reddish-black sand.

- **Fleas are opportunistic little buggers.** Where there is wildlife, there are fleas. And plenty of them. Fleas can hitchhike right into your home on other pets, and although they can't live on humans, they can hitch a ride on your clothing or a picnic blanket, perhaps. And don't forget about the greatly appreciated, supervised trips your ferret takes to the wonderful outdoors. Through no fault of her own, your ferret may bring fleas into your house.

- **Fleas love warm, humid places.** Fleas seek all warm-blooded victims. Although it may be warm and humid for only several months a year where you live, your battle against fleas is year round.

Fleas can be more than a mere nuisance. A severe flea infestation can cause life-threatening anemia (a reduction in red blood cells, causing fatigue and weakness) in your ferret. Fleas also can carry parasites such as tapeworms and pass them along to both you and your fuzzy. The bottom line: If your ferret has fleas, you need to get rid of them as soon as possible.

The following sections let you know how to check for these annoying critters and give you steps to take to free your home from their terrible reign.

Checking for fleas

Some indications of a flea infestation include small bites (tiny, red raised marks) or reddened areas or lesions on the skin due to plenty of scratching. Severe infestations may bring poor fur quality, thinning patches of fur, and fur discoloration. You may find yourself suffering some of the same scratching effects; don't be surprised if you have some bites around your feet and ankles if the infestation is severe (fleas can jump over 100 times their body length). Herein lies one of the biggest problems with fleas: Their tiny bites are painfully itchy. To a flea-allergic pet, the situation can be almost unbearable as she scratches out her skin and her underbelly becomes irritated.

To check your fuzzy for fleas, ruffle back her fur with your hands and examine her skin closely — particularly the belly. You should also inspect your ferret's bedding and change it often. You can shake out her towels or other bedding onto a white floor or a piece of paper and then distinguish the specks of kitty litter from the flea dirt.

Ridding your ferret and home of fleas

After you discover that fleas have invaded your home, you need to act to get rid of them as quick as you can. The steps in the following sections give you the how-to. Before you treat your ferret for fleas, however, keep the following points in mind:

- ✔ **If one of your pets has fleas, all your pets have fleas.** If you have several pets, you must treat them all, whether or not you see evidence of fleas on each one.

- ✔ **What's safe for a dog may kill your ferret.** Controls such as sprays, dips, and flea collars aren't meant for fuzzies. Ferrets are hypersensitive to most of these products — particularly organophosphate pesticides. Even "ferret-safe" products can be harmful to a sick, geriatric, young (under 12 weeks old), or nursing ferret.

- ✔ **You must see a veterinarian before applying any flea product on your ferret (or any pet, for that matter).** Your vet will make sure the product is safe and that your pet is healthy enough to withstand chemical treatment.

Step 1: Treat your ferret

To rid your ferret and home of fleas, begin by bathing all your warm-blooded furry pets with safe flea shampoos. After you purchase a ferret-safe flea shampoo — preferably one made with pyrethrins or other natural ingredients — follow these steps:

1. **Gently bathe your ferret from head to toe — and remember the tail (tails have fleas, too).**

   Refer to Chapter 9 for detailed information on bathing your ferret. Here are some highlights: Don't forget your goggles, snorkel, and shoulder-length rubber gloves, and remember to prevent the shampoo from getting into the eyes, nose, mouth, and ears.

2. **When your ferret is dry, use a flea comb to remove any flea corpses from her coat.**

3. **Move the fuzzy to a warm, dry, flea-free place before you tackle her cage.**

   A travel carrier works well in times like these. After all, putting a squeaky-clean furball into a flea-infested cage doesn't make much sense.

Step 2: Treat your ferret's cage, bedding, and other stuff

When your ferret is bathed and flea-free, you're ready to tackle her cage and bedding. (*Note:* You have to do the same with your other pet stuff, too.) Follow these steps to treat these fuzzy fixtures:

1. **Remove all bedding from the cage and machine wash it in hot water.**

   If you prefer, you can place it in a sealed plastic bag and throw it away.

2. **Scrub the cage thoroughly with hot, soapy water and then dry.**

3. **Spray the cleaned, dry cage with a cat-safe flea spray and allow it to thoroughly dry.**

Step 3: Treat your home

The third step — treating your entire home — is probably the most inconvenient and time-consuming of all the steps. You may have killed the fleas on your ferret and the eggs on her bedding, but thousands of eggs may be getting ready to hatch all over your house, including in the baseboards, carpeting, and furniture.

You have several options for treating your home for fleas. The easiest way is to hire a professional exterminator. Other hands-on methods are foggers, sprays, and powders that you apply. As you decide what method to use, keep in mind that ferrets are remarkably sensitive to chemicals, so choose the safest and most natural method whenever possible. And always follow product directions when going it alone.

Before treating the environment with sprays or powders, it's imperative that you completely remove all your pets, including your ferret (and her cage/toys/bowls), from the premises until everything settles and dries. It isn't good for your ferret to be walking through wet sprays or having the powders settling on her body/stuff. Nor is it healthy for her to inhale the chemicals. Follow the directions on the bottles/can before returning your pet to your home.

Because most commercial flea-killing products don't successfully kill all the eggs, larvae, and pupae, you may need to repeat this step 7 to 21 days after the first treatment, depending on which product you use. Make sure you acquire the advice of an expert.

Step 4: Stop fleas from coming back

You must make a regular effort to prevent reinfestation after you take the first few steps to treat for fleas. Here are some general suggestions:

✔ Keep your pet's environment clean by vacuuming and scrubbing regularly.

✔ Empty the vacuum bag after vacuuming each time, because fleas can survive in the bag and continue to lay eggs. The babies will hatch and leave the vacuum.

✔ Inspect and de-flea all incoming pets before they enter your home.

The following list presents products that you should use only in conjunction with your vet's blessing:

✔ **Advantage (Bayer):** Made with the ingredient imidacloprid, Advantage is said to kill 98–100 percent of the fleas within 24 hours.

Applying a small amount of the liquid directly on the skin at the base of your ferret's skull provides up to 28 days of protection. The liquid spreads evenly across your ferret's skin to provide full-body coverage. Monthly applications are advised to protect against newly hatching fleas. Reapplication is recommended after bathing, but your ferret should receive no more than one application per week.

✔ **Frontline Top Spot (Merial):** Made with the active ingredient fipronil, this product targets both fleas and ticks (see the following section). It's designed to be continually released onto the ferret's skin and fur for at least one full month after initial application.

Frontline Top Spot becomes waterproof two days after application; therefore, don't bathe your ferret during this period. If you must bathe your ferret before applying the product, wait at least five days after the bath before applying Frontline Top Spot. Some ferret owners prefer to use the Frontline spray because it's easier to dose.

One reason Frontline Top Spot is deemed so safe for mammals is because it isn't absorbed into a pet's bloodstream. Like Advantage, Frontline should be applied monthly.

✔ **Revolution (Pfizer):** Made with the active ingredient selamectin, Revolution is a topically applied product that prevents heartworm, kills adult fleas, prevents flea eggs from hatching, and treats and controls ear-mite infestation. It's also said to treat and control sarcoptic mange.

Unlike Advantage and Frontline, Revolution enters the bloodstream and tissues through the skin. You can bathe your pet after letting Revolution absorb for four hours. Talk to your vet about the correct dosage for your ferret.

Revolution has a very low adverse-reaction rate, and when compared to other products on the market, Revolution has the broadest spectrum of prevention and treatment of parasites.

The wonderful thing about these products is that they kill the fleas before they lay eggs. If you stick with one of the products with all your pets, chances are you won't often (if ever) need to go through the frenzied treatment process I describe in the previous sections.

Ticks

Ticks look like tiny brown crabs. When filled with blood, they resemble a raised mole on the skin. Ticks will appear without warning. They don't generally occur as an infestation, but rather as a single incident; perhaps you'll find up to several at a time if your ferret has been walking through infested brush areas. You should always check for ticks carefully after walks. The ticks may be flat, attached, but not yet filled with blood. Or they may be attached and already starting to fill up.

Here are a couple things to know about ticks:

✔ Finding ticks can be difficult. You must feel beneath the fur for the tiny lumps. Ears are also great hiding spots for ticks.

✔ Ticks can harbor some diseases, including Lyme disease, that can affect both humans and other animals. Some spot-on products (see the previous section) used to control fleas are also effective in killing ticks.

Fortunately, ticks are relatively easy to deal with. If you find one hitched to your fuzzy's skin, follow these steps:

1. **Using a pair of tweezers or forceps, grab the tick as close to the ferret's skin as possible.**

2. **Gently pull off the tick, being sure not to leave the tick's barbed mouth parts still attached to the fuzzy's skin.**

3. **After removal, crush or burn the tick.**

Don't burn the tick off of your ferret. Many people suggest this, but you run the risk of seriously burning your fuzzy.

Cuterebra flies

Cuterebra flies, which don't bite or sting, look like big hunched-back bumblebees. They lay their eggs along well-traveled paths and around the burrows of typical hosts, such as rabbits and rodents. The heat and moisture emitted from the host animals as they pass by triggers the eggs to hatch into larvae, called *warbles*. Although ferrets aren't the main target hosts, they can become infested when they're playing outside.

The tiny warbles enter the ferret's mouth or nose or sometimes through a tiny open wound on its skin. Contrary to some beliefs, warbles can't burrow into the healthy skin of an animal from the outside. Warbles can remain in the nose or mouth for several days before migrating to various spots beneath the skin where they pupate — usually on the head, neck, or trunk. The warbles remain under the skin for approximately 30 days while they undergo some astonishing changes.

As a warble enlarges, a swelling beneath the skin begins to appear, which is when you should notice a problem. Depending on the stage of growth, a warble can range in size from a few millimeters to a couple of centimeters. The lesion looks a little like an abscess, but if you look closely, you'll see a tiny opening at the top of it, which is where the larva breathes in air. Occasionally, you may see a discharge coming from the opening, but this isn't common. You may see your ferret biting or scratching at the lump, or his fur around the lump may be matted.

To treat the warble, you need to head to the vet's office. Your vet needs to enlarge the wound and remove the warble carefully so as not to rupture it. A rupture can cause a secondary infection or trigger the ferret's immune system to attack the material as if it was a foreign body. The resulting wound, when thoroughly cleaned, should remain open during the healing process. New, healthy tissue will slowly fill in the hole. Your vet will give you all the details about caring for the wound after his work is done.

Ear mites

Blood-sucking ear mites are common in ferrets. You can identify the issue by checking your fuzzy's ear canals for brownish-black gunk. Ferrets with ear mites may show the following symptoms:

- ✔ Scratching feverishly at their ears
- ✔ Walking with a slight head tilt
- ✔ Shaking their heads due to the extreme discomfort

Their ears may also stink and be slightly discolored.

Treatment for ear mites is relatively easy (if you stick with it) and is necessary to prevent secondary infections that can be extremely painful and even result in deafness. Some vets may prescribe an ear ointment such as Tresaderm. Others may use injectible ivermectin. Ivermectin (the same as injectible ivermectin) mixed with propylene glycol or used by itself and applied directly into the ear canal also works. You can even use Revolution, which is a flea treatment I discuss in the earlier flea section.

Here are some other things you need to know about ear mite treatment:

- ✔ Ear mites can pass between fuzzies and other household pets and vice versa, so it's important to treat all animals.
- ✔ Wash all bedding frequently during treatments.
- ✔ You can't eradicate ear mites with one application of medicine; you have to use a series of applications. A minimum of two treatments, 7 to 10 days apart, is usually necessary, so it's crucial to be painstakingly thorough.

Medications designed to kill the mites won't kill the eggs, which is why you have to repeat treatment. Mites hatch out after the first treatment. The second treatment kills the second batch of mites before they have a chance to lay eggs again and start the cycle over.

Sarcoptic mange (scabies)

As someone who's suffered from the dreadful pest known as sarcoptic mange (scabies), I can testify that the condition is unbearably itchy and definitely no fun. This external bug is in the mite family and passes quite easily from animal to animal or from animal to human. Depending on your ferret's case, her symptoms may include itchy patches of hair loss on the belly, face, or legs or crusty skin with oozing, pimple-like sores. Sometimes, the scabies infestation attacks only the feet and toes, causing severe inflammation. Marked by scabby, swollen, red feet, foot rot often results in the claws falling out if left untreated. A vet can make a diagnosis with skin scrapings.

For treatment, you can choose really, really stinky vet-prescribed lime sulfur dips and shampoos, or you can go the simple route with oral or injectible ivermectin. You can also use Revolution, which I discuss in the earlier flea section.

Battling the Internal Bugaboos That Threaten Your Fuzzy

It's bad enough that pests want to invade the outside of your little fuzzbutt, but some also want to take over your fuzzy's insides. Some internal parasites can be life threatening and require immediate attention. You must stay vigilant for the warning signs and always take your little one to the vet if you suspect that something's wrong. In the following sections, I introduce some dangerous internal parasites and detail the warning signs that wave red flags so you can rush your fuzzy to the vet.

Never, ever take on the role of doctor and medicate your ferret without your vet's guidance. Ferrets are tiny creatures and can overdose very easily. Some medications can be lethal in certain combinations. Also, you may cause more harm if you misdiagnose or fail to see other underlying health problems. Don't be hasty. Always get help from an experienced ferret vet who can diagnose and come up with the proper course of action (see Chapter 12 for more on finding one).

Intestinal worms

Ferrets are susceptible to many intestinal worms, including roundworms, hookworms, tapeworms, flukes, and lungworms. Almost all intestinal infestations harbor the same symptoms:

- Dry, brittle fur
- Weight loss
- Diarrhea, mucousy or bloody poops, and/or worms in the poop (in rare, serious infestations)
- Abdominal bloating
- Weakness or lethargy
- Itchy heinie
- Increased appetite with weight loss
- Increased gas
- Tender belly

Some intestinal worms are passed from one animal to another or to a human through an animal's infected poop. Some, like tapeworm, are passed through fleas or other intermediate hosts. Others can get into the system just by having their tiny larva burrow through the skin.

Although the symptoms generally are the same, treatment of intestinal parasites can vary depending on the organism you're dealing with. Some worms require oral medication in liquid or pill form. Others can fall to an injection (often ivermectin). Whatever the case, intestinal parasites left untreated can cause your ferret to have chronic intestinal problems and be prone to poor health. In rare instances, severe cases of intestinal worms can cause death.

 If you have more than one ferret and one of them has internal parasites, chances are you have more than one wormy fuzzy. Treat all your ferrets thoroughly, according to your vet's instructions. Don't forget to change their litter boxes and clean the cage to prevent reinfestation. If you also have dogs and cats, check them for parasites, too. Animals just love to get into poop!

Giardia

Giardia, a lovely protozoan, can get into you or your ferret via a water source (streams, lakes, ponds, and infected tap water, for example) or through the ingestion of infected poop. After gaining access to the intestinal tract, these buggers attack the inner lining of the intestine, causing an uncomfortable inflammation. Signs of giardia infestation include weight loss, bloating, diarrhea, and mucousy poops.

Giardia can be difficult to find under the microscope. You need a very fresh poop sample looked at immediately — like, while it's still steaming. Better yet, have your vet take a swab from the rectum. The very best course of action is to send a sample in a special solution to the lab for proper analysis and identification. Some people believe giardia is rare in ferrets, but others believe that it's very common and only shows its ugly warning signs when the fuzzy is stressed out. This is one parasite that's still being investigated.

The treatment suggested by a vet is oral medication — usually Flagyl (metronidazole). Some vets suggest Panacur (fenbendazole) as another option, although this medication isn't made specifically to combat giardia. For healthy fuzzies, some experts think that the symptoms may go away without treatment. I always suggest getting help. It may take up to a month to cure your furball, but your effort is well worth it.

Some medications — especially Flagyl and Pepto-Bismol — are so offensive to fuzzies that they projectile-ptooey them all over you. A treat such as Linatone can come in handy. Mixing the medication with a yummy supplement can save you a laundry bill and reduce the rebellion on your ferret's part. Keep in mind, though, what you're medicating the fuzzy for in the first place; for example, ferrets with insulinoma shouldn't have sweet stuff.

Coccidia (coccidiosis)

Coccidia is a protozoan infection common in ferrets as well as other animals. The infection is picked up through the ingestion of infected poop and can be diagnosed by your vet if you provide a stool sample. However, a stool sample isn't always a fail-proof test. Your fuzzy may shed the oocysts (eggs) only periodically, which means you may test a poop on a day when no oocysts were shed. For the most accurate results, pick a poop that's bloody and mucousy.

Severe coccidia infestations can cause diarrhea, lethargy, dehydration, weight loss, loss of appetite, and, in severe cases, death. Kits (baby ferrets) are most susceptible to severe coccidia infestations and may have thin, brittle fur and a sparse coat. The kit's whiskers are stubby and broken off. In prolonged conditions, her heinie may appear red and swollen. Treatment often is successful if you catch the condition early enough. Many vets prescribe Albon (sulfadimethoxine) to treat coccidia.

Chapter 15

Handling Viruses, Infections, and Other Conditions and Illnesses

....

In This Chapter

▶ Addressing many common ferret diseases and conditions

▶ Finding out what you can do to diagnose and treat your ferret

....

No matter how hard people try to stay healthy with good eating, exercise, and proper immunizations, millions of humans manage to get the worst viruses, respiratory infections, and flu every year. Your fuzzy is no different.

Experts have written entire books on the diseases and illnesses ferrets can contract. This isn't one of them. In this chapter, you simply get the basics on what you need to know about common ferret diseases and what you can do about them. This chapter deals with the most common diseases and conditions, in alphabetical order, from the simple (flu) to the deadly (rabies) and from the serious (cardiomyopathy) to the not-so-serious (eye problems). As I make clear throughout this book, recognizing changes in your ferret's appearance and behavior early on can mean the difference between life and death. Even some of the presumably innocent conditions I describe in this chapter can take a turn for the worst or can be indicative of another more serious condition.

A handful of signs seem to show up with almost all fuzzy ailments, which is just one more reason to leave the diagnosing and medicating to your experienced vet. Your ferret may be suffering from more than one malady. Also, you need to be aware that signs aren't set in stone. Your ferret may exhibit one sign or a combination of several. She may show none at all, especially in the beginning stages of an illness. The signs I list in this chapter are the most common ones for each illness and are here for reference purposes only. Don't wait until more signs appear before hauling your fuzzbutt to the vet.

Gastrointestinal (GI) Diseases

Gastrointestinal diseases refer to all those things that can go wrong with the stomach, intestines, or esophagus. The next few sections cover those GL ailments that can affect ferrets, and what you can do if you spot the symptoms involved.

Epizootic Catarrhal Enteritis (ECE)

Epizootic Catarrhal Enteritis (ECE) is an inflammation of the intestinal lining. In addition to the intestinal damage, as the disease progresses, the ferret's liver can be seriously affected, and the results can be deadly! Ferrets with ECE can't absorb food and water properly, causing life-threatening diarrhea. The disease is transmitted when a ferret comes in contact with the bodily fluids or feces of a sick ferret or via handlers of ill ferrets. Experts have strong evidence that a coronavirus causes ECE.

The fuzzies most at risk are older carpet sharks and very young ferrets. Ferrets that are already battling other illnesses, such as lymphosarcoma, adrenal disease, and/or insulinoma (see Chapter 16), also are at high risk. Healthy young and middle-aged furkids seem to get over ECE the fastest with the right support, almost as if the condition were the flu. In multi-ferret homes, you can expect most, if not all, of your fuzzies to get this disease within 48 to 72 hours after it enters the door. Baby ferrets bought from pet stores are frequent *asymptomatic carriers* of ECE, which means they can show no signs of having the condition. ECE also can enter your home on your clothes after you've handled a ferret with ECE.

This nasty disease can last anywhere from several days to several months. Watch your ferret closely and get her to a vet the moment the signs become apparent. ECE is typically diagnosed by its characteristic timeline and clinical signs.

Prevention

ECE is an extremely contagious disease that spreads from ferret to ferret very quickly. To safeguard your ferret, you need to clean, clean, clean. Follow these tips:

- Don't let other people handle your ferret without taking precautions.
- Wash thoroughly before and after you handle any ferrets.
- Change clothing before handling your own little one after visiting with strange ferrets.

✔ Make sure all new ferrets you get have been checked by the vet for parasites and given an overall clean bill of health before exposing them to others.

Quarantining newcomers for ECE is a bit unrealistic because any ferret can carry the disease for months and months. If she comes in with it, your other ferrets will be exposed. That's the bottom line. Quarantining in this case only gives you a false sense of security.

Clinical signs

Some typical signs of ECE include the following:

✔ Diarrhea that's initially bright green to yellow and full of mucous; it may be bubbly, foul-smelling, or slimy, and it may or may not be projectile diarrhea

✔ Seedy poop, often yellowish in color (indicating undigested food)

✔ Dehydration, often severe (see Chapter 13 on dehydration)

✔ Lethargy and sleepiness

✔ Extreme weight loss (up to 50 percent in severe cases)

✔ Vomiting

✔ Squinted, watery eyes (which is a sign of pain)

✔ Oral and stomach ulcers

✔ Coma

Treatment

We have no cure for ECE as of press time. Also, no vaccine is currently available to protect against ECE, although experts are working diligently to develop one. And because ECE is probably viral, no medication can effectively combat it directly. However, some medications can be useful to manage some of the secondary effects of the disease, such as intestinal ulcers and intestinal pain. In addition, secondary bacterial infections may occur in an already weakened animal, and these too require treatment.

Some medications that have been successful (possibly in certain combinations) in treating secondary infections that occur along with ECE are

✔ Amforol

✔ Amoxicillin

✔ Clavamox drops

✔ Cefa drops

✔ Baytril

Over-the-counter anti-cramping medications and tummy coaters have been used in the past for treatment, but they aren't necessary and may cause more harm than good. Cimetidine may be used to prevent ulcers and excretion of excess stomach acid. Some veterinarians use an oral antiviral called "alpha interferon" with mixed results.

Treatments vary by degree of illness and should be administered only under the guidance of your veterinarian. Not all medications work for every ferret. Your vet may find, through trial and error, the perfect medication to get your fuzzy through her ordeal. Every case needs to be evaluated on an individual basis. Please note that treatments of ferrets evolve over time as new medications are developed and new knowledge of diseases is gained. Your vet should be aware of current treatment protocols as they become available.

In healthier or younger ferrets, the disease should be treated like the flu unless signs become severe. The treatment, in addition to the secondary medications, is more complicated for other ferrets. An affected ferret will die of dehydration more quickly than she will starve to death, so keeping her hydrated is the most important part of supportive care. You must combat serious bouts of dehydration with subcutaneous fluids and/or electrolyte replacers, such as Pedialyte or Gatorade. Of course, you must pay attention to feeding your ailing fuzzy, too. The following bullets point out the care procedures:

✔ Your vet should show you how to administer subcutaneous fluids. It takes 20 CCs or 4 teaspoons of fluids per pound of body weight three times a day to keep a healthy ferret alive. A dehydrated ferret needs more than that to stay alive. Your vet should determine how much subcutaneous fluids to administer and when to administer them. It's important to strictly use your vet as your guide, because it's possible to overhydrate or drown your ferret in fluids!

✔ Supplemental feedings with Assist Feed Recipe (see Chapter 13) three to four times a day has proven very helpful in supportive care. Assisted feeding is critical if your ferret isn't eating on her own. It also plays a role in reversing fatty liver disease, which is often the result of severe bouts of ECE. Additionally, assist feeding ensures that your ferret gets enough nutrition and helps keep her hydrated.

When your ferret is back on her paws again, be aware that her intestinal lining will be abnormal for some time, even after the signs seem to go away. She may suffer from periodic bouts of diarrhea and dehydration. Monitor your recovering fuzzy closely and for several months. Long-term damage to the lining of the intestinal tract may mean abnormal stools on and off for quite some time.

Oral fluids are equally important to a recovering ferret, so you can try to give water via spoon or syringe if your ferret isn't drinking from a bowl. The Assist Feed Recipe also will provide some oral fluids.

Intestinal and stomach blockages

The leading causes of death in ferrets under 2 years old are intestinal and stomach obstructions. Young ferrets mouth and taste everything from fingers to foam rubber. But older fuzzies aren't immune to this affliction. Blockages can occur when your overzealous carpet shark eats something that's too big to pass on through his system. Hairballs frequently cause clogs in ferrets (see the later "Hairballs" section). No matter the cause, if the ferret's body can't push the blockage out the other end, everything in her system backs up.

Blockages can occur anywhere in the digestive tract, from the throat to the stomach to the small intestine. Stomach blockages may move around, causing signs to appear and subside. A clog in the belly can last a long time and cause a slow wasting away. If it's a hairball, the mass slowly grows.

Signs

Here are some signs that your fuzzy may be blocked up:

- Constipation
- Tiny poop (looks like string cheese) or black, tarry poop
- Bloating
- Painful belly
- Loss of appetite
- Loss of weight
- Vomiting
- Mouth pawing
- Severe dehydration
- Teeth grinding
- Face rubbing
- Lethargy
- Coma
- Seizuring (occurs after the blockage is complete and has been there 24 hrs or longer)

Diagnosis and treatment

Attempting a diagnosis by feeling around the ferret's belly isn't fail-proof. Sometimes, large tumors cause similar signs and feel like an obstruction. Often, your vet will confirm your suspicions with an X-ray.

If you suspect that your fuzzy ate something she shouldn't have and it isn't life threatening, you can start giving her Laxatone a couple times a day. Watch for foreign objects in anything that comes out the other end (*if* anything poops out).

Poop mixed with water makes identifying foreign bodies quite a bit easier. You can put some poop in a small sandwich bag, add a little water, and squish away!

Keep in mind that it often takes more than Laxatone to fix a blockage problem. If you don't see the object coming out, get straight to the vet. Left untreated, a stopped-up fuzzy can die an agonizing death. Don't wait until the last minute to go to the veterinarian.

Exploratory surgery may be necessary to cure the ailment. After the blockage moves into the small intestine, surgery is imperative, or else a painful death can occur within a day or two. Vets recommend a soft diet for several days following the surgery (see Chapter 8 for tips on changing your ferret's diet).

Because dehydration from failure to eat and drink is a serious problem, administering oral or subcutaneous fluids every few hours is imperative.

If you think pumpkin-pie filler is just for Halloween, think again. This stuff is a great way to flush out your ferret's intestinal tract. If you think your ferret could have a blockage, offer her this tasty treat — as much as she wants. Most ferrets love it! Hopefully, it will flush out any foreign bodies. Word of caution: This doesn't work if the ferret's GI tract is completely blocked. If you think this is the case, contact your vet immediately.

Helicobacter Mustelae (H. mustelae) Infection

Helicobacter mustelae (H. mustelae) is a bacterium that resides in the stomachs of most ferrets. Although your ferret may harbor it after ingesting contaminated poop, she likely got it from mom, because it passes from mom to kit via exposure to the mom's poop. Unfortunately, this bacterium can be serious and cause disease.

Of course, H. mustelae may reside in your ferret's stomach for a lifetime without causing any disease. What makes the bug go from benign to gravely destructive isn't clear. What *is* clear is that serious bouts of H. mustelae infection may result in gastric problems, such as *chronic atrophic gastritis*. Some ferret experts believe that this little bug can be serious enough to cause gastric ulcers — a theory that has mounting evidence to support it. In fact, almost all fuzzy ulcer patients are infected with H. mustelae. Most ferrets adversely affected by H. mustelae are over the age of 4.

Atrophic gastritis is a chronic inflammation of the stomach lining, which leads to loss in function of many of the cells and the replacement of scar tissue. As a result, the stomach's ability to produce stomach acid is impaired, leading to severe digestive problems.

The presence of the infection causes an inflammation of the stomach lining. By attaching to the cells responsible for producing the protective mucosal lining of the stomach, the bacterium hinders the body's ability to produce mucous. This makes the stomach vulnerable to strong stomach acid, and the result can be burns or ulcers. H. mustelae infection also increases the pH of the stomach and impairs the stomach's ability to produce stomach acid; the latter is needed to digest food.

Here are the signs of an infection:

- ✔ Vomiting
- ✔ Loss of appetite
- ✔ Loose stools
- ✔ Excessive salivating
- ✔ Dark, tarry stools
- ✔ Lethargy
- ✔ Teeth grinding
- ✔ Painful belly
- ✔ Enlarged mesenteric lymph nodes
- ✔ Weight loss

It seems as though a ferret's own system can control this bacterial invasion under normal circumstances. Unless your fuzzy becomes extremely stressed out or is already weakened by disease or illness, the signs may not appear at all. The relationship between stress, disease, and illness, however, hasn't been proven to cause the bacterial rebellion. It's currently recommended that you treat only those ferrets that show signs of H. mustelae infection. After the signs appear, your ferret should be treated by a veterinarian immediately. Medication combinations that have been successful include Amoxicillin, Flagyl, and Pepto-Bismol for 4 to 6 weeks, or Biaxin in combination with Amoxicillin for 2 to 3 weeks. These are just two of the current treatments out there. Other treatments are available, and there will undoubtedly be new and improved treatments in the future.

Eosinophilic Gastroenteritis

Eosinophilic gastroenteritis most commonly presents as a disease of the intestinal tract. However, it can involve other organs such as the liver, abdominal lymph nodes, pancreas, or skin. Eosinophils are a type of white blood cell that are released when some types of foreign invaders enter the body. These cells release a substance called *histamine* in their attempt to do battle, but unfortunately in large amounts histamine can instead start attacking the tissue around it. Histamines, by the way, are the same substances that cause your skin to swell after a bee sting. In the intestine they cause damage to intestinal lining. When the intestinal lining isn't functioning normally it can't absorb nutrients or water properly, resulting in diarrhea and weight loss. The foreign invaders that cause eosinophilic gastroenteritis are unknown at this time. Some veterinarians believe a food allergy is involved, but this hasn't been as yet substantiated. These vets may suggest a more natural diet may prevent eosinophilic gastroenteritis or help heal a ferret with the disease. Again, there is yet no scientific, only anecdotal findings.

Signs of eosinophilic gastroenteritis

The following list presents the common signs of eosinophilic gastroenteritis:

- Severe diarrhea
- Loss of appetite
- Weight loss
- Swollen ears and feet (in severe cases)
- Skin ulcerations (in severe cases)
- Abdominal pain (in severe cases)

Diagnosis and prognosis

Your vet can begin to make a diagnosis after reviewing the gastrointestinal signs I list in the previous section. Next comes a complete blood-cell count, which almost always shows a dramatic increase in eosinophils. The predominant signs coupled with the blood test should be almost conclusive. Definitive diagnosis, however, can be made by taking biopsies of the affected tissues — including intestinal or stomach tissue and the lymph nodes around the intestines. These areas often include large numbers of eosinophils in cases of eosinophilic gastroenteritis.

The prognosis should be good if you catch the disease early. With early diagnosis, medication and diet can work their magic and heal your fuzzy. Managing the signs and preventing future damage is your number-one priority. Unfortunately, too many ferrets are diagnosed with eosinophilic gastroenteritis when tissue damage is already profound. In these cases, prognosis is guarded to poor.

Treatment

Because the exact cause of eosinophilic gastroenteritis remains unknown, we have no cure for the condition. Treatment is geared toward managing the current signs and preventing further damage to the tissues. A maintenance dose of a corticosteroid, such as prednisone, may be a lifelong necessity to prevent a relapse and further damage. *Corticosteroids* suppress inflammation and prevent large groups of eosinophils from forming; they also prevent them from breaking down as easily, thus blocking further tissue damage.

A diet change is a must for ferrets with eosinophilic gastroenteritis, because it's suspected that food allergens may be culprits in this disease. If your ferret will eat mice or raw meat, a natural diet is the best choice in my book. (Chapter 8 has the full scoop on dietary options and changing your fuzzy's diet.) If not, you can start off by feeding your fuzzy turkey baby food in the beginning and graduate to Hills z/d diet, which you can get from your vet. Some vets even go so far as to say that the switch to a "hypoallergenic" diet can successfully wean a ferret off of corticosteroids. Vets recommend a food without any grains, such as Wysong's Archetype freeze-dried diet.

Megaesophagus

Megaesophagus is a relatively uncommon disease in ferrets. It's the result of the absence of or the decrease in the ability of the esophageal muscles (located in the throat and torso) to move food into the stomach. This breakdown in the muscles' ability can be a problem all its own, often with unknown causes, or it can be the result of an obstruction or damage to the nerves supplying the esophageal muscles.

The result of this loss of motility is that the esophagus swells as it fills with food and/or liquid. Some of the food may flow back up and out of the mouth, mimicking vomiting; some food may enter the ferret's stomach, making a sound much like water going down a drain. It isn't unusual to hear gurgling or notice that your ferret's breathing is impaired. *Aspiration pneumonia,* the result of inhaling food, also is a dangerous problem that these little ones face.

Your vet can make a diagnosis by using a barium swallow and X-ray, an endoscopy, a fluoroscopy, or clinical observation. There is no cure for this disease. The prognosis is guarded and depends a great deal on controlling the signs and meeting the nutritional needs of the ferret. You need to show a lot of care and dedication, because significant weight loss and dehydration are common with megaesophagus.

Your vet will use many different meds when dealing with megaesophagus, depending on which signs you're treating. You'll probably have to hand feed your ferret small, liquid meals three to five times a day for the remainder of your ferret's life. In the beginning, however, your ferret needs five to six meals a day to get her back on her feet. You can use the Ferret Feeding Formula (FFF), which I describe in Chapter 13. You want to start off with a soupy mixture and feed 10 to 15 CCs per feeding, using a syringe!

Although a soupy mixture is needed, it can increase the danger of aspiration. You need to take great care during feeding. Keep your ferret's head in an elevated position and in line with its neck. Use a syringe to gently feed the soupy mix to the ferret. A little choking is common. If the choking continues or regurgitation occurs, allow your ferret to bring her head down to assist in bringing the food back up. Let her rest 20 to 30 minutes before trying to feed her again.

Some people suggest that you massage your ferret's throat and chest to stimulate swallowing. However, this practice can lead to regurgitation and aspiration. Holding your ferret in the upright position with her head at a 45-degree angle to the floor during feeding, and for 15 minutes or so after feeding, will help gravity take over and facilitate the flow of food into the stomach.

Never use a water bowl for a ferret with megaesophagus, because her head position with the bowl can cause choking. You need to hang a water bottle high in her cage so that she has to stretch her neck up to reach for the water. This will minimize the risk of choking.

Dental Problems

Many things can go wrong with an animal's teeth. No toothy critter can hide from this fact — not even ferrets. Some fuzzy dental problems probably are genetic. Others can result from overuse and misuse of the chompers. Diet and physical health also may play a major role in the destruction of a ferret's teeth. Do your part and make sure your ferret gets a dental checkup during her routine exams at the vet's office (see Figure 16-1). The following sections look at some problems that can occur in your fuzzy's mouth.

Faulty teeth

If you spend enough time with your fuzzy, you'll see her rough and tumble pretty hard with other fuzzies and her imaginary fuzzmates. She'll fall and crash into things. When she's cage crazy, she may gnaw frantically at the cage bars until someone rescues her. Plus, most ferrets are fed a hard kibble diet, too (see Chapter 8). Because of these things, fuzzy teeth endure a lot of wear and tear and abuse. For other fuzzies, teeth issues may be something they were born with. The following sections look at wear and tear and born problems.

To help you get through the dental reading and your life as a fuzzy owner, here are a few terms that you need to be familiar with:

- *Plaque* is a clear "biofilm" that's made up of cellular debris, oral secretions, plenty of bacteria, and some white blood cells. It adheres to the teeth rather quickly and stays there until it's removed.

- *Tartar* and *dental calculus* are interchangeable words and result when minerals are added to the plaque, causing the plaque to harden. All tartar comes from plaque, but not all plaque mineralizes into tartar. Tartar is a hard material that starts to build up on the teeth at the gum line. It also adheres to the teeth and stays there until removal.

- In the presence of plaque or plaque and tartar, *gingivitis* can occur. This is an infection of the gums, or *gingiva,* caused by bacteria — usually those found in the plaque biofilm. Gingivitis is marked by red, inflamed gums.

- *Periodontal disease* often is next to come and is marked by recession of the gum lines and actual bone loss. This is the stage where teeth lose their support, become loose, and fall out. Damage from periodontal disease is permanent, so you need to provide care to prevent the condition. (For more on this condition, see the following section.)

Wear and tear

Chipped, broken, and worn teeth aren't necessarily things to gnash *your* teeth over, unless you notice an obvious problem. But always let an experienced vet make that decision for you if you have any doubt. A vet can smooth out a chipped tooth if the surface is rough and irritating the inside of your ferret's lip. Breaks can be a little more serious. Exposed tooth pulp is painful and can lead to infections. Usually, a root canal or complete removal is warranted.

A chipped tooth may hide a more serious problem, such as a hidden crack leading into the pulp chamber of the tooth. The crack can result in a tooth infection that can spread to other teeth. Even worse, the infection can spread into the body and various vital organs such as the heart, kidneys, and liver. All chipped teeth should be checked by a vet; you can probably wait until her yearly physical, as long as you see no changes (such as discoloration, smell, or drainage). *Note:* All chipped teeth are at risk of future fractures and need to be watched.

Worn teeth are facts of life and will worsen as your ferret ages. Chewing hard kibble into manageable sizes for swallowing may be more difficult, so older fuzzies with worn teeth may need a softer diet (see Chapter 8 for more on switching a ferret's diet).

Growing issues

Your ferret may end up looking more like a Bulldog than a fuzzy weasel. Some poor furkids have teeth that protrude outward — usually, the canines are the culprits. Because these teeth prevent the lip flap from resting against the gums, the ferret's gums may become dry. And the inside of the lip gets irritated from the constant rubbing of the teeth. I've only had this situation happen to one ferret, and the offending teeth were the two lower canines. The problem was fixed by surgically clipping the teeth as far down as necessary and filling them with a safe, hardening substance (acrylic is commonly used).

If a ferret's tooth is severely deformed, completely removing it may be necessary. However, in small animals like ferrets, each tooth is an important part of the strength of the jawbone. Pulling teeth can compromise the jaw by removing a part of the load-bearing strength, along with the subsequent loss of bone that naturally occurs after the loss of a tooth. Therefore, this should be a last resort.

Some furkids actually grow extra baby teeth. Albino kids are notorious for this condition. Usually, all baby teeth are pushed right out when the adult teeth come in. Other times, they linger for several days before finally being squeezed out. If you notice a baby tooth that overstays its welcome, you probably should have your vet uproot it to prevent problems down the road. *Note:* Some adult ferrets have an extra incisor tooth (called a *supernumery tooth*); this condition is harmless.

Says ferret expert Bob Church: "About 5 percent (2 to 9 percent) of ferrets have an extra incisor tooth, and maybe 1 out of 100 of those have two extra teeth. A fewer number of ferrets don't grow all their teeth — usually a front premolar or the bottom tiny mandibular molar. On rare occasions, a ferret will have a tiny extra molar in the roof of her mouth. All these conditions are benign."

The dreaded dental disease

Gum disease, or *periodontal disease,* occurs with great frequency in ferrets — especially ones that are over 5 years old. Come to think of it, it happens in humans even more frequently. Humans are poor tooth brushers; and if we can't take care of our own teeth, we probably won't spend a lot of time on our pets' teeth.

The main cause of periodontal disease is the lack of a natural diet (see Chapter 8). Hair, bone, and other particles from a natural diet are extremely effective at massaging the gums and wiping away plaque and tartar. Other diseases, such as lymphoma, also can play a role in periodontal disease. Experts agree that you can greatly reduce the severity of the disease with daily tooth brushing and with more extensive cleanings performed by an experienced vet, as often as needed.

Dealing with dental dominoes

Friend and ferret expert Bob Church has this to say about dental issues: "All visible dental damage is considered more or less permanent because the ability of the tooth to repair enamel is extremely limited. Thus, dental damage is accumulative over time. Every tooth injury adds to the last one and helps set up the next one. For example, eating kibble wears flat spots on the tooth, which increases the risk of platform fractures (slab fractures) and changes the dental tartar accumulation patterns — both of which help increase gingivitis and periodontal disease, which leads to infections and major tooth loss. I call the disease risk factors 'Dental Dominos.'"

Unqualified people shouldn't scrape a ferret's teeth because they can cause scratches on the teeth that make tartar worse. Vets scrape the teeth free of the tartar and then polish them, making the scratches less of a problem.

The signs of periodontal disease include

- ✔ Loose teeth
- ✔ Discolored teeth
- ✔ Stinky breath
- ✔ Red, inflamed, or receding gums
- ✔ Drooling
- ✔ Mouth ulcers
- ✔ Difficulty eating
- ✔ Tartar and plaque buildup
- ✔ Refusal to floss (okay, just kidding)

At the very least, you should add dental checkups to your weekly or monthly grooming habits. In addition to checking for lumps, bumps, bruises, and other abnormalities, stick your head in your fuzzy's mouth and look for dental problems. For more on general care and grooming habits, head to Chapter 9.

Gum disease and ulcers of the mouth are serious problems by themselves. But did you know they can also be caused by renal disease, especially in ferrets five years and older? Renal disease can be diagnosed with blood tests and a urinalysis.

In addition to the lack of proper texture in a traditional diet, which provides gentle abrasiveness, eating fine particles of carbohydrates and changes in the oral pH contribute to periodontal disease. My answer to combating periodontal disease is to opt for the evolutionary or alternative diet, which offers various food items with varying degrees of texture. (See Chapter 8 for details about the diet.)

Heart Disease

Sadly, heart disease is a rather common problem in middle-aged and older ferrets. The most common type of heart disease seen in ferrets is dilated cardiomyopathy. We focus on these topics in the sections that follow, explaining the signs, diagnosis, and treatment phases of the diseases (and prevention when applicable). (Ferrets also can also suffer from hypertrophic cardiomyopathy and from heart valve disease.)

The ultimate means of establishing a diagnosis of heart disease is an ultrasound of the heart. An ultrasound is the only way to determine the actual cause of the heart problems:

- ✔ If the heart walls are stretched and thin, a doctor can diagnose dilated cardiomyopathy.

- ✔ If the heart walls are much thicker and bigger than normal, the doctor can diagnose hypertrophic cardiomyopathy.

- ✔ If the heart valves are thicker than normal and not working well, the doctor can diagnose valvular heart disease.

- ✔ If heartworms are seen in the heart, the doctor can diagnose heartworm disease.

Because the treatment for these four problems is different, a cardiac ultrasound is necessary to make the correct diagnosis and to select the correct treatment plan for your fuzzy with heart disease.

Dilated cardiomyopathy

Dilated cardiomyopathy is most common in ferrets over the age of 3. It's a form of heart disease that causes damage to the heart muscle. Eventually, during the course of the disease, the heart stretches, enlarges, and weakens. Some of the heart muscle is replaced by scar tissue, making it impossible for the heart to contract normally. Inevitably, the blood flowing out of the heart decreases, and the heart becomes less efficient.

The exact cause of dilated cardiomyopathy is unknown at this time. Possible causes include viral infections and nutritional problems, such as deficiencies of taurine, l-carnitine, l-arginine, or perhaps even a deficiency of Coenzyme Q10 in the diet. The relationship of a taurine deficiency causing dilated cardiomyopathy has already been proven in cats. Unlike cats, however, ferrets don't improve when extra taurine is added to their diets.

How long your big-hearted fuzzy will live with dilated cardiomyopathy really depends on how fast her heart is deteriorating. If your ferret is diagnosed early, and you and your vet manage the signs properly, she may live for 2 or 3 more years.

Signs

Following are the signs of the dilated cardiomyopathy form of heart disease:

- Labored breathing
- Coughing
- Pale or bluish gum coloring
- Decreased or no appetite
- Heart murmur
- Lethargy
- Frequent rests during play
- Muffled heart sounds
- Hypothermia (low body temperature)
- Fluid buildup in the chest and abdominal areas

Ferrets with cardiomyopathy often have enlarged livers or spleens, as well. Frequently, a suffering fuzzy has a swollen belly. In this case, she probably has congestive heart failure, and the swollen belly results from a buildup of fluid in the abdomen. The ferret likely also has fluid accumulating in her chest and lungs.

Diagnosis

Heart disease usually begins long before the diagnosis is made; however, a diagnosis also can be made before the onset of the signs. X-rays can be taken to look at the size and shape of the heart. Dilated cardiomyopathy heart disease causes the heart to be bigger and rounder than normal. An EKG can check for abnormal rhythms and conduction disturbances. And, of course, the best diagnosis method is an ultrasound, which I discuss earlier in this section.

Treatment

Dilated cardiomyopathy generally is irreversible and has no cure. Treatment is designed to control the disease and slow down its progression. You can manage dilated cardiomyopathy with medication. The medications that vets commonly prescribe are

- ✔ **An ACE inhibitor** — such as benazepril or enalapril
- ✔ **A diuretic** — such as furosemide
- ✔ **A muscle contraction strengthener** — such as digoxin or pimobendan

Only your vet and/or vet cardiologist can determine which medications and what dosages should work for your ferret.

Heartworms

Heartworm disease is a parasitic roundworm *(Dirofilaria immitis)* infestation that attacks the heart. Where many mosquitoes buzz around, vets and ferret owners will see plenty of cases of heartworm. Ferrets are just as susceptible to this deadly disease as cats and dogs. In fact, many carnivores are. Even if your ferret doesn't go outside, mosquitoes can come inside.

Infected mosquitoes inject the larva into the ferret's bloodstream with a single piercing bite. The deadly parasite then develops and migrates to the fuzzy's heart, where the adult worms wreak cardiac havoc. It only takes a single worm to produce devastating results.

Signs

Signs of heartworm disease include the following:

- ✔ Coughing or hacking
- ✔ Lethargy
- ✔ Fluid buildup in the chest and abdomen
- ✔ Labored breathing
- ✔ Pale lips, gums, and tongue
- ✔ Hypothermia (low body temperature)
- ✔ Heart murmur
- ✔ Muffled heart sounds
- ✔ Green color to the urine

Prevention

The best course of action against heartworm is prevention. Fortunately, you can acquire several effective options to prevent your ferret from getting heartworm:

- ✔ **Heartgard:** You can use Heartgard for cats or ¼ of the Heartgard for small dogs once a month. Be aware: Most fuzzies don't like the stuff!

  Merial, the maker of Heartgard, advises against splitting the pills or chewables. The company states that the effective ingredient (ivermectin) isn't evenly distributed throughout the pills or chewables, so you don't know for sure if your fuzzy is really getting an effective dose. Ferrets can handle large dosages of ivermectin. A whole feline chewable Heartgard has less ivermectin in it than a dose a fuzzy would receive for treatment of ear mites.

- ✔ **Ivermectin:** Some vets prefer giving ferrets liquid ivermectin orally (or through injection) on a monthly basis.

- ✔ **Interceptor:** These tablets are small and easy to crush, and you can mix them into some baby food or Ferretone. Interceptor tablets need to be given once a month.

- ✔ **Revolution:** This medicine for cats is a liquid that you apply directly to the skin on the neck or above the shoulders (you do this monthly). In addition to heartworm prevention, Revolution kills fleas, ticks, and ear mites.

  Most vets prescribe the kitten dose of Revolution for a ferret when protecting her from fleas and ticks. This makes sense considering how little ferrets weigh! Some vet cardiologists, though, have suggested that this dose isn't strong enough to protect a ferret against heartworms; they say that the cat dose is the effective dose against heartworms. This may seem quite high, because cats can weigh so much more than ferrets, and you don't want to risk the life of your beloved pet! Therefore, always discuss this subject with your vet to make sure your ferret is kept healthy and adequately protected.

- ✔ **Advantage Multi:** This product is new to the U.S. market. The two main ingredients are imidacloprid (Advantage) and moxidectin. Like Revolution, it's a monthly topical applied directly to the skin on the neck or above the shoulders. In addition to heartworm prevention, Advantage Multi kills fleas, ear mites, and intestinal worms. The kitten size (2 to 5 pounds) is the size recommended for ferret use.

Before beginning a heartworm preventative, your ferret should test negative for heartworms, if possible. Fuzzies can be tested with the same in-clinic test that dogs get. Another detection method is a cardiac ultrasound, but it takes an experienced ultrasounder to visualize the heartworms in the ferret's heart.

None of these preventatives are approved for use in ferrets or have been tested in ferrets, so are used at the owner's risk. Manufacturers of these medications will not help out if there's a reaction or problem, such as not protecting the ferret against heartworms, because the use in ferrets is what's considered "off" label. They are used extensively by ferret owners, however.

Treatment

Infected ferrets usually die without treatment. Heartworm treatment, however, is relatively new in ferrets. Some vets report a 60- to 75-percent survival rate when using Immiticide to treat heartworms. Prednisone is often used during and after the treatment period. The safer option is to treat more conservatively with ivermectin, furosemide, and prednisone. High doses of ivermectin slowly kills the adult heartworms. Furosemide treats the fluid retention, and prednisone prevents dangerous blood clots from forming as the heartworms die. (Occasionally diltiazem will also be used to treat the right-sided congestive heart failure that the heartworms can cause.)

Vets highly recommend cage rest during heartworm treatment. As you can see, prevention is much better and safer than treatment!

What extra care you can give your ferret

Along with extra rest, ferrets with heart disease should embark on a gentle exercise routine, with plenty of close supervision during playtime. Over-stimulation may worsen the condition. Of course, common sense also dictates that frightening or startling these little heart breakers isn't a good idea. No barking dogs, firecrackers, or tuba playing, please. Ferrets with heart disease benefit from a low-sodium diet. Use only treats and baby food (such as turkey and turkey gravy) with a low salt content.

Influenza (The "Flu")

Don't sneeze on your fuzzy, and don't let her sneeze on you, either! Your ferret is highly susceptible to human influenza A; you can pass it back and forth to each other if you're not careful. Influenza is the most common respiratory infection in ferrets. In healthy ferrets, recovery takes about five days. In weak or old ferrets, the sickness can be a little more serious, lasting several weeks.

Disseminated Idiopathic Myofasciitis

Katrina D. Ramsell, PhD, DVM

Disseminated idiopathic myofasciitis (DIM), also known as "Polymyositis," is a relatively new disease in domestic ferrets. The earliest documented case is from 1999, and the disease was first described in 2003. DIM causes a severe inflammatory condition that primarily affects a ferret's muscles (myositis). The disease generally affects ferrets less than two years of age and is suspected when a ferret exhibits particular clinical signs and has blood values consistent with the disease. Muscle biopsies are currently the only way of confirming the disease in a living ferret. Until 2006, DIM was considered a fatal disease. There are now some confirmed cases and several suspected cases that have responded favorably to the current treatment protocol and are doing well.

Initial signs of DIM usually come on relatively quickly and commonly include:

- A severe, persistent, fluctuating fever (often 104-108($^\circ$F)

- Severe lethargy and weakness

- Dehydration

- Enlarged lymph nodes or masses under the skin

- Abnormal stools

- Decreased appetite

Other signs that may occur with DIM include:

- Sensitivity/pain when touched, especially in the hind end

- Increased heart and respiratory rates

- Clear discharge from the nose and sometimes eyes

- Tiny orange dots on the skin

- Pale gums

Ferrets with DIM often have a dramatic increase in their white blood cell count, with most of these cells being neutrophils (cells involved with inflammation and infection). DIM ferrets are also commonly anemic (too few red blood cells), and chemistry results often show a decrease in the blood protein albumin and an increase in blood glucose.

Despite many diagnostic tests, a cause for DIM still has not been identified. It does not appear to be a contagious disease, and it has not been associated with any particular breeders, foods, or environmental agents. DIM is likely an immune-mediated disease, and vaccines are currently being investigated as a potential cause for this condition. There is no apparent link between this disease and ferret vaccines that are *currently* available on the market.

Although DIM was considered a fatal disease for three years, a few ferrets confirmed to have DIM and several ferrets suspected to have the disease have responded well to the current treatment protocol. All confirmed, untreated cases have died. If you suspect your ferret has DIM you should contact a ferret knowledgeable veterinarian immediately. Contact information for consultation on DIM and more complete information on the disease is available through the American Ferret Association Web site at: www.ferret.org.

Here are the signs that your ferret has influenza (ones we all, unfortunately, know so well):

✔ Sneezing and coughing

✔ Runny nose and eyes

✔ Fever over 104° Fahrenheit

✔ Lethargy

✔ Wheezing

✔ Diarrhea

✔ Face rubbing

✔ Loss of appetite

Unfortunately, the signs are so general and so common to other conditions that it can be difficult to identify the flu.

A little tender, loving care usually is all it takes to get your ferret through. However, antibiotics, fluids, and tummy-coaters may be necessary to combat severe bouts of the flu. Be sure to consult your vet. For severe sneezing, some vets may recommend an antihistamine. Be sure to wash your hands frequently after and in between handling your sicky. Your ferret won't think twice about sharing her miserable illness with you or other ferrets.

Tylenol (acetaminophen) is extremely toxic to ferrets, even in very low doses. The liver metabolizes the medicine, which will send your ferret reeling into liver failure quickly before killing him. Many over-the-counter medicines contain acetaminophen. It's important that you don't use any over-the-counter products without your vet's guidance and approval. You can prevent many fatal mistakes.

If the signs persist for longer than a week, or your fuzzy shows signs of refusing to eat at all, you may not be dealing with the flu. Get to a vet immediately. A ferret with the flu is crabby and tired, but she isn't knocked completely on her butt. Also, look for abnormal discharge from her nose. A flu discharge is clear.

Bacterial pneumonia can bubble up for several reasons — often due to a flu gone from bad to worse. In addition to having flu-like signs, pneumonia causes open-mouthed breathing or labored breathing along with severe, sometimes discolored, nasal goo. Bacterial pneumonia can kill your fuzzy quickly. The treatment depends on the type of bacteria producing the pneumonia. To make the diagnosis and prescribe the defense, your vet can perform a tracheal wash by introducing a small amount of saline into the trachea and then sucking it back up to perform a culture. This can be safely done under a general anesthetic and oxygen. Depending on the type of bacteria present, your vet may prescribe a dosage of penicillin, sulfadiazine, or trimethoprim.

Ferrets, contrary to popular belief, don't catch the common cold, which is caused by a rhinovirus. However, ferrets can catch bacterial sinus infections, influenza A, and upper-respiratory infections, all of which can mimic cold-like signs.

Urinary Tract Problems

Several urinary tract problems can pop up in carpet sharks. Many of the problems have similar signs, so a trip to the veterinarian is advisable upon the outset of signs — especially when you consider that urinary tract infections can become serious enough to cause kidney damage and even death. You need to have a correct diagnosis made and begin treatment as soon as possible.

Bladder or urinary tract infections

Bladder or urinary tract infections are caused most often by that irritating resident bacteria *E. coli* (found in poop, so keep that litter box clean). Staphylococcus is another bacterium that can be the evildoer. Although both males and females are susceptible to this type of infection, it seems more common in females in heat and females with adrenal disease (see Chapter 16).

Signs of a bladder or urinary tract infection include

- ✔ Straining to urinate
- ✔ Painful urination
- ✔ Frequent piddles
- ✔ Discolored or smelly urine

If you notice any of these signs, take your critter to the vet immediately. Bladder infections can travel to the kidneys and cause major damage and death. By the time a full-blown kidney infection develops, your fuzzy may be so gravely ill that treatment can prove futile, so correct and early diagnosis is imperative.

Most experts agree that treatment with the proper antibiotics should continue for a minimum of two weeks; some opt for a three-week course of treatment. Stopping the medication too soon may cause the infection to flare up again. And the bug may be even stronger and more resistant to medications the next time around.

Prostate problems

Although male ferrets can get urinary tract infections — they may exhibit similar signs — your vet should first rule out a prostate problem, such as inflammation, cysts, tumors, or abscesses. Prostate woes may be diagnosed just by feeling for an enlargement. You may get to see a little pus ooze out of the fuzzy when his infected prostate is squeezed. Eeeeew! Because this male condition always is a result of adrenal disease (see Chapter 16), it may go away when you treat that condition.

Stones and blockages

Bladder stones aren't that common in fuzzies, and the cause still isn't fully understood. Some experts speculate that a poor diet high in ash or plant-based protein plays a major role. Other possible causes include bacterial or viral infections and even genetic links. Whatever the cause, a bladder stone is a painful condition. The signs are similar to those of a urinary tract infection. Other signs may include bloody or gritty urine (the grit or sand actually is mineral deposits).

If the stones in your fuzzy's system get big enough or collect in the same area, blockages can occur. Your fuzzy will no longer leave piddle puddles at this point. This situation is painful and deadly and requires immediate attention and treatment.

Because stones and blockages mimic infections, diagnosis can be difficult. Often, your vet can feel the large, urine-filled bladder or even the stones themselves. Use of X-rays has been successful in identifying stones in the bladder.

Treatment depends on the severity of the situation. It may be as simple as a change in diet (see Chapter 8), or it may require more drastic measures — such as surgery. A vet will put your ferret on a regimen of antibiotics to help combat the problem.

Eye Problems

I believe that most every living thing with eyeballs is prone to cataracts and other afflictions of the eye. Naturally, ferrets fall into the group of susceptible animals. I have several fuzzies with cataracts, which are quite common. Some of these furballs are completely blind; others have partial vision. Very often, however, most eye problems in ferrets can be corrected surgically or medically. Don't worry if your ferret's eyes aren't fixable; a blind ferret or one with limited vision can find trouble as well as or better than a carpet shark with perfect vision.

Living with cataracts

Most of us know people who've had cataracts removed from their eyes so that they could see better. Ferrets are prone to this eye disorder, and they can have their cataracts removed just like we can. The condition is easy to spot, because the ferret's eye becomes opaque or filmy behind the pupil. Cataracts eventually cause blindness because they prevent light from reaching the retina.

If your ferret has a cataract and is under 1 year old, the problem probably is genetic (that is, the result of poor breeding). Some cataracts can be caused by an injury (even while a furkid is inside her mom), a disease, or even an improper diet. Cataracts also may be a developing sign of old age. Although your ferret may be treated for cataracts, blind ferrets adapt very well, as I explain in the "Eye Problems" section.

What sort of things cause interference with sight in the ferret? To name just a few:

- ✔ Retinal Disease
- ✔ Disease of the lens (cataracts or luxated (twisted) lens)
- ✔ Disease of the optic nerve
- ✔ Central nervous system problems that affect the vision center (stroke, head trauma)
- ✔ Trauma to the eye globe causing rupture or puncture
- ✔ Corneal Disease (scarring from ulcers or trauma)

Following are sure-fire signs of eye problems:

- ✔ Your ferret seems more cautious about moving around.
- ✔ She startles and backs off or snaps at you when you reach in to grab her.
- ✔ She walks into things.
- ✔ She avoids open spaces and runs along walls or large objects.
- ✔ Cataracts are visibly present in her eyes.
- ✔ She places a call to your health-insurance carrier to see if laser surgery is covered.

If you're not sure if your ferret is blind, you can do the finger test. All my sighted ferrets rapidly chase, follow, or watch my finger as I move it from side to side. My blind guys just pop up their heads and listen to figure out what everyone else is doing. I love these guys. They're so cute!

What? Is your ferret deaf?

Having a deaf ferret isn't the end of the world, much like blindness can be overcome. Deafness is common and can be caused by many things. Perhaps the most common cause is a genetic defect. Breeders manipulate many genes to achieve the pretty white markings on ferrets, which can also be associated with deafness. Other causes of deafness include head trauma, infections such as meningitis, seizures, severe and ongoing ear-mite infestations, and ear infections. Certain medications, such as Gentamicin, Gentocin, and Streptomycin, also have been proven to cause deafness in ferrets.

Not sure if your ferret is deaf? Want to find out for sure? Do you want to know what type of behaviors deaf ferrets exhibit, and what you can expect in the future? How do you care for a deaf ferret? What considerations must you make? Well, there are several ways you can determine, but first remember to test in your own home with no distractions, no other ferrets, and no use of vibrations. Do not use visual cues. Do not use odors. It's also important to wait until the ferret has explored the room and is comfortable with his surroundings.

- ✔ Use a squeaky toy, and when he isn't looking, squeak it to see if he responds.

- ✔ Same thing as above, but clap loudly or slam a book shut.

- ✔ Put some pennies in a coffee tin and shake it when the ferret turns his back to you.

I have oversimplified the subject of deafness in this brief overview. I can point you to easy explanations for all your questions! You can find an extraordinary amount of information on deaf ferrets on my friend Wolfy's Web site: www.wolfysluv.com/deaf.html. I encourage you to visit this site to educate yourself on the topic of deafness.

Blind ferrets adapt and function very well. However, you must take special precautions when dealing with a blind ferret. For example, you don't want to sneak up on her or startle her. You may need to take extra care when ferret-proofing your home to keep her away from falling dangers such as furniture or stairs. You can use scent mapping to help her learn her way around. You have many ways to improve your relationship with your visually impaired ferret! For more information, visit www.wolfysluv.com/blind_ferrets.html.

Aleutian Disease Virus (ADV)

Aleutian Disease (AD) is a contagious and potentially fatal ferret disease caused by a parvovirus. No vaccine is currently available for ferrets. Named after the Aleutian mink, which is highly susceptible to infection with this disease, ADV was first diagnosed on a mink ranch in the 1940s and then in ferrets in the 1960s. The biggest problem with this virus for the ferret isn't the virus itself, but the ferret's immune-system response to the invader.

When a virus enters the body, the body usually forms antibodies. These antibodies attach to the virus to help the body's immune system identify the virus as a foreign invader, thus triggering a defensive response to destroy it. In the case of ADV, a large complex of substances, not just the antibodies, bind with the viral particles and form antibody or immune complexes. These large complexes circulate throughout the body until they're deposited into the tissues of various organs; here, due to their size, the complexes cause inflammation. In small amounts, the complexes won't cause outward signs of disease; however, if the body deposits enough of these complexes into one area, the clinical disease may result.

Although transmission of ADV can occur through the air, typical transmission occurs through direct contact with the bodily fluids of an infected ferret, or from contaminated cages, supplies, or humans. Practicing good husbandry and sanitation is the best way to prevent the spread of ADV. ***Note:*** The ADV can remain in a ferret-free home for up to two years.

Aleutian Disease Virus (ADV) is the actual organism that causes the disease and Aleutian Disease (AD) is the disease caused by the virus. ADV is not interchangeable with AD.

Doctors are still researching AD, and vets don't yet agree on how easily or quickly it can be passed. What they do agree on is that not all ADV-positive ferrets will develop the clinical signs of the disease. Some may never show signs at all. The bad news is that these seemingly healthy animals may be able to shed the virus, or pass it to other ferrets, at any time. According to Susan Brown, DVM, co-author of *Essentials of Ferrets: A Guide for Practitioners,* "We know very little about this 'carrier state,' including how often or under what conditions the virus is shed by the carrier, how long the infection can last, and whether the ferret can ever completely rid its body of the virus."

Clinical signs

Yes, many ADV-positive ferrets may never show clinical signs; and no one can predict if or when the ADV-positive ferret will show signs. It can be months or even years, if ever. The signs of AD are variable and depend largely on what organs are affected and what, if any, secondary infections have arisen as a result. The following list presents the possibilities; upon seeing a sign, head to your vet on the double:

- ✔ Weight loss
- ✔ Bloody (black, tarry) stools
- ✔ Hind-end weakness
- ✔ Lethargy

> ✔ Anemia
>
> ✔ Body twitching or seizures
>
> ✔ Enlarged liver or spleen
>
> ✔ Difficulty breathing

Diagnosis and prognosis

Signs of AD vary by type and severity, and they can't be used as the sole diagnostic tool of the disease. Unfortunately, many other ferret illnesses and diseases have the same or similar manifestations as AD. The vet will use the ferret's history, along with the clinical signs, to rule out the most likely non-AD causes of your ferret's illness.

Doctors may run a specific test on either blood or saliva to confirm or rule out ADV, provided by Avecon Diagnostics, called the ELISA test. Unfortunately, as of press time, the accuracy of this test hasn't been determined. Additionally, a positive result doesn't necessarily mean that ADV is what's causing the clinical signs you see; it only means that the virus likely is present. Perhaps the most definitive diagnosis comes from taking biopsies of multiple organs.

Science currently has no cure for AD and no way to predict how long a ferret that exhibits clinical AD-related signs will live. It all depends on the severity of the damage to the organs. Unfortunately, most active cases of AD aren't diagnosed until the later stages of the disease, thus shortening the ferrets' lives. Based on the clinical signs present, the positive presence of ADV and its infectious nature, and the likely prognosis, you and your vet must discuss the best plan of action for your ferret.

Treatment

You and your vet can manage the clinical signs to a degree with supportive care. The care will vary according to what signs are present and the degree in which they're manifested. Your ferret may require assisted feedings and additional fluids to help keep her hydrated. Your vet also may prescribe anti-inflammatory drugs and other medications to treat the clinical signs.

You need to put AD into perspective and not panic. AD has been around for decades and has thus far been far less of a serious issue than problems such as cancer, ulcers, intestinal blockages, and Helicobacter. You should always practice good husbandry procedures to prevent the spread of any disease from ferret to ferret, especially if you own multiple fuzzies or come into contact with fuzzy strangers.

Canine Distemper

Canine distemper is an unforgiving and miserable disease that's 99.9 percent fatal. In extremely rare instances, ferrets have survived, but all survivors have suffered neurological impairments. Because no treatment is available, prevention is critical. You can do your part to prevent the disease by vaccinating your fuzzy.

The canine distemper virus is extremely contagious and can be transmitted to your fuzzy via other infected animals. If you think your fuzzy is safe from canine distemper because she never leaves the house, you're dead wrong. You can carry this virus into your household on your shoes and clothing. The distemper virus also can live a long time outside of the victim's body. So be careful and do the right thing: Vaccinate your fuzzy. ***Note:*** Humans can't catch this disease from the poor victims.

The *incubation* period (the time it takes from the day of infection to the onset of signs) in your ferret may be as little as 7 days or as long as 21 days. When the signs appear, death usually occurs quickly, because the virus attacks many organs at once. On rare occasions, a fuzzy may suffer a longer, more miserable death. Because the prognosis is hopeless and the signs are unbearably miserable, if your vet makes a positive diagnosis, he should humanely euthanize your ferret as soon as possible. The extremely rare survivor will just suffer severe neurological damage and her quality of life will be poor.

Clinical signs of distemper include

- ✔ Eye infection/discharge
- ✔ Severe lethargy
- ✔ Loss of appetite
- ✔ Rash on chin, lips, and nose
- ✔ Rash on belly and heinie
- ✔ Hardened/thick paw pads
- ✔ Diarrhea
- ✔ Vomiting
- ✔ Seizures
- ✔ Coma

Pet owners who decide against vaccinating for distemper run the risk of not only a single ferret becoming infected with distemper, but also the entire group. A single ferret can come into contact with the virus — perhaps from the owner's shoe or during a vet checkup where an infected dog was in the office — become ill, and infect all the ferrets in the household before the owner realizes what's going on.

Enlarged Spleen (Splenomegaly)

The spleen (in ferrets and in other animals and humans) has several functions: For example,

- ✔ It serves as a blood purifier, filtering out bacteria and damaged cells.

- ✔ It provides the perfect environment for the cells of the immune system to learn how to counterattack an invasion of possible marauding organisms.

- ✔ It stores iron from old red blood cells, which is used to make new red blood cells. In ferrets and many other species, the spleen is an additional site for red and white blood cell production.

- ✔ In some species, the spleen stores blood and releases it in times of need.

An enlarged spleen, or *splenomegaly,* is extremely prevalent in fuzzies, and no one really knows why. This problem often appears by itself, with no other underlying diseases. The ferret's spleen normally gets larger with age, but sometimes this growth is accelerated. One common thought is that the use of certain anesthetics rapidly causes this condition. The enlargement in this case is temporary only while the animal is under the effects of the anesthetic. Then the spleen goes back to normal. The spleen is very elastic, and may enlarge and go back to normal on its own as well when responding to the body's needs for more cells

Diagnosing an enlarged spleen is relatively easy. Most experienced vets should be able to feel the enlarged organ by simply squishing around the ferret's abdomen. And an X-ray often confirms the size and condition of the organ. Care should be taken not to apply enough pressure to rupture a severely bulging spleen.

The shared expert opinion regarding treatment is to leave the spleen in if it isn't causing discomfort or other problems. In other words, "If it ain't broke, don't fix it." Fuzzies generally can live long, healthy lives with big spleens. Removing a spleen unnecessarily can put your baby in more jeopardy. On the other hand, if the oversized spleen is causing discomfort, lethargy, or loss of appetite, removal of the organ is necessary. Surgery to remove the spleen actually is straightforward, and the survival rate is extremely high — especially when no other illnesses are present.

It's always a good idea to have your vet send out a sample of the spleen to a pathologist to determine the cause of the enlargement. Remember, illnesses or diseases caught early have a better chance of being treated more effectively.

Hairballs

Ferrets are prone to developing gastric hairballs, and hairballs can lead to intestinal blockages. Unlike cats, ferrets won't leave colorful wads of urped-up fur on your newly shampooed carpet. Ferrets are capable of throwing up, but usually the fur accumulates in the ferret's body until it becomes a large mass — a mass too big to go either up or down. Hairballs and other blockages (see the section "Intestinal and stomach blockages") can cause ferrets to become seriously ill — and they often cause death.

You should give your ferret a hairball preventative such as Laxatone, Petromalt, or Laxaire on a regular basis to help clean out her system. I give each of my ferrets ¼ teaspoon of a hairball preventative a few times a week. Most ferrets like the taste of the stuff, although some need to get used to it. With more difficult types, you may need to insist that they take it — by squeezing it directly into their mouths. You can find hairball remedies or preventives at many pet stores and certainly at the larger pet supply stores. Some ferret shelters and veterinarians also carry these products. You absolutely must have a tube of this type of product on hand at all times.

If you think your fuzzy has ingested something that can cause major internal damage, increase the hairball remedy to ½ teaspoon twice a day to help pass the object through. Monitor her health and behavior closely and get her to the vet immediately if her health deteriorates. If you don't have a yummy-tasting hairball preventative on hand for some reason, a good substitute is petroleum jelly (Vaseline). You may need to mix it with a little Ferretone or another liquid treat to help the ferret swallow it.

Rabies

Although ferrets are highly unlikely to contract rabies, the possibility does exist. Rabies, caused by a rhabdovirus, is passed through the saliva of an infected animal, most frequently through a bite that penetrates the skin. After entering the body, the deadly virus attaches to nerve bundles, reproduces, and migrates to the victim's brain. The virus then travels along nerve bundles until it reaches the salivary glands, where the animal can then pass it to another victim through a bite.

Many different strains of the rabies virus exist, including rodent, raccoon, fox, and skunk strains. Studies suggest that fuzzies are most susceptible to the raccoon strain, which they can pass on before death.

Rabies can manifest itself in one of two ways:

- **Furious rabies:** With furious rabies, the infected animal exhibits intense aggression, biting, and foaming at the mouth.

- **Dumb rabies:** With dumb rabies, the animal becomes lethargic and deathly ill, and wants little to do with people or other animals. Animals with dumb rabies don't attack and usually die quickly. Although ferret infection is extremely rare, studies indicate that ferrets will likely exhibit dumb rabies, with death occurring seven days (on average) after the ferret has been infected.

The following signs also suggest that your ferret may have rabies (although they can indicate a host of problems):

- Disorientation

- Loss of coordination

- Muscle spasms

- Difficulty breathing

- Drooling

- Nervousness

- Hind-leg weakness

- Passiveness

- Hind-end paralysis

Today, unlike many years ago, you have a choice on how much life "insurance" you're willing to buy for your lovable fuzzbutt, because you can give her a rabies vaccine. Some people want to weigh the pros and cons of vaccinating (the only viable con being a history of life-threatening allergic reactions), but the pros weigh heavily on the scale. Failure to vaccinate your ferret can lead to a miserable disease and death. To the true fuzzy human, the emotional cost of losing a ferret to a preventable disease is immeasurable. Proof of vaccination also may calm the fears of people who get bitten or scratched — and perhaps prevent confiscation of your pet (see Chapter 3).

Ulcers

By the time you're done reading about all that can go wrong with your fuzzy, you may be suffering from an ulcer yourself! Ulcers are one of the most common ferret diseases. An *ulcer* is an open sore, which can occur on the skin, eyes, or mucous membranes. For this section, I talk about ulcers of the gastrointestinal tract. The causes of ulcers are just about the same for fuzzies and humans:

- **Stress, stress, and more stress:** The stress can come from illness, disease, grief (loss of a cagemate), low-quality food, injury, or even anxiety over the environment (overcrowding, abuse, small cage, poor husbandry, no exercise, and so on). (For more on helping your fuzzy grieve, check out Chapter 17.)

- **Possible bacterial invasion:** The bacteria *H. mustelae's* presence may trigger a progressive inflammatory reaction in a ferret's stomach's lining. The reaction weakens the lining and predisposes it to further damage. Ulcers, perhaps? No one knows for sure if bacteria can be directly linked to ulcers, but it sure can cause some serious damage to the tummy.

- **Ulcer-causing substances:** These substances include alcohol, aspirin, and certain medications.

- **Hairballs or other stomach foreign bodies:** Rubbing on the lining of the stomach in the same area over and over can cause severe irritation.

Signs

The signs of an ulcer include the following:

- Lethargy
- Tender belly
- Face rubbing
- Black, tarry stools
- Teeth grinding
- Loss of appetite
- Vomiting (may be bloody)
- Weight loss
- Pale gums
- Bad breath
- Hunched posture (painful abdomen)
- More aggression (pain)

If you notice any of these signs, take your ferret to the vet for an exam and diagnosis.

Diagnosis

Having an ulcer diagnosed as soon as possible is important, because it's a very painful condition that may lead to death. Besides being unable to adequately digest their food, ulcer patients bleed internally from oozing blood vessels. For some reason, ulcer signs often are misdiagnosed as another intestinal or stomach problem. An effective diagnostic tool is a barium X-ray, which shows any signs of burned-out bellies or intestine.

Treatment

Treatment of ulcers usually begins with antibiotic therapy, with medicines such as Amoxicillin and Biaxin to combat H. mustelae. Some veterinarians use Flagyl. To treat the ulcer itself, most vets use Carafate (which is most effective when given 10 minutes prior to feeding; consult your vet). Your vet may prescribe OTC acid relievers such as Pepcid AC or Tagamet to relieve the burning and nausea that accompany ulcers. A bland diet is recommended during treatment (see Chapter 8 for tips on changing diet).

Because a ferret's body is always secreting stomach acid to help break down food, treatment can be long and tedious. It can and usually will take over a month for a ferret's ulcer to heal, and you should be prepared to treat the ulcer for a minimum of ten days after all signs have disappeared. Also, don't be surprised if your ferret gets another ulcer down the road. After she gets one, she'll be prone to getting more.

If you allow your ferret's ulcer to progress without proper treatment, it may become so deep that it hits a major blood vessel and causes the suffering fuzzy to bleed to death internally. (The black, tarry stool associated with ulcers, for example, actually is digested blood and a sign of bleeding in the digestive tract.) If your ferret doesn't bleed to death, anemia may result from the constant rupturing of small blood vessels in the belly. Ulcers can also go all the way through the lining of the stomach and perforate, leading to the dumping of stomach contents into the abdomen and resulting in peritonitis and death.

Chapter 16

Finding and Treating the Big C and Other Lumps

In This Chapter

▶ Surveying the top three ferret cancers

▶ Identifying and removing skin tumors and chordomas

▶ Reviewing your treatment and manageability options

*U*nfortunately, whether you own one ferret or ten, you're likely to encounter ferret cancer during your time as a ferret owner. The three most prevalent cancer conditions are adrenal disease (which may or may not be cancerous), insulinoma, and lymphosarcoma. Symptoms and treatments vary, as well as prognoses.

As you'll see in this chapter, the Big C diagnosis is rarely an immediate death sentence. Many cases are treatable. Others are manageable, and your ferret may live a few more quality years after the diagnosis, with or without ongoing medical intervention. However, early detection and treatment are instrumental in adding quality months or even years to your fuzzy's life, so you need to watch for changes in your fuzzy's appearance, habits, and behavior. A good vet will trust your judgment that something isn't quite right with your fuzzbutt (see Chapter 12 for tips on finding a good vet). In this chapter, I discuss the three main types of ferret cancer. I also discuss chordomas and skin tumors.

Adrenal Gland Disease

Everyone has adrenal glands, including ferrets. These tiny organs are located very close to the kidneys. In a nutshell, *adrenal glands* produce extremely important hormones that help regulate blood glucose levels and electrolyte levels, increase musculature, and help the ferret in times of stress. Different areas of the adrenal glands are responsible for producing different hormones. For instance, small amounts of sex hormones, or "sex steroids," are produced by these glands.

Adrenal gland disease is extremely common in ferrets, but no one knows exactly why. The adrenal glands can start overproducing sex steroids that act the same way excessive amounts of the sex hormones testosterone and progesterone would act. Usually starting out as hyperplasia, the adrenal glands produce more gland tissue, which results in excessive hormone production. As the disease progresses, however, neoplasia (cancer) can develop. Fortunately for ferrets, *metastasis,* or spreading of the cancer beyond the adrenal gland(s) to other organs, doesn't happen often.

The disease can strike ferrets as young as 2 years old, but it commonly hits ferrets that are 3 and older. Many theories exist pertaining to the cause:

- ✔ Some people suspect the problem has something to do with early neutering, which I define as neutering before puberty or prior to sexual development.

- ✔ Others believe adrenal gland disease is caused by the unnatural light cycles that ferrets experience while living in people's homes. These light cycles differ greatly from what the ferrets would experience naturally in the wild.

- ✔ Still others believe that prolonged stress may be a factor. Perhaps the cause is a combination of all these things.

The signs of adrenal gland disease depend largely on which hormones are being produced, the gender of the ferret, and the stage of the disease's development. Within these factors, the signs may include the following:

- ✔ Hair loss on the tail/body

   Hair loss on the tail and/or body is one of the most common signs of adrenal gland disease. However, it doesn't have to be present for adrenal gland disease to exist. Hair loss can come and go. A ferret may lose all her tail fur only to have it grow back thick and fluffy later on. Some may attribute this phenomenon to a seasonal coat change. It is, however, thought to be the early stage of adrenal gland disease — hyperplasia that temporarily resolves itself. As the disease progresses, hair loss usually starts on the tail and progresses up the body. The hair loss, if adrenal-gland related, is always symmetrical. Sometimes, ferrets lose all but their socks and hats.

- ✔ Excessive itchiness, with or without crusts, redness, or flaking

- ✔ Swollen vulva in spayed females (see Figure 16-1)

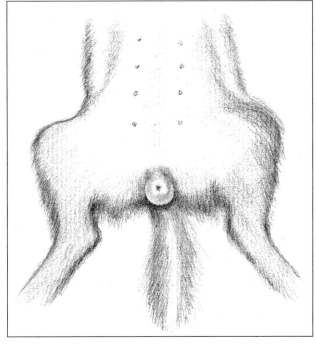

Figure 16-1:
Female ferret with swollen vulva caused by adrenal gland disease.

- ✔ Aggressive mating behavior (in neutered males)
- ✔ Unusual aggressive behavior (in either gender) toward owners or cagemates
- ✔ Difficulty urinating for males that develop enlarged prostates
- ✔ Anemia in females
- ✔ Some muscle thinning, weakness, or a potbellied appearance

Making the diagnosis

Diagnosing adrenal gland disease can, at times, be pretty easy. In many cases, just looking at the ferret is enough. If she's experiencing serious hair loss alone or if the hair loss is coupled with any of the other common signs, she probably has adrenal gland disease. However, it's very important that you take your fuzzy to your vet as soon as you notice a symptom of the disease. The unfortunate thing is, a fuzzy can be suffering from adrenal gland disease and show no signs for a very long time. Your vet may get lucky and detect an enlarged adrenal gland during a routine physical examination, but this doesn't usually happen.

Because the adrenal glands are so tiny, an ultrasound of the abdomen often will miss the early stages of adrenal gland disease. Running more bloodwork and taking X-rays won't help in diagnosing adrenal gland disease, either. However, it's common for a ferret with adrenal gland disease to have another disease present, as well. Therefore, you should consider asking for additional bloodwork and X-rays anyway so that you and your vet can develop a treatment plan that's suitable for your pet's special needs.

After you discover some symptoms, you and your vet may opt to send your fuzzy's blood to the University of Tennessee, where experts can perform a test that's helpful in diagnosing adrenal gland disease. The experts can perform an adrenal-gland panel to evaluate the levels of sex steroids in your ferret's system. This is one way to zero in on a diagnosis — especially in cases where the diagnosis isn't so obvious.

Many vets will suggest surgically removing the affected adrenal gland(s) without going to extreme diagnostic measures if the major signs of the disease are already there.

Treating the disease

When it comes to treating adrenal gland disease, you have a few options to consider, which may be used independently or together. Many variables will come into play, such as the age and health of your ferret and your financial situation, but undoubtedly your vet will help you decide what's best for you and your ferret. One option, which is frequently recommended, is surgery. However, some medications may also have a positive effect in treating adrenal gland disease and/or managing its signs.

Surgery

The adrenal gland disease treatment most effective and most often opted for is surgical removal of one or both adrenal glands. Adrenal gland surgery is a fairly common procedure. Your ferret may be a candidate if she's in good health otherwise and can withstand general anesthesia. Another option is to *debulk,* or surgically remove, as much adrenal tissue as possible, followed by medical therapy. Post-operative prognosis is pretty good but depends on the tumors present and what else is going on inside the ferret's body. After the diseased gland(s) is removed, the signs gradually disappear. The ferret's fur usually grows back, although it can take many months. The fur also may be thinner and a different color.

Ferrets are prone to developing multi-organ diseases, so when your vet performs an abdominal exploratory surgery on your ferret, ask him to take a good look around inside your fuzzy. Your vet should check the condition of her adrenal glands, pancreas, stomach, intestines, spleen, and kidneys, which only takes a couple extra minutes. Biopsies can be performed on anything suspicious, and your vet can remove anything obvious right then and there. Early detection of disease can prolong your fuzzy's life and make medical management more successful.

What if surgery isn't the right option for your ferret? Reasons may include the following:

- ✔ Your fuzzy is at an advanced age.
- ✔ Your fuzzy has other complicating diseases, such as advanced heart disease.
- ✔ Maybe your own fears are preventing you from going the preferred surgical route.

Well, if surgery isn't an option for you, fuzzies can live up to three years completely untreated. However, your ferret may experience behavioral changes, or other medical conditions may develop, such as prostate problems, as a result of untreated adrenal gland disease. Sometimes her fur will grow back at the next seasonal coat change. But affected ferrets usually lose more hair the next time around. And it may not grow back at all.

Other treatment options

You do have alternative medical options to treat adrenal gland disease — some of which have been used with great results. The following list outlines some of these options and what they can do for your sick fuzzy: (*Note:* Not all adrenal ferrets are candidates for alternative treatments. Speak with your vet about what's right for your furkid.)

- ✔ Medical therapy alone is an alternative treatment option.
- ✔ Lupron depot (the long-acting lupron), also known as Lueprorlin in Europe, is currently the most widely used adrenal medication because it's safe for ferrets. The medication has very few, if any, known side effects and can be ordered directly from your vet. It acts by stopping the LH (Luteinizing Hormone) stimulation to the adrenal glands. In turn, the adrenal glands stop overproducing adrenal androgens and sex hormones. In carcinomas (cancer), Lupron may keep tumors from getting bigger, but Lupron does nothing directly to shrink tumors. Lupron can be an expensive treatment option, and it's necessary for the remainder of the ferret's life.

  Suprelorin implants are currently being used in Australia, New Zealand, and a few other countries. Perhaps in the near future this option will be available to our ferrets, as well. This medication works like Lupron, stopping the LH stimulation to the adrenal glands and turning off the overproduction of sex hormones and adrenal androgens.

✔ Giving a ferret melatonin (orally or through implants) is another popular medical approach to treating adrenal disease. Some ferret owners have used this option as a preventative. It works by lowering LH, sex hormone, and androgen levels. However, some are concerned that ferrets may develop immunity to melatonin after long-term use, rendering it relatively useless. Like Lupron and Suprelorin, it does nothing directly to stop the progression of the disease. Also, because it's a relatively new treatment, the long-term effects are as yet unknown.

Melatonin implants can be used in conjunction with adrenal surgery or along with Lupron. In fact, your veterinarian may recommend it.

Prostate problems in the male ferret often are associated with adrenal gland disease. The overproduction of the testosterone-like sex steroid causes the prostate to enlarge. Some enlarged prostatic tissue can apply pressure on the urinary tract, leading to the ferret having difficulty urinating or creating urinary blockage. Ferrets can develop bacterial infections in the prostatic tissue leading to more serious disease. (Bacterial infections need to be treated with appropriate antibiotics.) Lupron, in high doses, inhibits the production of sex steroids, causing the prostate to shrink back to normal size.

Insulinoma

Insulinoma is one of the most diagnosed ferret cancers. A ferret with *insulinoma* has cancer of the insulin-secreting pancreatic cells, or *beta cells*. One of the pancreas's main roles is to release insulin as needed to regulate the ferret's blood sugar levels. It does its job by facilitating the movement of glucose out of the bloodstream and into the cells, which use it as a primary fuel source. In ferrets with insulinoma, tumors cause an overproduction of insulin. Too much glucose moves out of the bloodstream quickly, which causes rapid drops in blood sugar, or *hypoglycemia*. And without blood glucose, the ferret's brain and red blood cells are left with little to no fuel to maintain.

Insulinoma most often strikes ferrets after the age of 3. Sometimes, the disease goes unnoticed for a long time as the ferret's system fights to regulate its own blood sugar levels. During this time, the signs may not be overly apparent. When they do show up, some of the signs may include

✔ Weakness and lethargy

✔ Excessive salivation

✔ Pawing at the mouth

✔ Dazed and confused look

✔ Tremors and seizures

✔ Loss of coordination

✔ Rear leg weakness

✔ Enlarged spleen

✔ Coma

With insulinoma, the signs may come and go as the ferret's body works to counteract the swings in blood glucose by producing more glucose from the liver. Things that can trigger and aggravate the signs include exercise, stress, and diet (see the upcoming sidebar for more on diet and the possible causes of insulinoma). However, any of the signs warrants a trip to the vet.

Making the diagnosis

A vet usually obtains a diagnosis by drawing a *fasting* blood sugar level, in which the fuzzy goes three to four hours without food before the blood is drawn. Anything longer than three to four hours is too long for a ferret with insulinoma to go without food. Normal blood glucose levels are between 90 and 120. Having a fasting blood glucose level of less than 70 generally is considered diagnostic for insulinoma. If you want to take the diagnostic process a step further, exploratory surgery will confirm the presence of insulinoma tumors.

Treating the disease

Your vet can help you determine the best course of action to treat insulinoma, based on your ferret's history and current condition. Surgery is frequently an option and may stop or slow the progression of insulinoma. Unfortunately, pancreatic tumors can be small and seedy nodules, located throughout the pancreas, making the treatment process surgically challenging. In some cases, the tumors are isolated nodules that can be more easily removed. And although surgery can stop or slow the progression of the disease, the condition is never completely curable. Tumors frequently return at a later date.

Your fuzzy may live an additional ten months or longer after diagnosis, with a lot of tender, loving care and a consistent management program, including dietary changes (see Chapter 8). Some of the medications that vets have found to be successful in managing insulinoma are diazoxide (Proglycem) and corticosteroids (such as prednisone). Only your vet can determine what's best for your ferret.

People often recommend that you add Brewer's yeast to the insulinoma patient's diet. I suggest that you *not* do this. The chromium in Brewer's yeast has been shown to actually lower blood sugar levels as opposed to stabilizing them, as once thought.

Every ferret owner should keep some Karo syrup or honey on hand, especially if you have a ferret with insulinoma. If your fuzzy *crashes* (shows extreme lethargy, weakness, or has seizures) due to low blood sugar, take a cotton swab and dab a little honey or Karo syrup on her gums. The sugar helps to stabilize the ferret until you can get her to a vet, which you should do as quickly as possible. Follow up with some high-protein food like chicken baby food.

Use this type of sugar boost in emergency situations only — to bring your ferret out of a hypoglycemic episode. Too much sugar can be dangerous for a fuzzy with insulinoma.

Lymphosarcoma (Lymphoma)

Very common in beloved furballs is *lymphosarcoma,* a cancer of the lymphatic system (the organs and cells designed to fight disease). Many fuzzies suffering from this type of cancer can have severely impaired immune systems, while other ferrets are *subclinical* — they have no overt signs of the disease at all. The cause of lymphosarcoma remains a bit of a mystery. Environmental and genetic influences are possible factors. Some experts are convinced that lymphosarcoma is linked directly to some type of virus. The condition sometimes shows up in multiple cagemates, reinforcing the viral theory by implying some sort of viral transmission.

The two most common types of lymphosarcoma in ferrets are *juvenile lymphosarcoma* (lymphoblastic form), which hits furkids typically under the age of 14 months, and *classic lymphosarcoma* (lymphocytic form), which generally is diagnosed in middle-aged and older ferrets. Because of the instances of subclinical ferrets, lymphosarcoma isn't always easy to recognize. Thankfully, many ferrets may show signs, including

- Lethargy
- Extreme weight loss
- Diarrhea
- Labored breathing
- Loss of appetite
- Enlarged spleen
- Enlarged lymph nodes (locally or throughout the body)

Making the diagnosis

In juvenile lymphosarcoma, death can occur suddenly and with no signs, because the disease raids many organs at once. Vets often misdiagnose any warning signs that do exist in the youngsters as an upper respiratory infection, pneumonia, or cardiomyopathy. This is due mainly to respiratory and circulatory distress resulting from large, fast-growing tumors that invade the chest cavity and squish the lungs.

Classic lymphosarcoma, on the other hand, is more often recognized by vets. Unlike with the juvenile version, classic lymphosarcoma frequently causes enlarged lymph nodes that a vet can easily feel under the armpits and on the neck. The vet should confirm diagnosis with a biopsy of a lymph node, bone marrow, spleen, or chest fluid. Often, irregularities in the ferret's complete blood count raise a red flag, but that isn't always the case. It's always best to send out biopsy samples to a pathologist.

Treating the disease

Some fuzzy cancers, including lymphosarcoma, respond pretty well to chemotherapy. For many ferrets, chemotherapy provides a decent remission rate (with the exception of the intestinal form of lymphosarcoma), with life often prolonged 6 to 36 months from the start of treatment. However, this form of treatment can be very expensive, and not all cancer patients are good chemo candidates. You must talk to your vet about all your possible treatment options.

Some signs of lymphosarcoma can be alleviated temporarily with steroids, but this treatment isn't a cure for the condition.

Chordomas

Chordomas are the most common musculoskeletal tumors found in the ferret. It's difficult to explain these icky tumors without first giving you a simple lesson on a complex matter of development. All developing embryos have certain tissues that develop to form their basic support systems, such as the spine (including the tail). Leftover embryonic tissue that doesn't develop into the skeletal structure rests in between the vertebrae. These remnants sometimes continue to grow, causing the formation of chordomas.

The mass often grows slowly at the tip of the ferret's tail, eventually giving the tail a club-like appearance. The tumor itself is made up of a bony center beneath a layer of cartilage and rough cells that resemble red, raw elephant skin. For the Herculean fuzzbutt, this tumor can be quite a weapon.

Chordomas are easily diagnosed and typically appear in fuzzies over 3 years old. The most common ferret chordoma is located on the tip of the tail. In some rare instances, a chordoma grows in between the vertebrae near the head, in a tumor called a *cervical chordoma.* This more serious tumor can cause compression of the spinal cord, at which point the ferret becomes physically impaired. Cervical chordomas also are more apt to spread and cause severe pain and neurological problems.

Chordomas can present more than just cosmetic problems for your ferret. They frequently cause hair loss on and surrounding the tumor. Often, the mass becomes ulcerated and oozy. Because of its vulnerable location and the probability of trauma to the tail, vets generally recommend removal, which is a relatively simple procedure.

Itchy Growths: Skin Tumors

Skin tumors appear in all shapes and sizes on fuzzy friends. The good news is that the majority of these skin tumors are *benign,* or non-cancerous. However, all are capable of becoming *malignant,* or cancerous. Vets usually recommend the removal of the lump, bump, or ugly formation. Although the most common ferret skin tumors rarely develop into cancer, the possibility will always remain if you don't have a tumor removed.

Also, several types of skin tumors are itchy and easy to rub and irritate. Removing a tumor from your ferret eliminates the risk of her developing secondary infections from open sores. Be sure to send a tumor tissue sample to a lab for analysis, just for peace of mind. If your vet suspects cancer, removal of a nearby lymph node for biopsy also is a good idea to determine if the cancer has spread. You and your vet can determine a course of treatment from there. Remember: The earlier you act, the better chance you give your fuzzy!

Many types of skin tumors can afflict ferrets. The following sections touch on the most common skin tumors.

Mast cell tumors

Mast cells are directly related to the immune system. They produce histamines to combat foreign bodies in the ferret's system. For reasons unknown, these cells may migrate and form small tumors on the ferret's skin. The growths can appear anywhere on your fuzzy as a single tumor or multiple tumors.

Tumor talk

Allow me to try to unravel the mystery of tumors and the terms used to describe them. *Neoplasia* is the process in which cells grow in an abnormal and uncontrolled manner. The result is a *neoplasm,* also known as a *tumor,* which is made up of cells that serve no useful purpose to the body. Tumors may occur just about anywhere on the ferret's body — either externally on the skin or internally.

There are two types of tumors: *Benign* (noncancerous) and *malignant* (cancerous). A benign tumor remains local, or at the site where it originally grows. Although it doesn't spread, or *metastasize,* to other parts of the body, it may grow big enough to become medically dangerous. Some tumors also have the potential to become malignant. A malignant tumor can metastasize through neoplastic cells being shed; these cells then travel to other areas of the body, such as the lungs, liver, brain, and lymph nodes. The rate of metastasis depends on the type of tumor and many other factors relating to the individual animal.

The suffix –oma doesn't designate a tumor as benign or malignant. For instance, lymphoma usually is malignant but may occur as a solitary tumor that doesn't spread; this is rare but possible (in people). An *adenoma* is a benign tumor — specifically a benign epithelial tumor having a glandular origin and structure. Adenocarcinoma is a malignant tumor originating in the glandular tissue. Carcinoma always means malignant; it's an invasive malignant tumor derived from epithelial tissue that tends to metastasize to other areas of the body. Approximately 80 percent of all malignant tumors are carcinomas (in humans).

You can't always tell whether a tumor is benign or malignant just by looking at it with the naked eye or by where it resides. A pathologist examines the tissues microscopically to determine the tumor type, which is why sending tissues off to a lab is so important.

Mast cell tumors often are round, slightly raised red lumps — button-like in appearance. Sometimes they're flat and scaly in appearance. Because of the ferret's constant production of histamines, this type of tumor is extremely itchy. You'll know something's up if you witness your poor ferret scratching feverishly at her skin (at the area of the tumor), causing excessive bleeding and oozing. Also, the site usually shows some hair loss and may be scabbed over from the constant irritation.

Although mast cell tumors often are malignant in other animals, they rarely become cancerous in ferrets. Nonetheless, because of the risk of infection and the obvious discomfort your fuzzy feels, you should be a nice human and have any mast cell tumors removed. Always have a biopsy done. You should also expect more, though, because they frequently pop up in other places.

Basal cell tumors

Basal cell tumors are slow-growing, wart-like nodules that feature little craters in the middle. They can pop up anywhere on your ferret. They're loose on the skin and move freely when you push on them.

Because of their raised presentation and mobility, basal cell tumors are easy to rub or scrape, which presents the possibility of infection. For these very same reasons, basal cell tumors are easy to remove, and you *should* have them removed. If removed properly by your vet, the tumors shouldn't recur in the same place.

Sebaceous cell tumors

Sebaceous cell tumors generally are tumors of the skin's oil glands or hair follicles. They're really funky in shape — sometimes branching out like cauliflower. They may appear as bluish-colored lumps just under the skin, although on the outside they can range in color from tan to brown to blue. Like the other common skin tumors, sebaceous cell tumors can appear anywhere on the fuzzy's body, and they're usually firm to the touch.

Removing sebaceous cell tumors is important because they often grow rapidly and can become cancerous. Besides, your ferret won't like sporting a vegetable-shaped mass for all the world to see.

Chapter 17

Saying Goodbye When the Time Comes

In This Chapter

▶ Knowing when to let go

▶ Ordering a postmortem to get answers and further fuzzy science

▶ Putting your deceased pet's body to rest

▶ Mourning for your lost pet

▶ Coming to the aid of your surviving pets

*W*ell, I suppose this topic had to come up eventually: death, the taboo and rarely-talked-about elephant in the room. Naturally, humans are never quite prepared for the death of a greatly cherished pet. The end always seems to come way too soon. And what's so unfortunate is that many humans don't know what they have until it's gone. Thankfully, many more humans cherish every breath their pets take, knowing all too well that each breath could be the last.

It's difficult to watch a beloved pet suffer. And for the true animal lovers, it never seems to matter how long the pets have been with them. I can still remember and feel the passing of every single fuzzy that has died since they first graced me with their presence. And with each death came the same questions, over and over and over again: Did I do something wrong? What more could I have done? Was this the right time to let go? Why this little girl? Why now?

This chapter deals with death head-on. In this chapter, I talk about knowing when to euthanize your pet. I discuss what you can learn from a postmortem examination. I present some options for humanely and compassionately taking care of your deceased pet's body. Finally, I cover coping with the grieving process. I try to help you with your grief and your other fuzzies' grief so you can move on — but never forget.

Letting Go of Your Family Member

Sometimes, the only way people can truly show their love for their pets is to let them go. Pets count on humans day after day to make the right decisions for them, and the day will come when they must count on us to make that final, heartbreaking decision — to be selfless instead of selfish and end their suffering. In their eyes we'll see. In our hearts we'll know.

It's time to let go when your fuzzy no longer enjoys life. His illnesses or injuries have been treated as well as they can be, yet he continues to suffer. Little hope exists, and your fuzzy's time from here on out will be filled with pain and misery. Stop. Look. Listen. Your fuzzy will tell you he's ready to go if you're willing to listen closely.

You can set up your fuzzy's final day with your vet. Humane euthanasia is painless to your fuzzy. It involves overdosing the ferret on an anesthetic, either by gas or by injection. Your baby will slowly fall to sleep. For the first time in a long time, he'll feel no pain; he'll be free from the suffering. In only a few short moments, he'll pass over the Rainbow Bridge — a term that comes from a poem by the same name, referring to an animal's passage from life to death — and be greeted by all the other pets that went before him. He'll once again be able to romp and play, and he'll watch you from afar until the day you can join him again.

And as hard as it may be for you, it will be comforting for your fuzzy if you're there with him. He'll want to hear your soothing voice and feel your touch while he leaves this world.

Many people ignore another important aspect to consider upon the death of a pet, be it from euthanasia or from a natural death at home. The other animals that the deceased pet had contact with — particularly any siblings or animals that were part of the fuzzy's social group — should be able to see and smell the deceased pet. It may seem "gross" to some people, but the remaining animals should be able to understand what happened so they can settle back into a normal life instead of always being concerned about where the deceased pet is. Other animals can have abrupt and dramatic behavioral changes when a beloved companion "disappears."

The other animals will have a far smoother transition if they have time to smell and see their dead cagemate. This may mean bringing the other social members to the vet's office, or at least a cagemate or two, or bringing the body home for a while and then returning it to the vet.

Learning from Fuzzy's Death with a Postmortem

It seems an impossible thought right after your fuzzy dies. No way will you allow a vet to operate on your newly deceased baby and examine him just out of curiosity. Well, you may want to think twice about your apprehensions. *Necropsies,* or *postmortems,* are performed shortly after the death of an animal and serve many important functions, which I outline in the following list.

A *necropsy* is simply a postmortem examination of an animal. An *autopsy* is a postmortem examination of a human, "auto" meaning "self" or "of the same species." *Postmortem* is Latin for "after death."

✔ **A postmortem may shed light on sudden, unexpected ferret deaths.** Not all animals give many warning signs before leaving this world. Some die quite unexpectedly and throw their humans into emotional tailspins. You may want some answers to the questions buzzing around in your head.

✔ **You and your other pets could have something to worry about.** The fear of something contagious enters everyone's head at one time or another. If your ferret's death is a surprise, you may want to know if you can expect more problems down the road or if you can prevent other surprises. And remember, animals can pass some icky cooties to humans, too.

✔ **A postmortem can provide invaluable information to the veterinary community about ferret disease and treatments.** Your fuzzy's death can assist other ferrets and their owners by providing precious data to veterinarians — data that can strengthen or weaken theories relating to ferret diseases and illnesses. The postmortem can also give clues as to what does and doesn't work in terms of treating fuzzies. The more a vet sees and learns, the greater help the vet will be to ferrets in the future.

✔ **A postmortem may reveal internal genetic abnormalities, which sometimes are the result of poor breeding.** An examination can reveal diseases or illnesses that hadn't previously been identified in your ferret. As horrible as this may sound, if your ferret was a new purchase, you may be able to use the information from a postmortem to get your money back or to get a new fuzzy. At the very least, you may be able to help future fuzzies and owners from the fate you've witnessed.

✔ **You can find out if husbandry played a role in the ferret's death.** Diet and environment play big parts in the health of a fuzzy. Experts aren't the only ones who can learn from their mistakes. I know I'd want to correct any deficiencies on my part and prevent future pet losses.

For an accurate and complete postmortem, your fuzzy's body must be fresh. So what should you do if your pet passes at home and you want a vet to perform a postmortem? Place his body in a bag (double bagging is recommended) or container and put him in the fridge until the time comes. Don't freeze him or leave him at room temperature, because these environments can damage tissues and organs. Freezing, for instance, causes changes in tissues microscopically and makes it more difficult to do pathology or microscopic examinations. You can, however, freeze a body if you need to for just a gross postmortem or if you're looking for viral problems.

Your vet may or may not charge you for the postmortem. Most vets do charge a fee. It depends on their curiosity and desire to learn more about fuzzies. Some vets do the gross necropsy (dissecting and evaluating) for free and charge only for samples sent to pathologists or laboratories for testing.

If you choose to have a postmortem performed, your vet will, upon request, stitch up any incisions after the exam is completed. Your ferret won't look exactly like your little baby, but he won't look like Frankenfert, either. Keep in mind that the body is only the package that your fuzzy arrived in. He's no longer in there; he's opted for a superior package deal over the Rainbow Bridge.

Having a necropsy performed is a difficult decision. I've always been told never to make a decision when I'm hungry, angry, lonely, or tired (HALT). You can probably throw grieving into that mix, too, but then it wouldn't spell a word. Chances are you aren't reading this material to figure out what to do at this very moment. You should think about postmortems now, before you're too emotional, and make a decision about what you'll do when your beloved ferret dies.

Selecting Fuzzy's Final Burrowing Place

What comes after the death of your ferret? Grieving, sadness, emptiness, anger, fear, loneliness. The list goes on and on. An important part of grieving, though, is putting some closure on the loss. A big part of getting closure is deciding what to do with your deceased pet. You have several options. It's no longer a choice between burying him in the backyard, tossing him out with the trash, or leaving him at the vet for convenience:

✔ Some people have their pets cremated.

✔ Some people have elaborate funerals at pet cemeteries complete with caskets and grave markers.

✔ Some people have their pets freeze-dried or stuffed (taxidermied).

✔ Some people opt for a simple or extravagant backyard funeral.

The following sections present some of these popular options.

Choosing cremation

Your vet will, upon request, properly store your deceased pet and arrange for a pet crematory to pick up the body for cremation. You also can take your pet directly to a pet crematorium with prior arrangement. Your cremation options are offered for different prices and vary from vet to vet and from crematorium to crematorium. If you choose this route, though, you usually have two main options:

✔ A mass cremation without the return of your pet's ashes. The crematory disposes of all ashes according to the law.

✔ A special cremation with the return of your pet's ashes. This includes a guarantee (complete with a certificate) that your deceased pet was cremated separately from other animals, assuring that all ashes are your pet's and only your pet's.

If you choose a special cremation, you need to think about your options for the returned ashes:

✔ You can keep each pet separated in special containers. These containers can sit on special shelves or in other special places of honor.

✔ You can have one big urn in which you keep all your pets together as a family.

✔ You can bury the ashes or spread them in your pet's favorite *outdoor* place. I emphasize outdoor because your fuzzy's favorite hidey-hole in the play area probably isn't a good idea!

Your vet or the pet crematorium should be able to give you prices for these services and show you several urn styles. You can bypass your vet or the crematorium and even purchase urns online. Some urns are simple, and some are elaborate. The style you choose depends on your taste and your budget. You can add an engraved nameplate or simply have the pet's name etched in wood. Some people even add a little picture of the pets to the containers. This is a time for celebration of your pet's life.

If you choose to receive only the ashes back without a special urn, be prepared for what you may get. Most of my pets' ashes were returned in small, white, plastic bottles or decorative tins. One time, though, some ashes came back in a clear plastic bag, which was both startling and disturbing to me.

Not all pet crematoriums are up to snuff. People, in some cases, get back way more than just their pets' ashes, or it may be apparent that not all the ashes could've possibly been returned. Be careful which crematorium you choose. Speak with your vet about the crematorium she uses. Call a referred crematorium and ask questions. If you're unhappy with the answers you get, you can take your pet to another place. The choice is yours. Some crematoriums even let you stay there while the service is performed.

Proceeding to a pet cemetery

No, a pet cemetery isn't anything like author Stephen King's portrayal. Thank heavens! In fact, pet cemeteries look a lot like human cemeteries, except much smaller. Many people love this resting option because they'll always have a special place to visit their beloved pets. Finding them, however, can be challenging, although some crematoriums have cemeteries on site. Pet cemeteries aren't all that popular, and many people don't even know they exist. Ask your vet to point you in the right direction, or contact a friend who has some experience with one. You can also perform an Internet search or check out the phone book under "pet cemetery."

The burial for your pet can be simple, such as you picking out a tiny site and delivering the body to the cemetery. Or it can be extravagant. You can have your ferret set up in a special coffin, and you can view the body in the funeral home before saying goodbye, just like at a human wake. Some places allow you to deliver the pet, in coffin, to the burial site and bury the pet yourself. Or you can follow a somber ground crew as they lead you to the burial site. You can purchase a headstone so that your fuzzy's gravesite will always be marked with sentiment.

The pet cemetery burial option can be a costly endeavor. Pet cemeteries vary in policies and practices. I'm sure they also differ in prices and available packages.

Opting for a backyard burial

Backyard burials can be personal, private, and inexpensive, and they can mean everything to a grieving human. Many families with kids know exactly what I'm talking about. How many of you, as tearful children, made your family members gather around the toilet to bid farewell to the bravest, coolest goldfish that ever lived?

Together through eternity

Due to popular demand, some human cemeteries are making ground-breaking changes to allow pets to be buried alongside their humans.

I love this idea! Except that even after all our deaths, my spouse would still be complaining that there are too many cats "hogging the bed."

Before you decide to bury your pet in the backyard, be sure to check city ordinances; backyard burials may actually be illegal in your area.

Headstones are optional for your backyard burial. For my old dog Ara, I custom-designed a headstone and had it etched in heavy granite by the stonecutter at the local cemetery. It took forever for the stone to arrive, but it was well worth the wait. Of course, after I spent $350, I started getting dozens of pet catalogs offering low-cost, simple pet headstones. But none could compete with my personal touch. (Read the sidebar "A personal story" for more about my sweet wolfdog, Ara.)

If your deceased pet was especially close to your child, you may want to encourage your child to celebrate the pet's life by personally making a headstone or grave marker. It's a wonderful way for the child to put a little closure on this huge matter of loss.

Note (actually a ***Hubby Alert***): Just as a matter of clarification, my buried pets will be packed up and moved with me if I ever move from my house. They'll then be reburied in a beautiful place in my new yard. I've warned you, Hubby! You think I'm kidding? Here it is in writing!

Grieving for Your Lost Fuzzy

I'll tell you right off the bat: There's nothing worse than grieving a loss that no one seems to understand. People can sometimes make you feel worse about the death of your pet. Someone who has never had a pet may proclaim, "It's only an animal." Well, not exactly. Pets are family members that you grow extremely attached to. Your ferret has been a source of comfort and joy, as well as sadness and frustration. Many people view pets just as they view human children, but other people out there just don't understand.

I'm surrounded by people who just don't understand how I can cry over the loss of a ferret or any other small critter. A dog or a cat they'd understand — at least a little, so they say. And those who really have no clue rationalize, "It's not like they were humans." Those are the people to avoid. Those are the people who make me like animals more than people.

A personal story

One of the hardest decisions I've ever made was to put my 16½-year-old wolfdog, Ara, to sleep, but it was one I had to make. In the morning, he struggled to rise from his bed. He looked at me with sad, helpless eyes as I lifted his back end up for him. I saw that dignity still glowed dimly in his eyes, but the light was fading and I could tell he knew it. We romped slowly in the yard before our vet, Mike, arrived to put him to sleep. I questioned my decision as Ara walked up almost briskly to greet Mike. Maybe it wasn't time. I'd made this decision several times in the months before then and selfishly changed my mind just as Mike arrived. But Ara was almost 17 years old and was no longer happy. He fought to stay with us much longer than anyone had expected such a large dog to. We moved Ara's bed outside, and he quickly went to it. As he looked up at me, I could tell he trusted me to make the right decision. I held him closely while he left his broken-down body and passed over the Rainbow Bridge.

In my backyard, I have a beautiful group of large pine trees set in an imperfect row. Directly below their towering branches are many unmarked graves where dozens of critters rest. Directly north of these graves lies underground the most handsome, majestic, and loyal dog anyone's ever met. Ara Glen. His headstone reads, "Always Faithful, Always Loved." Ara is the keeper and protector of my critter graveyard. He watches over the little guys and guides them over the Rainbow Bridge. I visit his grave often when I need to talk, and I know he understands. This is why I planted him close to my heart.

After the death of your furry friend, surround yourself with people who do understand and don't think you're strange. I've seen people spend hundreds of dollars to remove tumors from mice, rats, and guinea pigs. It isn't the size or cost of the animal that matters; it's how much room he takes up in your heart.

So, you have my first bit of advice: Surround yourself with the right people. In the following sections, I give you more advice for dealing with your grief and for helping others through their grief.

Know you're not alone

You may feel crazy for feeling the way you do. Well, let me tell you, many of us out there feel crazy and silly right along with you. Don't let others kick you when you're down.

Many support groups are out there that deal directly with the loss of a pet. You can do a search on the Internet. If you can, visit the Web site www.rainbowsbridge.com. It's a neat site that has many wonderful tips and links to other pet-loss sites. It's also a virtual memorial site. If you visit this site or other sites like it, you'll find many hotlines and chat groups and even books dealing with grief issues, all available for you and your family members.

Face the feelings

A variety of different feelings will pop up at any given time after the death of your fuzzy. Feel them. Don't run from them. Remember that you're not alone. Your feelings are powerful, but they aren't unique. Among the emotions that will creep up for you to face are denial, anger, guilt, sadness, and emptiness.

Facing your feelings, however, doesn't mean beating yourself up about what you couldn't help. We all think we could've been better pet humans after our animals are gone, but hindsight is 20/20. Chances are, you were a wonderful parent. Feelings are temporary. Your memories will last forever, but the pain slowly fades after a while.

Give yourself time

Many people think that they should run right out and get new pets as soon as they lose the ones they loved so dearly. They think that doing so will fix the grief they're feeling. It won't. You know better than that. You can never replace a lost family member.

Give yourself time to grieve your loss. Pets aren't replaceable. You can certainly add to your family when you feel better, but taking on a new responsibility when you're grieving isn't fair to you, your family, or the new pet. Likewise, you shouldn't try to fix someone else's grief by giving a pet as a gift. Grief isn't something that can be fixed. It's something that you must work through over a period of time.

And when you're truly ready for a new pet, toss any feelings of guilt or betrayal out the window. Your deceased pet would've wanted you to move on and be happy with a new pet.

Help others deal with their loss

You may want to giggle inside when you see a child dragging an adult to the toilet for the ultimate farewell to Moby the goldfish. But you should recognize that the child is hurting. It's very possible that another person will feel the loss of your pet just as, or even more, deeply than you do. Respect other people's feelings by acknowledging them and providing as much support as you can. Each person is unique, and everyone has the right to grieve.

Don't forget that you have to help your other animals with their loss, too. Animals bond deeply with both humans and other animals. When my wolfdog, Ara, died, my hyper Doberman, Cassie, wanted to do nothing but sleep. She was lethargic and depressed. Several months later, I introduced two puppies to her, and she hated me for it. But they all play and get along today. However, she has never bonded to them the way she did with Ara. My point is, show all your grieving family members extra attention and love during the grieving period. (See the following section for much more advice on this topic.)

Do pets really grieve? Many people, myself included, tend to project human emotions such as grief onto pets. The fact is, no one knows for sure if animals grieve, and the topic is a subjective one. Some will say the changes in behavior that an animal experiences after a death are due to the changes in environment — the safety and security of their "world" has been altered (a cagemate suddenly disappears or social structure is disrupted). Depending on the species and on the age of the animals and their health, it can affect them more or less dramatically. You need to understand the social behavior of a pet species to understand how the animals can respond to environmental changes.

Helping a Surviving Ferret Cope

Depression in animals isn't much different than depression in humans, except that animals don't have complex self-destructive thought patterns. The loss felt by a surviving ferret isn't to be underestimated, though. Surviving ferrets are affected very deeply. The signs are there. Lethargy and lack of appetite may be glaringly obvious, as well as their reclusiveness or clinginess. And it isn't unheard of for a lone ferret to die soon after his cagemate passes on. But you can do your part to help your surviving ferret get through these hard times. It isn't difficult. Ferrets are by nature solitary animals and usually do just fine on their own after a period of adjustment.

You need to give your sad fuzzy a lot of extra attention during his grieving stage. Spend more time developing and implementing enrichment plans to keep him busy and entertained (see Chapter 10). The worst thing you can do is isolate him. But be careful not to make too many abrupt changes in his life by suddenly carrying him around more often than usual and stressing him out. Over-babying him will only cause him to have more anxiety. Be aware of your own agitation and depression and keep him out of contact with that. He doesn't need to take on your stress as well. Realizing that life moves on will also help with your grief. If you get stuck in your grief, you won't be doing any favors to your ferret.

When dealing with a grieving ferret, many people ask, "Should I get another ferret? When will we know if it's the right time?" Many factors come into play when deciding whether to get a new ferret to keep your surviving ferret company. How old is your surviving ferret? If he's old and sickly, adding a newcomer is probably not a great idea. A surviving youngster may be a completely different story, because he may have many healthy years to share with another ferret. Take health and personality factors into consideration. What if your survivor doesn't get along with a new ferret? Are you ready to set up and maintain another cage and split playtimes? And the biggest question of all: Are *you* ready for a new ferret?

Many ferrets will benefit greatly from the company of a new ferret. But first and foremost, you need to make a commitment to your surviving ferret to truly meet his needs for consistent enrichment, which will keep him thriving. Enrichment is vital to a ferret, but even more so to a ferret that lives alone.

Part V
Ferret Psychology 101: Behavior and Training

The 5th Wave   By Rich Tennant

ⒸRICHTENNANT

"Hey – that's a record! Honey, I just clocked the ferret at 28 mph coming through the living room."

In this part . . .

"**G**ood heavens! You mean I have to know more than just how to feed, burp, and change diapers?" Well, only if you want a truly happy and healthy carpet shark living in your home. This part deals with understanding ferret behaviors, quirks, and training issues. At the very least, this part is designed to show you what is and isn't normal behavior. After all, how can you meet the needs of any pet if you don't understand its needs in the first place?

If, after reading the first two chapters in this part, you still believe your furball is crazy, turn to the third chapter of the part where I discuss behavior modification tips. I'm here to tell you that you're not alone. Being owned by ferrets can be challenging, but understanding them is the key to making it all work.

Chapter 18

Understanding What Fuzzy Is Trying to Tell You

- -

In This Chapter

▶ Responding to various ferret sounds

▶ Reacting to your ferret's dance moves

▶ Recognizing your ferret's body language

▶ Considering other ways your ferret communicates

- -

Ferrets are extremely interactive critters. They use many different types of communication to get their points across — from body language to vocalizations to crazy behaviors. They can be notorious thieves and affectionate lap warmers at the same time. Watching them can be both amusing and baffling, but knowing what they're trying to say to you is important. It can mean the difference between a lick on the nose and a nip of the nostrils.

You'll surely encounter all sorts of captivating behavior, both good and bad, during your ferret rendezvous. My experience has been that the good encounters are far more plentiful than the bad. I spend more time laughing with my furballs, even when they're being devilish. In this chapter, I cover the main types of ferret communication so you can properly manage, care for, and play with your ferret. I discuss ferret vocalization, ferret dancing, fuzzy body language, and other unique behaviors. Hopefully, this chapter will help you recognize that you're not alone in thinking your ferret may be a little crazy . . . and will put to rest any fears you have that you're crazy for loving every minute of it.

Say What? Speaking Ferret-ese

For the most part, fuzzies are quiet. I mean, goodness, they sleep for hours on end! Occasionally, one of my furkids has a ferret dream and does a little whimpering in her sleep, but that's a rarity. During playtime, though, the vocabulary comes out. Ferrets use vocalization to send signals. Seasoned ferret humans (sprinkled with ferret poo) have personal terms for ferret vocalizations that they've come up with over the years. These terms are sort of like understood jokes between ferret and human. However, most fuzzy humans recognize a few terms universally. I cover these vocalizations in the sections that follow so you can speak the ferret language and understand what your ferret wants.

People who don't understand ferret communication can become frightened or intimidated when encountering vocalizations for the first time. Recognizing the difference between a dook of happiness and a screech of anger is important. Not knowing may cause you to react improperly to the message being given. Humans often run into this difficulty with their human partners, too!

The dook

The most common ferret babble is known as *dooking* (also known as clucking or chuckling). It sounds like sort of a low-pitched, grumbling gibber. My ferrets frequently get a case of the verbal "hee hees" while they're dooking. Dookings are awesome sounds made out of sheer giddiness or excitement. The stimulation felt from wrestling with another ferret, rapid counter cruising, or even from exploring new smells, toys, and hidey-holes can cause carpet sharks to dook. Nothing to worry about here; just enjoy!

Mother jills (female ferrets) make a slightly different but similar noise to help their kits (baby ferrets) locate them when the babies are exploring their environment. Experts suggest that polecats also use a similar noise when first meeting each other, during dancing used to avoid conflict, and before and during ritual fighting.

The screech

The opposite of the dook is the certified sign of terror, the *screech*. These noises are high-pitched reactions to extreme pain, fright, or anger. The screech is a common defense mechanism and often is accompanied by or even replaced by rapid chattering. When you hear this warning cry, your job as a concerned parent is to jump to your fuzzy's defense. Her tail may be puffed and her back arched. She may have her mouth gaped open, and she may even be scooting backward. Go to her rescue immediately, but be sure to assess her body language before reaching down with your vulnerable hands.

When rushing to help your fuzzy, do so with care. Most animals engrossed in pain, anger, or fright are capable of unpredictable behavior, and ferrets are no exception to this rule.

The bark

Sometimes your ferret will surprise you and utter a noise that resembles a bark. Usually, the bark is one or two very loud chirps that come from a very excited or frightened furball. A friend of mine has a ferret that will bark if he tries to take away its treasured dried fish or jerky. Some humans bark if you prematurely remove their dinner plates, too.

A ferret that's traumatized or excited enough to screech, hiss, or bark can take temporary leave of her senses and nail you good with her chompers — and it won't be her fault. Many situations can cause screeching, barking, hissing, or chattering — from a serious fight between two rival ferrets to having a tail caught in a door to coming face to face with a large, unfamiliar dog.

The hiss

The *hiss* is a warning noise in the ferret's vocabulary. I find a ferret's hissing noise quite amusing, even if she doesn't; it's sort of a cross between a "hee hee" and chattering. The noise can be in the form of long bursts of sound or short, hissy spats, depending on the situation. A hissing fuzzy is a very annoyed or angry fuzzy. Take care when handling this girl, because she's liable to lash out at you.

You Make Me Feel Like Dancin'! Interpreting Your Ferret's Jig

If you haven't figured it out by now, ferrets are animated critters with a complex array of behaviors. Often, a ferret's vocalizations (described in the previous section) are accompanied by particular movements and body language — such as opening the mouth, puffing the tail, arching the back, and so on — that resemble dances. Reading between the lines can be difficult, if not alarming, to people who don't know how to read ferret music. In the following sections, I help you interpret your ferret's dances and take action accordingly.

The dance of joy

I don't know of a ferret that hasn't mastered the dance of joy (see Figure 18-1). If you run across one, her ferret human is most certainly doing something terribly wrong. All healthy, happy ferrets partake in this frequent and brilliant performance. The dance of joy is an unadulterated sign of pure happiness and delight. (*Note:* These dancers are professional ferrets. Don't try these moves at home. Doing so may cause irreparable damage to your skeletal structure and harm your ego!)

To perform the dance, the ferret moves in all directions, sometimes at the same time. She may hop forward and sashay sideways, with a double twist back. No two dances are the same, yet all are amusing.

The dance of joy is a great way to gauge whether your ferret is in shape. A very fit and energetic fuzzy will be the last one on the dance floor. Short bursts of dancing performed between short ferret naps are also common. If you find that your ferret is sleeping more than playing when she gains her daily freedom, try giving her more exercise (see Chapter 10). If her energy still seems low over time, take her to the vet for a checkup. You want to make sure that her lack of energy isn't more than just being flabby and out of shape.

It's probable that the dance of joy does a few things for the polecat:

✔ The arched back, piloerection (frizzed-out tail), and sway make the animal look bigger than it is.

✔ The side-to-side swings may confuse a potential predator or make the animal attack the tail rather than the head.

Figure 18-1:
The ferret
dance
of joy.

✔ Several different species of weasels and polecats have used war dancing to confuse or distract potential prey, increasing the odds of getting a meal.

Ferrets do the dance as part of their "play fighting" behaviors. When doing the dance for a human or to play with another ferret (or just on their own), ferrets also open their mouths and sometimes dook.

The war dance

I like to call the war dance "dooking it out," even though dooks aren't associated with angry or fearful fuzzies (see the earlier section "The dook"). Sometimes, recognizing the war dance can be difficult because the dance of joy covers all the same basic body movements, including the notorious arched back. But an angry ferret often hisses or screeches as an additional warning. The war dance can be performed with or without a ferret partner. Your ferret may choose you as a partner or the family dog. Or she may pick out an inanimate object that happened to catch her off-guard.

The war dance often features an arched back, which is the furball's way of appearing bigger than life. I call it basic trickery. The dance can be slow or fast, depending on the situation. Many angry ferrets back themselves into a corner, arched back and all, and screech or hiss with their mouths wide open. A very angry or frightened ferret also will let loose an A-bomb — a spray of musk. Although a frizzed-out tail often is appropriate attire for the war dance, it isn't always worn.

If your ferret is in a bad situation, rescue the furkid quickly, but do so very cautiously. A bite that results from an upset ferret is rarely the fault of the ferret.

Decoding Your Ferret's Body Language

Ferrets do a lot more than dance when they're playing, inspecting, or exploring their environments. They always seem to be on mysterious quests, which sometimes feature about as much grace as a weasel in a lingerie drawer (not that I would know). Some ferrets appear to feel bored and frustrated at times. Some seem happy and silly. And others may just want to cool out in their hidey-holes. In the following sections, I cover some peculiar behaviors that ferrets exhibit alone and with each other. Hopefully you'll get the insight you've been looking for. Ferrets can be weird creatures!

The frizz look

A true sign of excitement, both good and bad, is the frizzed-out tail. I call it the "pipe cleaner tail," and others call it the "bottlebrush tail." The official term is *piloerection.* When humans get piloerection, we call it goosebumps. When ferrets get it, people call it frizzed or fuzzed. No matter what you call it, if you aren't reading the other signs that accompany the pipe cleaner tail, you may be in for a surprise. Remember, the frizzed tail is a sign of extreme emotion, good or bad. This ferret can be unpredictable.

The situation is similar to when dogs get hackles or when cats do that thing with the fur on their tails. Ferrets puff out the fur on their tails when they're frightened or angry (and are more prone to biting). However, the frizzy look can also be a sign of surprise or happy excitement. Each one of my furballs has a frizzed tail for several minutes after bath time. They're excited and overstimulated while they search for creative ways to dry off and undo all the cleaning.

The alligator roll and wrestlemania

Okay, so your ferret doesn't look like an alligator, but boy, can she flip and roll her partner in seconds flat! I've seen all my ferrets perform the alligator roll many times. The flip is just a form of playing or wrestling. The alpha fuzzy, or head cheese, is the master. She quickly grabs another fuzzy by the back of her neck and flips her upside down. Both carpet sharks then rapidly roll and wrestle about.

There are several variations of wrestling that almost always come into play when your ferrets are out of the cage. Many species of mammals participate in these mock battles to sharpen their survival skills and establish their rankings in the group.

Ferrets can appear to be quite aggressive during normal play. The rough play, besides being fun, often is a way of establishing dominance. A ferret's skin is tough, and what appears to be ruthless biting may in fact just be a bothersome pinch to the recipient. (Ferrets use their paws for grabbing at other ferrets, for tackling, and for wrestling them to the ground, but their teeth are their main weapons.) One opponent may scream briefly in protest. Don't interfere unless you truly feel the game has turned into more than a game.

The trouble comes when a fuzzy chooses a human hand or toe or a piece of clothing to perform an alligator roll on. Youngsters and overexcited ferrets in play mode do this a lot. Although it can be amusing and innocent at first, this behavior shouldn't be encouraged. If you choose to play along with the roll and wrestle with your ferret, use a toy to tackle and wrestle with rather than your hand. You don't want to encourage the fuzzy to bite your hand, and biting is almost always a part of this game.

The treasure hunt

Next time you get invited to a party in which the host sends you and the rest of the guests on a treasure hunt, grab your fuzzy to help in the search. Ferrets make excellent detectives. The job of the fuzzy is to explore every inch, every crack, and every scent of her environment, leaving nothing unexamined. A ferret's nose will be glued to the ground as she follows scent trails this way and that. She'll stop at nothing to get to know everything she can.

Because of a ferret's determination and persistence to explore, proper ferret-proofing is essential to your ferret's safety (see Chapter 6). A ferret can find anything that you don't hide well enough. And when she finds it, she'll hide the stuff even better. This is called *cache behavior.* I've had ferrets present me with cherished items I thought I'd never see again. At first I wanted to show my excitement at the discoveries by rewarding the treasure hunters, but then I realized that they probably hid the treasures in the first place.

The chase is on

Most animals love to chase each other, but ferrets are the masters at the high-speed chase. The behavior may be the inner predator coming to the surface, or it may just illustrate the ferret's desire to have a good time. Regardless, you don't have to be a fuzzy to partake in chases. I've seen my cats and several furkids cruising around the house at the speed of fuzz. I've even done the ferret shuffle as quickly as I could to get away from a tailing carpet shark.

Overly excited or happy ferrets can appear to be quite nuts. They bounce off the walls, furniture, and body parts, often with their mouths gaping wide and teeth showing. This behavior is normal. Many people mistakenly believe this open-mouth gesture is aggression. Rather, it's an invitation to play, and it's all part of ferret fun and games.

A ferret chase *can* be a dangerous behavior, though. Many dogs don't like to be chased by ferrets and will snap at them in retaliation. And kids who don't know how to properly perform the ferret shuffle shouldn't chase because they can easily step on fuzzies. The safest way for a person (adult or child) to play chase with a ferret is to be on all fours on the ground. The fuzzy almost always wins this way, and you reduce the risk of accidentally crushing her.

Did you know that ferrets and polecats aren't typically chase hunters? They hunt most of their food by uncovering it or by cornering it in tunnels. They move very rapidly if you startle them, however, as if to avoid becoming food for an owl!

Fuzzy stalking

Sometimes a ferret remains very still before pouncing on another ferret or toy. I call this behavior *fuzzy stalking* or *the ambush*. In this way, fuzzies are similar to cats, although ambushing isn't the preferred method of hunting by the ferret's wild relatives. A more serious variation of stalking is lunging. You may encounter the lunge when a ferret is becoming overprotective of a special toy or hidey-hole.

Tail wagging

Some ferrets wag their tails out of sheer excitement or stimulation. Some may even do it when they're upset. Tail wagging isn't as common in fuzzies as it is in cats, but it's hardly cause for alarm when it does happen. Youngsters seem more prone to this funny behavior. If your fuzzy is a tail wagger, you can say that you have a furkid with a tad more character than the rest of the furkids.

"Why Does My Ferret Do That?" Understanding Other Fuzzy Behaviors

Besides understanding vocalizations and body language, you need to know what other behaviors come with the ferret package. I get calls from people who proclaim excitedly that their ferrets hate the litter they've chosen. The ferrets toss or dump the litter constantly. They ask me what secret litter I use and what they can do to fix the problem.

Some ferret humans are relieved when I tell them that the problem probably isn't the litter. It's a natural ferret behavior to dig. Or it can be due to boredom and stress (see Chapter 10 for ideas on enrichment for your ferret). Some ferret humans want a quick fix and seem frustrated with my answers. I tell these people that ferrets are crazy, which is why people love them so much. In the sections that follow, I cover digging and the remaining fuzzy behaviors that you should recognize and understand.

Digging to China

A ferret's long claws weren't put there just for looks, you know. Any ferret owner will tell you that digging comes as naturally to a ferret as pooping. Normal targets of digging include cage corners, litter boxes, potted plants, and carpeting. If you think about it, though, the digging behavior makes sense:

✔ Polecats, relatives of the ferret, are burrowing critters.

✔ Polecats and ferrets hunt by sense of smell. When a wild polecat locates food with her sniffer, her claws dig in for the kill.

✔ Ferrets inherently know that digging drives humans right up the wall!

Another reason for digging that some people overlook is boredom or frustration. Although you can't take the urge to dig out of the ferret, you must recognize that ferrets need a lot of stimulation. Digging can, at times, be a way of saying, "Pay attention to me!" or "I'll get you for taking away my toy!" Or she may simply be attempting to get out of her cage. For tips on how to enrich your ferret's life and prevent stress and boredom, refer to Chapter 10.

Although you can't prevent a ferret from digging, you can do some things to prevent damage done by your excavator (for more on ferret-proofing, see Chapter 6):

✔ Keep your plants up high or cover the soil with wire, large decorative rocks, or tin foil.

✔ For carpeting, you can try to use plastic carpet runners or simply remove the carpeting where your fuzzy will be playing. Tile certainly is easier to clean, also.

Ferret fixations

Your ferret may become fixated on a certain object and treat it with extra-special care — even preventing others from getting near it. For some ferrets, "fixation" is the understatement of the year. When a ferret claims her love for an object, she often guards it tooth and nail.

My ferret Elmo discovered a toy from one of those fast-food kid's meals before I could even get it out of the plastic. It was a hard-plastic lion that he grabbed and ran off with to his hidey-hole. After he'd familiarized himself with it, he proudly brought the toy out to show off to his friends. But Elmo never allowed anyone to get too close to it. Like a mother protecting her vulnerable baby, this oversized carpet shark hissed warnings to the other ferrets to keep a safe distance.

Even today, Elmo has many toys, but this one is never far from his sight. He carries it to the food bowl and drops it in while he eats, and then he carefully buries it in his bedding when he's through. The toy even accompanies him to the litter box. Now that's true love!

The movers are here

What happens if your ferret becomes obsessed with something she just can't get her teeth around? Why, she simply tucks it under her belly and secures it there with her front paws. From there, the thief amuses any onlookers with her unique ability to scoot backward with the object in tow. Balls and small, hard objects often are subjected to this tuck-and-scoot method of moving.

And what if the object is too big to tuck and scoot? Well, her pointy honker isn't just for smelling and leaving nose prints on your eyeglasses. And her feet weren't made just for walking. Ferrets can not only drag around heavy objects, but also push them around (different from bossing us around). They use their noses and/or front feet to push items to the desired destinations. They'll try for hours to shove oversized items into obviously undersized locations. My fuzzies frequently try to drag me under the couch. I never have the heart to point out the flaw in their plan. I'm rather amused at watching them try to make it work no matter what.

A felon on your hands?

Ferrets would make excellent crooks if they weren't so darned blatant about their thieving ways. It's absolutely normal, even if sometimes annoying, for ferrets to steal objects and carry them off to their secret hidey-holes. Heck, the animal's name appropriately means "thief" (see Chapter 2). This thieving or hoarding is a *caching behavior.* It serves an important role in the survival of wild polecats: as a way for them to stock up on food for future shortfalls.

Almost anything the ferret can grab with her paws or carry in her mouth is fair game. From pieces of food to cigarette butts, you'll find the most unusual collections of goodies in the most unusual places. Purses, pockets, and backpacks are frequent targets for ferret raids. If you value any items your ferret may steal — such as car keys, shoes, and jewelry — I suggest that you keep these items up high or away from the ferret's play area altogether.

Hoarding is one of the ferret's most endearing traits, but it can lead to trouble. Some stolen items are big, but others are dangerously small. Ferrets can ingest small items that can cause blockages. Remember this characteristic about your ferret when you ferret-proof your home (see Chapter 6). Plus, food that your fuzzy stashes can spoil or mold.

Blame the ferret!

In several plays written thousands of years ago, Aristophanes made fun of political opponents by calling them ferrets. He would imply that they stole public trust and funds in the same way ferrets stole bits of meat and shiny objects. The wording of these quotes may differ, and the animal mentioned by Aristophanes has been called a cat, marten, ferret, polecat, and house ferret. Thanks to Bob Church for providing these gems!

✔ In *The Acharnians* (425 BCE): "Happy he who shall be your possessor and embrace you so firmly at dawn, that you fart like a house ferret." **Note:** Reference to poofing.

✔ In *Wasps* (422 BCE): "But to-day men-at-arms are placed at every outlet to watch me, and two of them are lying in wait for me at this very door armed with spits, just as folks lie in wait for a house ferret that has stolen a piece of meat." **Note:** Reference to stealing meat.

✔ In *Peace* (421 BCE): "Let someone bring me the thrush and those two chaffinches; there were also some curds and four pieces of hare, unless the house ferret stole them last evening, for I know not what the infernal noise was that I heard in the house." **Note:** Reference to stealing meat.

✔ In *The Thesmophoriazusae* (411 BCE): "And how we give meats to our pimps at the feast of the Apaturia and then accuse the house ferret . . ." **Note:** Reference to giving meat (treasure) to others and blaming the ferret for stealing it.

✔ In *Plutus* (380 BCE): "Quick she drew back her hand, slipped down into the bed with her head beneath the coverlets and never moved again; only she let flee a fart in her fear which stank worse than a house ferret." **Note:** Reference to poofing.

The zig-zag

Have you ever heard the saying a straight line for a ferret includes six zigs and seven zags? When zig-zagging, your ferret isn't trying to evade a pursuer, though that would be an excellent guess. Your ferret has inherited a unique hunting technique from her wild polecat relatives. Scanning the ground from side to side as she moves forward allows your ferret to cover more surface area and increases the odds of catching or unearthing a meal — or a dirty sock, in the case of your domesticated ferret.

Butt scooting

A skid mark here, a skid mark there: The unmistakable signs of the infamous ferret butt scoot! Ferrets and polecats may drag their butts across the yard or floor after going to the bathroom. This is your ferret's way of saying, "I was here!" Not all butt scoots leave visual evidence, but they all leave olfactory trails that tell other ferrets and animals that the area has been or is currently occupied by your fuzzy.

Coveting thy hidey-hole

Hidey-holes go hand in hand with ferrets, and the good spots are highly coveted if you have more than one fuzzy. In the wild, polecats use the burrows of other animals to nest in, but if none are readily available, they'll dig their own holes in tree root balls. They don't seem to stay in one spot for long; they'll pack up and move frequently. Domesticated ferrets also take advantage of hidey-holes when they find them. They'll hole up in them to sleep or rest and occasionally have to defend them from other ferrets. When your ferret can't find hidey-holes, she'll create them herself by digging or burrowing into mattresses, couches, or even your underwear drawer.

Scoping out boundaries

Wild polecats spend a lot of time patrolling their territories in the wild, and a good amount of time is spent along the boundaries. Boundary patrols are conducted so that intruding polecats know the territory is currently occupied and they shouldn't enter. This reduces the amount of fights and decreases the chances of injury.

Domesticated ferrets inherited this territorial patrolling behavior. When first released from her cage or after a long nap, your ferret will first patrol the area before she starts to play. Along the walls, behind couches and curtains; she's simply retracing her territory and looking for intruders. Although you certainly hope she'll aim for the litter box, pooping along the edges, in corners, and even in doorways where intruders may enter is your ferret's way of putting up a fence, so to speak.

Chapter 19

Putting Your Ferret through Basic Training: Easy as 1-2-3?

. . . .

In This Chapter

▶ Discouraging biting

▶ Heading to the "bathroom" for toilet training

▶ Going for walks

. . . .

*L*ike a dog, a fuzzy doesn't come preprogrammed for use. You teach a dog how to sit, come, and heel; you must teach a fuzzy certain things, too — like how to mind his manners, use the litter box, and tolerate a harness and leash. These are basics of ferret life that every furkid should know. Some ferrets take to basic training quite quickly, but others need constant reminders of who's the boss. Teaching the basics of good manners means putting on your professor's hat and doing a little home-schooling with your new fuzzy. If your new ferret is an adult, chances are someone else has already home-schooled him, so you just need to keep him current on his skills.

As with any animal, including humans, patience and consistency are the keys to training success. You'll see what I mean when you bring your furball home. But just remember that the patience and effort are well worth it, because nothing can compare to the joy a socialized and greatly loved ferret will bring into your household. In this chapter, I cover the three basic training areas that require your effort, patience, and consistency: eliminating biting, bathroom training, and harness and leash socialization.

Just Say NO to Biting

Ferrets are similar to kittens and puppies in that they need to be trained not to bite. If you watch a human toddler closely, you'll be amazed at all the stuff that ends up in the kid's mouth. Chewing is how babies, human and animal, explore their environments and ease the pain of teething. Eventually the toothaches go away, but the nipping lingers on. Although the urge to nip lessens with age, an untrained adult ferret can be dangerously bold and aggressive with his chompers. Your job is to let your fuzzy know while he's young what is and isn't acceptable behavior. If you begin proper socialization and training when your ferret is young, you decrease the chances of him biting as an adult. (In this section, I talk about training baby ferrets, not adults that haven't been properly socialized. I cover getting help for the difficult adult carpet shark in Chapter 20.)

Sometimes, training a youngster not to nip takes a lot of time and patience. The key to being successful is consistency. It can seem so cute at times to get the little guy all riled up and allow him to play-bite your hand. But you can't let your ferret bite during play and expect him to know that it isn't acceptable at other times and with other people. He won't understand that nipping is okay only when you're in the mood, so don't confuse him. Teach him one thing — not to bite — and stick to your guns. Believe me, if you have multiple fuzzies, the other ferrets will tell the kit just how far he can go with them. You should do the same!

It's important that you pay special attention to the do's and don'ts of nip-training your ferret. The following list presents some suggestions to help with training your fuzzy not to bite:

- ✓ **Provide plenty of hard chew toys.**

- ✓ **Use a toy to wrestle with him rather than your hand.**

- ✓ **Mist a bitter pet spray on your hand when playing with him.**

  After he gets a taste, he probably won't come back for seconds. Bitter spray is a nasty-tasting but harmless substance used to deter chewing in all kinds of pets. The substance is clear, too, and won't harm your furniture or fingers. Most pet stores carry it.

- ✓ **Correct a nip immediately by scruffing the kit and very loudly saying "No" or "No bite."**

  Scruffing is when you firmly grasp the loose skin on the back of the ferret's neck with your thumb and fingers and dangle the ferret. Hissing (not screaming) loudly at the ferret after you say "No" is also very effective. Hissing is the tool a Mother Ferret or other ferrets would use to discipline kits. You can also lay (not tap) your finger gently across his nose after you scruff, say "No bite," and then hiss at him.

- ✓ **If you're holding the kit when he nips, don't reward him by giving him his freedom (in other words, don't put him down to roam free).**

  Instead, place him in jail (cage him).

- ✓ ***Don't ever* hit your ferret in an attempt to discipline or train him, because aggression leads to aggression.**

  Your fuzzy may also think that you're encouraging him to play harder. Hitting is an ineffective technique and frequently leads to bigger behavioral problems.

This Way to the Bathroom

If you read the other chapters of this book, you'll notice that I talk rather frequently about the ferret's bodily functions; that's because ferrets seem to poop about every 15 minutes or so while they're awake. And most ferret people spend more time telling animated stories and jokes about their fuzzies' notorious bathroom habits than they do cleaning up after their kids. (Okay, I'll admit it, that's a little weird.)

Mother Fuzzy, if given the chance, will teach her kits to use the litter box. However, because many kits are delivered to new homes or halfway houses before mom gets the chance to teach them, the new human caretakers must do this dirty deed.

It's pretty simple to train a furkid that the litter box is his designated toilet. Although teaching ferrets the purpose of the litter box is pretty easy, getting them to use it consistently is a crapshoot. Ferrets, unfortunately, don't have the greatest toilet habits. The following tips should help (for more on effective litter boxes and incorporating them into your ferret's kingdom, check out Chapter 5):

✔ **Keep your fuzzy's litter box in the corner of his cage.** A corner area is a magnet for a fuzzy butt. Ferrets prefer to back into a loading zone and unload.

✔ **Limit baby ferrets — or any ferret that's just learning to use a litter box — to smaller cages and play areas until the bathroom concept has sunk in.** Move your ferret to a larger cage only after he's potty trained, and add litter boxes to the higher levels if needed (see Chapter 5 for more on ferret cages).

As you expand your ferret's out-of-cage play area, increase the number of litter boxes you put in it. If a litter box is close by, your ferret will be more likely to use it. If you pay attention, your fuzzy will show you which corners are the best spots for litter boxes. Frequently pick him up and place him in a box until he goes. If he refuses, let him play for a few minutes and then repeat the process.

✔ **If your ferret is tiny (or ill), make sure his litter box has a low side or is small enough for him to climb in.**

✔ **When you wake your ferret for playtime, place him immediately in his litter box and wait until he does his duty.** When he does, you can let him come out. Don't be fooled by a faux poo; make sure he's really gone to the bathroom.

✔ **Until your fuzzy starts going consistently in his litter box, keep a little poo in the box as a reminder that the litter box is a toilet.**

✔ **If you catch your ferret straying from the plan (by backing into a corner, for instance), pick him up, firmly say "No," and then place him in the litter box until he goes.**

✔ *Always* **praise your ferret for a job well done.** Use verbal schmoozing as well as petting.

Now that you have some tips in your potty-training arsenal for getting your fuzzy to use his box, you need to know the don'ts of bathroom training. The following list presents these don'ts:

✔ *Never* **hit your fuzzy for having an accident.** Just be thankful he isn't a Great Dane!

✔ **Never rub a ferret's nose in his waste when he has an accident.** This practice is abusive and serves no purpose. (It doesn't work with dogs, either.)

✔ **Don't offer your fuzzy food rewards for going in his box.** You'll just teach him how to fake a poopy to get a treat.

I have some ferrets that back up to the edge of the litter box and then poop outside on the tile. This just proves that even when you do everything right, things can still go wrong. Go figure!

Harnessing Your Fuzzy for a Walk

Fuzzies are explorers by nature and can cover a lot of ground in only a few seconds. A fuzzy loves to wander around the backyard and explore outside, and it's nice for a ferret and his human to explore the outside world together. Unfortunately, without the proper restraint, it won't take your fuzzy long to get beyond your safe reach and into trouble. If you want to take your ferret outside to play, I advise you to always keep him leashed.

And nothing goes better with a ferret's leash than a harness for his long, slender body. I suggest that you choose an H-shaped harness designed specifically for ferrets (see Chapter 5). A tight collar (but not too tight) works, as long as you keep a close eye on your traveling ferret and he doesn't attempt to escape. I personally don't like using collars. A tug on a collar can send the startled ferret into a frantic roll to get away from you. Also, a struggling fuzzy can often slip right out of a collar and scurry for freedom. I prefer harnesses because ferrets need less time to adjust to these new articles of clothing, and they're much more secure and safe.

As an extra precaution, you should consider fastening an identification tag to your fuzzy's harness in case he does escape. Some people even attach bells to the harness to keep track of the fuzzy's whereabouts.

The sections that follow show you how to familiarize your fuzzy with his harness and give you basic rules to follow when taking your fuzzy to the great outdoors to explore.

Getting fuzzy used to a harness

Before you take your ferret outside, get him accustomed to his harness and leash inside. Most ferrets struggle when you first put on the harness or collar, but after awhile, most go about their business of exploring. Once in a while, though, I come across a rebellious carpet shark who takes more time to get used to the new constraint.

Start off slowly by following these simple steps:

1. **Get your ferret used to wearing his harness in the house while you supervise — but without a leash attached.**

   His harness should be just tight enough to prevent him from slipping out during a struggle.

2. **When he begins to forget about his new piece of clothing, add the leash and walk him around the house.**

3. **When he seems to accept his limited freedom, you can move to the outside world.**

I like to have my ferrets get all their struggling out inside the house, just in case. There's nothing like the panic that races through you as you're trying to catch a loose ferret outside.

Wah-lah. There's little more to this training than just harnessing your little guy. Some ferrets may need time to get used to having dead weight holding them back, but I've never seen a ferret revolt the way a puppy sometimes does. Ferrets don't heel or walk peacefully by your side like a pooch. The harness-and-leash method is merely a convenient way to tow you behind them as they go on their merry little ways.

A lot of people keep harnesses or tightly fitted collars on their ferrets all the time. Perhaps they leave the harnesses or collars on due to frustration or anxiety about having to put them back on later. I think this is a dangerous practice. Ferrets can and will get into everything and like to squeeze into small places. I advise you to never leave a collar or harness on your ferret while he's unsupervised, because it's very easy for him to get caught up on something and either get stuck or strangle himself, even in his own cage. If you have to battle to get the harness on, simply practice more often.

Following basic rules when you're out and about

The following list presents some basic rules for safety and sanity when you're outside with your fuzzy:

- ✔ **Never tie your tethered ferret to something and leave him unsupervised.** Besides being an easy target for predators, your ferret will get bored and frustrated and do everything he can to escape, and he may just succeed.

- ✔ **Never let your leashed ferret wander into shrubbery.** He can become entangled in the branches, and it will be difficult for you to rescue him. Worst-case scenario, he can get stuck and wiggle his way out of his harness or collar.

- ✔ **Never use stretchy collars.** This collar variety is easy to pull off.

- ✔ **Never use plastic collars or harnesses.** Your fuzzy will be tempted to chew on them and swallow the pieces. Even if the ferret wearing the collar doesn't chew it, a visiting playmate may.

- ✔ **Never ignore the temperature.** You wouldn't walk your fuzzy across hot coals, so don't walk him on hot pavement. The fuzzy's paw-paws are very sensitive, you know. Likewise, those of us who've hopped frantically across a sandy beach know how brutally hot sand can get, and they don't make sandals for carpet sharks! Walking on snow is okay as long as your ferret isn't in it for too long.

Chapter 20

Dealing with the Behaviorally Challenged Ferret

In This Chapter

▶ Knowing the reasoning behind your ferret's aggression

▶ Handling and taming the biting fuzzbutt

Some potential ferret owners, even after reading many books and magazines on ferrets, still aren't prepared for the endless behavioral possibilities they may face. You really can't know what all to expect until you've actually walked several miles with fuzzies attached to your shoes. It isn't just the newcomers who get all the surprises; many experienced fuzzy owners encounter unexpected problems after years of perfect fuzzdom. And consider this: It may be the ferret owner who's the problem and not the poor fuzzy.

This chapter is mostly about problem-solving and preparing you as much as possible for the issues you may face. It deals with some of the reasons people give up their ferrets — in other words, it deals with the behaviorally challenged carpet sharks. I discuss the biters, the misunderstood ferrets of the world, and the aggressive beasts. You get the information needed to understand these fuzzies and reform them into acceptable members of the family.

Understanding Your Dracula in Fuzzy's Clothing

Once in a blue moon, a person will adopt a ferret that's just plain mean — in other words, she's a biter — and nothing much can be done about it. This is common in all pets, and ferrets are no exception. Most ferrets are loving and playful family members. Out of all the ferrets that have passed through my shelter or have remained as permanent residents, I've only encountered four severe biters. My experience has been that a lovable pooch is still far more dangerous than the typical fuzzy. But problem biters do exist, and you may adopt one someday.

The good news is that there's hope for the biting ferret. Most aggressive ferrets can be turned into gentle critters if their owners are willing to work on their relationships. If you're serious about being a fuzzy human, dumping a problem carpet shark at the nearest shelter should be your absolute last resort. This section is for the ferret lover who's willing to work to keep the ferret a part of the family.

Ferrets can bite for many reasons. Although you may not have all the colorful information about your fuzzy's personal history, you may be able to put the pieces together just by being a good observer. It may mean learning how to deactivate the bomb before it goes off, or it may mean taking time to convince your fuzzy that not all humans are evil. Usually, it's the latter (humans are the root of most biting evils).

Not all ferret bites should be considered attacks. In fact, most aren't. Ferrets often have a good reason to bite; biting is sometimes the only way a ferret can communicate her needs or wishes. For example, a fuzzy can't reach up and smack you on the back of the head to say, "Tag, you're it." However, a nip on the ankle may be just as effective. Tag, by the way, is a favorite ferret game.

After you identify why your ferret is biting, you can address the situation appropriately. The following sections take a look at the most common reasons ferrets bite. (The later section "Socializing Your Biting Beast" explains what you can do to correct the problem, and Chapter 19 deals with training your ferret not to bite.)

You must recognize the difference between playful biting and aggressive biting and try to correct both. An aggressive biter may bite you and hold on, or she may bite so hard that she draws blood. The pain caused by an aggressive biter is unmistakable. Playful bites include mouthing, light nips, and even "nip and runs." Although playful bites cause little to no discomfort, they may cause future problems.

I'm having growing pains

Baby ferrets are natural nippers. They are, by nature, animals that face predation pressure. Young kits may react to startles by biting, simply as an instinctive reaction. Nothing is wrong with them; they just tend to react instinctively. And like all mammals, they explore the world with their mouths. And they have teething pains that can be severe at times, and gnawing on the closest available thing — your arm or a chew toy — helps to alleviate the pain. If your biting furball is a kit, I tend to think the situation really doesn't fall into the classification of "problem" — yet (see the following section).

Nobody told me not to bite

Many owners fail to nip-train their ferrets at an early age, when training is so crucial. The kit stage is the time when members of the ferret litter teach each other their biting limits. It is how a large male kit can play with a small female and not harm her. The rule ferrets learn is to never play harder than another ferret. An untrained fuzzy may be the owner's fault, the fault of a previous caretaker, or even the fault of a pet shop that failed to handle the cute babies on display. Perhaps the fuzzy you've adopted hasn't had limits set for her. Unfortunately, innocent kit nippers turn into bold biters if you don't stop the nipping early.

Often, people dump their nipping ferrets because they just don't know how to set limits and be the human bosses. The reason is due purely to frustration and lack of education. Chapter 19 covers how to nip-train a fuzzy. Educate yourself and don't give up on your little furball!

I'm in pain, darn it!

Your ferret has limited ability to say "Hey, my belly aches" or "I have these nasty bugs in my darn ears," so she may bite instead. Your biting furball may be suffering from a treatable condition, such as a severe ear-mite infestation, or a more chronic disease, like adrenal disease. There are many, many medical conditions that can lead a ferret to bite.

Be a good human and be mindful of sudden changes in behavior. Many times she just isn't feeling well and needs your help. If the biting seems out of character, take your biter to the vet (warn the vet in advance about the aggression) for a complete physical. Rule out any illness or injury that may be causing your ferret to lash out in pain.

I'm a manly or bully ferret

Unneutered male ferrets can (and probably will) be more aggressive than their altered counterparts. As with some teenage boys, it's the male ferret's hormonal duty to dominate whomever he can. Usually, an unneutered ferret chooses other male ferrets to bully. Female ferrets can also be targets of this type of male aggression. Sometimes, he'll bully the human who unknowingly tests his ferret manlihood. If you want to fix the aggression problem for this type of ferret, neuter that boy!

I'm facing a lot of change right now

Change, whether good or bad, is scary. Imagine this: Some giant picks you up, rips you out of your house, and plops you down in the middle of who knows where. Strangers are poking at you. Everything smells and looks funny. Some big, wet nose is sniffing at you and blowing snot on you. The new noises are enough to make your head explode. If you had a tail, it would be puffed out like a bottlebrush! You don't know whether to poop, run away, or bite. Heck, for all you know, you're in for the nightmare of your life.

A ferret in a strange situation may act scared and confused. Whether she's with a human she's loved and trusted for years or in the care of a brand new human, she doesn't know what to expect. When a ferret is under this much stress, she may bite. Give this ferret time to acclimate to big changes before rushing in and forcing her to bond with you. It may take hours, days, or weeks. But go slowly and let her explore new surroundings or new people.

Biting always worked before!

If your ferret was once under the care of another human (or perhaps you were the culprit), it's possible that she may have been trained to bite inadvertently. I don't mean "Caution: Guard Ferret on Premises!" I'm talking about a weenie human who gave the ferret her way every time she nipped. For instance, if the person picked up the fuzzy and she nipped, the person put her down and gave her freedom. Or perhaps when the ferret bit, the human thought that she must be hungry, so the person rewarded her with food. In other words, the ferret was training the human.

Never positively reinforce a biting ferret. You shouldn't view biting as a cute way to tell you something.

I'm still fighting back

The main cause of a biting ferret is mistrust of humans. Humans can be pretty nasty animals. Some humans react violently or impulsively to stuff they don't understand; others are just jerks who thrive on being cruel. Unfortunately, animals are frequent victims of human abuse. In these cases, you can't blame a rescued fuzzy for remaining aggressive. Abused fuzzies learn several things during their abuse: 1) Attack or be attacked. 2) Hands equal hitting, feet equal kicking, and humans equal pain. 3) Every ferret for herself.

Working with an abused ferret takes extra time and patience. If you've ever been badly hurt by someone, physically or emotionally, you know how long it can take to trust again. Head to the following section to start the road to recovery with your scared fuzzy.

Some other reasons for my biting

Some ferrets react aggressively to particular noises, smells, or objects. My ferret Sybil (appropriately named), for example, came to my shelter with two other nutcases, Buster and Fidget. Sybil reacts aggressively when the dogs start barking, no matter where they are or why they're barking. How does she react? She runs up and bites me when they bark. Many ferrets react similarly to other stimuli, such as

✔ New smells (especially on the hands or clothes)

✔ The ruffling of newspapers

✔ Vacuum cleaners

✔ Brooms

✔ Loud music

The list goes on. This is called *displaced aggression,* and there isn't always a reason why it happens. Some ferrets just get extra freaky around freaky people. This type of carpet shark may chase a timid person around the room and nip at his ankles. Most of these quirky ferrets are otherwise lovable and sweet, as most fuzzies are. The bottom line: If you're smart enough to identify the trigger, you should be smart enough not to trigger your fuzzy when she's out of her cage. (Oh, and by the way, most ferrets do have foot fetishes!)

Socializing Your Biting Beast

Not many fuzzies are just determined to be aggressive no matter what their owners do. A hopeless fuzzy case is a rarity. If you think you have an eccentric head case that you just can't handle, I suggest that you just haven't found the right approach or haven't been consistent with your technique. Your fuzzbutt may even be suffering from a combination of neuroses or a serious medical condition. Every ferret is a unique individual and responds differently to different methods of resocialization. Your job as your fuzzy's human is to find the best combination of love and gentle discipline.

In the following sections, you find out the best way to handle the biting ferret, as well as what to do if you should find yourself with a ferret hanging off your finger. With patience and consistency, using the tips here, you'll be able to turn your Dracula into a charmer in no time.

Norm and his magic touch with aggressive ferrets

Norm Stilson of the Greater Chicago Ferret Association uses the same method to socialize all biting ferrets, and he has a tremendous success rate. He admits that his reconditioning process can take anywhere from a few weeks to a couple years. It depends largely on the severity of the ferret's mistrust of humans (in other words, how big of a jerk her previous human was) and how much time Norm has to work with the biter. Still, I've seen him in action, transforming the most hopeless biters into snuggly, happy fuzzbutts.

Norm uses the upper body grip, which I describe in the "Getting a grip" section, and spends a lot of time talking gently to the ferret. He uses his free hand to stroke the fur on top of the fuzzy's head and neck at the same time. He cuddles the fuzzy up against him (keeping control of the ferret's head) and even kisses the top of the fuzzy's head. Norm's version of the method, in my opinion, is the best.

Getting a grip

I find that the best way to handle an aggressive carpet shark is to firmly hold the upper part of her body from underneath, but with more control over her head — the *grip* method. You may have to distract her a little to seize her this way, but it allows you to hold her so she can't twist her head around to latch onto some vital part of your body. Simply follow these steps:

1. **Grab your fuzzy by the scruff of the neck.**

2. **Take your free hand and hold her from underneath, just above her chest.**

3. **Wrap your fingers around the fuzzy's neck.**

   A paw may also go in between your fingers.

4. **When you're confident that you have the ferret safely but firmly in your grip, you can release the scruff.**

5. **Now you can use that free hand to smother her with gentle petting.**

This is a great handling method and doesn't require gloves (see the upcoming sidebar). And it usually works, too.

Getting unstuck

If a ferret bites you and doesn't want to let go (an uncommon behavior), you can use some techniques to get her off. Unless you're an experienced ferret handler, though, you'll probably be too busy panicking and overreacting to think about these techniques logically. Most people just try to fling the ferret from whichever body part she's latched onto.

With a little preparation and knowledge, you may be able to keep your wits about you in a latching situation and get unstuck. Some of the following tips may come in handy:

✔ Place a tiny amount of bitter solution into the corner of the ferret's mouth (use a cotton swab or small controlled spray). You can find this bitter solution at most pet stores. While she's ptooeying out the taste, your finger will be ptooeyed out along with it.

Don't spray bitter solution directly into the ferret's face. Ever. Doing so is painful and cruel, and the fuzzy's next bite will be justified.

✔ Dip a cotton swab in rubbing alcohol and touch the corner of the ferret's mouth. This method usually works wonders!

✔ Ask a helping hand to gently squeeze the carpet shark's jaws open and aid you in prying her off, one tooth at a time.

A real fear biter can "jump bite," moving from your skin to the helper's skin. Be extra cautious. (See the earlier section "Understanding Your Dracula in Fuzzy's Clothing" for more on the reasons for biting.)

✔ Have a helper thread a wooden chopstick behind the skin under attack. A gentle yet forceful twisting motion can loosen the bite grip just enough to allow for an escape without harming the ferret.

✔ Drip some Ferretone or olive oil over the tip of the ferret's nose. The ferret should automatically start licking the treat, releasing you in the process.

A gripping question: Gloves or hands?

Some people think that thick gloves, made of leather, are great for working to tame the aggressive ferret. Gloves can help protect your hands from the serious ouchies an aggressive biter can inflict. Using gloves allows you to handle the fuzzy confidently and without fear if you're serious about taming her. If you're skittish around your aggressive ferret to begin with, this option may be the way to go. Another option is a fillet glove, which is thinner and has metal armor that prevents bites from getting through. You can find these gloves at sporting goods stores.

Although many people advocate using gloves to tame the biter, I believe that doing so may actually defeat the purpose. I think fuzzies find the feel of a gentle but firm human paw a little more soothing than the feel of a stiff, groping glove. Being held with a glove may feel a bit more like being manhandled, which may be why your furball is so ticked off in the first place. I've never used gloves. They're too bulky on my tiny hands, and I can't seem to hold a fuzzy comfortably. Also, I never want to give a ferret the impression that my skin is tough and can withstand such torture!

"I will probably bite you even harder if you . . ."

If you opt for one of the following techniques to get your fuzzy to unlatch from a bite, you'll probably make the problem worse:

✔ Mist a bitter spray or another deterrent in your fuzzy's face

✔ Bite her back on the ear or head (some people actually do this)

✔ Flick her on the nose or head when she bites

✔ Hit her or throw her across the room

✔ Isolate her from the world for long periods of time

Although I often stress the importance of not rewarding biting with treats, giving a reward is justified during an extreme, prolonged bite. The object is to get unhooked without causing further trauma to you or the frightened ferret.

✔ Find a cold body of water — such as water in a toilet, bathtub, or sink — and submerge her until her desire to breathe overtakes her desire to mangle you.

This is a last-resort solution. Don't flush her down the toilet or drown her in the process. Bite wounds heal. Death is irreversible, and guilt haunts for a long time. You can also use cold running water from a faucet.

Don't try to get your ferret to release by pulling her or jerking her away. In other words, don't try to send her for a flying lesson. Doing so only causes more damage, and you'll feel really stupid if you further injure yourself or your fuzzy when you have many better options.

The main thing to remember when being bitten is don't panic. Panicking usually makes the situation worse. If you know you're dealing with an aggressive ferret, you can opt not to handle her unless someone else is around to come to your rescue.

Taming the critter

Depending on your ferret's personality and her past life experiences, she may or may not respond to certain methods of reconditioning. Some fuzzies learn quickly that humans can be trustworthy and can make great playmates. Others need quite a bit more time to come to this conclusion. This section

presents some ideas that may or may not work for taming your biting ferret. Unfortunately, some may even make matters worse, but it may only be temporary. Don't give up on a tactic right away just because it doesn't work the first time. Winning over a biter takes patience and consistency. If, however, the biting gets more severe and more frequent after much patience and consistency, you probably should try a new tactic.

This list gives you some of the more obvious solutions you can try:

- ✔ If your companion biter is an unaltered male, neuter him.
- ✔ Rule out medical reasons for biting through a veterinary exam and get veterinary care for any illnesses or injuries.
- ✔ If you know the biting trigger, such as barking dogs, don't subject your ferret to the trigger.
- ✔ If your fuzzy is visually or hearing impaired (or very young), take extra care not to startle her when handling her.
- ✔ Make sure that your ferret is well fed and given a proper diet.
- ✔ Spend more quality time with your ferret instead of keeping her cooped up in the cage for days on end.

And here are some more creative ideas; you can use these in combination with the previous solutions and with each other:

- ✔ Put a bitter spray, such as Bitter Apple (the spray works but the cream is better), on your hands so a bite doesn't taste as good.
- ✔ Screech, growl, hiss, or loudly yell "Ouch!" or "No!" when the ferret bites (use simple words, not sentences). Some people do a quick, firm shake while verbally reprimanding the biter. Many ferrets see this as a sign that biting definitely isn't a good thing to do.

  Some ferrets may bite harder if a verbal reprimand is accompanied by a scruff, especially if you include a firm shake. This is a definite individual thing.

  Another method is to tell her, "I'm in charge, darn it!" and place her submissively on her back with a scruff. Hold her firmly in that position high up on her body to keep control of her head. After a few minutes, give her a timeout in her cage.

- ✔ Sentence the ferret to short-term (no longer than 30 minute) jail time by placing her in a small carrier for biting. A fuzzy should always get a timeout immediately after biting.

Timeouts are important for many forms of ferret discipline but should be used with care. Some people believe that an immediate timeout after biting is a reward to a ferret that wants to be left alone anyway. So, if you can, try to physically hold the fuzzy for several minutes after the bite occurs before you put her away for a timeout (see the section "Getting a grip"). However, if you're too angry to be rational or too busy cleaning up your wounds, you should put away the fuzzy immediately. If these timeouts don't seem to work, try the "I'm gonna hold you anyway" method to see if this form of dominance works better. And get your tetanus shot updated!

✔ If your fuzzy currently has no playmate, try introducing a fuzzy friend so that she'll have someone to rough and tumble with. She may be bored to frustration.

✔ Immediately substitute a toy for the human body part and allow the ferret to only bite that.

✔ Wrap the fuzzy securely in a towel and carry her around like a bundled baby. Talk to her and stroke the top of her head gently.

Don't use your ferret's cage as a timeout place. This can work one of two ways. It can make the ferret view her cage as a "bad place" where she doesn't want to go at any time, or the timeout can be viewed as a reward because the cage is where the ferret wanted to go in the first place. I think it is better to have a special, very small timeout cage — a cat-sized carrier would work fine.

Aggression isn't a training or conditioning tool. In my opinion, aggression only leads to aggression, whether you're dealing with a human or a fuzzbutt. Chances are, what got you to this stage had something to do with a human who was being a jerk. So, throw away all the tough love and put on your compassionate hat. The biting ferret reacts positively only to a firm but consistently nonviolent approach. And don't forget to always reward your ferret for acceptable behavior. Ferrets are extremely intelligent and learn according to how you teach them. Heed what Bob Church, ferret guru and enthusiast, says: "A gentle hand grows a gentle ferret."

Part VI
Breeding Ferrets: The Facts, Fallacies, and Plain Ol' Hard Work

The 5th Wave   By Rich Tennant

"As you can see, this breed comes with a mask, although the big floppy shoes were our idea."

In this part . . .

*I*f you need to read a book about breeding, I must say that you probably aren't qualified to breed ferrets at this point in time. It takes the knowledge of many books, years of ferret ownership, and a great deal of research to even think about breeding carpet sharks. However, although I certainly don't advocate the indiscriminate breeding of ferrets, I do include this part about the basics of ferret breeding. And I do my best here to talk you out of bringing more ferrets into this world.

There are thousands of ferrets all awaiting good homes. Please read this part carefully and consider all the ramifications of breeding before you actually go through with it.

And even if you don't want to breed fuzzies, this part helps you know a little more about your lovable fuzzbutt.

Chapter 21

Should You Breed Your Ferret? Looking at the Big Picture

In This Chapter

▶ Considering the emotional, financial, and time commitments of breeding

▶ Understanding the ramifications of careless breeding

*B*eing able to breed ferrets responsibly and successfully requires years of ferret ownership and a great deal of research, among other things. Unless you meet the ownership requirement and can do the research, I strongly urge you to have your ferret altered and leave breeding to the people who know exactly what they're doing and why they're doing it.

However, kits are simply adorable. What's more satisfying than raising a beautiful, healthy fuzzy? (Maybe giving a good home to an old fuzzy that was abandoned in a shelter.) Responsible private breeders offer an alternative for fuzzy people who want kits but don't want to go to pet shops. Responsible breeders are more interested in a kit's well-being than money, thus are more concerned about weeding out the less-than-desirable fuzzy homes. And private breeders get to spend oodles of time sharing their wealth of information with people who seek them out.

This chapter discusses breeder requirements that many beginner breeders haven't thought about. Before you begin breeding ferrets, find out whether you have what it takes. And, even if you decide that you do, ask yourself whether you should. Also, I discuss ferret shelters and why they exist, because every ferret in a shelter was once somebody's little baby.

What It Takes to Be a Responsible Breeder

Breeding ferrets requires way more than just throwing two amorous fuzzies in a cage and hanging up the "Do Not Disturb" sign. Responsible breeders carefully choose their breeding pairs, and they breed for good temperament, good looks, and conformation. They're prepared for emergency medical situations and spend most of their free time caring for moms and kits (baby ferrets).

And responsible breeders don't just sell their kits to anyone. Money should be the last thing on a responsible breeder's mind. The honest truth is that unless you mass-produce hundreds of kits a year and sell them wholesale to pet shops, you probably won't make much money. If you're lucky, you'll break even. A responsible breeder does the work because he or she simply loves the ferret and wants to put the best ferrets in the best homes.

Alas, I can discuss much more that responsible breeders need to have and do, and I do so in the following sections.

Deep pockets

A ferret breeder must fork over money for the cost of caring for pregnant jills (unspayed females) and vulnerable kits (babies). In addition to normal care, breeders will always have unexpected expenses; have you thought about emergencies or unplanned situations? Responsible breeders must take the following costs into consideration:

- ✔ Purchasing excellent breeding stock to get started

  About 85 to 90 percent of the ferrets sold into the pet trade in the United States are altered and descented at weaning and are therefore unbreedable.

- ✔ Proper cages and setups for jills and kits (see Chapter 5 for more on ferret cages)

- ✔ Routine vet care for moms and kits, including supplements and any medication needed

- ✔ A first vaccination for kits before they go to their new homes

✔ Vet care for complications such as uterine infections and mastitis (infected and hardened mammary glands)

✔ Emergency C-sections for jills in trouble

✔ Humane euthanizing of kits that have severe deformities or the cost of providing lifelong care for these babies

✔ Spaying bad moms (see the following section) or retirees — and providing lifelong care for them if you can't find good homes

✔ Providing lifelong care for any kits that you can't sell

The emotional stake

Breeding isn't always smooth sailing, with happy births and successful adoptions; heartache is involved, and so are many decisions that you'd probably rather not have to face. Ferret moms, for example, may not be good moms at all. Kits can die from being cannibalized (eaten by mom) or neglected. It can be heartbreaking. Hand-rearing a newborn kit is next to impossible, so all you can do is watch.

Many breeders arrange to have two ferrets give birth within a few days of each other so that they can serve as foster moms if necessary. This plan doesn't always work, though — especially if the litters are large.

Before you decide to breed, ask yourself how you would feel about the following, because breeders face these situations at one time or another:

✔ Having kits die suddenly

✔ Moms cannibalizing or killing the kits

✔ Losing kits because a mom fails to nurse or is incapable of nursing

✔ Losing a mom during a difficult pregnancy or labor

✔ Getting your hopes dashed when you find out it was a false pregnancy (which is common in ferrets)

✔ Worrying about all the kits you help into the world and stressing over how they're doing in someone else's care

✔ Having kits with severe birth defects euthanized

✔ Having fuzzies returned to you for one reason or another

Retiring a breeding myth

Breeding animals isn't a way to teach a child about the miracle of life (and death, in many cases). If you feel your child is missing out in this area of knowledge, rent a video, buy some books, or tune in to the Discovery Channel or Animal Planet. These are great ways to spend quality time with kids and still teach them the value and beauty of life. Of course, also explain to your kids the devastating effects of overpopulation so that they'll understand why a video may be far more responsible than the real thing (see the final section of this chapter for more).

Time to care

Breeding ferrets, providing support during and after pregnancies for moms and kits, and finding perfect homes for your precious babies can be extremely time-consuming. You'll probably have to forgo your karate classes to do the following:

- ✔ Search for (and research) a source of quality breeder ferrets, which are your initial financial and emotional investments.

- ✔ Keep diligent records (financial and pedigree).

- ✔ Talk to and learn from other responsible breeders.

    Responsible breeding isn't a competition; it's a shared interest.

- ✔ Check your kits' weights regularly to make sure that they're gaining weight, and take the necessary steps to correct problems upon discovery.

- ✔ Chauffeur your ferrets to and from the vet.

- ✔ Spend time socializing kits and begin training before they go to their new homes.

    Good breeders hang onto kits until they're at least 8 weeks old.

- ✔ Spend an enormous amount of time on the phone talking to potential buyers and new fuzzy parents. Good breeders should be choosy about whom they sell their babies to, and they should provide ongoing before- and after-sales support.

- ✔ Take care of kits that owners have brought back to you. A responsible breeder takes back kits that don't work out in their homes, which can be a burden over time.

If you think you have what it takes to be a responsible fuzzy breeder, research the subject a little more. Call your local ferret shelter and put in a few hours of volunteer work each week. If you don't have time to do that now, you certainly won't have the time to breed ferrets responsibly.

Willingness to find out what you don't know

Responsible breeding means knowing a lot about ferret biology and genetics. For example, did you know that ferrets are similar to chinchillas in that breeding certain color variations may cause lethal genes? Additionally, new, exotic ferret colors being produced may be the result of mutant or recessive genes. No one knows for sure whether funky-colored ferrets will have more health problems down the road. How can you know whether you're creating one of these tragic situations?

In addition to biology and genetics, you need to know the rules governing the sale of ferrets. For example, when it comes to selling your kits, did you know that breeders who wholesale their ferrets (sell to pet shops, for example) are required to be USDA licensed? (Some breeders also have to be licensed by their state's Department of Agriculture; USDA is a separate federal licensing.)

This places even more emphasis on the need to keep good records and maintain good husbandry practices. Inspectors can pop in at any reasonable time — unannounced — to inspect your facility, animals, and records. Also, ferret breeders may be required to have additional permits or licenses, depending on where they live.

Avoiding a Need for More Shelters

If you love ferrets (and presumably you do if you want to breed them), you don't want to bolster the need for shelters. Most people have heard at one time or another the statistics on how many dogs and cats are killed each year in shelters. The senseless deaths of these once-loved pets number in the millions. As ferrets gain popularity as companion pets in households, the number of furballs that wind up in shelters also increases, as does the number of deaths of these homeless fuzzies.

Careless breeding by humans is the cause for overpopulation. The population of fuzzbutts at ferret shelters such as the Greater Chicago Ferret Association can fluctuate between 60 and 100 ferrets at a time. That's a lot of displaced furkids. Many are geriatric fuzzies that no longer fit into the perfect pet mold their humans have illogically created. These unfortunate souls get dumped for younger or different pets.

No ferret breeder can guarantee that every one of his or her kits will remain in permanent, loving homes. Too many people treat animals as property; they put little thought into getting pets and end up abusing them, neglecting them, selling them to the highest bidders, or giving them away to whoever shows up first. Some people even dump fuzzies into the wild to futilely fend for themselves, or they abandon them at shelters where their futures are unknown. This revolving-door syndrome gets passed on by example to children. It's morally and ethically wrong to treat any life with such disregard; this cycle needs to be stopped.

You can help stop this cycle by thinking long and hard about whether you should breed ferrets at all. If you can't meet the points listed previously in "What It Takes to Be a Responsible Breeder," you'll for sure be adding to the vicious cycle. But even responsible breeders can't guarantee they won't be a part of the cycle, because there are no guarantees on where the ferrets end up. Although it's true that overpopulation is a problem and breeding needs to be curtailed, the true problem lies with a human mentality that pets are disposable and the job of the shelter is to take in the unwanteds. The cycle stops with education and a change in mentality.

Chapter 22

Unmasking the Details of Ferret Love

In This Chapter

▶ Reviewing the fertile fuzzy

▶ Understanding the unbred ferret

▶ Caring for your ferret during her pregnancy

▶ Dealing with easy and difficult deliveries

▶ Recognizing and taking care of problems after birth

*E*ven if you've identified the perfect pair of fuzzies to breed (see Chapter 21), getting them to cooperate may be difficult. We humans tend to think that guys, no matter what species, have one thing on the brain and are always in the mood; the male ferret, or *hob,* however, has long bouts of "Not now, dear — I have a headache" syndrome.

Headaches aside, ferret courtship and mating often are primitively brutal and unromantic. After the deed is done and the male scoots off to put another notch in his chew toy, the female, or *jill,* needs some extra-special attention. Being the good human that you are, your job is to see that her needs are adequately met. This means more than just running out for a late-night pickle purchase; you must provide a whole lot of tender, loving care, supply a good place for her to hunker down, and fill her belly with extra-good stuff.

In addition to addressing the needs of a pregnant ferret, this chapter gives you an overview of the ferret's reproductive system and mating habits. We give a lot of emphasis to the do's and don'ts of breeding ferrets. This chapter also discusses the actual birth of the kits. Because the mortality rate in newborn fuzzy kits is high, I outline the basic things that can go wrong and explain what you may be able to do to help. This is a particularly important chapter to pay attention to if you're considering bringing more fuzzbutts into the world. It's also great for people — especially shelter workers — who unexpectedly find themselves with pregnant ferrets on their hands.

This chapter isn't meant to be a step-by-step guide to breeding fuzzies. The breeding process takes years to learn. Consider the information here as background basics and an overview of typical things people encounter when breeding ferrets. If anything, this chapter is meant to further convince you to leave fuzzy breeding to experienced and responsible experts.

Fine-Tuning the Organs

Hormones and sexual maturity can cause wondrous changes in the appearance, behavior, and habits of our lovable ferrets. These changes occur over time as the body develops and peak during the mating seasons, or *ruts,* when sexual maturity has been reached.

You need to know how ferrets develop and what changes you can expect to encounter in unaltered ferrets if you're considering breeding them. This brief section gives you an overview of the ferret's reproductive system and mating habits.

The boy (hob)

The male ferret's testicles begin to mature approximately six weeks after his birth. Full maturity takes close to three months. You can tell when a hob is beginning that confusing time of puberty because his testicles begin to increase in size, mainly due to the increase in the male hormone testosterone. Also testicle size can change according to the photoperiod. Ferrets are tuned into the photoperiod to determine times of fertility. The testicle size is small and may appear "immature" in the non-breeding season (winter) and increase greatly in size in the breeding season — spring to fall. The increase in testosterone also causes the ferret to notice the girls a little more.

Boy ferrets that are ready to breed wear a discolored, yellowish undercoat, caused by an increase in oil production in the skin glands. They're at their smelliest during this time.

Mature males may tease the girls (only because they like them) and grab the backs of their necks to show them how much they care. Like with the overactive male dog, behaviors such as pelvic thrusting and mounting various objects occur frequently. They may also begin to stash ferret magazines under their snooze sacks and spend way too much time on the phone! After breeding season, however, the male ferret returns to being just one of the stinky guys.

If you haven't already figured it out, unaltered male ferrets are quite the smelly boys. They can be extremely aggressive toward other males and even their humans — especially when they're out to capture a female's heart. For this reason, unaltered boys don't usually make good pets when they're in breeding season.

The girl (jill)

Unaltered female ferrets become sexually mature at about 6 months of age under normal lighting conditions. The onset of *estrus* (the heat period) is closely associated with the increase in daylight during the normal seasonal change. Females that are exposed to shorter light days are late bloomers that reach sexual maturity as late as 12 months of age.

A female in estrus is easy to identify. Her pink vulva swells due to an increase in the female hormone estrogen (see Figure 22-1). You may see a clear or slightly discolored discharge.

The female in heat may get crabby and sleep less (I refer to it as PMS, or Pre-Mustelid Syndrome). But unlike female humans, the ferret in estrus usually cuts back on her food intake. Some other stuff is going on inside her body, too. The lining of her uterus begins to swell, and follicles containing eggs develop in the ovaries. Then she just sits back and waits for her dream ferret to come by and sweep her off her fuzzy feet.

Making a love connection: Enter Neanderthal ferret

A female ferret should be bred about two weeks after the swelling of her vulva becomes noticeable (see the previous section). Typically, you should bring the female to the male's condo for the rendezvous. I recommend that you stay close to chaperone the first date to be sure the chemistry isn't overly explosive. Expect a lot of noise and commotion. The female may even adamantly reject the hob's advances. If he persists, she usually wins after a horrific fight ensues.

Many bree-ders recommend that you keep the breeding pair together for two to three days. Any longer than that and the male quickly gets on the female's nerves, causing arguments (and an occasional throwing of dishes). A lack of tolerance on the female's part often indicates that she has little buns in the oven.

Breeding the female two days in a row may cause her to produce a bigger litter. If the fuzzy has fewer than five kits to nurse, she may go back into heat two to three weeks after the kits are born. This occurrence is called *lactational estrus.*

Romance and schmoozing are the last things on a male fuzzy's mind when he meets up with his dream girl. The male ferret practically tackles the female when he grabs her by the nape of the neck to mount her. He uses her to mop every corner of his condo, even though she may be screaming and biting in protest. When she goes into submission, he has his way with her, and it isn't uncommon for him to return for second or third helpings. No courtship is involved — unless you call clubbing her over the head and dragging her off by the fur to the nearest cave romantic. Some males are actually gentle, and their mates actually seem to enjoy themselves. But, for the most part, unaltered boys are no Don Juans.

The typical Mustelid love lasts an hour or so on average, with ten minutes being noted for some unimpressive fellows and an awesome three hours being noted for some marathon guys.

The following list presents a couple things you should be aware of so you don't panic or cause injury:

- ✔ Females often receive puncture wounds on the neck during the mating ritual. Blood is common, but violently shaking the female and/or causing wounds serious enough for profuse bleeding isn't. Separate the pair immediately.

- ✔ The typical mating ritual of ferrets — specifically the neck biting and prolonged intercourse — causes the release of hormones, which stimulates ovulation. Without the hormone, the female won't release her eggs and will remain in heat.

- ✔ The male ferret's penis has a bony hook at the tip that causes it to become latched inside the female after he penetrates. And the male remains hooked until he decides that he's had enough — no sooner. Don't try to separate ferrets in the middle of the act. Besides ruining the mood, forcing a separation may injure one or both fuzzies.

Female carpet sharks are induced ovulators, which means that their eggs aren't released until mating actually takes place. Pressure on the cervix, caused by the act of mating, and neck biting stimulates the release of the eggs (ovulation) 30 to 40 hours after the deed is done. Sperm can survive in the female for 36 to 48 hours. As many as 18 (typically 5 to 13) eggs are fertilized. The vulva begins to dry and shrink after a week and returns to normal size in three to four weeks (longer if breeding took place long after estrus began).

If the shrinkage doesn't begin after a week or so, your fuzzy hasn't established pregnancy, and you should set a new date with the male ferret.

What Happens If Your Unaltered Ferret Isn't Bred?

What if you decide not to breed your fuzzy after she goes into estrus? Not every ferret is bred every season for many reasons. But because female ferrets are induced ovulators, they remain in heat indefinitely until they're bred, and the result of a prolonged estrus can be deadly.

When a ferret is in estrus, her level of estrogen rises dramatically. This raised level of hormone, when in heat, suppresses the production of blood cells in the bone marrow. Prolonged suppression results in a condition called *aplastic anemia*. This condition is almost always fatal if left untreated because the ferret's red blood cells aren't replaced as needed and/or she'll succumb to bacterial infections from the lack of white blood cells. Some signs of aplastic anemia may include pale gums, hind-end weakness, patches of fur loss, and small areas of bleeding under the skin.

You have several ways to bring your female ferret out of estrus and harm's way:

- Breed her to an unaltered male.
- Breed her to a vasectomized male. (The hormones are still going strong, but the road is blocked.)
- Have a ferret-knowledgeable vet give her a hormone injection to fake her out of heat (see Chapter 12 for tips on finding a vet).

  A hormone injection and breeding to a vasectomized male are short-term solutions that cause a false pregnancy in your female. She'll eventually come back into heat and have the same problem. If you've decided that breeding your female isn't for you, you should proceed to the last suggestion.
- Spay her! (See Chapter 12 for more information.)

Mothering the Mom-to-Be

About two weeks into your fuzzy's pregnancy, you should be able to gently palpate her belly and feel the small walnut-sized babies. However, she may not show the typical bulging signs of pregnancy until one month has passed. The kits should arrive in about 41 to 43 days (usually 42 days), barring any unforeseen circumstances. Until then, get ready to pamper and schmooze your fuzzy even more than you already do — for at least a couple of months. If you're a true ferret lover (and you'd better be if you plan on breeding ferrets), mothering isn't too difficult a job for you. Just triple your current efforts. Your care may very well be rewarded with a healthy litter of adorable kits. On the other hand, you must accept that complications are common no matter how well you care for her.

This section details what kind of care you should give to the mother fuzzy, from her feedings to her environment.

You should handle your pregnant fuzzy gently and very frequently to get her as comfortable with you as possible. This positive interaction between you and the mom is critical, especially if you need to physically intervene during or shortly after the birth. An unfamiliar hand poked into her nest may cause mom to reject and/or cannibalize her kits. For this reason, the person who handles momma ferret most often during pregnancy should be the only person to invade the nest if invasion becomes absolutely necessary.

I suggest that you, as a serious ferret breeder, find another breeder (if you don't have another female to breed yourself) who will have a ferret giving birth around the same time as your little girl. Make prior arrangements to place your kits with the other nursing female if your mom proves to be an unfit mother (ferret moms aren't always good moms; see the later section "Some Problems You May Face"), because hand-rearing kits is next to impossible. (See the final two sections of this chapter for more on foster moms and hand rearing.)

Depending on the time of year, the new mom will go back into heat either two or three weeks after her kits are weaned or when the next breeding season arrives. A healthy ferret can have up to three successful litters per year, although most reputable breeders stick with one or two litters a year per ferret.

Strange craving? Keeping mom nourished

Pickles and ice cream aren't likely to be on the list of things your pregnant fuzzy will crave. However, a pregnant ferret does need some extra nutrition to maintain her strength, good health, and body condition before the kits arrive. Extra nutrition is necessary during the nursing period as well.

The following list presents some tips for keeping your pregnant fuzzy in good health and ready to deliver:

✔ Experts recommend that a pregnant ferret's diet contain 35 to 40 percent protein and 15 to 20 percent fat. You should increase the number of daily feedings when the fuzzy begins to lactate, or produce milk. Most nursing moms are extra thin, so keep up on the extra nutrition.

✔ Keep meat baby food or other healthy foods on hand for treats to feed during playtime and cuddling. Your fuzzy should also have her basic food (kibble, if you choose) available at all times, as well as plenty of fresh water (see Chapter 8 for more on normal fuzzy diets).

✔ Many breeders supplement the pregnant and nursing ferret's basic diet with cooked meat and eggs. You can use a thicker Ferret Feeding Formula or Bob's Chicken Gravy (see Chapter 25), or you can come up with your own creative recipes.

Pregnant and nursing ferrets are prone to some ailments that can be life-threatening to both mom and the kits. It's important that you monitor your female's health and behavior closely. (For more information on mother fuzzy's ailments, see the sidebar "Conditions your female may encounter.")

Providing a maternity ward

You can keep pregnant fuzzies with other pregnant fuzzies, but you must separate them and give them private rooms at least two weeks before the kits are due. The private room should be a secure enclosure with extra bedding and a snuggly nest box. Providing a nest box is imperative, because it helps to keep the babies close together and warm. A baby that gets separated from the nest quickly chills and dies. The box also provides much-needed privacy for the new family. The following list runs through the many considerations you should make for your fuzzy's maternity ward, from the nest box to the environment of the entire room:

✔ You need to create an enclosed nesting area to simulate the underground den area that a ferret would nest in the wild. You can use a wooden parrot nest box, which are better ventilated and control moisture better than plastic. If you prefer plastic, head over to the section on building your own nest boxes in Chapter 5. The box should be clean and smooth to prevent injuries to the mom and kits. Openings to nest boxes should also be very smooth to protect mom when she enters and exits the box. Her belly and nipples will be vulnerable to abrasions.

✔ Make sure the cage contains no openings greater than ¾"-x-¾" because newborns are about the size of the average pinky finger. If necessary, you can kit-proof the nursery by safely attaching cardboard, sheet metal, or acrylic glass "guards" inside the cage around the entire perimeter (they should extend 5 to 6 inches high).

✔ Provide the appropriate bedding for the cage and box. Be careful about what type of bedding you choose. Avoid cloth or other materials that can snag little claws or unravel (stray fibers can strangle tiny heads and limbs). Also babies have been lost and died in the "folds" of cloth. Cross shredded paper can work well, as can clean straw or hay.

Conditions your female may encounter

Unfortunately, your mother ferret may develop the following conditions, all of which require immediate veterinary attention:

✔ **Eclampsia:** Possibly related to diet and stress, this occurs late in pregnancy but before kits are born. Can kill both the mom and unborn kits. *Signs:* Loss of appetite, lethargy, dehydration, black/tarry poop, severe coat shedding. Exact cause is unknown.

✔ **Mastitis:** Bacterial infection in the mammary glands that occurs during the early stages of lactation. A common cause of mastitis is having rough edges on the nest box or too high an opening on the nest box. As mom drags herself in and out of the box, she continually irritates her swollen breast tissue, often receiving little abrasions or cuts that allow bacteria to enter. *Signs:* Swelling, hardening, discoloration, and tenderness of mammary glands; anorexia; lethargy; inability to nurse kits (in severe cases).

✔ **Nursing sickness:** Possibly related to diet and stress, this occurs shortly before or shortly after the kits are weaned. *Signs:* Loss of appetite, weakness, weight loss, lack of coordination, dehydration. Exact cause is unknown.

✔ **Vaginitis:** Results from general irritation to the vulva and secondary bacterial infection, often caused by bedding material such as hay, straw, and wood chips. *Signs:* Yellow discharge from the vaginal area.

✔ **Pyometra:** Bacterial infection of the uterus that occurs in unaltered, non-pregnant females. *Signs:* Pus discharge from vaginal area, distended abdomen from pus-filled uterus, lethargy, depressed appetite, increase in water consumption, fever.

✔ Don't remove any extras that momma ferret adds. As her due date draws close, mom will begin to arrange her baby room just perfectly. She'll always pluck some fluffy wads of fur off her abdomen to line the nest with. The soft fur will be an extra comfort to the helpless kits. This also gives the kits access to the nipples later on and puts her skin closer to the kits for body heat.

✔ Be quiet and limit your activity around the maternity ward as delivery approaches. No playing your bongos or allowing the dogs to romp around and shake the cage. Disturbances may cause mom to panic and eat her kits when they finally do arrive.

Heading Off to the Delivery Room

This is an exciting time for you as you wait for the big day to arrive. You can be comforted by the fact that most ferrets give birth with little difficulty. A few will require your or your vet's intervention. But most of the work will be done by your ferret. The following sections take you through a normal delivery and a difficult delivery to show you what to expect and what you need to be prepared to handle.

No matter the delivery style, never assume (you or your vet) that the delivery is complete. Making sure that no kits are left behind is essential to the life of your fuzzy mom. Watch your ferret's behavior. If she seems distressed, make sure that you (if you're qualified) or your vet feels the jill's belly to rule out the possibility that another kit (dead or alive) is still inside her. Failing to check may lead to the death of your new mom and any unborn kits. If possible, wait to do any exams on her until she's at least fed her kits.

The typical delivery

A normal kit delivery can happen quite quickly; two to three hours is typical for average-sized litters. In larger litters, the birthing process may take a little longer, with several kits arriving each hour. You and your vet should quietly observe mom for arising problems during this time, but don't disturb her unless absolutely necessary.

Watch for kits still stuck in the placental sack. You'll have to help them out if mom fails to do so. She'll lick them clean and stimulate their breathing when they do get out. A kit stuck in the sack for too long will suffocate.

Allow mom to chew the umbilical cords in half instead of you cutting them. The crushing force of her chomp will keep the loose ends from bleeding. Also, make sure that mom eats all the placental material. As disgusting as this practice seems to humans, the placenta provides much-needed nourishment for the fatigued mom. It contains hormones that help the uterus to shrink and is also rich in iron (to promote milk production).

After this process, the new fuzzy mom usually curls up around her new kits, and they in turn immediately begin to suckle. Many ferret breeders agree that the first three days of the kits' lives are the most crucial. If the kits survive these difficult days, the chances of long-term survival are greatly heightened.

Don't mess with that nest! Mom is a great housekeeper and will clean up after the birth, eating most of the afterbirth. You may remove any dead babies if necessary, but mom will usually eat them before you can get to them. Disturbing the nest during those first three days increases the likelihood of cannibalism or mom rejecting the babies.

The difficult delivery

Many kit deliveries are far from typical, unfortunately. Many things can go wrong with a delivery and lead to the death of a kit, the death of your fuzzy mom, and/or the need for an emergency cesarean section. The following list presents some common occurrences:

✔ Kits born too quickly for mom may be a mass of entangled umbilical cords, resembling a small pile of spaghetti and pinky meatballs. Entangled kits can't nurse, and they get cold quickly and die. Also, limbs and lives may be lost due to the constriction of the drying cords and placentas around body parts.

✔ Even though most kits die inside mom if they aren't delivered by the 44th day, some overdue kits can continue to grow, presenting problems if delivery ensues (by blocking the birth canal, for instance).

✔ A kit in an unusual birthing position (such as its head tucked into its chest) almost always blocks the birth canal, where it can die and prevent the other kits from making their grand entrances. Unfortunately, those poor kits also die. And then mom cries, neglects the kits already delivered, and acts restless.

✔ Kits with congenital defects often become stuck in the birth canal and die.

✔ Small or overdue litters can produce dangerously large kits. Large kits can cause a holdup in the birth canal.

Depending on the cause of the difficult delivery, your vet may inject a labor-inducing drug or perform a cesarean section. It's a procedure that some fuzzy moms face. If the healthy mom is well cared for after the surgery, she almost always is physically capable of nursing and caring for her kits properly.

Some Problems You May Face after Birth

Hopefully all your kits will arrive safely and soundly. If so, you'll be happy as a clam and looking forward to helping raise the fuzzy family (or rehome them when they're old enough). What could possibly go wrong now? Many things, actually. You still have a long way to go before the babies are out of the woods.

Some ferrets just aren't cut out to be moms (or a human may make a mistake during a pregnancy to cause the ferret to become a bad parent; see the first section of this chapter for more). And even if you have the perfect mother fuzzy, situations may arise that prevent her from nursing her babies. In these situations, which I describe in the following sections, a foster mom is vital in helping keep the kits alive — unless the kits have already been cannibalized.

And if your fuzzy mom dies during pregnancy or delivery, the role of the foster mom becomes even more vital. As sad as it seems, the possibility isn't that far-fetched.

A difficult mother

New moms that are nervous or uncomfortable often make poor ferret mothers. Some ferrets just weren't meant to be moms, so they reject or cannibalize their babies for no apparent reason. But reasons do exist, and they are valid to the fuzzies. The following list shows you how to avoid possible difficult situations:

- ✔ **Fuzzy moms like their kits warm, so cold babies almost always are rejected.** If mom is away for a period of time (at a surgery, for instance), keeping the babies warm while she's away is essential. Or, if the kits wander away and get chilled, warm them up before returning them to the nest. (See the earlier section "Providing a maternity ward" for some tips.)

- ✔ **Some moms require a meal before cozying up to their new babies.** If your ferret mom seems uninterested after delivering all those kits, offer her some warm canned food or her kibble moistened with warm water.

- ✔ **Fluctuations in cage temperature, noise, and/or activity surrounding the nest can make a mom cannibalize or reject her youngsters.** Keep the area around the cage and nest calm. Now isn't the time to let the kids come in to see the new arrivals (see the earlier section "Providing a maternity ward" for more tips).

A mother incapable of nursing

Some fuzzy moms simply don't produce enough milk, or any milk at all, for their kits to nurse on. One possible cause is mastitis (see the earlier sidebar "Conditions your female may encounter"). You (along with your vet) need to monitor the activity level and growth of all the kits at all times while they're nursing. Kits should gain weight daily, tripling by day 10 (see Chapter 23 for more). A kit that doesn't get enough nourishment slowly starves; he loses the desire to suckle, chills, and eventually dies. Weigh your babies daily, because a newborn fuzzy can live only three days without eating before he dies.

If the ferret mother is producing some milk, you can leave the kits with mom as long as you supplement the feedings with kitten milk replacer. The best solution, however, is receiving the assistance of a foster mom (see the following section).

Hand-rearing kits as a last resort

Hand-rearing a kit is an emotionally and physically exhausting endeavor that rarely pays off. The mortality rate, even with experienced fuzzy humans, is high. Kits need a mother's milk for at least ten days in the early stages of their lives. Successful hand-rearing is possible if you start with healthy kits that are 2 weeks old. In any case, you should give it your best shot if hand-rearing is your only option.

To hand-rear, give the kits kitten-milk replacer every four to six hours via a plastic eyedropper or bottle. Make sure you give the food in small amounts and very slowly to avoid aspiration pneumonia. Tube feeding is difficult, even for the experienced, so take it slow. If you make it to week three, introduce the babies daily to a soft diet, such as canned cat or ferret food. The kits still need supplemental feedings until they reach 4 to 5 weeks old.

Calling on the foster mom

A breeder should try to have a foster fuzzy mom waiting in the wings in case an emergency arises with your momma — whether it's one of your own ferrets or a fellow ferret breeder's ferret. Most foster ferrets readily take new kits into their nests. Hopefully, your foster fuzzy is already nursing kits close in age to the ones being introduced. If she's a good milk producer, foster-nursing shouldn't be a problem for her, because ferrets can nurse more kits than they have available nipples.

The best way to introduce the "orphans" into the foster mom's nest is to first remove the foster mom. Allow the new kits to intermingle with the existing kits so that the new kits' scent becomes less distinct from the others' scent. If everyone smells the same, no one can complain!

In the rare instance that the foster mom rejects the kits (be sure to monitor them closely to watch for this), you need to find an immediate replacement. If you can't locate one, hand-rearing the kits is an option, but a very difficult one (see the sidebar "Hand-rearing kits as a last resort"). If the kits are less than 10 days old, they'll most likely die. The success rate increases with older kits.

Chapter 23

From Birth to Bundle of Energy: Walking a Fuzzy's Timeline

In This Chapter

▶ Raising your fuzzies from newborns through their terrible twos

▶ Surviving adolescence and the teenage years

*I*f you make it through the pregnancy and birthing ordeal — hey, it's stressful for all involved — you may be fortunate enough to watch a kit or two grow up. Healthy kits grow rapidly, both physically and emotionally. It won't be long before you're wiping away the tears in your eyes as you proclaim, "It seems like only yesterday Scooter was covered with newborn fuzz!"

This chapter takes you step by step through the developmental stages of carpet sharks. Some stages aren't too pleasant, but they'll be only temporary if you do your part as a good fuzzy human. From physical changes to behavioral changes, I tell you what to expect almost every step of the way and how to handle the changes to produce happy and healthy ferrets. However, keep this in mind: When it comes to fuzzbutts, nothing is set in stone!

Fuzzy Infancy: Birth to 3 Weeks

Kits (baby ferrets) are born into the world completely helpless and dependent on their mothers for survival. Their eyes and ears are sealed shut, rendering them blind and deaf. A small layer of fuzz covers their tiny bodies, which are smaller than a normal tube of lipstick (see Figure 23-1). Newborns typically weigh in at a whopping 6 to 12 grams. Most kits are born without any teeth, although baby incisors usually appear by day ten.

Healthy newborn kits have only two goals: getting food and keeping warm. Immediately after birth, they'll latch onto one of mom's nipples if allowed and remain there for a long period of time, gorging themselves on rich milk. Adequately fed newborns should gain between 2½–3 grams per day during their first week of life, doubling their birth weight by day five. Despite having just been squeezed through the birth canal and dropped into the cold world, newborn ferrets are active and mobile, although they have nowhere to go just yet. They explore their nest a tiny bit and start to develop the little muscles in their legs. They're able to recognize mom and siblings through smell. During the first few weeks, however, the young kits need to be stimulated by mama fuzzy to go to the bathroom.

Figure 23-1:
These 3-week-old ferrets aren't much bigger than a tube of lipstick.

During the second week of life, kits should gain about 4 grams per day. By 10 days old, they should've tripled their birth weight and should average about 30 grams. During the third week, the daily weight gain should be about 6 grams. And by 3 weeks old, your kits should be at least ten times heavier than when they were born.

At three weeks, the males and females are easier to tell apart (without cheating and turning them over). Females are daintier and have narrower heads. Boys are butterballs with their wide heads and stockier builds.

Even though fuzzies are born with their eyes closed, you can tell which ones are albinos because the color of their eyes shows through their thin skin. If you can't see dark color behind a fuzzy's semitransparent eyelids, you know you have a bouncing baby albino. (For more on fuzzy colors and what they entail, head to Chapter 2.)

Furball Toddlerhood: 3 to 6 Weeks

Kits that hit 3 weeks of age are working to rapidly develop their nest legs as they boldly explore their environment. Mom is still a part of their lives, keeping a close eye on kits that may wander too far away. Although the kits still rely on mom for the majority of their nourishment, natural weaning should begin at this age. The baby canine teeth and some baby premolars are beginning to erupt, and permanent incisor teeth are breaking through and pushing the baby incisors out. You can offer these kits a soft mush or canned food a few times a day (for more on diet, see Chapter 8).

Weaning doesn't involve caging mom and plopping down a crock of odd-smelling mush in front of your confused kits. Weaning is a gradual process that should begin at the age of 3 weeks and be completed at around 6 weeks. Kits need time to adapt to the nutritional change. To wean effectively, first familiarize yourself with the diet information in Chapter 8. This is imperative, because you need to understand nutrition in ferrets. Starting out with canned food or a soft mush made with moistened kibble is only one way to start your babies. As kits get older, you should offer a variety of other foods, such as chicken and beef (either raw or cooked). A change of kibble and canned food is recommended. This is also the time to introduce small mice and insects if desired. The more variety offered, the better. The weaning process is messy as the kits delve face first into their food, but it's a relatively easy process. During these three weeks, the kits will naturally begin to rely less and less on mom and start to prefer the replacement diet you offer.

The fourth week is somewhat of a turning point in a kit's new life. His eyes and ears begin to show signs of opening up to the world. His soft, white fuzz should start taking on some color and pattern, giving you a glimpse into his future. More baby premolars also start to erupt around this time. Healthy kits should be eager to dive into the bowl of soft mush you provide and stuff themselves while still taking advantage of mom's milk supply. And although mom may still want to remind the kits to go to the bathroom, the kits should show signs of being the self-proficient poopers that their parents are!

By week five, a kit's eyes and ears have opened and he's ready to get into trouble! Kits at this age are extremely active and are starting to rough and tumble with their siblings. By week six, the kits should start eating more soft food and start relying less and less on mom for nutritional support. Some breeders introduce the dreaded first distemper vaccination at this age (see Chapter 12).

The Terrible Fuzzy Twos: 6 to 10 Weeks

Emotionally, at 6 to 7 weeks old, furball kits should be spending a lot of awake time playing mock-combat with their siblings. This play is important in developing hierarchy among the youngsters and preparing them for their futures as possible top furballs in their new homes!

At around seven weeks, ferrets should quit hanging on mom so much and start relying almost completely on the soft food you serve. Permanent canines are pushing through their sensitive gums, sometimes erupting just beside the baby canines. This is a pretty painful ordeal to the small fuzzbutt and can cause him to wallow in the throes of teething behavior (see Chapter 20). It isn't unusual to have kits with canine teeth side by side for several days until their baby canines finally fall out.

At 8 weeks old, kits should have four permanent canine teeth. They're now capable of eating the hard kibble that most other ferrets rely on. A kit should have a well-developed and varied diet by now, but if you haven't started this process yet, now is the time to introduce him to new tastes and smells. Babies are so impressionable!

Many private breeders begin to let their kits go to their new humans at around the age of 8 weeks (see Figure 23-2). Babies are usually using the litter box by now, and drinking from the water bottle comes easily. Some breeders, however, wait as long as 12 weeks before letting their babies go. The decision is up to the breeder and may be based on how comfortable he or she is with the person buying the ferret. Or it may just be based on personal policy. Whatever the case, there's really no disadvantage to waiting the extra four weeks for your youngster, other than possibly being a bit delayed in getting him on a varied diet.

Figure 23-2:
These
8-week-old
kits are just
about ready
for their
new homes.

For those kits that received their first distemper shots at 6 weeks old, 9 weeks of age is the perfect time for the second attack on their heinies. For complete information on vaccination schedules, head to Chapter 12.

Kits in the 6- to 10-week age range are extremely active in testing their humans to the limits. This age range is the critical training period, which many ferret humans fail to recognize. You need to handle your furkids frequently and gently. They need consistency and someone who's willing to teach them what is and isn't acceptable behavior. Because many kits arrive at pet shops at this age, they frequently don't receive the proper human guidance (for more on pet shops, see Chapter 4). Many of these toddlers become troubled teenagers for their unsuspecting humans. Therefore, as a responsible ferret breeder, you need to begin training as early as possible. (For information on ferret training, head to the chapters of Part V.)

Adolescence Already? 10 to 15 Weeks

Your kits should have almost all their permanent teeth by 10 weeks of age. The little indentations on your fingers and arms are proof enough (see Chapters 19 and 20 for tips on biting training)! Kidding aside, if your kits received the proper fuzzy guidance during their terrible twos stage (see the previous section for advice and the chapters of Part V for tips), adolescence shouldn't be too bad.

By 3 months old (12 weeks), well-adjusted kits are discovering that humans can be fun companions. Although the activity level of kits this age still far surpasses the average human's energy levels (even with a double espresso), kits do begin to mellow a little bit (emphasis on a little bit). Ferret personalities become well-formed and defined during adolescence. Even though these kits are still highly influenced by the humans who interact with them, it's relatively easy to pick out the alpha males and females (top furballs) by watching them interact with their siblings and humans.

Part VII
The Part of Tens

The 5th Wave   By Rich Tennant

"What I don't understand is how you could put the entire costume on without knowing the ferret was inside."

In this part . . .

*1*f I could keep writing on and on about ferrets, I would do just that. But there's just too much information out there to put into one book. This part focuses on a couple of specific issues. Here I give you a head start on creating new and exciting ferret recipes to keep your fuzzy from getting bored with his cuisine. I also discuss ten common ferret myths and misconceptions so you can wade through bad information and educate others about fuzzies.

Chapter 24

Ten Common Ferret Myths and Misconceptions

In This Chapter

▶ Debunking incorrect views of the ferret's nature and history

▶ Clearing the air in terms of diseases and hygiene tendencies

▶ Telling the truth about the ferret's eating and sleeping habits

*W*hat kind of ferret book would this be if I didn't dedicate at least one chapter to beating the tar out of common ferret myths and misconceptions? Not a complete one. Why do little fuzzies often get unfairly judged? Well, you always seem to see at least one or two poor groups of animals out there getting a bad rap. Although some ferret misconceptions are way out in left field, I suppose one or two have a *little* merit. (I emphasize little because the misconceptions are usually little things that people blow way out of proportion and attach to the entire business of ferrets.) All pets have their ups and downs, their pros and cons — just like people. But to stereotype an entire group of animals based on a few misconceptions is just plain irresponsible.

The following sections present ten misconceptions commonly associated with ferrets; and, for the sake of thoroughness, I'll give you reasons why they aren't true!

Ferrets Are Rodents

You think ferrets are rodents? Get out of here. Ferrets are much cuter. Contrary to popular belief, not all small, furry animals are rodents. Ferrets are relatives of polecats, actually. Ferrets are carnivores, and most carnivores like to eat rodents. Most ferrets, however, are too busy sleeping or playing to care! (Head to Chapter 2 for more on the ferret's history.)

Ferrets Are Wild, Dangerous Animals

Some uninformed folks think that ferrets are wild, dangerous animals. Sure. And pigs can fly. Occasionally, ferrets get wild with excitement during play-time. And the most dangerous thing about them is that you may pull a muscle when laughing as you watch them do ferret things. Except in Hawaii, where ferrets are classified as wild animals, and in California (boo, hiss), ferrets legally meet the definition of domestic: They're fond of home life and house-hold affairs. (I like that definition — too bad they don't cook!) Ferrets are tame and fit for domestic life. They've adapted or have been bred to live with and be of use to man. (For more on the laws concerning ferrets, check out Chapter 3.)

In fact, ferrets can't survive on their own; they require human assistance. Like dogs and cats (which have more bite incidents than ferrets ever will), all domestic fuzzies have their moments. They can have bad days and need timeouts. In the majority of cases, however, a well-treated ferret is a very, very loving and trusting ferret (to find out how to deal with an abused ferret, see Chapter 20).

Feral Ferrets Will Take Over!

A *feral* ferret is one that reverts back to its natural state of wild behavior and can successfully live and reproduce in the wild. Many people fear that escapee ferrets will form feral colonies and destroy native wildlife. This fear is unfounded and virtually impossible for several reasons:

- ✔ The majority of would-be escapees in the United States are already neutered or spayed.

- ✔ Unless some little old lady is leaving piles of ferret food under her bushes and the ferrets actually get a chance to snarf down the food before other animals steal it, escapee ferrets frequently die of starvation. Olfactory imprinting on kibble makes it unlikely that ferrets can recognize enough food to survive.

- ✔ There is no natural niche for escapee ferrets to fill in the wild. Most environments already have efficient predators filling all the possible niches. A domestic ferret let loose in North America's wild would be low on the food chain. (To see how difficult it is to reintroduce even wild ferrets — like black-footed ferrets — into nature and have them establish viable colonies, read Chapter 2.)

New Zealand has the only established feral colony of ferrets, and these ferrets were purposely conditioned and introduced to control the rabbit population (another of many introduced species). New Zealand had no other predators when the ferret was introduced, and the colony of ferrets successfully maintains itself on other prey animals (which they've been conditioned to eat).

Ferrets Are Vicious Biters

I won't kid you by saying that ferrets never bite. They can bite for many reasons (see Chapter 20 to get the full rundown). But the vast majority of ferrets aren't vicious biters. Comparatively speaking, ferrets are safer than dogs and cats in terms of inflicting injury or the likelihood of causing death with an attack. Some ferrets are more temperamental than others, and these buggers may need more patience.

Like most domestic animals, the more love you give, the more you receive. Ferrets need daily handling and loving care (see Chapter 10). This daily attention reduces the possibility of biting, which can happen because of fear or overstimulation in a rarely handled fuzzy. Even the toughest ferrets can be turned around with proper handling, time, and patience.

Ferrets Pose a Serious Rabies Risk

Believe it or not, ferrets are extremely resistant to the rabies virus. I know of no documented case of a human contracting rabies from a ferret. Studies have indicated that ferrets may not even pass the virus through their saliva, via a bite, and they note that the amount of rabies virus found in the saliva of an infected ferret is negligible. And the pet community saw less than a handful of reported rabies cases in domestic ferrets in the 20th century. Although some states are still paranoid and automatically impose the "off with its head" sentence to a misunderstood biting or scratching ferret, most states have come out of the fog and issue quarantine sentences instead. Hooray for the smart states! (For more on ferret laws, refer to Chapter 3.)

Still, all ferrets can and should receive their annual rabies vaccination, which is formulated especially for ferrets, just to be safe (see Chapter 12 for more on vaccinations).

A Ferret's Stink Will Never Go Away

All ferrets have scent glands, from which they can on rare occasions emit a foul odor, next to their heinies. Unneutered, non-descented males are the worst smell offenders. However, most ferrets are descented and altered at a young age — at least in the United States. In other countries, descenting is considered animal abuse, so you have to deal with the occasional poof.

Basically, the stink of a ferret depends on your attentiveness as a ferret mom or dad. Descented ferrets can stay odorless for quite some time, but skin glands produce a smell over time as well. You need to bathe your ferret as she approaches the borderline of tolerable stink — but no more than once every few months or so.

And even better than routine bathing is providing your ferret with a tub of clean potting soil to dig in (see Chapter 10). The soil will absorb the excess oil on her skin and leave her smelling quite fresh!

A poor diet can cause your ferret to smell a little muskier than a ferret on a high-protein, low-ash diet (see Chapter 8). Make sure that you feed your fuzzy a high-quality diet. Also, bad teeth and dirty ears are two more causes of stink, so take care of your fuzzy's grooming and get her regular veterinary checkups (Chapter 9 covers grooming basics).

Although I always push altering in ferrets, I don't think descenting is necessary in order for you to live with your ferret. A ferret usually lets loose an odor when she's scared, overstimulated, or aggressive (the three Fs: Fear, Fun, Fight). Unlike with the skunk, a ferret's smell dissipates rapidly. And believe it or not, some people actually enjoy the smell of ferret and skunk spray. Manufacturers have even bottled the skunk smell and marketed it with good results! Go figure.

Ferrets Can Catch the Common Cold

No! No! No! Ferrets can't catch the common cold. Colds are caused by rhinoviruses, which are species-specific. Fortunately, they don't attack ferrets.

On the other hand, ferrets can catch influenza A, the flu virus humans are all too familiar with. They can also catch bacterial respiratory and sinus infections, which they can pass back to you. Take extra care when handling your ferret when you or she has the flu.

Ferrets Were Domesticated in Egypt

The notion that ferrets were domesticated in Egypt is about two-and-a-half centuries old and began with a reference to Libyan ferrets made by Roman romantic authors Strabo and Pliny. Linnaeus used this reference to state that ferrets were native to Africa. The rest is history — or, should I say, mis-history. To add insult to injury, one author claimed to have a hieroglyph that depicted a ferret. Although the author never produced or published the hieroglyph, the claims were used to assert that not only were ferrets domesticated in Egypt, but also domesticated prior to cats. This unproven idea spread like wildfire and the ferret community ran with it because of the desperate need to prove domestication in ferret-free states (see Chapter 3).

According to author Bob Church, as published in John Lewington's *Ferret Husbandry, Medicine and Surgery, 2nd Edition* (Saunders/Elsevier Limited), "There are no zooarchaeological reports, genetics studies, theological support, historical documents, hieroglyphs or biogeographical or ecological evidence that document the presence of either the ferret or polecat in Egypt during the window of domestication. Such ruminations are conjectural suppositions, which, through repetition and decades of reprinting, have taken on a 'truthfulness of familiarity' or 'common knowledge.' Unfortunately, these suppositions are regarded as factual by many in the ferret community despite a singular lack of substantive evidence."

You can also take into consideration the Egyptian culture, where mummifying was common practice. The Egyptian people mummified mammals, birds, reptiles, and even eggs. In the long list of animals excavated, not one is a ferret or polecat. Not a single bone or body of a ferret or polecat has ever turned up during archeological excavations in or around Egypt. Consider also the ecological conditions of Egypt and the ferret's inability to withstand heat and go long periods without water. In fact, no place in the world with ecological conditions like Egypt houses ferrets or polecats. (For more on the history of the ferret, check out Chapter 2.)

Ferrets Sleep 20+ Hours per Day

Ferrets aren't quite the lazy bums that people claim they are — not if they're happy and healthy, that is! A ferret caged all day may sleep 18–20 hours, but she's likely to be bored and depressed. Like their polecat relatives, healthy, free-roaming ferrets with little cage time should sleep only 15–18 hours a day.

Your ferret should be out and about four hours a day at the very least. If she isn't used to getting exercise, she may become sluggish and she'll constantly look for a place to just curl up and sleep away. Get your ferret out to play (see Chapter 10)!

Ferrets Need to Have Food Available at All Times

Most fuzzies don't need a constant food flow. Only ferrets that are insulinomic need to have food available at all times! Personally, I believe people put too much emphasis on making sure the ferret has food at all times. Fuzzies wouldn't have a free buffet in the wild, so why do people think domestication is any different? Physiologically, ferrets are designed to go considerable periods of time without food (well, it's a little more complicated than that).

Ferret owners influence how often their ferrets need to eat, because ferrets adapt their eating cycles to what they're being fed. For example, if you feed your ferret a kibble that's high in carbs, blood-sugar fluctuations can drive your ferret to eat more often — perhaps as often as every four to five hours. A very poor diet can drive her to eat even more often, perhaps every three to four hours. However, giving your fuzzy a diet that's high in fat- and meat-based protein can leave her satisfied much longer — perhaps as long as eight to ten hours.

I feed my ferrets mice, Wysong Archetype freeze-dried diet, and/or some high-quality kibble twice a day. I leave them with no food overnight. And they're all healthy, muscular, and happy! (For more on giving your fuzzy the proper diet, chomp your way over to Chapter 8.)

Chapter 25
Ten Recipes Your Ferret Will Love

In This Chapter

▶ Whipping up gourmet dishes with chicken and tuna

▶ Getting creative with snacks and stews

▶ Giving your fuzzy the BARF treatment

Recipes in This Chapter

▶ Bob's Chicken Gravy

▶ Bob's Chicken Ferretisee

▶ Foster's Tuna Shake

▶ Bear's Jerky

▶ Stella's Super Soup

▶ Tui's Chewies

▶ Carnivore Store

▶ Mickey's Meatloaf

▶ Clyde's Seaside Chunks

▶ Bluto's BARF

▶ Bob's Chicken Gravy

1 believe that the key to good health for any animal is a well-balanced and varied diet. Whether you want to add some variety into your ferret's diet or need that perfect homemade "soup" for the sick or recovering ferret, I have the right recipe for you! This chapter provides some great recipes, compliments of my friend Bob Church, ferret guru and fellow fuzzy lover, for you to try with your ferret.

With a few exceptions (Bob's Chicken Gravy, for instance, has sent dozens of blenders to the great garbage dump in the sky), most of these recipes are easy to make. You may even get inspired to come up with one or two recipe ideas of your own.

Bob recommends his recipes with some simple caveats:

✔ He assumes that your vet has checked your ferret and has reviewed the recipe to determine if your fuzzy's health allows you to give him the food.

✔ Ferrets are olfactory imprinted, meaning they set their food preferences by the time they're 6 months old, so an older ferret may not want to try the foods right away (see Chapter 8 for more information on olfactory imprinting and converting your fuzzy to a new diet). If you put in some time and effort, though, you'll find that your fuzzy will accept most of these recipes. Younger ferrets and kits will accept them right away.

✔ Most of these recipes represent snacks or meals, not long-term diets. The recipes are designed to increase enrichment (see Chapter 10), offer variety, and increase dietary choice. Make sure you consult with your vet in order to ensure your ferret is getting a complete and balanced diet.

✔ Ferrets that eat a soft diet often will develop dental tartar. This also happens with hard, crunchy kibble, but the rate of deposit seems faster with the soft diet. Make sure you don't hurt your ferret while you're trying to help him! Tooth brushing and annual dental checkups are a must, regardless of the food your ferret eats.

All these recipes have been taste-tested and fuzzy-approved by ferrets all over the world! However, you'll notice that the exact ingredient measurements are missing from most of the recipes. Bob wants to leave this part mostly up to you so that you can modify the food for the specific needs of your ferret, as advised by your vet. The measurements may require some trial and error on your part. It's likely that you'll never make two recipes the same, unless you write down exactly how much you choose to use of this, that, and the other thing.

Bob's Chicken Gravy

Bob's Chicken Gravy is easy to digest and gentle on the stomach, making it great for ferrets that aren't feeling too well or are coming off a liquid diet and moving back onto solid foods. This recipe is about 70 percent chicken and 30 percent animal fat, so you need a heavy-duty blender (or a hand-cranked meat grinder) and probably some goggles. If you need to, you can cut the recipe in half.

1 whole roasting chicken, cut into small pieces (don't remove the skin, fat, bones, or giblets)

1 tablespoon olive oil

1 tablespoon fatty-acid supplement (Ferretone or Linatone)

1 cup ferret, mink, or high-quality feline kibble

2 tablespoons fine bran, whole oats, or Metamucil

1 tube Nutri-Cal (use ½ half or ¼ tube for insulinoma ferrets)

3 or 4 eggshells

4 tablespoons honey

1 cup fat trimmings from any meat source safe for human consumption (uncooked)

1 Put on your goggles (if you have them). Puree the chicken with the fat, kibble, and eggshells. Add water until you make a thin gravy. Remove your goggles.

2 Pour the mix into a pot and cook on the stove for 30 minutes or until it has the consistency of cream or thick gravy.

3 Add the rest of the ingredients to the pot and mix well.

4 Let the mixture cool before serving.

> **Bob's Tip:** *The best way to get your ferret used to Bob's Chicken Gravy is to dip your finger into the mixture and touch it to the nose of your ferret. He'll lick it off as he cleans his nose, and eventually he'll learn to love the food. Here's another tip: Take what's left over after a meal and pour the stuff into zipper bags or ice-cube trays. Store in the freezer. When serving the gravy, add water or Pedialyte to get the desired consistency, and microwave it until it's warm. Be sure to mix it well to get rid of any "hot spots" resulting from the microwave! (**Note:** You can blend to desired consistencies for a ferret's special needs.)*

The Metamucil/bran/oats helps to control loose stools that sometimes happen when a ferret is first placed on chicken gravy. It's supposed to represent the 2 percent to 4 percent indigestible fiber (fur, connective tissue, and so on) consumed when a ferret eats whole prey (see Chapter 8).

Why Nutri-Cal? Ferrets that eat a kibble diet have made physiological adaptations for a carbohydrate diet that include a decrease in ability for gluconeogenesis. (Gluconeogenesis is the formation of glucose from noncarbohydrate sources.) It takes about two weeks for the ferret's physiology to make the shift from a sugar-based energy system to a protein-based system and full efficiency of liver and kidney gluconeogensis to occur. Because Bob's Chicken Gravy was designed to get ferrets off a liquid diet and back onto kibble (as stated in the intro), the sugars in the Nutri-Cal and the honey are designed to prevent low blood sugar and the physiological shift. If Bob's Chicken Gravy is used as a long-term diet, after two weeks the honey and Nutri-Cal should be removed from the recipe and a vitamin replacement should step in.

The sugars in honey are roughly half fructose and half glucose. The metabolism of these two sugars is different. The glucose immediately enters the bloodstream and raises the blood sugar. This gives the ferret the energy needed to fuel the initial metabolism of protein to glucose (gluconeogenesis requires glucose to initiate the process). Fructose isn't digested as effectively as other sugars. Fructose is absorbed in the jejunum and is metabolized in the liver, usually into triglycerides. This helps the ferret put on fat weight without causing a high increase in the blood sugar. There is some evidence that fructose reduces the effectiveness of insulin, which can be a help in insulinomic ferrets.

Bob's Chicken Ferretisee

This recipe reminds me of a springtime salad, almost good enough for humans to eat over a crisp bed of lettuce. It's easy to make and store, is highly nutritious, and its small pieces make it great to offer as a treat and training aid. Chicken Ferretisee isn't designed to be a complete meal, however.

½ chicken

1-2 tablespoons lard or olive oil

Fatty acid supplement (such as Ferretone or Linatone)

½ cup kibble, ground up (a coffee grinder works well)

1 Cut pieces of whole chicken (including the bone) into ½- to 1-inch cubes. Use a cleaver when the chicken is partially frozen.

2 Melt some lard (or heat olive oil) in a wok until it's about ⅛-inch deep.

3 Quick-fry the chicken cubes in the lard until they reach a golden-brown color. (The goal is to kill any possible bacteria but leave the inside as raw as possible.)

4 Set the chicken cubes aside to drain and cool.

5 Place the chicken cubes in a bowl and lightly spray them with Ferretone or Linatone (use an atomizer).

6 Add the ground-up kibble to the bowl and toss the mixture like a salad.

Bob's Tip: Freeze the unused portions and thaw as needed.

Foster's Tuna Shake

You may not like the idea of drinking fish, but your ferret will lap it up and shake for more. Foster's Tuna Shake is a great occasional snack and it can be frozen, so a single batch can last a long time. Bob advises that most ferrets will be so olfactory imprinted that they'll ignore this food, so start off with the young ferrets (see Chapter 8 for diet conversion tips).

1 can tuna (packed in spring water)

⅛ cup heavy cream

1 teaspoon smooth peanut butter

4 chicken bones — a back, 2 legs, and a wing

Pedialyte (optional)

1 Dump the tuna (including the spring water) into a blender.

2 Add the heavy cream, the peanut butter, and the four chicken bones.

3 Blend to a milkshake-like consistency. (You can add a little Pedialyte if you want for taste.)

> *Bob's Tip: For any recipe that includes heavy cream or another dairy product, you can blend in a Lactaid tablet if you know that your ferret is a little lactose intolerant or shows signs (gets diarrhea, for instance) after eating it. Most ferrets tolerate the lactose in heavy cream, though. Because this recipe is so fat-rich, some ferrets with liver or gall bladder problems may have a hard time eating it. Be sure to discuss this treat with your vet if your ferret has a problem with it.*

Bear's Jerky

The jerky made for humans has a lot of salt and seasonings ferrets don't really need. Making Bear's Jerky solves that problem and makes the occasional treat much cheaper to dole out.

1–2 pounds brisket (cheap cut)

Fatty-acid supplement (such as Ferretone or Linatone)

High-quality bone meal fit for human consumption

1 Cut the fat off the brisket.

2 Slice the remaining meat into ¼-inch-thick strips.

3 Place the strips onto a dehydrator screen, and spray the surface of the meat with the Ferretone or Linatone.

4 Sprinkle the bone meal on the top of the meat.

5 Let the meat dehydrate before serving.

> *There's a possibility of meat spoilage if you don't dehydrate the meat properly. Always follow the instructions to ensure that the meat is safely and completely dried.*

Stella's Super Soup

This is a yummy meal that you can dish out on a daily basis to your appreciative ferret, but don't replace his diet with it. If you divide your basic stock into three parts and then add kibble to one, heavy cream to another, and both to the third, you'll have three "flavors" that are sure to enrich your ferret's palate.

½ gallon of water

Leftovers from your last turkey or chicken dinner

1 teaspoon chicken soup stock

Ground kibble or heavy cream

1 Bring the water to a boil.

2 Add the leftover bones from your last turkey or chicken dinner.

3 Cut up the skin, giblets, fat, and meat into small pieces. Add the pieces to the boiling water.

4 Boil the mixture until the bones begin to get soft (about 20 minutes). Add the chicken soup stock.

5 Add ground kibble or heavy cream to thicken the stock to your desire.

6 Remove from the stove.

7 Let the mixture cool before serving.

The bulk of the nutrients in Stella's Super Soup come from the chicken leftovers and chicken soup stock. The kibble and/or heavy cream are just meant to be thickening and flavoring agents. I've left it up to the owners which one to choose, because you know the food preferences of your individual ferret. The kibble and cream can be left out without problem; they are just there to help address the ferret's olfactory imprinting.

Tui's Chewies

Ferrets love to gnaw, and this treat will give your floor monkey something healthy and fun to gnaw on. Tui's Chewies aren't designed to be a replacement for commercially made chews, but rather an occasional alternative.

Water

Non-flavored gelatin

Chicken or beef, finely chopped

Beef or chicken bouillon

1 Dissolve the non-flavored gelatin in boiling water, per the instructions on the gelatin box.

You can make a super-saturated solution by adding enough water to where no more gelatin will dissolve; you'll still see some bits floating around.

2 Toss in the finely chopped chicken or beef.

3 Add some flavor with the chicken or beef bouillon.

4 Pour the mixture onto a cookie sheet (or cookie molds). Cut the mixture into rectangular shapes when it dries.

5 Place the shapes in a cool dehydrator until they're rubbery and hardened.

Bob's Tip: *You can also store the small, rectangular yummies uncovered in the freezer. Sometimes, the chewies will end up more like gummies; when that happens, you can just freeze them and serve them cold. Ferrets like them either way!*

Carnivore Stew

If used as an occasional meal, Carnivore Stew will enrich your ferret's stomach as much as it will enrich his life. It's a great occasional alternative to a monotonous diet of kibble.

Leftover trimmings from a meat-based meal (skin, bones, giblets, fat, and meat waste)

Whole bits of kibble

Lard or fish oil (optional)

1 Boil the leftover trimmings until they're cooked completely.

2 Add the kibble so that it makes up ⅛ of the stew.

3 If the mixture is low on fat (should be about ⅛ of the total trimmings), add a little lard or fish oil.

You can add the kibble during boiling or after; it makes little difference. The kibble should absorb most of the moisture, creating a gravy-like thickness. Carnivore Stew should be slightly warmed up before serving to make it more palatable.

Mickey's Meatloaf

Okay, not everyone likes mother's meatloaf, but your ferret will love this one. You can cut Mickey's Meatloaf into small pieces that are wonderful for use in training or as special treats.

Ground chicken or turkey — uncooked

Chicken broth

One egg

Ground kibble

Whole kibble

Olive or fish oil

Spray oil

Ice cube tray

1 Mix all the ingredients (except the whole kibble and spray oil) like you're making a meatloaf (a mound of ground meat mixed with other ingredients).

2 Add just enough whole kibble to spread a crushed piece per square inch.

3 Give the ice cube tray a light coating of spray oil and then fill the tray with the meatloaf.

4 Microwave the tray for a minute or two to harden the food, and then remove the miniature loaves from the tray areas.

You can store the pieces in plastic food containers in your freezer until needed.

Bob's Tip: *To serve, place a small meatloaf on a dish and microwave until you cook it throughout. Allow it to cool so you don't burn the mouth of your little floor monkey. Also, you can substitute ground beef or pork for the chicken or turkey if your ferret will accept it.*

Clyde's Seaside Chunks

The acceptance of this occasional meal is dependent on how olfactory imprinted your ferret has become, but if he's open to seafood, he'll gobble up the Seaside Chunks. You can cut up the food into tiny chunks to use as treats.

Crawdads, fish, small shrimp, and/or crab

Artificially sweetened gelatin

1 Make the gelatin according to the instructions, except that while you're mixing the gelatin, add small bits of seafood, just as you would fruit. (Do not add fruit!)

2 Put the mix into small ice cube trays and store in the refrigerator until used.

Bob's Tip: *You can use any flavor of gelatin your ferret likes; Bob's ferrets seem to like the lemon, banana, and grape flavors best.*

Bluto's BARF

BARF stands for Bones and Raw Food or Biologically Appropriate Raw Food (see Chapter 8 for all the details). Although this treat may make you want to barf, your ferrets should love it as an occasional meal or offered as a special treat. Plus, you can be happy that Bluto's BARF is an excellent source of protein for your ferret.

½-inch frozen chicken chunks

Beef or chicken liver, partially frozen

Chicken hearts or gizzards, partially frozen

Chicken bones

Chicken broth

Frozen fat trimmings (about ⅛th by volume)

1 Mix the frozen meat ingredients (chicken chunks, liver, hearts or gizzards, and fat trimmings) in a bowl and cover the mixture with the broth.

2 Boil the chicken bones until the ends start to scratch under the pressure of your fingernail.

3 Cut the bones with poultry scissors into small chunks.

4 Add maybe a half-dozen pieces of bone to the bowl containing the meat and broth mixture.

5 Place that bowl in the microwave and heat until the broth is near the boiling point. Allow it to cool.

Bob's Tip: *This recipe seems to work better if you freeze the meat ingredients first and cut them with a cleaver into ½-inch chunks while still partially hard. You can serve this recipe as a soup, freeze it into small blocks for a treat, cook it into a paste, or add it as gravy to soften kibble.*

 None of these recipes should take the place of your ferret's base diet (see Chapter 8). Ferrets are small animals with small stomachs and giving too much of a supplement, treat, or snack can unbalance the rest of the diet. Here's a handy guide:

- ✔ Meals: 100 percent of average meal weight

- ✔ Snacks: 10 percent of average meal weight

- ✔ Treats: 1 percent of average meal weight

- ✔ Samples: A bite or a few licks

I think all the dishes in this chapter are safe to use as samples, treats, and snacks. Snacks and treats should be limited to once per day. Samples should be limited to twice a day. A few of the recipes, as indicated, can even be used as occasional meals (a couple times per week, for instance) for most ferrets that don't have health problems. Always check with your vet before making any significant changes to your ferret's diet.

Index

• A •

AA (arachidonic acid), 140
AAFCO (Association of American Feed Control Officials), 130
acetaminophen, 204, 215, 262
acupuncture, 215
AD (Aleutian Disease), 266–268
adenoma, 285
adopting ferrets. *See* choosing a ferret
adrenal gland disease, 275–280
ADV (Aleutian Disease Virus), 178, 266–268
Advantage (Bayer), 237, 259
Africa, 360
aggression
  during breeding season, 52
  from eating live prey, 134
  in new pets, 56
  during play, 306
  reason behind, 319–323
  warning signs, 55
air returns, ferret-proofing, 92
airplane, traveling by, 185–186
ALA (alpha-linoleic acid), 139
albino color, 30
Albon, 242
alcohol, 142
Aleutian Disease Virus (ADV), 178, 266–268
allergic reactions of ferrets, 199, 201–202, 251
alligator roll, 306
alpha-linoleic acid (ALA), 139
altering ferrets. *See* neutering; spaying
alternative diets
  BARF, 125–128
  commercial raw diets, 128–130
  evolutionary diets, 130–135
  exploring, 135–139
  freeze-dried raw diets, 128–130
  natural diet, 123–125, 128, 135–139
American Ferret Association, 29, 32, 176, 261
Amforol, 245
Amoxicillin, 245, 249, 274

anaphylaxis, 199, 201–202
anemia, 51–52, 341
animal shelters
  adopting from, 59–61
  boarding ferrets at, 190
  ferret populations at, 336
aplastic anemia, 51–52, 341
arachidonic acid (AA), 140
Archetype freeze-dried diet (Wysong), 251, 362
Aristophanes, 24, 311
Aristotle, 24
Arizona, 37
artificial insemination, 36
Assist Feed Recipe, 217–220, 246
assist feeding, 219–220
Association of American Feed Control Officials (AAFCO), 130
atrophic gastritis, 249
Audubon, John James, 35
Augustus, Caesar, 24
automobile, traveling by, 183–185
Avecon Diagnostics, 268

• B •

baby ferrets (kits)
  adolescence (10-15 weeks), 353–354
  birth–3 weeks, 349–351
  birthing problems, 346–348
  choosing, 49, 56–57
  delivering, 344–346
  hand-rearing, 348
  introducing to other ferrets, 109
  litter box considerations, 79
  nipping behavior in, 320–321
  survival boot camp, 36
  terrible twos (6–10 weeks), 352–353
  toddlerhood (3–6 weeks), 351–352
  vaccinations, 49, 199–200
  vet office visit, 200
baby food, 136, 141, 203
Bachman, John, 35

backyard burials, 291–293
bad breath, 159
Balearic Islands, 24
BARF diet, 125–128, 130, 371
barking, 303
basal cell tumors, 286
baseboards, ferret-proofing, 91
bathing ferrets
  controlling odor, 16
  frequency of, 147
  introducing to other ferrets by, 110
  location, selecting, 148
  process for, 149–152
  shampoo, selecting, 147–148
bathrooms, ferret-proofing, 94
Baytril, 245
Bear's Jerky, 367
bedding
  cleaning, 145
  controlling ferret odor, 16, 66, 71, 110
  fleas in, 236
  food caching considerations, 139
  nest boxes, 72–73
  during pregnancy, 343–344
  safety considerations, 71, 85
  for traveling, 183
beeswax, 156, 223
behaviors. *See also* aggression; biting
  boundary patrols, 312
  burrowing, 67
  butt dragging, 212–213, 311–312
  caching, 307, 310
  from cage stress, 69
  chasing, 307
  curbing through enrichment, 164
  digging, 66, 308–309
  fixations, 309
  hidey-holes, 312
  hissing, 109, 303
  neutering for, 51
  normal, 210–213
  socializing ferrets, 323–328
  suckling, 212
  tuck-and-scoot moving, 310
  tunneling, 83
  zig-zag, 311
Belair, Randy, 179

Benadryl, 204
Bene-Bac, 204
Bennett, Christopher, 180
Betadine solution, 204
Biaxin, 249, 274
birthing process, 344–346
biting
  from hybrids, 27
  myths about, 359
  nip-training, 313–314
  from other animals, 231
  reasons for, 14, 320–323
  socializing ferrets, 323–328
Bitter Apple spray, 327
black color, 30
black sable color, 30
black-footed ferret, 32–38
Black-Footed Ferret Recovery Plan, 35–38
blackheads, 148
bladder problems, 263
blaze pattern, 31
bleeding, 222–223, 340
blockages
  bladder, 264
  diagnosis and treatment, 247–248
  possible malady, 225
  remedies for, 203–204
  from toys, 85
  from vegetables, 142
Bluto's BARF, 371
boarding ferrets, 190
Bob's Bone Broth, 127
Bob's Chicken Ferretisee, 366
Bob's Chicken Gravy, 364–365
body language, 305–308
bonding, 101, 163, 169–170
bones in diet, 125–128
boundary patrols, 312
breeders/breeding
  altering practices of, 52
  delivering kits, 344–346
  emotional commitment, 333
  financial commitment, 332–333
  handling pregnancy, 341–344
  hybrids, 29
  mating habits of ferrets, 338–341
  problems after birth, 346–348

selecting, 58–59
time commitment, 334–335
Brewer's yeast, 282
broth, 127
Broth, Bob's Bone, 127
Brown, Susan, 126, 217–218, 267
brushing, 159–160
bubonic plague, 35, 37
bupivicaine, 215
burns, 232
burrowing behavior, 67
butt dragging, 212–213, 311–312
buying ferrets
  age considerations, 49–50
  altered versus whole, 51–53
  gender considerations, 51
  list of basic tips, 48
  number of ferrets, 53–55
  potential sources, 56–62

• *C* •

cabinets, ferret-proofing, 91, 94–95
cache behavior, 307, 310
caffeine, 142
cage stress, 69
cages. *See also* bedding
  carpeting in, 66
  cleaning, 65–66, 68, 110, 143–147
  design considerations, 64–67
  fleas in, 236
  food caching considerations, 138–139
  introducing, 100–101
  materials for, 66
  multilevel, 66–67
  nest boxes, 72–73, 83, 343–344
  placement indoors, 68–69
  placement outdoors, 69–71
  size considerations, 64
  travel, 87–88, 183, 186
  ventilation in, 64, 68
  water bottles, attaching, 77
California, 40–41
Californians for Ferret Legalization, 41
cancer
  adrenal gland disease, 275–280
  insulinoma, 159, 229, 280–282

lymphosarcoma, 282–283
  malignant tumors, 285
canine distemper
  in black-footed ferrets, 35, 37
  vaccinations for, 199, 269
canned food, 121–122, 136, 203
captive breeding, 36
car, traveling by, 183–185
Carafate, 274
carcinoma, 285
cardiomyopathy, dilated, 256–258
cardiovascular fitness, 165
Carnivore Care, 203, 217–218
Carnivore Stew, 369
carnivores, 118, 125, 129
carpeting in cages, 66
carriers, pet, 87–88, 183
cat food, 119, 136
cataracts, 265
cats
  bites from, 231
  introducing ferrets to, 103–104
Cefa drops, 245
cereals, as treats, 142
cervical chordoma, 284
champagne color, 30
chasing behavior, 307
checkerboard wall, 175
children
  bonding enrichments, 163
  considerations when selecting
    ferrets, 49
  permit stipulations regarding, 40
  preparing for ferrets, 101, 106–108
  supervising with ferrets, 19, 106
chiropractic care, 215
chocolate, 142
chocolate color, 30
choosing a ferret
  age considerations, 49–50
  altered versus whole, 51–53
  gender considerations, 51
  list of basic tips, 48
  number of ferrets, 53–55
  potential sources, 56–62
chordomas, 283–284
chronic atrophic gastritis, 248–249

Church, Bob, 133, 137, 254–255, 311, 361–372
cinnamon color, 30
classified ads, 61
Clavamox drops, 245
claws, 13, 154–157
clay litter, 81–82
cleaning. *See also* bathing ferrets
    cages, 65–66, 68, 143–147
    importance with raw food diet, 135
    teeth, 131
clipping nails, 154–157
Clyde's Seaside Chunks, 370
coat and skin
    color categories, 29–31
    color patterns, 31–32
    showing ferrets, 177
    skin tumors, 284–286
coccidia (coccidiosis), 242
Coenzyme Q10, 257
coffee products, 142
collars, 86
Colorado, 37
colors
    categories, 29–31
    distinguishing, 14
commercial diets, 119–123, 128–130, 136
common cold, 263, 360
corncob litter, 82
Corner Creek Acres, 65
corticosteroids, 251, 281
costume contest, 179
coughing, 212
cremation, 290–292
crepuscular nature, 15
crinkle tub, 174
cuterebra flies, 238–239

• D •

da Vinci, Leonardo, 24
dairy products, 142
dance of joy, 303–305
dark-eyed white (DEW) color, 30–31
deafness in ferrets, 30, 266
death of a ferret
    backyard burials, 291–293
    cremating remains, 290–292

grief in surviving companions, 55, 288, 296–297
grieving process, 293–296
    knowing when to let go, 288
    pet cemeteries, 290, 292
    postmortems, 289–290
debulking tissue, 278
declawing, 13
dehydration, 221–222
dental calculus, 253
dental care. *See* teeth
descenting ferrets, 16
DEW (dark-eyed white) color, 30–31
DGLA (dihomo-gamma-linolenic acid), 140
DHA (docosahhexoenoic acid), 139
diarrhea, 204, 224–226
digging behavior, 66, 308–309
dilated cardiomyopathy, 256–258
DIM (disseminated idiopathic myofasciitis), 261
diseases and illnesses
    adrenal gland disease, 275–280
    Aleutian's Disease, 178, 266–268
    aplastic anemia, 51–52, 341
    from cage stress, 69
    canine distemper, 35, 37, 199, 269
    chordomas, 283–284
    dental problems, 252–256
    enlarged spleen, 270
    expectant/new mothers, 344
    eye problems, 229, 264–266
    gastrointestinal, 244–252
    hairballs, 203, 271, 273
    heart disease, 256–260
    heartworm, 201
    hypoglycemia, 229, 280
    influenza, 260–263
    insulinoma, 159, 229, 280–282
    lymphosarcoma, 282–283
    polymyositis, 261
    sylvatic plague, 35, 37
    ulcers, 272–274
    urinary tract problems, 263–264
disseminated idiopathic myofasciitis (DIM), 261
distemper vaccine, 199
distilled water, 118
diving for treasures trick, 173–174

docosahhexoenoic acid (DHA), 139
dog food, 119
dogs
  ferrets chasing, 307
  introducing ferrets to, 104–106
domesticated pets, ferrets as, 21–23,
    360–361
dooking, 302, 305
doors, ferret-proofing, 91–92
dry commercial food, 120–121, 123, 141

• **E** •

E. coli bacteria, 129, 144
ear care, 152–154, 177, 204
ear mites, 239–240
ECE (Epizootic Catarrhal Enteritis), 244–246
eclampsia, 344
eggs, as treats, 140
Egypt, ancient, 23, 360–361
eicosapentaenoic acid (EPA), 139
electric shock, 231–232
electrical cords, 93
elimination (pooping)
  in food dishes, 74
  with natural diet, 128
  preferred locations for, 78
ELISA test, 268
Elizabeth I, Queen of England, 23–24
emergencies
  animal bites, 231
  bleeding, 222–223
  burns, 232
  dehydration, 221–222
  diarrhea, 204, 224–226
  electric shock, 231–232
  evacuation kits, 205–208
  eye injuries, 229
  feeding sick ferrets, 217–220
  first-aid kits, 202–205
  fractures, 230
  heatstroke, 227–228
  hypothermia, 228–229
  pain management, 213–215
  poisoning, 203, 230–231
  preparing for, 205–208
  seizures, 226–227
  setting up aftercare, 216–217
  shock, 220–221
  spinal injuries, 230
  vomiting, 224
Endangered Species List, 35, 38
enrichment activities
  benefits of, 162–165
  need for, 162
  recommended, 167–175
eosinophilic gastroenteritis, 250–251
EPA (eicosapentaenoic acid), 139
Essentials of Ferrets (Brown), 217, 267
estrus, 339, 341
evacuating ferrets, 205–208
evolutionary diet, 130–135
exercise(s)
  physical enrichment, 164–165, 169
  time available for, 14–15
  training, 170–174, 316–317
exotic animals, classification as, 40–41
eye problems, 229, 264–266
eyesight, 14, 28, 167

• **F** •

feeding ferrets. *See also* recipes; water
    bottles
  after birthing, 347
  assist feeding, 219–220
  commercial diets, 119–123
  digesting fiber, 118
  evolutionary diets, 130–135
  ferrets as carnivores, 118
  financial considerations, 17
  food dishes, selecting, 74–76
  foodstuffs in first-aid kit, 203
  free choice, 133
  insects to, 130–135, 137
  lactose intolerance, 119
  myths about, 361–362
  natural diets, 123–130, 135–139
  olfactory imprint of food, 118, 136, 166
  during pregnancy, 342–343
  setting schedules, 122
  supplementing diet, 139–140
  treats, 140–142
  water bottles, selecting, 76–78
  when sick, 217–220
feeding schedules, 122

female ferrets. *See also* spaying
  expectant, 341–344
  genitals of, 13, 52–53
  selecting, 51
  sexual maturity in, 339
feral colonies, 42–43, 358–359
Ferret Aid Society, 179
ferret clubs, 175–179
Ferret Health List (FHL), 180
Ferret Husbandry, Medicine and Surgery
    (Lewington), 70, 361
Ferret Mailing List (FML), 180
ferret shows, 175–179
Ferret Symposium, 179
ferret-free zones, 39–43, 182
ferret-friendly zones, 39
ferreting, sport of, 24–26
ferret-meister, 25
Ferretone, 204, 325
ferret-proofing your home
  baseboards, 91
  bathrooms, 94
  cabinets, 91, 94–95
  challenges in, 18–19
  electrical cords, 93
  fireplaces, 93
  floor vents and air returns, 92
  food caching considerations, 138
  furniture, 93–94
  general guidelines, 90
  heights, 92
  kitchen, 91
  laundry room, 90
  moldings, 91
  plants, 92
  recommended daily actions, 95–96
  trash cans, 95
  windows and doors, 91–92
ferrets
  classification, 10, 41
  history of, 22–25
  myths and misconceptions, 357–362
  scientific name, 10, 41
Ferrets Anonymous, 41
FHL (Ferret Health List), 180
fiber in diet, 118
fillet gloves, 325

financial commitment, 17–18, 332–333
fireplaces, ferret-proofing, 93
first-aid kits, 183, 202–205
fixations, 309
Flagyl, 242, 249, 274
fleas, 148, 234–237
floor vents, ferret-proofing, 92
flukes, 241
FML (Ferret Mailing List), 180
Foley, Dave, 24
food dishes, 74–76, 144
Foster's Tuna Shake, 366–367
fractures, 230
Frederick II, Emperor, 24
free choice feeding, 133
freeze-dried raw diets, 128–131
Frontline Top Spot (Merial), 237
fruits, as treats, 141–142
fun matches, 178–179
fur. *See* coat and skin
furniture, ferret-proofing, 93–94
fuzzy stalking, 308

• **G** •

garbage cans, ferret-proofing, 95
gastrointestinal diseases, 244–252
gates, security, 90
Gatorade, 203, 227
gender. *See* female ferrets; male ferrets
Genghis Khan, 24
genitals
  in adrenal gland disease, 277
  of female ferrets, 13, 52–53
  of male ferrets, 13, 52, 338
giardia, 241–242
gibs, 51
GLA (gamma linolenic acid), 140
Greater Chicago Ferret Association, 324, 336
Greece, ancient, 24
grieving process
  for companion ferrets, 55, 288, 296–297
  for humans, 293–296
grooming ferrets
  bathing, 16, 110, 147–152
  bonding through, 102
  brushing, 160

ear care, 152–154
nail care, 154–157
teeth care, 157–159
washcloth rubdown activity, 169–170
Gruber, Bill, 180
guardhairs, 31
gum disease, 158–159

• *H* •

hairballs, 203, 271, 273
hammocks, hanging, 83
hand-rearing kits, 348
harnesses, 85–86, 183, 316–317
Hawaii, 40
health issues. *See also* diseases and
    illnesses; emergencies; veterinarian(s)
    financial considerations, 17
    lack of exercise, 15
    physical enrichment, 165
health records, 187, 203
hearing, sense of
    deafness in ferrets, 30, 266
    frequency range, 166
heart disease, 256–260
heart rate, 213
Heartgard, 259
heartworm disease, 201, 258–260
heatstroke, 227–228
Helicobacter mustelae infection, 248–249
herbal care, 215
hiccuping, 212
hidey-holes, 312
hissing behavior, 109, 303
histamines, 250, 284
hobs, 51, 338
holding ferrets, 99–100, 102, 107
homeopathic care, 215
hookworms, 241
hotels, pet-friendly, 182
hybrids, ferret, 26–29
hygiene. *See* cleaning
hypercarnivores, 118
hypoglycemia, 229, 280
hypothermia, 228–229

• *I* •

identification tags, 208
Illinois, 39
illnesses. *See* diseases and illnesses
influenza, 260–263
insects, feeding to ferrets, 130–135, 137, 141
insulinoma, 159, 229, 280–282
intelligence of ferrets, 28, 161
Interceptor tablets, 259
International Ferret Congress, 179
Internet clubs and lists, 179–180
intestinal blockage
    diagnosis and treatment, 247–248
    possible malady, 225
    remedies for, 203–204
    from toys, 85
    from vegetables, 142
introducing ferrets
    to additional ferrets, 108–112
    adjusting to environment, 98–102
    assessing social tendencies, 98
    to cats, 103–104
    to children, 106–108
    to dogs, 104–106
    forcing relationships, 110–111
    to other small animals, 106
    quarantine, 62, 97
    to strangers, 112–113
itching and scratching, 210
Ivermectin, 259

• *J* •

Jerky, Bear's, 367
jills, 51, 339
jumping through hoops, 172–173
juvenile lymphosarcoma, 282–283

• *K* •

Kaopectate, 204, 224
Karo syrup, 203, 211, 227, 282
kibble (dry food), 120–121, 123, 141
kitchen, ferret-proofing, 91

kits (baby ferrets)
  adolescence (10–15 weeks), 353–354
  birth–3 weeks, 349–351
  birthing problems, 346–348
  choosing, 49, 56–57
  delivering, 344–346
  hand-rearing, 348
  introducing to other ferrets, 109
  litter box considerations, 79
  nipping behavior in, 320–321
  survival boot camp, 36
  terrible twos (6–10 weeks), 352–353
  toddlerhood (3–6 weeks), 351–352
  vaccinations, 49, 199–200
  vet office visit, 200
kitten food, 119, 136
Kritter Koncepts, 66

• L •

LA (linoleic acid), 140
labels, pet food, 120
lactational estrus, 340
lactose intolerance, 119
laughter, 165
laundry room, ferret-proofing, 90
Laxatone, 248, 271
leashes, 85–86, 183
legal considerations
  breaking the law, 43–44
  descenting, 16
  feeding live animals to ferrets, 132
  ferret-free zones, 39–43, 182
  ferreting, sport of, 25–26
  licensing, 20, 39–40
Letterman, David, 25
Lewington, John H., 70, 361
licensing requirements
  for breeding ferrets, 335
  for owning ferrets, 20, 39–40
lidocaine, 215
life span of ferrets, 11–12
lighting for cages, 68
Linatone, 204, 242
Linnaeus, 360

linoleic acid (LA), 140
litter boxes
  cleaning, 145
  controlling ferret odor, 16
  design considerations, 78
  picking litter for, 81–82
  selecting, 79–81
  training ferrets, 315–316
  when traveling, 183
lodgings, pet-friendly, 182
lost ferrets, 62
Lueprorlin, 279
lungworms, 241
Lupron, 279–280
lymphosarcoma (lymphoma), 282–283

• M •

male ferrets. See also neutering
  aggression in, 321
  genitals of, 13, 52
  selecting, 51
  sexual maturity in, 338
mange, sarcoptic, 240
M*A*S*H (television series), 25
mast cell tumors, 284–285
mastitis, 344
mating habits, 338–341
McNicholas, June, 29
meat. See also raw meat diets
  stink trail activity, 170
  as treats, 141
Meatloaf, Mickey's, 370
medications, 90, 215
megaesophagus, 251–252
melatonin, 280
metastasis, 285
Mexico, 37
Mickey's Meatloaf, 370
microchips, 62
military installations, 40
minks, 62
mitts pattern, 31
moldings, ferret-proofing, 91
Montana, 37

mothers
   delivering kits, 344–346
   handling pregnancy, 341–344
   problems after birth, 346–348
moving, tuck-and-scoot method, 310
multipet households
   additional ferrets in, 108–112
   pet introductions, 103–106
   supervising ferrets, 64

● *N* ●

nail care, 154–157, 177, 222–223
name, calling by, 171–172
National Animal Poison Control Center,
   203, 231
natural diet
   components of, 123–130
   converting to, 135–139
   for eosinophilic gastroenteritis, 251
   evolutionary diet, 130–135
   periodontal disease, 254
   pooping with, 128
necropsies, 289–290
neoplasia, 285
neoplasm. *See* tumors (neoplasm)
Neosporin ointment, 204
nest boxes, 72–73, 83, 343–344
neutering
   controlling ferret odor, 17
   permit stipulations regarding, 40
   selection considerations, 51–53
New Zealand, 359–360
newspaper, as litter, 82
nipping. *See* biting
noise, 68, 84
Nolvasan, 204
Northern California Ferret Alliance, 41
novel objects, 174–175
NSAIDs, 215
nursing, 347
nursing sickness, 344
Nutri-Cal, 142, 203
nuts, as treats, 142

● *O* ●

obligate carnivores, 118, 125
odor of ferrets
   in bedding, 16, 66, 71
   controlling when introducing ferrets, 110
   myths about, 359–360
   scenting mechanism, 15–17
older ferrets (senior), 76, 79
olfactory imprint on food, 118, 136, 166
omega-3 fatty acids, 139–140
omega-6 fatty acids, 140
OPIOIDS, 215
Oxbow Pet Products, 203, 217

● *P* ●

pain management, 213–215
Panacur, 242
panda pattern, 31
paper bag escape, 179
parasites, external
   cuterebra flies, 238–239
   ear mites, 239–240
   fleas, 148, 234–237
   sarcoptic mange, 240
   ticks, 238
parasites, internal
   coccidia, 242
   giardia, 241–242
   heartworm disease, 201, 258–260
   intestinal worms, 241
patterns, color, 31–32
Pedialyte, 203, 227
Pediatric Liquid Benadryl, 204
pelleted litters, 81
Pepcid AC, 274
Pepto-Bismol, 204, 242, 249
periodontal disease, 158, 253–256
permits, 40
pet carriers, 87–88, 183
pet cemeteries, 290, 292
pet shops, 56–58
pet sitters, 187–189

petroleum jelly, 204
Petromalt, 159
physical characteristics
  color categories, 29–31
  color patterns, 31–32
  of ferrets, 11–14
piloerection, 304, 306
plane, traveling by, 185–186
plants, ferret-proofing, 92
plaque on teeth, 253
play. *See also* enrichment activities
  aggression during, 306
  bonding through, 101
  in multiferret households, 54
Pliny, 360
poaching with ferrets, 25
point pattern, 32
points, 31
poisoning, 203, 230–231
polecats
  ferrets' relationship to, 21–22, 41
  natural diets of, 125
  solitary nature of, 98
polymyositis, 261
poop sample, 201
poop(ing)
  in food dishes, 74
  with natural diet, 128
  preferred locations for, 78
postmortems, 289–290
prairie dogs, 34–35, 37–38
prednisone, 260, 281
pregnancy, 341–344
preparing ferret quarters
  cages, setting up, 63–71
  food dishes, selecting, 74–76
  hanging hammocks, 83
  leashes and harnesses, 85–86
  litter boxes, selecting, 78–82
  nest boxes, 72–73, 83
  toys, selecting, 84–85
  travel taxis, 87–88
  water bottles, selecting, 76–78
problem solving, 164
Proglycem, 281

prostate problems, 264
pyometra, 344

quarantine, 62, 97, 187

rabies
  diagnosing, 271–272
  risk in ferrets, 43, 359
  in stray ferrets, 62
  vaccinating for, 42, 183, 200, 272
raisins, 142
Ramsell, Katrina D., 261
raw meat diets
  commercial, 128–130
  cooked versus, 131
  E. coli bacteria, 129
  freeze-dried, 128–130
  importance of hygiene, 135
  natural diets, 124–125
  salmonella infections, 129
recipes
  Assist Feed Recipe, 217–220, 246
  Bear's Jerky, 367
  Bluto's BARF, 371
  Bob's Bone Broth, 127
  Bob's Chicken Ferretisee, 366
  Bob's Chicken Gravy, 364–365
  Carnivore Stew, 369
  caveats for, 363–364
  Clyde's Seaside Chunks, 370
  Foster's Tuna Shake, 366–367
  Mickey's Meatloaf, 370
  Stella's Super Soup, 368
  Tui's Chewies, 368–369
respiration rate, 213
Revolution (Pfizer), 237, 259
roan pattern, 31
rodents, 357
roll over trick, 173
roundworms, 241, 258–260
Royal Canin canned diet, 203

• S •

sable color, 31
safety issues. *See also* ferret-proofing your home
  with bedding materials, 71, 85
  with cage placement, 70–71
  with collars, 86
  when introducing ferrets, 106, 109
salmonella bacteria, 129, 144
salty foods, 142
sarcoptic mange (scabies), 240
scabies (sarcoptic mange), 240
scenting mechanism. *See* odor of ferrets
scoopable litter, 82
screeching, 302
scruffing, 99–100, 155
Seaside Chunks, Clyde's, 370
sebaceous cell tumors, 286
security gates, 90
seeds, as treats, 142
seizures, 226–227
selecting a ferret. *See* choosing a ferret
sense(s)
  enriching, 163–164
  of hearing, 14, 30, 166
  of sight, 14, 28, 167
  of smell, 14, 110, 166
  of taste, 166–168
  of touch, 14, 167
sexual dimorphism, 12
shelters, animal
  adopting from, 59–61
  boarding ferrets at, 190
  ferret populations at, 336
shivering, 210, 228
shock, 220–221, 231–232
Siamese pattern, 32
Siberian polecat, 33
sit up and beg trick, 171
sleeping, excessive, 211, 361
Sleeping Not Dead (SND), 211
sleeping patterns, 15
small animals
  feeding to ferrets, 130–135, 141
  introducing ferrets to, 106

smell, sense of, 14, 110, 166
Smothers, Dick, 23–24
SND (Sleeping Not Dead), 211
sneezing, 212
socialization
  assessing, 98
  for biting ferrets, 323–328
  enrichment activities, 169–170
  in hybrids, 27
solid pattern, 32
solitary ferret, 55
Soup, Stella's Super, 368
South Dakota, 37
space needed by ferrets, 18
spaying
  controlling ferret odor, 17
  permit stipulations regarding, 40
  selection considerations, 51–53
spinal injuries, 230
splenomegaly (enlarged spleen), 270
sprites, 51
standards pattern, 32
Staton, Valerie, 56
Stella's Super Soup, 368
Stew, Carnivore, 369
Stilson, Norm, 324
stink trail, 170
Strabo, 360
strays, rescuing, 61–62
stress, 69, 163, 273
suckling behavior, 212
supplements, dietary, 139–140, 142, 203
Suprelorin, 279–280
sylvatic plague, 35, 37

• T •

Tagamet, 274
tails
  blackheads on, 148
  chordomas, 283–284
  piloerection, 304, 306
  wagging, 308
tapeworms, 241
tartar on teeth, 158, 253
taste, sense of, 166–168

taurine, 119
tea products, 142
teeth
  brushing, 159
  characteristics, 14
  checking, 157–159
  cleaning, 131
  dental problems, 158, 252–256
  design of, 119
  showing ferrets, 177
  water bottle considerations, 76
temperature
  birthing problems, 347
  heatstroke, 227–228
  hypothermia, 228–229
  normal body, 149, 213
  outdoor cage placement, 70
  travel considerations, 186
  walking considerations, 318
theobromide, 142
ticks, 238
time commitment, 14–15
timeouts, 327–328
toilets, ferret-proofing, 94
touch, sense of, 14, 167
toys
  cleaning, 146–147
  fuzzy stalking, 308
  selecting, 84–85
  when introducing ferrets, 54
  when traveling, 183
training
  bodily functions, 315–316
  enrichment exercises, 170–174
  in litter box usage, 78
  not to bite, 313–314
  walking with harness, 316–317
  in water bottle usage, 78
trash cans, ferret-proofing, 95
travel cages, 87–88, 183, 186
traveling with ferrets
  by car, 183–185
  internationally, 186–187
  by plane, 185–186
  preparing for, 181–183

treats
  enrichment activities, 170
  feeding during grooming, 149–150,
    155
  recommended, 140–142
tricks
  at fun matches, 179
  teaching ferrets, 171–174
tube racing, 178
Tui's Chewies, 368–369
tumors (neoplasm)
  chordomas, 283–284
  skin, 284–286
Tuna Shake, Foster's, 366–367
tunneling behavior, 83
Tylenol, 204, 215, 262

• U •

ulcers, 272–274
United States Department of Agriculture,
    40, 186
urinary tract problems, 263–264
urine, drinking, 213
U.S. Fish and Wildlife Service, 35–36
Utah, 37

• V •

vacations
  by car, 183–185
  international, 186–187
  by plane, 185–186
  preparing for, 181–183
vaccinations
  allergic reactions to, 199, 201–202
  for black-footed ferrets, 37
  for canine distemper, 199, 269
  for kits, 49, 199–200
  permit stipulations for, 40
  for rabies, 43, 183, 200, 272
vaginitis, 344
vegetables, as treats, 142
ventilation in cages, 64, 68

veterinarian(s)
  boarding ferrets, 190
  financial considerations, 17
  office visits, 198–201
  on raw meat diets, 124–125
  selecting, 96, 194–198
vision, 14, 28, 167
vocalization, 301–303
vomiting, 224

• W •

Waardensburg syndrome, 30
war dance, 305
water, distilled, 118
water bottles
  cages, attaching to, 76–77
  cleaning, 144
  training to use, 78

weight of ferrets, 12–13
wildlife, classification as, 40, 42
windows, ferret-proofing, 91–92
Winsted, Wendy, 25
wood stove pellets, 81
Wyoming, 35, 37

• Y •

yawning, 211
yawning contest, 178
younger ferrets. *See* kits (baby ferrets)

• Z •

zig-zagging behavior, 311
zoos, ferrets in, 36